THE PHILADELPHIA NEGRO

A Social Study

W. E. B. DuBois

Introduction by E. Digby Baltzell

Together with
A Special Report on
Domestic Service
by Isabel Eaton

SCHOCKEN BOOKS • NEW YORK

First published in 1899
First SCHOCKEN edition 1967
Introduction by E. Digby Baltzell, Copyright © 1967 by Schocken Books Inc.
Library of Congress Catalog Card No. 67–26984

Manufactured in the United States of America

TABLE OF CONTENTS.

Contents.

Contents.

SPECIAL REPORT ON NEGRO DOMESTIC SERVICE IN THE SEVENTH WARD.

Contents.

INTRODUCTION TO THE 1967 EDITION

by E. Digby Baltzell

IN AN appendix to his famous study of the American Negro, *An American Dilemma*, Gunnar Myrdal discussed the need for further research in the Negro community. "We cannot close this description of what a study of a Negro community should be," he wrote, "without calling attention to the study which best meets our requirements, a study which is now all but forgotten. We refer to W. E. B. DuBois' *The Philadelphia Negro*, published in 1899."[1] One would hardly expect a greater tribute to this early classic in American sociology. It is no wonder that there has not been a scholarly study of the American Negro in the twentieth century which has not referred to and utilized the empirical findings, the research methods, and the theoretical point of view of this seminal book.

A classic is sometimes defined as a book that is often referred to but seldom read. *The Philadelphia Negro,* written by a young scholar who subsequently became one of the three most famous Negro leaders in American history, surely meets this requirement. Though always referred to and frequently quoted by specialists, it is now seldom read by the more general student of sociology. For not only has the book been out of print for almost half a century; it has been virtually unobtainable, as my own experience of almost twenty years of searching in vain for a copy in second-hand bookstores attests. Even at the University of Pennsylvania, under whose sponsorship the research was undertaken and the book published, although one copy has been preserved in the archives and one on microfilm, the sole copy listed in the catalogue and available for students in the library has been unaccountably missing from the shelves for several years. In writing this introduction, I am using a copy lent me by my good friend, Professor Ira Reid of Haverford College, a one-time colleague and friend of the late Professor DuBois at Atlanta

---

1. Gunnar Myrdal, *An American Dilemma,* p. 1132.

University. Modern students, then, will certainly benefit from a readily available paperback edition of this study of the Negro community in Philadelphia at the turn of the nineteenth century.

In order to gain a full understanding of any book, one ought to know something of the life and intellectual background of its author, the place of the book in the history of the discipline (in this case sociology), as well as the climate of intellectual opinion and the social conditions of the era in which the book was written. Because *The Philadelphia Negro*—like all his other writings—was so intimately a part of the life of W. E. B. DuBois, I shall begin this introduction with a brief outline of his career. DuBois himself wrote in his seventies: "My life had its significance and its only deep significance because it was part of a problem; but that problem was, as I continue to think, the central problem of the greatest of the world's democracies and so the problem of the future world."[2]

It is one of the coincidences of American history that in the year 1895, Frederick Douglass, a crusading abolitionist and the first great leader of the Negro people, died, and Booker T. Washington rose to national leadership with his "compromise" speech at Atlanta, in which he made the famous statement that "in all things that are purely social we can be as separate as the fingers, yet one as the hand in all things essential to human progress." In that same year, which marked the passing of Negro leadership from the fiery and moralistic Douglass to the compromising and pragmatic Washington, a young New Englander, W. E. B. DuBois, obtained the first Ph.D. degree ever awarded a Negro by Harvard University.

William Edward Burghardt DuBois "was born by a golden river and in the shadow of two great hills," in Great Barrington, Massachusetts, in 1868, the same year "Andrew Johnson passed from the scene and Ulysses Grant became President of the United States."[3] He was a mulatto of French Huguenot, Dutch, and Negro ("thank God, no Anglo-Saxon") ancestry. The Burghardt family had lived in this area of the Berkshires ever since his

2. W. E. B. DuBois, *Dusk of Dawn* (New York: Harcourt, Brace and World, 1940), p. vii.

3. In writing of DuBois' life, I have tried to quote him directly where possible. I have profited greatly from the following biographical studies:

mother's great-grandfather had been set free after having served for a brief period in the Revolution. (In 1908, DuBois was accepted by the Massachusetts branch of the Sons of the American Revolution but was eventually suspended from membership by the national office because of his Negro ancestry.) DuBois grew up in a community of some five thousand souls which included between twenty-five and fifty Negroes. Social position in the small town was more a matter of class than of color. The rich people in town, mostly farmers, manufacturers, and merchants, were "not very rich nor many in number." Like the wealthier white children whom he "annexed as his natural companions," young Will DuBois judged men on their merits and accomplishments and felt, as was natural in that day, that the rich and successful deserved their position in life, as did the "lazy and thriftless" poor. He "cordially despised" the immigrant mill-workers and looked upon them as a "ragged, ignorant, drunken proletariat, grist for the dirty woolen mills and the poorhouse."

As his father, apparently a charming but irresponsible almost-white mulatto, died when he was very young, DuBois was brought up by his mother. Though always very poor, she did her best to pass on to her only son her own pride of ancestry and old-established position in the local Negro community. Fortunately, young Will was a precocious and brilliant boy, possessed of an infinite capacity for work and an abiding passion to excel. His stern New England upbringing was reflected in the following description of his values as a senior at Fisk: "I believed too little in Christian dogma to become a minister," he wrote many years later. "I was not without faith: I never stole material or spiritual things; I not only never lied, but blurted out my conception of the truth on many untoward occasions; I drank no alcohol and knew nothing of women, physically or psychically, to the incredulous amusement of most of my more experienced fellows: I above all believed in work—systematic and tireless."[4]

Francis L. Broderick, *W. E. B. DuBois: Negro Leader in a Time of Crisis,* and Elliott Morton Rudwick, "W. E. B. DuBois: A Study in Minority Group Leadership" (unpublished doctoral dissertation, University of Pennsylvania, 1956).

4. W. E. B. DuBois, "My Evolving Program for Negro Freedom," in Rayford W. Logan, ed., *What the Negro Wants,* p. 38.

From an early age, DuBois planned to go to college and was fortunately encouraged to do so by his friends and teachers. "A wife of one of the cotton mill owners, whose only son was a pal of mine," he wrote more than half a century later, "offered to see that I got lexicons and texts to take up the study of Greek in high school, without which college doors in that day would not open. I accepted the offer as only normal and right; only after many years did I realize how critical this gift was for my career."[5]

Among the Negroes of Great Barrington, young Will DuBois soon came to have a very special place. He was the only Negro in his high-school class of twelve and one of the two or three boys in the whole class who went on to college. After school and on weekends he worked at all sorts of jobs. Through his friendship with the local newsdealer, he obtained, for a brief period, a position as local correspondent for the *Springfield Republican*. He also contributed local news to two Negro newspapers, one in Boston and the other in New York. With a few harsh exceptions as he reached adolescence, he was accepted on his merits by his peers. Though not particularly good at sports, he was highly respected intellectually. At fifteen, he began annotating his collected papers, a practice he scrupulously followed until his death, in Ghana, at the age of ninety-five.

DuBois was, of course, aware of the color line as he grew up, but he had his first experience with a large Negro community at the age of fifteen, when he went to visit his grandfather in New Bedford. "I went to the East to visit my father's father in New Bedford," he later wrote, "and on that trip saw well-to-do, well-mannered colored people; and once, at Rocky Point, Rhode Island, I viewed with astonishment 10,000 Negroes of every hue and bearing. I was transported with amazement and dreams; I apparently noted nothing of poverty and degradation, but only extraordinary beauty of skin color and utter equality of mien, with absence so far as I could see of even the shadow of the line of race."[6]

DuBois graduated with high honors from high school in the

5. *Ibid.*, p. 34.
6. *Ibid.*, p. 35.

spring of 1884. His mother died soon after graduation day. Too poor—and also thought to be too young—to go to college, he finally took a job as timekeeper for a contractor who was building a fabulous "cottage" for the widow of Mark Hopkins, whose father-in-law had made a fortune in railroads and founded one of the first families in San Francisco. He learned a great deal about the ways of men on this responsible job, and was also able to save a little money. In the fall of 1885, he obtained some scholarship aid and entered Fisk University in Nashville, Tennessee, as a sophomore. He would have preferred Harvard, but Fisk in many ways proved to be a very valuable experience. Here for the first time he lived among, and learned about, his fellow Negroes. Though he did learn about a certain segment of the Southern Negro community at Fisk and in Nashville, he was, nevertheless, determined to see it whole. "Somewhat to the consternation of both teachers and fellow students," he obtained a job teaching school in the summer months in West Tennessee. "Needless to say, the experience was invaluable," he wrote. "I traveled not only in space but in time. I touched the very shadow of slavery. I lived and taught school in log cabins built before the Civil War. My school was the second held in the district since emancipation. I touched intimately the lives of the commonest of mankind— people who ranged from barefooted dwellers on dirt floors, with patched rags for clothes, to rough, hard-working farmers, with plain, clean plenty. I saw and talked with white people, noted now their unease, now their truculence and again their friendliness. I nearly fell from my horse when the first school commissioner whom I interviewed invited me to stay to dinner. Afterwards I realized that he meant me to eat at the second, but quite as well-served table."[7]

His years at Fisk, in contrast to his youth in New England, left DuBois with a strong and bitter sense of the "absolute division of the universe into black and white." Yet it was probably a good thing that he went there before finally realizing his boyhood dream of going to Harvard, which he entered on a scholarship, as a junior, in the fall of 1888. "I was happy at

7. *Ibid.*, pp. 37-38.

Harvard, but for unusual reasons," he wrote much later. "One of these unusual circumstances was my acceptance of racial segregation. Had I gone from Great Barrington high school directly to Harvard I would have sought companionship with my white fellows and been disappointed and embittered by a discovery of social limitations to which I had not been used."[8]

On the whole, his days at Cambridge were very lonely. He made friends with only a very few of his classmates and reserved his social life for the stimulating Negro community in and around Boston: "I asked nothing of Harvard but the tutelage of teachers and the freedom of the library. I was quite voluntarily and willingly outside of its social life."[9]

Fortunately, the members of the faculty were far more friendly than the students:

> The Harvard of 1888 was an extraordinary aggregation of great men. Not often since that day have so many distinguished teachers been together in one place and at one time in America. . . . By good fortune, I was thrown into direct contact with many of these men. I was repeatedly a guest in the house of William James; he was my friend and guide to clear thinking; I was a member of the Philosophical Club and talked with Royce and Palmer; I sat in an upper room and read Kant's Critique with Santayana; Shaler invited a Southerner, who objected to sitting by me, out of his class; I became one of Hart's favorite pupils and was afterwards guided by him through my graduate course and started on my work in Germany. It was a great opportunity for a young man and a young American Negro, and I realized it.[10]

Apparently, even the haughty Anglophile and defender of Anglo-Saxon traditions Barrett Wendell knew a good man when he saw one. And DuBois never forgot the following experience:

> I have before me a theme which I wrote October 3, 1890, for Barrett Wendell, then the great pundit of Harvard English. I said: "Spurred by my circumstances, I have always been given to systematically planning my future, not indeed without many

---

8. *Dusk of Dawn,* p. 34.
9. *Ibid.,* p. 35.
10. *Ibid.,* p. 37.

mistakes and frequent alterations, but always with what I now conceive to have been a strangely early and deep appreciation of the fact that to live is a serious thing. I determined while in school to go to college—partly because other men went, partly because I foresaw that such discipline would best fit me for life. . . . I believe foolishly perhaps, but sincerely, that I have something to say to the world, and I have taken English 12 in order to say it well." Barrett Wendell rather liked that last sentence. He read it out to the class.[11]

W. E. B. DuBois did indeed have something to say to the world and he soon went on to write and speak more eloquently in behalf of his race than any other man of his generation. But first he finished his work at Harvard, obtaining an A.B. in 1890, an M.A. in 1891, and completing most of the requirements for the Ph.D. before going abroad for two years on a scholarship. DuBois set sail for Europe on a Dutch boat in the summer of 1892, a year, as he put it, which marked "the high tide of lynching in the United States, when 235 persons were publicly murdered." He studied at the University of Berlin, where he listened to Max Weber and was accepted into "two exclusive seminars run by leaders of the developing social sciences." During the vacations, he traveled all over Europe where he was pleased to find far less racial discrimination than in the United States. He later summed up his experiences in Europe as follows:

From this unhampered social intermingling with Europeans of education and manners, I emerged from the extremes of my racial provincialism. I became more human; learned the place in life of "Wine, Women, and Song;" I ceased to hate or suspect people simply because they belonged to one race or color; and above all I began to understand the real meaning of scientific research and the dim outline of methods of employing its technique and its results in the new social sciences for the settlement of the Negro problems in America.[12]

DuBois returned from Europe in 1894 with an almost blind faith in science and a determination to engage in a career of research, writing, and teaching. He had originally wanted to be a

11. *Ibid.*, pp. 38-39.
12. Logan, *op. cit.*, p. 42.

philosopher but "it was James with his pragmatism and Albert Bushnell Hart with his research method, that turned me back from the lovely but sterile land of philosophic speculation, to the social sciences as the field for gathering and interpreting that body of fact which would apply to my program for the Negro."[13]

After spending a year teaching the classics at Wilberforce, where he was frankly horrified at the low standards and especially the overly emotional religious atmosphere (as contrasted to his own rearing in the Congregational Church in Great Barrington), he was called to the University of Pennsylvania, where he was given an opportunity to carry out his program of applying the methods of science to the Negro problem. In the meantime, he received his Ph.D. from Harvard and had his thesis, *The Suppression of the African Slave-Trade to the United States of America, 1638-1870,* published as the first volume in the Harvard Historical Series, in 1896, the year he began his research on the Philadelphia Negro.

W. E. B. DuBois was brought to Philadelphia largely on the initiative of Susan P. Wharton, a member of one of the city's oldest and most prominent Quaker families. She had long been interested in the problems of Negroes and was a member of the Executive Committee of the Philadelphia College Settlement, which had been founded in 1892. It is important to see that *The Philadelphia Negro* was a product of the New Social Science and Settlement House movements, both of which grew up in this country and in England during the closing decades of the nineteenth century.

"The best account of this new period," writes Nathan Glazer, "and indeed the most important book, to my mind, for an understanding of the rise of the contemporary social scientific approach, is Beatrice Webb's *My Apprenticeship.* Beatrice Webb describes the rise of her interest in social problems, and the unique vantage point afforded to her by the Potter family (she was Beatrice Potter) and its connections to further his interest. Although the most distinguished visitor to her home was Herbert Spencer, two other distinguished Victorians who played a central

---

13. *Ibid.,* p. 39.

role in the development of social science were often there. One was Francis Galton, whose discoveries in correlation were to be largely responsible for moving social statistics from the level of simple enumeration to that of a scientific tool of great precision and value. The other was Charles Booth, who, with his own fortune acquired from industry, was to conduct, beginning in the 1880's, the first great empirical social scientific study, an investigation into the conditions of life among all the people of London."[14]

It was in 1883, the year Karl Marx died, that young Beatrice Potter deserted the social life of fashionable Mayfair and went to the East End of London to work on her friend Charles Booth's famous and seminal study of the life and living conditions of the London poor. The next year, a group of Protestant clergymen, followers of Charles Kingsley and Frederick Dennison Maurice and their Christian Socialism, along with some young college men from Oxford and Cambridge, founded Toynbee Hall, which was an important landmark in the Settlement House and Social Gospel movements in England and also in this country. At the same time, Jane Addams, who had just graduated from college and was traveling abroad, made her first visit to the slums of London's East End. She was so horrified by what she saw there, and so impressed with the work being done at Toynbee Hall and with her newly acquired friend Beatrice Potter, that she came back and founded Hull House, in 1889, in the heart of the Chicago slums. Other settlement houses soon sprang up in most of the major cities along the Eastern seaboard. In the meantime, the famous *Hull House Papers and Maps* were published in 1895, based directly on Charles Booth's methods of research; even the colors on the maps, which indicated different degrees of poverty, were the same.

While the more famous founders of sociology, such as Auguste Comte, Karl Marx, and Herbert Spencer, were predominantly armchair theorists in their approach to understanding the causes and consequences of the industrial and urban revolutions, the rise of capitalism and the problems of labor, it was the more empirical and pragmatic tradition of Charles Booth in England

14. Nathan Glazer, "The Rise of Social Science Research in Europe," in Daniel Lerner, ed., *The Human Meaning of the Social Sciences* (New York: Meridian, 1959), pp. 58-59.

and the Hull House work in this country, as the following paragraph suggests, that inspired young DuBois when he came to Philadelphia.

> Herbert Spencer finished his ten volumes of Synthetic Philosophy in 1896. The biological analogy, the vast generalizations, were striking, but actual scientific accomplishment lagged. For me an opportunity seemed to present itself. . . . I determined to put science into sociology through a study of the condition and problems of my own group. I was going to study the facts, any and all facts, concerning the American Negro and his plight, and by measurement and comparison and research, work up to any valid generalization which I could.[15]

It was in this same spirit that Susan P. Wharton went out to the Wharton School, which a member of her family had founded at the University of Pennsylvania, and prevailed on the Provost, Charles C. Harrison, to undertake a study of the Negro problem in the city's Seventh Ward (where, incidentally, Provost Harrison, Miss Wharton, and many of Philadelphia's more fashionable families lived at that time). Provost Harrison, heir to one of the great sugar fortunes in America, had turned away from business in his later years to devote himself to education and social reform. He was immediately receptive to her plans. (The project was outlined at a meeting at the Wharton residence, 910 Clinton Street, situated only a few blocks from the heart of the Negro ghetto and the College Settlement House at Seventh and South Streets [see map].) It was indeed fortunate for the University, Miss Wharton, and the city as a whole, that a young scholar of DuBois' ability, background, education, and scientific point of view was obtained for the job by a member of the Sociology Department of the Wharton School, Samuel McCune Lindsay. DuBois came to the city in August, 1896, and, except for a brief period of two months during the summer of 1897, when he studied rural Negroes in Virginia because so many of them had recently migrated to Philadelphia at the time of the study, he remained in the city until January, 1898. Many years later, DuBois described his call to Philadelphia and his stay there:

---

15. *Dusk of Dawn*, p. 51.

In the fall of 1896, I went to the University of Pennsylvania as "Assistant Instructor" in Sociology. It all happened this way: Philadelphia, then and still one of the worst governed of America's badly governed cities, was having one of its periodic spasms of reform. A thorough study of causes was called for. Not but what the underlying cause was evident to most white Philadelphians: the corrupt, semi-criminal vote of the Negro Seventh Ward. Everyone agreed that here lay the cancer; but would it not be well to elucidate the known causes by a scientific investigation, with the imprimatur of the University? It certainly would, answered Samuel McCune Lindsay of the Department of Sociology. And he put his finger on me for the task.

There must have been some opposition, for the invitation was not particularly cordial. I was offered a salary of $800 for a limited period of one year. I was given no real academic standing, no office at the University, no official recognition of any kind; my name was even eventually omitted from the catalogue; I had no contact with students, and very little with members of the faculty, even in my department. With my bride of three months, I settled in one room over a cafeteria run by a College Settlement, in the worst part of the Seventh Ward. We lived there a year, in the midst of an atomosphere of dirt, drunkenness, poverty and crime. Murder sat on our doorsteps, police were our government, and philanthropy dropped in with periodic advice.[16]

These are bitter words. And apparently DuBois was not quite true to the facts of the case. There was no evidence in the minutes of the University's Board of Trustees of any "opposition" to the appointment. On a request for information on the case from a DuBois biographer, the late Professor Lindsay replied that DuBois was "quite mistaken about the attitude of the Sociology Department. It was quite friendly, I am sure, and as far as I know that was true of the entire Wharton School faculty."[17] I have quoted this passage from DuBois' writings, nevertheless, because it suggests his own bitterness in 1944, when he wrote the passage, at the general neglect in this country of the Negro problem in the four decades following his publication of *The*

16. Logan, *op. cit.*, p. 44.
17. Rudwick, *op. cit.*, p. 32.

Philadelphia Negro. More important, I think, it may very well reflect the spirit if not the letter of the thoughtless rather than malicious attitudes of whites of that era toward an educated and fastidious Negro like DuBois. For DuBois was very sensitive to the climate of opinion at that time which, by and large, assumed the inferiority of all Negroes, whether educated or not.

The life and thought of every age, one would suppose, is always marked, like the life of every individual, by ambivalence, paradox, and contradictions. In other words, just when many men and women like Beatrice Webb, Jane Addams, or Miss Wharton were dedicating their lives trying to understand and alleviate the horrible conditions that surrounded the lives of the downtrodden at the turn of the century, the dominant values of the comfortable and complacent middle classes were crudely materialistic, smugly racist, and somewhat self-righteous, to say the least. In short, the 1890's were indeed marked by materialism at the top and misery at the bottom of both the class and racial scales. Thus DuBois, for instance, noted that the year 1892 marked the high tide of lynchings in the United States; it was also the year of the bitter and cruel Homestead Strike. In 1894, Coxey's Army marched on Washington. In 1895, South Carolina, following the lead of Mississippi, and under the leadership of the extreme racist Ben Tillman, disfranchised its Negroes; in the same year, the Supreme Court of the United States, in the Plessy vs. Ferguson case, sanctioned the "separate but equal" standard that Booker T. Washington compromised with in his Atlanta speech; and between 1895 and 1909, the Negro was systematically disfranchised throughout the South. It is no wonder that many Americans responded to Bryan's plea, in the campaign of 1896, that Wall Street should not "crucify mankind upon a cross of gold." Perhaps Kelly Miller, the son of former slaves who rose to become a professor of sociology at Howard University, caught the spirit of the "Gay Nineties," as seen from the Negro point of view, in the following summary of the distinction between Frederick Douglass and Booker T. Washington:

> The two men are in part products of their times, but also natural antipodes. Douglass lived in the day of moral giants; Washington lived in the era of merchant princes. The contemporaries of Douglass emphasized the rights of man; those of

Washington, his productive capacity. The age of Douglass acknowledged the sanction of the Golden Rule; that of Washington worships the Rule of Gold. The equality of men was constantly dinned into Douglass' ears; Washington hears nothing but the inferiority of the Negro and the dominance of the Saxon.[18]

The Anglo-Saxon complex Kelly Miller was referring to was, of course, a reflection of the inevitable racial implications in Social Darwinism, which was the overwhelmingly dominant ideology in America at that time. In an age when men thought of themselves as having evolved from the ape rather than having been created in the image of angels, the Negro, it was almost universally agreed among even the most educated people, was definitely an inferior breed and situated at the very base of the evolutionary tree. "Now as to the Negroes," Theodore Roosevelt wrote to his friend Owen Wister, "I entirely agree with you that as a race and in the mass they are altogether inferior to the whites." And Roosevelt never repeated his "mistake," as he called it, of asking Booker T. Washington or any other Negro to the White House. For he was very sensitive to the opinions of an age in which, as the historian Rayford W. Logan has written, "both newspapers and magazines stereotyped, caricatured and ridiculed Negroes in atrocious dialect that shocks the incredulous reader today. Few newspapers in the Deep South today portray the Negro in such outlandish fashion as did the spokesmen for the 'Genteel Tradition in the North.' "[19] Nor must we forget that very distinguished and objective social scientists, almost without exception, agreed with the "Genteel Tradition" and Roosevelt's point of view. With calipers and rulers and all sorts of statistical devices, they were busy building up elaborate classifications of the "inborn" mental and psychological traits of Nordics, Aryans, Semites, Teutons, Hottentots, Japs, Turks, Slavs, and Anglo-Saxons—with Negroes of course at the very bottom of this biological hierarchy.

---

18. Quoted in E. Franklin Frazier, *The Negro in the United States*, p. 545.

19. Rayford W. Logan, *The Negro in the United States*: A Brief History, p. 54.

Finally, it is important to place this dominant American ideology in a larger frame. For it was between the publication of Darwin's *Origin of Species by Natural Selection, or The Preservation of Favored Races in the Struggle for Life,* in 1859, and the Boer War in 1902, that white Western men conquered, explored, fought over, and partitioned among themselves the continent of black Africa below the Sierra. The year of 1896, when DuBois went to Philadelphia, also witnessed Queen Victoria's Diamond Jubilee celebration, a symbol of the high tide of "white supremacy" throughout the world.

It was, then, in the most discouraging and deplorable period in the history of the American Negro since the Civil War that young DuBois came to Philadelphia and set about doing a thorough and objective study of the Negro community. That the book, when finally published in 1899, succeeded in being objective, most modern readers, I think, will recognize. But even at the time of its publication, its reviewers were equally impressed with the author's critical and thorough methods of research. In the *Yale Review,* a reviewer found the book to be "a credit to American scholarship . . . the sort of book of which we have too few. . . . Here is an inquiry, covering a specific field and a considerable period of time, and persecuted with candor, thoroughness and critical judgment."[20] The reviewer in *The Annals* of the American Academy of Political and Social Science (a Southerner) found the book to be "exceptional and scholarly. . . . It is a critical, discriminating statement of the conditions and results of Negro life in a large, northern seaboard city a little more than thirty years after the Civil War . . . and its permanent national value to the scholar and the statesman is predicted."[21] The reviewer in *The Nation* was especially impressed with the historical material included in the book and only criticized the author for taking "too gloomy a view of the situation."[22] The *Outlook* review was long, detailed, and filled with praise: the historical background alone, thought the re-

---

20. *Yale Review,* IX (May, 1900), 110-11.
21. *The Annals* of the American Academy of Social and Political Science, XV (January-May, 1900), 101.
22. *The Nation,* LXIX (1899), 310.

viewer, "would of itself give this volume exceptional value."[23] And he went on to praise DuBois' objectivity: "In no respect does Dr. DuBois attempt to bend the facts so as to plead for his race . . . he is less apologetic than a generous-minded white writer might be. . . . Professor DuBois' aim is always to keep well within the field where his generalizations cannot be disputed."[24]

Thus the reviews at the time of publication invariably praised the book and remarked on the objectivity of the author. In fact, between the lines one has the impression that most of the white reviewers were rather surprised that a Negro author could have been capable of a work of such careful scholarship and objectivity. In spite of this, one is amazed to find that the reviewers did not come out openly and criticize DuBois' definitely environmental, rather than racial, approach to the problems of the Philadelphia Negroes. There was only a hint of this in the *American Historical Review,* in which the reviewer praised the book but questioned the author's optimism in regarding the Negro problem as soluble, in the long run, in terms of status and environmental improvement. The reviewer also, incidentally, appeared to be worried about "race pollution.' The tone of the review is suggested by the following lines:

> The book is not merely a census-like volume of many tables and diagrams of the colored people of Philadelphia. The author seeks to interpret the meaning of statistics in the light of social movements and the characteristics of the times, as, for instance, the growth of the city by foreign immigration. . . . He is perfectly frank, laying all necessary stress on the weaknesses of his people. . . . He shows a remarkable spirit of fairness. If any conclusions are faulty, the fault lies in the overweight given to some of his beliefs and hopes.[25]

After praising DuBois' fairness and outlining some of his findings, the reviewer criticizes DuBois' hopes:

> This state of things is due chiefly, in Dr. DuBois' judgment, to a color prejudice, and this he believes can be done away with in time, just as the class prejudices of earlier centuries in

23. *Outlook,* LXIII (1899), 647-48.
24. *Ibid.*
25. *American Historical Review,* VI (1900-1901), 163.

Europe are being wiped out gradually . . . but we need, what
Dr. DuBois does not give, more knowledge of the effects of the
mixing of blood of very different races, and the possibilities of
absorption of inferior into superior groups of mankind. He
speaks of the "natural repugnance to close intermingling with
unfortunate ex-slaves," but we believe that the separation is
due to differences of race more than of status.[26]

The hereditarian or racial as against the environmental or
cultural approaches to the causes of the differences between
Negroes and whites, both in America and in other parts of the
world, divide men to this day. Perhaps the ultimate truth lies in a
"both/and" rather than an "either/or" approach. Nevertheless—
and especially in an age such as our own which tends to assume,
often dogmatically, the greater importance of environment and
culture—one must look back on *The Philadelphia Negro* as a
pioneering attempt to objectively advance this modern approach
in an era when most men deeply and sincerely felt that fixed
hereditary aptitudes differentiated the races of men and consequently precluded any possibility of eventual integration on a
plane of social, cultural, and political equality. Thus, in answer to
his hereditarian opponents such as the reviewer in the *American
Historical Review*, DuBois fell back on his own broad historical
perspective by reminding his readers in the closing pages how
many once-held hereditarian dogmas had already been eroded by
the passage of time and the changing social situation:

> We rather hasten to forget that once the courtiers of English
> kings looked upon the ancestors of most Americans with far
> greater contempt than these Americans look upon Negroes—
> and perhaps, indeed, had more cause. We forget that once
> French peasants were the "Niggers" of France, and that
> German princelings once discussed with doubt the brains and
> humanity of the *bauer* (p. 386).

It was, then, not only DuBois' painstaking methods of
research and his objective interpretations of the evidence that has
given *The Philadelphia Negro* a permanent place in the socio-

---

26. *Ibid.*, p. 164.

logical literature. It was also the fact that DuBois brought a thoroughly sociological point of view to bear on this carefully collected evidence. In other words, the book, in emphasizing an environmental point of view, made a definite theoretical contribution. Some four decades later, for example, the authors of an important modern study of the Negro community in Chicago, *Black Metropolis,* explicitly referred to this contribution as follows:

In 1899, Dr. W. E. B. DuBois published the first important sociological study of a Negro community in the United States— *The Philadelphia Negro* (University of Pennsylvania). At the outset, he presented an ecological map detailing the distribution of the Negro population by "social condition," and divided his subjects into four "grades:" (1) the "middle classes" and those above; (2) the working people—fair to comfortable; (3) the poor; (4) vicious and criminal classes. Despite the economic emphasis in this classification and his extensive presentation of data on physical surroundings, Du Bois concluded that "there is a far mightier influence to mold and make the citizen, and that is the social atmosphere which surrounds him; first his daily companionship, the thoughts and whims of his class; then his recreation and amusements; finally the surrounding world of American civilization" (p. 309) This emphasis upon the *social* relations—in family, clique, church, voluntary associations, school, and job—as the decisive elements in personality formation is generally accepted. The authors feel that it should also be the guiding thread in a study of "class". . . all serious students of Negro communities since DuBois have been concerned with the nature of social stratification. . . . In the Thirties this interest was given added stimulus by the suggestive hypotheses thrown out by Professor W. Lloyd Warner and by a general concern in anthropological and sociological circles with social stratification in America.[27]

As this quotation from *Black Metropolis* suggests, there has been a direct intellectual line between DuBois' emphasis on class and social environment as major causal agents in personality formation and a whole subsequent tradition in American soci-

27. St. Clair Drake and Horace R. Cayton, *Black Metropolis,* pp. 787-88.

ology. Thus, for example, Franz Boas in his Lowell Lecture, *The Mind of Primitive Man* (1911), was echoing the findings and conclusions of DuBois when he wrote that "the traits of the American Negro are adequately explained on the basis of his history and his social status . . . without falling back upon the theory of hereditary inferiority."[28] And the tradition continued through W. I. Thomas and Florian Znaniecki's classic and pioneering study of the adjustment to the urban environment of Polish peasants in Chicago and Warsaw (*The Polish Peasant in Europe and America* 1918-21), through the whole school of urban sociology which Robert E. Park (for some time an assistant and colleague of Booker T. Washington at Tuskegee) inspired at the University of Chicago during the 1920's, to the later W. Lloyd Warner school of community studies at Harvard and Chicago, which inspired *Black Metropolis* and *Deep South* as well as the classic *Yankee City* Series. The origins, in both method and theoretical point of view, of all of these studies are to be found in *The Philadelphia Negro*.

In many ways, DuBois' whole life experiences before coming to Philadelphia in 1896—his youth, when he competed on his merits with his peers in the white community in Great Barrington, his observations of the faculty and students at Fisk as well as the poorest and most primitive Negroes in West Tennessee, his own achievements at Harvard as well as his contacts with great teachers like William James, and his witnessing the attitudes of educated Europeans toward himself—all combined to prepare him to see that racial inequality was partly a matter of class inequality and to emphasize the need for stratification and the creation of an open and talented elite class within the Negro community. And, above all, he emphasized the fact that this class, already existing in nascent form in Philadelphia, must be recognized by members of the white community who were forever judging all Negroes on the basis of the behavior of the "submerged tenth." "In many respects it is right and proper to judge a people by its best classes rather than by its worst classes or middle ranks," he wrote in the excellent chapter on "The Environment of the Negro" (p. 316). "The highest class of any

---

28. Franz Boas, *The Mind of Primitive Man* (New York, 1911), p. 272.

group," he continued, "represents its possibilities rather than its expectations, as is so often assumed in regard to the Negro. The colored people are seldom judged by their best classes, and often the very existence of classes among them is ignored." Thus DuBois saw very clearly that the white community's propensity to see all Negroes as part of one homogeneous mass served as a rationalization for their own racist thinking. Much of the charitable work among the depressed classes of Negroes, moreover, only served to reinforce white prejudices: "Thus the class of Negroes which the prejudices of the city have distinctly encouraged," wrote DuBois, "is that of the criminal, the lazy and the shiftless; for them the city teems with institutions and charities; for them there is succor and sympathy; for them Philadelphians are thinking and planning; but for the educated and industrious young colored man who wants work and not platitudes, wages and not alms, just rewards and not sermons—for such colored men Philadelphia apparently has no use" (p. 352).

While DuBois was rightly critical of the white community, he also criticized upper-class Negroes for not taking the lead among their own people:

> The aristocracy of the Negro population in education, wealth and general social efficiency . . . are not the leaders or the ideal-makers of their own group in thought, work, or morals. They teach the masses to a very small extent, mingle with them but little, do not largely hire their labor. Instead then of social classes held together by strong ties of mutual interest we have in the case of the Negroes, classes who have much to keep them apart, and only community of blood and color prejudice to bind them togethere. . . . The first impulse of the best, the wisest and richest is to segregate themselves from the mass . . . they make their mistake in failing to recognize that however laudable an ambition to rise may be, the first duty of an upper class is to serve the lowest classes. The aristocracies of all peoples have been slow in learning this and perhaps the Negro is no slower than the rest, but his peculiar situation demands that in his case this lesson be learned sooner (pp. 316-17).

In emphasizing the need for a properly functioning class structure within the Negro community, DuBois was anticipating one of the major themes of the late E. Franklin Frazier's classic study of the emerging Negro middle class in America. Half a century after DuBois' study of Philadelphia, Professor Frazier (the first Negro to be elected president of the American Sociological Society) wrote in his *Black Bourgeoisie*:

> Because of its struggle to gain acceptance by whites, the black bourgeoisie has failed to play the role of a responsible elite in the Negro community . . . they have no real interest in education and genuine culture and spend their leisure in frivolities and in activities designed to win a place in Negro "society." The single factor that has dominated the mental outlook of the black bourgeoisie has been its obsession with the struggle for status.[29]

In the long run, one of the most important contributions of this book, as more than one reviewer at the time of its publication noted, may well be the fact that it is the best documented historical record of an urban and Northern Negro community in existence. Fortunately, DuBois was well trained in, and devoted to, the historian's craft. But it was also fortunate that the city of Philadelphia possessed the oldest and, in 1896, the largest Northern Negro community in the nation, exceeded in population only by the three Southern Negro communities of New Orleans, Washington, D.C., and Baltimore (a border city).

In fact, Negroes had been brought up the Delaware by the Swedes before Penn founded the Colony in 1682. In the city where the Declaration of Independence was written and the nation founded, the Negroes also had an important history, which DuBois carefully documented: here in Philadelphia was the first expression against the slave trade, the first organization for the abolition of slavery, the first legislative enactments for the abolition of slavery, the first attempt at Negro education, the first Negro convention, and so forth.

Since DuBois himself, in this study and in many others, contributed so much to the understanding of his people's history, it seems most appropriate to close this introduction with a brief history of some of the more important sociological changes in the

---

29. E. Franklin Frazier, *Black Bourgeoisie*, pp. 235-36.

Philadelphia Negro community since the turn of the nineteenth century.

The Philadelphia Negro Since DuBois

The most striking thing about the development of the Philadelphia Negro community since DuBois' day is its steady increase in size. In fact, the steady migration of Southern Negroes to Philadelphia began in the decade of the 1890's (see Table 1)

Table 1

PHILADELPHIA NEGRO POPULATION
Increase by Decades (1890–1960)

| | | INCREASE | |
DECADE	POPULATION	NUMBER	PER CENT
1880	31,699		
1890	39,371	7,672	24
1900	62,613	23,242	60
1910	84,459	21,846	33
1920	134,229	49,770	58
1930	219,599	85,370	63
1940	250,880	31,281	14
1950	376,041	125,161	50
1960	529,239	153,198	30

and kept up throughout the twentieth century. DuBois saw this increasing pace of migration and consequently went to Virginia during the first summer of his study in order to see how the Negroes lived in the rural areas, the better to understand their problems of adjustment to urban life. The pace of migration, of course, was greatly increased during World War I and the 1920's. At the same time, anti-Negro attitudes increased, producing racial strife, increasing segregation in public places, and a rapid rise in residential ghettoization. Migration slowed down during the 1930's, then increased again during World War II and the postwar years, until today the Negroes constitute over one fourth

Table 2

PHILADELPHIA NEGRO POPULATION DISTRIBUTION BY CITY SECTIONS
IN 1890 AND 1960

	1890				1960			
	Number Negro	Number Total	Per Cent Negro	Per Cent of Negro Total	Number Negro	Number Total	Per Cent Negro	Per Cent of Negro Total
Center City	15,627	104,154	(15)	(40)	7,476	38,323	(18)	(1)
South Phila.	7,914	218,506	(4)	(20)	66,621	260,767	(30)	(13)
West Phila.	4,080	99,182	(4)	(10)	169,100	402,161	(42)	(32)
North Phila.	7,504	267,044	(3)	(20)	234,646	342,857	(70)	(44)
Kensington	1,329	250,555	(1)	(3)	8,148	257,508	(3)	(2)
Northwest-Far North	1,891	72,229	(2)	(5)	36,506	347,464	(10)	(7)
Greater Northeast	1,026	35,294	(3)	(2)	6,742	353,432	(2)	(1)
City Total	39,371	1,046,964	(37)	(100)	529,239	2,002,512	(26)	(100)

Source: Population of Philadelphia Sections and Wards 1860–1960, Philadelphia City Planning Commission, 1963 (Mimeo.).

Table 3

THREE NEGRO GHETTO WARDS IN PHILADELPHIA 1890–1960

YEAR	30TH WARD SOUTH PHILA.			32ND WARD NORTH PHILA.			24TH WARD WEST PHILA.		
	NUMBER NEGRO	NUMBER TOTAL	PER CENT NEGRO	NUMBER NEGRO	NUMBER TOTAL	PER CENT NEGRO	NUMBER NEGRO	NUMBER TOTAL	PER CENT NEGRO
1890	1789	30614	6%	382	30050	1%	930	42556	2%
1900	5242	28874	20%	962	39889	2%	2193	53200	4%
1910	9999	29209	34%	1517	40293	4%	3958	54370	7%
1920	15481	29471	51%	3926	47540	8%	8152	60408	13%
1930	19537	27783	70%	14476	45663	31%	13041	54947	24%
1940	22185	27605	82%	24975	50062	50%	18343	53803	34%
1950	23789	27208	88%	44872	60860	73%	36741	63391	58%
1960	21587	23527	96%	52191	54497	96%	45666	57987	80%

Note: These three wards, whose boundaries have remained unchanged since 1890 (see Map p. 59), lay in the heart of the three Negro ghettos of Philadelphia as of 1960 (see Table 2). The 30th, the oldest ghetto ward in the city, became half-Negro for the first time in 1920; the 32nd, over half foreign born or foreign stock in 1920 (largely Jewish), first became over half Negro during World War II. In 1960, the 32nd was the largest Negro ward in the city.

Source: Population of Philadelphia Sections and Wards 1860–1960, Philadelphia City Planning Commission, 1963 (Mimeo.).

of the city's residents in contrast to the less than 5 per cent minority of DuBois' day.

With the steady increase in the size of the Negro population, the pattern of residential distribution also changed. In contrast to 1890, when most of the city's Negroes lived in the center of the city and close to their white neighbors, by 1960, a majority of Negroes had moved to the southern, northern, and western sections of the city (Table 2). In 1960, for the first time in the city's history, one whole city section contained more Negro than white residents (Table 2: 70 per cent Negro in North Philadelphia). The changing size and residential distribution of the Negro population has, of course, been both cause and result of changing social relations between the races.

In Philadelphia in the 1890's, the largest concentration of Negroes was in the Seventh Ward which DuBois studied in detail. But this Ward was, at the same time, the center of the city's "silk stocking" or upper-class neighborhood. The majority of the Negroes in the Ward were employed as domestic servants, and lived in close proximity to (if not in the homes of) their employers. Social relations between whites and Negroes, therefore, were marked by clear status differentials and high social interaction, rather than by the residential segregation, and low social interaction which characterizes the relations between the races today. In 1960, the Seventh Ward, as in its heyday of fashion in the 1890's, is still about one-third Negro. But most of the members of the white upper class have migrated to the suburbs. Though there are still a few fashionable white blocks, many of the old mansions have long since been converted into cultural institutions, apartments, rooming houses, and offices for physicians and other professional people. Both the white and Negro populations have steadily declined in absolute numbers: In 1890, the Seventh Ward had 30,179 residents of whom 8,861 (or 30 per cent) were Negroes; in 1960, there were only 17,079 residents in the Ward, of whom 6,308 (or 35 per cent) were Negroes.[30] And of course, in our modern, mechanized world of smaller middle-class households, live-in domestic servants are no

---

30. *Population of Philadelphia Sections and Wards 1860-1960.*

longer fashionable or economically feasible, producing a consequent decline in social relations between the races.

Following a pattern set by the Georgetown community in Washington, D.C., in an earlier day, the Seventh Ward has been witnessing, during the 1960's, a steadily increasing pattern of white invasion of the Negro areas of the Ward. Though the Ward has recently been absorbed into one all-inclusive center-city ward, its traditional area will be largely white by 1970. More and more white, suburban families are now moving back to the city, both those who have raised their children and those of the younger generation who are disenchanted with the suburban way of life. But they will be moving back to a more and more segregated city, as the figures in Tables 2 and 3 clearly show.

Fortunately for the historian and the sociologist, there were three major ghettoized Negro wards in the city in 1960 which had not had their boundaries changed since 1890 (Table 3). The changing racial composition of these three wards reflects the history of the Negro community in the city in the twentieth century. As an inspection of the figures in Table 3 will show, all three of these wards contained a small minority of Negro residents in 1890. But, as the size of the Philadelphia Negro community steadily increased in the twentieth century, each ward eventually became ghettoized in a definite historical pattern. The Thirtieth Ward, which lies just to the South of the Seventh (see Ward Map in 1890, p. 60), became the city's first Negro ghetto (51 per cent Negro in 1920). It was no accident that Philadelphia's first race riot in the twentieth century, in the summer of 1918, took place on the southern boundary of the Thirtieth Ward. Thus in her Ph.D. dissertation at the University of Pennsylvania, published in 1921, Sadie Tanner Mossell (now Mrs. Raymond Pace Alexander, wife of a noted jurist, and herself a lawyer and chairman of Philadephia's Commission on Human Relations) wrote that "a colored probation officer of the Municipal Court, a woman of refinement and training and an old citizen of Philadelphia, purchased and took up residence at the house numbered 2936 Ellsworth Street. The white people in the neighborhood resented her living there and besieged the house. A race riot ensued in which two men were killed and sixty injured."[31]

The steady migration of Negroes into the city during the war years and the 1920's not only contributed to the ghettoization of the Negro community; it also contributed to the segregation of Negro children in the schools and the closing of most of the city's commercial and entertainment centers to Negroes: As Miss Mossell noted, "such social privileges as the service of eating houses and the attending of white churches and theaters by Negroes, were practically withdrawn after the influx of Negro migrants into Philadelphia."[32] The older Negro residents of the city were naturally upset by this new segregation. The Mossell study continued:

> The old colored citizens of Philadelphia resented this. Placed the blame at the migrant's door and stood aloof from him. Negro preachers invited the new arrivals into the church but many of the congregations made him know that he was not wanted. In some cases the church split over the matter, the migrants and their sympathizers withdrawing and forming a church for themselves.[33]

South Philadelphia, especially the southern part of the Seventh Ward running along Lombard and South (the oldest Negro commerical street in the city) streets, together with the whole Thirtieth Ward, was Philadelphia's first Negro ghetto. And it remained so from the 1920's through World War II. Beginning in the 1920's, however, another Negro ghetto began to develop in North Philadelphia (see Tables 2 and 3). Thus in 1920, the Thirty-second Ward was composed primarily of residents of foreign-born and foreign-stock (mostly Jewish) origins. In the course of the next decade, however, the Negro population increased almost fourfold, and by 1930 made up nearly one third of the Ward's residents (Table 3). By 1940, the Thirty-second Ward was about half Negro, as was the Forty-seventh, an immediately adjacent ward to the south (the

---

31. Sadie Tanner Mossell, "The Standard of Living Among One Hundred Negro Migrant Families in Philadelphia," p. 9.
32. *Ibid.*
33. *Ibid.*

Forty-seventh was cut out of the eastern half of the Twenty-ninth after the 1910 census and hence not used for Table 3). By 1950, the Thirty-second, the Forty-seventh, and three other North Philadelphia wards were over half Negro; by 1960, this whole section became the city's major ghetto (70 per cent Negro).

During the long, hot summer of 1964, a series of race riots broke out in major American cities, beginning in Harlem in July and ending in Philadelphia on the last day of August. Just as the riot of 1918 had broken out along the boundary of the Thirtieth Ward ghetto, so it was no accident that the racial disturbance in 1964 broke out on the boundary between wards Thirty-two and Forty-seven, along Columbia Avenue at 22nd Street, when a husband and wife, both intoxicated, were found quarreling by the police. Rioting soon spread throughout the North Philadelphia ghetto, killing two persons, injuring 339, and producing some $3 million worth of property damage.

The causes of any riot are many and complex. But DuBois would have agreed that one of the important causes in 1964 was the fact that the Negro masses in North Philadelphia were almost completely cut off from the more affluent and successful members of their own race. Most of the solid Negro citizens live in more suburban areas of the city and, like their counterparts whom DuBois criticized in his day, are more concerned with their own careers than with the problems of racial leadership. An exception was the local head of the NAACP, Cecil Moore, a flamboyant, charming, but often irresponsible individual who has stepped into the leadership vacuum left by the more solid Negro establishment. For unlike the establishment Negroes, Moore resides within the North Philadelphia ghetto and was on the scene during the riots, doing his best to calm his neighbors down. Lenora E. Berson, in her study of the riot, wrote:

> Today, only the National Association for the Advancement of Colored People (NAACP) has any real following in North Philadelphia. The Student Non-Violent Coordinating Committee (SNCC) and the Congress of Racial Equality (CORE) have made little headway in the city.
> Since his ascension to the presidency of the Philadelphia

Branch in January, 1963, Cecil Moore has transformed the NAACP from a conservative institution into a mass-membership action organization.

Much of Moore's strength within the local NAACP comes from its North Philadelphia members, whom he recruited into the organization. Unlike most Negro leaders, Moore lives in the riot area. He calls the North Philadelphians "my people," and many feel they are just that. In a poll of residents conducted by Radio Station WDAS, Moore was found to be far and away the best-known Philadelphia Negro.[34]

The last Negro ghetto to develop was that of West Philadelphia. By 1950, the Twenty-fourth Ward had more Negro than white residents for the first time. It has never reached the high proportion of Negroes which marks the Thirtieth in South Philadelphia, or the Thirty-second in North Philadelphia, largely because, since the 1950's, the southern part of the ward has developed into a bohemian and intellectual community. Once an elite residential neighborhood containing some of the finest examples of Victorian architecture in the city, this part of the Twenty-fourth, known as "Powelton Village," has become a more or less integrated and middle-class community, made up largely of graduate students and faculty members of the University of Pennsylvania and other local institutions, as well as other professionals possessing liberal or bohemian values. There is a great deal of neighborhhod pride in this area and some civic concern for life in the neighboring ghetto to the north.

By 1960, fourteen wards in the city—eight in North Philadelphia, three in South Philadelphia, and three in West Philadelphia—contained a majority of Negro residents. Indeed, the racial composition of the city and the residential distribution of its Negroes had changed beyond recognition since DuBois' day.

And so in many ways had the economic position of the Negroes, both for the better and for the worse. DuBois was vitally concerned with the depressed and segregated economic plight of the Negroes in the last decade of the nineteenth century, which was probably worse than it had been during the first decade of the century. He considered freedom and political rights

---

34. Lenora E. Berson, *Case Study of a Riot*, p. 30.

to be a mere sham unless Negroes were also able to take their rightful place in the city's economic life. He was, for instance, horrified to find that the depressed economic plight of his people pushed them into close social relationships with the most corrupt elements of machine politics. Above all he stressed the fact that the lack of opportunity to advance by education or hard work corrupted the Negro and drove him into the psychological environment of "excuse and listless despair." Thus he wrote: "The humblest white employee knows that the better he does his work the more chance there is for him to rise in business. The black employee knows that the better he does his work the longer he may do it; he can not hope for promotion" (p. 328). Aware of his own position in spite of his educational qualifications, DuBois saw that educational attainments of Negroes only led to frustration: "A graduate of the University of Pennsylvania in mechanical engineering, well recommended," he wrote, "obtained work in the city, through an advertisement, on account of his excellent record. He worked a few hours and then was discharged because he was found to be colored. He is now a waiter at the University Club, where his white fellow graduates dine." A graduate in pharmacy applied for a job and was given the following answer: "I wouldn't have a darky to clean out my store, much less stand behind the counter" (p. 328). Clerks and white-collar jobs were, of course, unobtainable, but so were both skilled and unskilled jobs in industry. DuBois noted one exception to this at the Midvale Steel Works, where the manager, dubbed a "crank" by many of his peers, had employed some 200 Negroes who worked along with white mechanics "without friction or trouble."* Finally, DuBois deplored the fact that, unlike other minority groups, Negroes were rarely found running their own businesses. Those that did exist were marginal. In short, the vast majority of Negroes in the city in DuBois' day were relegated to domestic service or allied personal services such as catering or hotel jobs as waiters, porters, shoe-shine boys (some in their fifties and sixties), and so forth.

As of the 1960's, though Negroes are surely a long way from

---

*Though DuBois did not mention it, the "crank" at the Midvale Steel Works was Frederick W. Taylor, who eventually became world famous as the "father of scientific management."

obtaining equal opportunity with whites, there is no question that opportunities for Negro employment in the city have improved greatly since the 1890's when DuBois painted a dismal picture of their plight. Perhaps the first wave of improvement in employment opportunities in the city, as well as all over the nation, came during World War I—incidentally a mixed blessing. While, as noted above, there was virtually no industrial employment of Negroes in 1896, Miss Mossell estimated that some 30,000 Negro laborers were employed by Philadelphia firms as of 1917. The Midvale Steel Company, which was the exception in 1896 when it employed some 200 Negroes, employed some 4000 Negroes in 1917. While this new employment was a change for the better in some ways, it also had unfortunate consequences. "The Pennsylvania Railroad," wrote Miss Mossell at the time, "was the only industry which provided any kind of housing for the migrant. The camps in which it lodged him, however, proved to be of little assistance, since the camps themselves, consisting of ordinary tents and box cars, did not provide adequate shelter."[35]

The living conditions of the Negro migrants were miserable enough during the war. But things were even worse when the war came to an end. Unemployment, idleness, racial riots, and continual strife marked Negro-white relations during what Eugene P. Foley has called "the warring Twenties."[36] In fact, racial unrest was continual up to and after the time of the passage by Pennsylvania of its first Civil Rights Act of 1935. Though Negroes were now employed in industry, their inferior position and pay was taken for granted. For example, the city went through the most crippling transit strike in its history in the early 1940's. The strike, which cost the taxpayers more than $10 million, was due to the fact that white workers refused to go back to their jobs as long as Negro workers were given equal pay for equal work. On the whole, then, it can be said that Negroes made very little headway in breaking down discrimination in employment throughout the 1920's and 1930's. Employment in industry, of

---

35. Mossell, *op. cit.*, p. 7.
36. Eugene P. Foley, "The Negro Businessman: In Search of a Tradition," p. 573. This is an excellent study of Negro business in America and is most relevant here because most of the empirical data was taken from the Philadelphia community.

course, picked up during World War II, but real gains awaited the postwar period.

The 1950's were definitely years of increasing opportunities for Philadelphia Negroes, even though in 1960 Negroes were twice as likely to be unemployed as whites (10 per cent vs. 5 per cent). In the first place there was a great decline in the proportion of Negroes engaged in domestic service.* DuBois found that 88.5 per cent of the females, and 61.5 per cent of the males in the Seventh Ward were domestic servants. By 1960, these proportions had declined on a city-wide basis to 0.6 per cent of the males and 3.3 per cent of the females.[37] The big change came in the 1950's, when male domestic service declined by 61.2 per cent, and female by 29.9 per cent, in the course of a single decade. In contrast to this decline in the proportion of Negroes in these occupations which stigmatized their inferior position, white-collar employment among Philadelphia Negroes increased in a relatively spectacular fashion. Between 1950 and 1960, for example, the proportion of Negro males employed as clerical workers increased by 58.9 per cent, that of females by 221.8 per cent. At the same time, the proportion of Negro males in professional occupations increased by 45.9 per cent, of females by 90.9 per cent; salesmen increased by 30.7 per cent, saleswomen by 88.4 per cent.

These statistics showing the quantitative increase in the proportion of Negroes in white-collar occupations during the 1950's reflect unprecedented changes in the quality of race relations in the center city. As of the 1930's, for instance, one rarely saw a Negro in the major downtown department and clothing stores, in banks, moving-picture houses, theaters, or other public places. No major department store or bank had Negroes in white-collar positions dealing directly with the public. No Negro lawyer could obtain office space in the center city business district. Negroes sat in the balconies of the big movie palaces. Hotels and restaurants were strictly segregated. Most of these strict taboos came in

---

*DuBois was very concerned about the low sex ratio (80) among Negroes and its effect on the family. It is consequently of interest that, in 1960, the sex ratio of Negroes in the city had increased to 90, partly a reflection of the decline of domestic service as the main Negro occupation.

37. *Philadelphia's Non-White Population 1960*, Tables 5 and 5a.

during and immediately after World War I; all of them were removed in the decade of the 1950's.

DuBois was particularly interested in the poor record of Negroes as businessmen. In 1896, there were no more than 300 Negro-owned businesses in the city. The majority of them were barbershops, catering establishments, and restaurants—all extensions of the servant role. And most of them were marginal, with the exception of a few well-known caterers. There is a direct relation, according to Eugene P. Foley, who has studied the Negro businessman in Philadelphia and elsewhere, between the ghettoization of the Negro and the growth of Negro businesses.[38] In fact, among Negroes, as among whites, immigrants to the city seem more likely to go into business for themselves than older residents. Thus in 1964, there were over 4000 Negro-owned businesses in the city, most of them located within the boundaries of the three Negro ghettos. Unfortunately, however, most of these businesses were pretty much of the same marginal character as those of DuBois' day. Along with the absence of responsible leadership this lack of success in business enterprise was certainly an important factor in the North Philadelphia riots of 1964. In her study of the riots, for example, Lenora E. Berson found this to be true.

The history of the Jews and of North Philadelphia combined to make the Jewish merchants the major representatives of the white establishment in the area. But it was as whites and as merchants and realtors rather than as Jews per se that they bore the brunt of the Negroes' attack. Anti-Semitism was not a primary factor in the rioting.

Nevertheless, the Jews do have a special and ambiguous position in the Negro ghetto. In every large city, Jewish organizations and individuals have long been in the forefront of the civil rights campaigns. In Philadelphia, two white board members of the NAACP are Jews, as is the only white elected official from North Central Philadelphia, State Senator Charles Weiner. The two Negro-oriented radio stations in the city are owned by Jews. It is likely that many, if not most, of North Philadelphia's residents are treated by Jewish doctors, advised by Jewish lawyers and served by Jewish community agencies.

---

38. Foley, *op. cit.*, p. 569.

But the landlord, too, is likely to be Jewish, as is the grocer and the man who owns the appliance store on the corner. All too often the Negro sees himself as a victim of their exploitation, and the contrast between himself and the more affluent businessmen of the community generates bitterness and resentment.[39]

The living conditions in the North Philadelphia ghetto are still deplorable and probably getting worse; and they are so dehumanizing largely because of the moral myopia of white residents of the City of Brotherly Love. At the same time, there is cause for hope if one takes DuBois' position that the ultimate salvation of the Negro community depends on its "Talented Tenth." He opened his famous essay on the "Talented Tenth" as follows:

The Negro Race, like all races, is going to be saved by its exceptional men. The problem of education, then, among Negroes must first of all deal with the Talented Tenth; it is the problem of developing the Best of this race that may guide the Mass away from the contamination and death of the Worst, in their own and other races.[40]

Opportunities for the Talented Tenth within the Philadelphia Negro community have opened up at an increasing rate since the end of World War II. Of non-white Philadelphians aged twenty-five and over, for example, the proportion that had finished high school tripled, the proportion that had finished college doubled between 1940 and 1960. Furthermore, in contrast to DuBois' day when employment for educated Negroes was almost non-existent, there are now more jobs available for educated Negroes than there are educated Negroes to fill them. Finally, DuBois would have been most gratified that, since World War II, talented Negroes have moved into elite positions on the local bar and bench, in business, in politics, and on the faculties of the local colleges and universities.

In closing, perhaps the best way to gain a historical perspec-

39. Berson, *op. cit.*, p. 46.
40. W. E. B. DuBois, "The Talented Tenth," in *The Negro Problem* (New York, 1903), p. 33.

tive on the dramatic changes in the opportunities that have opened for talented Negroes since DuBois' day, might be to speculate how he himself would now be received by the University of Pennsylvania. And certainly there is no question that today, if a gifted young Negro with a recent Ph.D. from Harvard, a book published in the Harvard Historical Series, and two years study abroad should apply for a position in the Sociology Department, he would be welcomed with open arms as an Assistant Professor at least, and at a salary of over $10,000 a year. In fact, he would hardly need to apply; for he would have been vigorously recruited; and he probably would not even consider Pennsylvania because of the great demand for young Negro sociologists at the very best sociology departments in the nation.

E.D.B.

University of Pennsylvania
June, 1967

SUPPLEMENTARY BIBLIOGRAPHY

The following selected bibliography will serve to bring DuBois' bibliography up to date.

I. *General Works on the Negro in America.* If available in a paperback edition, the citation is followed by (P).

Bardolph, Richard. *The Negro Vanguard.* New York: Holt, Rinehart & Winston, 1959. (P)

Breyfogle, William A. *Make Free: The Story of the Underground Railroad.* Philadelphia: Lippincott, 1958.

Broderick, Francis L. *W. E. B. DuBois: Negro Leader in a Time of Crisis.* Stanford, Calif.: Stanford University Press, 1959. (P)

Clark, Kenneth B. *Dark Ghetto: Dilemmas of Social Power.* New York: Harper & Row, 1965.

Deutsch, Morton, and Collins, Mary E. *Interracial Housing: A Psychological Evaluation of a Social Experiment.* Minneapolis: University of Minnesota Press, 1951.

Dollard, John. *Caste and Class in a Southern Town.* New Haven: Yale University Press, 1937. (P)

Drake, St. Clair, and Cayton, Horace R. *Black Metropolis: A Study of Negro Life in a Northern City*. New York: Harper & Row, 1962. (P)

DuBois, W. E. B. *The Negro in Business*. Atlanta, Ga.: Atlanta University Press, 1899.

———. "The Negroes of Farmville, Virginia: A Social Study," *Bulletin of the United States Department of Labor*, III (January, 1898).

———. "My Evolving Program for Negro Freedom," in Rayford W. Logan, ed., *What The Negro Wants*. Chapel Hill: University of North Carolina Press, 1944. (P)

Elkins, Stanley M. *Slavery: A Problem in American Institutional Life*. Chicago: University of Chicago Press, 1959. (P)

Foley, Eugene P. "The Negro Businessman: In Search of a Tradition," in Talcott Parsons and Kenneth B. Clark, eds., *The Negro American*. Boston: Beacon Press, 1965. (P)

Franklin, John Hope. *From Slavery to Freedom: A History of American Negroes*, 2d ed. New York: Alfred A. Knopf, 1956.

Frazier, E. Franklin. *Black Bourgeoisie*. New York: Free Press, 1957. (P)

———. *The Negro in the United States*, rev. ed. New York: Macmillan, 1957.

Glazer, Nathan, and Moynihan, Donald P. *Beyond The Melting Pot: The Negroes, Puerto Ricans, Jews, Italians and Irish in New York City*. Cambridge, Mass.: M.I.T. Press, 1963. (P)

Harris, Abram L. *The Negro as Capitalist: A Study of Banking and Business Among American Negroes*. Philadelphia: American Academy of Political and Social Science, 1936.

Logan, Rayford W. *The Negro in the United States: A Brief History*. Princeton, N. J.: Van Nostrand, 1957. (P)

Lubell, Samuel. *White and Black: Test of a Nation*. New York: Harper & Row, 1964.

McKay, Claude. *Harlem: Negro Metropolis*. New York: E. P. Dutton, 1940.

Myrdal, Gunnar. *An American Dilemma: The Negro Problem and Modern Democracy*. New York: Harper & Row, 1944. (P)

Redding, Saunders. *The Lonesome Road: The Story of the Negro in America*. New York: Doubleday, 1958. (P)

Silberman, Charles E. *Crisis in Black and White*. New York: Random House, 1964. (P)

Taeuber, Karl E. and Alma F. *Negroes in Cities*. Chicago: Aldine, 1965.

Washington, Booker T. *Up From Slavery: An Autobiography*. New York: Doubleday, 1901. (P)

Weaver, Robert C. *The Negro Ghetto*. New York: Harcourt, Brace & World, 1948.

Wilson, James Q. *Negro Politics: The Search for Leadership*. New York: Free Press, 1961.

Woodward, C. Vann. *The Strange Career of Jim Crow*. New York: Oxford University Press, 1957. (P)

II. Publications Relevant to *The Philadelphia Negro*.

Alexander, Ramond Pace. "The Struggle Against Racism in Philadelphia from 1923 to 1948." Speech delivered before The Business and Professional Group of the American Jewish Congress, Philadelphia, 1950.

Berson, Lenora E. *Case Study of a Riot: The Philadelphia Story*. New York: Institute of Human Relations Press, 1966.

Drexel Institute of Technology. *An Analysis of Little Businessmen in Philadelphia*. Philadelphia, 1964.

Mossell, Sadie Tanner. "The Standard of Living Among One Hundred Negro Migrant Families in Philadelphia," *The Annals* of the American Academy of Social and Political Science, XCVIII, 1921.

City of Philadelphia, Commission on Human Relations. *Philadelphia's Non-White Population 1960*. Report No. 1, Demographic Data; Report No. 2, Housing Data; Report No. 3, Socioeconomic Data.

————. *General Socio-Economic Characteristics and Trends, Philadelphia and Environs*. Public Information Bulletin 8-C, April, 1963.

The Philadelphia Colored Directory. Philadelphia Colored Directory Co., 1907.

Population of Philadelphia Sections and Wards: 1860–1960. Philadelphia City Planning Commission, 1963.

Scott, Emmett J. *Negro Migration During The War*. New York: Oxford University Press, 1920.

SEVENTH
WARD

[*Taken from publications of the American Academy, No. 150, July 2, 1895. The large figures refer to voting precincts.*]

THE PHILADELPHIA NEGRO.

CHAPTER I.

THE SCOPE OF THIS STUDY.

1. General Aim.—This study seeks to present the results of an inquiry undertaken by the University of Pennsylvania into the condition of the forty thousand or more people of Negro blood now living in the city of Philadelphia. This inquiry extended over a period of fifteen months and sought to ascertain something of the geographical distribution of this race, their occupations and daily life, their homes, their organizations, and, above all, their relation to their million white fellow-citizens. The final design of the work is to lay before the public such a body of information as may be a safe guide for all efforts toward the solution of the many Negro problems of a great American city.

2. The Methods of Inquiry.—The investigation began August the first, 1896, and, saving two months, continued until December the thirty-first, 1897. The work commenced with a house-to-house canvass of the Seventh Ward. This long narrow ward, extending from South Seventh street to the Schuylkill River and from Spruce street to South street, is an historic centre of Negro population, and contains to-day a fifth of all the Negroes in this city.[1] It was therefore thought best to make an

---

[1] I shall throughout this study use the term "Negro," to designate all persons of Negro descent, although the appellation is to some extent illogical. I shall, moreover, capitalize the word, because I believe that eight million Americans are entitled to a capital letter.

intensive study of conditions in this district, and afterward
to supplement and correct this information by general
observation and inquiry in other parts of the city.

Six schedules were used among the nine thousand
Negroes of this ward ; a family schedule with the usual
questions as to the number of members, their age and sex,
their conjugal condition and birthplace, their ability to
read and write, their occupation and earnings, etc. ; an
individual schedule with similar inquiries ; a home
schedule with questions as to the number of rooms, the
rent, the lodgers, the conveniences, etc. ; a street schedule
to collect data as to the various small streets and alleys,
and an institution schedule for organizations and institutions ; finally a slight variation of the individual schedule
was used for house-servants living at their places of employment. [2]

This study of the central district of Negro settlement
furnished a key to the situation in the city ; in the other
wards therefore a general survey was taken to note any
striking differences of condition, to ascertain the general
distribution of these people, and to collect information and
statistics as to organizations, property, crime and pauperism,
political activity, and the like. This general inquiry, while
it lacked precise methods of measurement in most cases,
served nevertheless to correct the errors and illustrate the
meaning of the statistical material obtained in the house-
to-house canvass.

Throughout the study such official statistics and historical matter as seemed reliable were used, and experienced
persons, both white and colored, were freely consulted.

3. **The Credibility of the Results.**—The best available
methods of sociological research are at present so liable to
inaccuracies that the careful student discloses the results
of individual research with diffidence ; he knows that they
are liable to error from the seemingly ineradicable faults of

---

[2] See Appendix A for form of schedules used.

the statistical method, to even greater error from the methods of general observation, and, above all, he must ever tremble lest some personal bias, some moral conviction or some unconscious trend of thought due to previous training, has to a degree distorted the picture in his view. Convictions on all great matters of human interest one must have to a greater or less degree, and they will enter to some extent into the most cold-blooded scientific research as a disturbing factor.

Nevertheless here are social problems before us demanding careful study, questions awaiting satisfactory answers. We must study, we must investigate, we must attempt to solve ; and the utmost that the world can demand is, not lack of human interest and moral conviction, but rather the heart-quality of fairness, and an earnest desire for the truth despite its possible unpleasantness.

In a house-to-house investigation there are, outside the attitude of the investigator, many sources of error : misapprehension, vagueness and forgetfulness, and deliberate deception on the part of the persons questioned, greatly vitiate the value of the answers ; on the other hand, conclusions formed by the best trained and most conscientious students on the basis of general observation and inquiry are really inductions from but a few of the multitudinous facts of social life, and these may easily fall far short of being essential or typical.

The use of both of these methods which has been attempted in this study may perhaps have corrected to some extent the errors of each. Again, whatever personal equation is to be allowed for in the whole study is one unvarying quantity, since the work was done by one investigator, and the varying judgments of a score of census-takers was thus avoided.[3]

---

[3]The appended study of domestic service was done by Miss Isabel Eaton, Fellow of the College Settlements Association. Outside of this the work was done by the one investigator.

Despite all drawbacks and difficulties, however, the main results of the inquiry seem credible. They agree, to a large extent, with general public opinion, and in other respects they seem either logically explicable or in accord with historical precedents. They are therefore presented to the public, not as complete and without error, but as possessing on the whole enough reliable matter to serve as the scientific basis of further study, and of practical reform.

CHAPTER II.

4. The Negro Problems of Philadelphia.—In Philadelphia, as elsewhere in the United States, the existence of certain peculiar social problems affecting the Negro people are plainly manifest. Here is a large group of people—perhaps forty-five thousand, a city within a city—who do not form an integral part of the larger social group. This in itself is not altogether unusual; there are other unassimilated groups: Jews, Italians, even Americans; and yet in the case of the Negroes the segregation is more conspicuous, more patent to the eye, and so intertwined with a long historic evolution, with peculiarly pressing social problems of poverty, ignorance, crime and labor, that the Negro problem far surpasses in scientific interest and social gravity most of the other race or class questions.

The student of these questions must first ask, What is the real condition of this group of human beings? Of whom is it composed, what sub-groups and classes exist, what sort of individuals are being considered? Further, the student must clearly recognize that a complete study must not confine itself to the group, but must specially notice the environment; the physical environment of city, sections and houses, the far mightier social environment—the surrounding world of custom, wish, whim, and thought which envelops this group and powerfully influences its social development.

Nor does the clear recognition of the field of investigation simplify the work of actual study; it rather increases it, by revealing lines of inquiry far broader in scope than first thought suggests. To the average Philadelphian the

whole Negro question reduces itself to a study of certain
slum districts.   His mind reverts to Seventh and Lombard
streets and to Twelfth and Kater streets of to-day, or to
St. Mary's in the past. Continued and widely known
charitable work in these sections makes the problem of
poverty familiar to him ; bold and daring crime too often
traced to these centres has called his attention to a problem of crime, while the scores of loafers, idlers and prostitutes who crowd the sidewalks here night and day
remind him of a problem of work.

All this is true—all these problems are there and of
threatening intricacy ; unfortunately, however, the interest
of the ordinary man of affairs is apt to stop here.   Crime,
poverty and idleness affect his interests unfavorably and
he would have them stopped ; he looks upon these slums
and slum characters as unpleasant things which should in
some way be removed for the best interests of all.   The
social student agrees with him so far, but must point out
that the removal of unpleasant features from our complicated modern life is a delicate operation requiring knowledge and skill; that a slum is not a simple fact, it is a
symptom and that to know the removable causes of the
Negro slums of Philadelphia requires a study that takes
one far beyond the slum districts.   For few Philadelphians
realize how the Negro population has grown and spread.
There was a time in the memory of living men when a
small district near Sixth and Lombard streets compre-
hended the great mass of the Negro population of the
city.   This is no longer so.   Very early the stream of the
black population started northward, but the increased
foreign immigration of 1830 and later turned it back.
It started south also but was checked by poor houses and
worse police protection.   Finally with gathered momentum the emigration from the slums started west, rolling on
slowly and surely, taking Lombard street as its main
thoroughfare, gaining early foothold in West Philadelphia,

and turning at the Schuylkill River north and south to the newer portions of the city.

Thus to-day the Negroes are scattered in every ward of the city, and the great mass of them live far from the whilom centre of colored settlement. What, then, of this great mass of the population? Manifestly they form a class with social problems of their own—the problems of the Thirtieth Ward differ from the problems of the Fifth, as the black inhabitants differ. In the former ward we have represented the rank and file of Negro working-people ; laborers and servants, porters and waiters. This is at present the great middle class of Negroes feeding the slums on the one hand and the upper class on the other. Here are social questions and conditions which must receive the most careful attention and patient interpretation.

Not even here, however, can the social investigator stop. He knows that every group has its upper class ; it may be numerically small and socially of little weight, and yet its study is necessary to the comprehension of the whole—it forms the realized ideal of the group, and as it is true that a nation must to some extent be measured by its slums, it is also true that it can only be understood and finally judged by its upper class.

The best class of Philadelphia Negroes, though sometimes forgotten or ignored in discussing the Negro problems, is nevertheless known to many Philadelphians. Scattered throughout the better parts of the Seventh Ward, and on Twelfth, lower Seventeenth and Nineteenth streets, and here and there in the residence wards of the northern, southern, and western sections of the city is a class of caterers, clerks, teachers, professional men, small merchants, etc., who constitute the aristocracy of the Negroes. Many are well-to-do, some are wealthy, all are fairly educated, and some liberally trained. Here too are social problems—differing from those of the other classes, and differing too from those of the whites of a corresponding

grade, because of the peculiar social environment in which
the whole race finds itself, which the whole race feels, but
which touches this highest class at most points and tells
upon them most decisively.

Many are the misapprehensions and misstatements as to
the social environment of Negroes in a great Northern city.
Sometimes it is said, here they are free; they have the
same chance as the Irishman, the Italian, or the Swede; at
other times it is said, the environment is such that it is
really more oppressive than the situation in Southern cities.
The student must ignore both of these extreme statements
and seek to extract from a complicated mass of facts the
tangible evidence of a social atmosphere surrounding
Negroes, which differs from that surrounding most whites;
of a different mental attitude, moral standard, and economic
judgment shown toward Negroes than toward most other
folk. That such a difference exists and can now and then
plainly be seen, few deny; but just how far it goes and
how large a factor it is in the Negro problems, nothing but
careful study and measurement can reveal.

Such then are the phenomena of social condition and
environment which this study proposes to describe, analyze,
and, so far as possible, interpret.

5. **Plan of Presentment.**—The study as taken up here
divides itself roughly into four parts : the history of the
Negro people in the city, their present condition considered
as individuals, their condition as an organized social group,
and their physical and social environment. To the history
of the Negro but two chapters are devoted—a brief sketch
—although the subject is worthy of more extended study
than the character of this essay permitted.

Six chapters consider the general condition of the
Negroes: their number, age and sex, conjugal condition,
and birthplace; what degree of education they have
obtained, and how they earn a living. All these subjects
are treated usually for the Seventh Ward somewhat

minutely, then more generally for the city, and finally such historical material is adduced as is available for comparison.

Three chapters are devoted to the group life of the Negro; this includes a study of the family, of property, and of organizations of all sorts. It also takes up such phenomena of social maladjustment and individual depravity as crime, pauperism and alcoholism.

One chapter is devoted to the difficult question of environment, both physical and social, one to certain results of the contact of the white and black races, one to Negro suffrage, and a word of general advice in the line of social reform is added.

CHAPTER III.

THE NEGRO IN PHILADELPHIA, 1638–1820.

6. General Survey.—Few States present better opportunities for the continuous study of a group of Negroes than Pennsylvania. The Negroes were brought here early, were held as slaves along with many white serfs. They became the subjects of a protracted abolition controversy, and were finally emancipated by gradual process. Although, for the most part, in a low and degraded condition, and thrown upon their own resources in competition with white labor, they were nevertheless so inspired by their new freedom and so guided by able leaders that for something like forty years they made commendable progress. Meantime, however, the immigration of foreign laborers began, the new economic era of manufacturing was manifest in the land, and a national movement for the abolition of slavery had its inception. The lack of skilled Negro laborers for the factories, the continual stream of Southern fugitives and rural freedmen into the city, the intense race antipathy of the Irish and others, together with intensified prejudice of whites who did not approve of agitation against slavery —all this served to check the development of the Negro, to increase crime and pauperism, and at one period resulted in riot, violence, and bloodshed, which drove many Negroes from the city.

Economic adjustment and the enforcement of law finally allayed this excitement, and another period of material prosperity and advance among the Negroes followed. Then came the inpouring of the new 'y emancipated blacks from the South and the economic struggle of the artisans to maintain wages, which brought on a crisis in the city, manifested again by idleness, crime and pauperism.

Thus we see that twice the Philadelphia Negro has, with a fair measure of success, begun an interesting social development, and twice through the migration of barbarians a dark age has settled on his age of revival. These same phenomena would have marked the advance of many other elements of our population if they had been as definitely isolated into one indivisible group. No differences of social condition allowed any Negro to escape from the group, although such escape was continually the rule among Irish, Germans, and other whites.

7. **The Transplanting of the Negro, 1638–1760.**—The Dutch, and possibly the Swedes, had already planted slavery on the Delaware when Penn and the Quakers arrived in 1682.[1] One of Penn's first acts was tacitly to recognize the serfdom of Negroes by a provision of the Free Society of Traders that they should serve fourteen years and then become serfs—a provision which he himself and all the others soon violated.[2]

Certain German settlers who came soon after Penn, and who may or may not have been active members of the Society of Friends, protested sturdily against slavery in 1688, but the Quakers found the matter too "weighty."[3] Five years later the radical seceders under Kieth made the existence of slavery a part of their attack on the society. Nevertheless the institution of slavery in the colony continued to grow, and the number of blacks in Philadelphia so increased that as early as 1693 we find an order of the

---

[1] Cf. Scharf-Westcott's "History of Philadelphia," I, 65, 76. DuBois' "Slave Trade," p. 24.

[2] Hazard's "Annals," 553. Thomas' "Attitude of Friends Toward Slavery," 266.

[3] There is some controversy as to whether these Germans were actually Friends or not; the weight of testimony seems to be that they were. See, however, Thomas as above, p. 267, and Appendix. "Pennsylvania Magazine," IV, 28–31; The *Critic*, August 27, 1897. DuBois' "Slave Trade," p. 20, 203. For copy of protest, see published fac-simile and Appendix of Thomas. For further proceedings of Quakers, see Thomas and DuBois, *passim*.

Council against the "tumultuous gatherings of the negroes of the towne of philadelphia, on the first dayes of the weeke." [4]

In 1696 the Friends began a cautious dealing with the subject, which in the course of a century led to the abolition of slavery. This growth of moral sentiment was slow but unwaveringly progressive, and far in advance of contemporary thought in civilized lands. At first the Friends sought merely to regulate slavery in a general way and prevent its undue growth. They therefore suggested in the Yearly Meeting of 1696, and for some time thereafter, that since traders " have flocked in amongst us and . . . increased and multiplied negroes amongst us," members ought not to encourage the further importation of slaves, as there were enough for all purposes. In 1711 a more active discouragement of the slave trade was suggested, and in 1716 the Yearly Meeting intimated that even the buying of imported slaves might not be the best policy, although the Meeting hastened to call this " caution, not censure."

By 1719 the Meeting was certain that their members ought not to engage in the slave trade, and in 1730 they declared the buying of slaves imported by others to be " disagreeable." At this milestone they lingered thirty years for breath and courage, for the Meeting had evidently distanced many of its more conservative members. In 1743 the question of importing slaves, or buying imported slaves, was made a disciplinary query, and in 1754, spurred by the crusade of Say, Woolman and Benezet, offending members were disciplined. In the important gathering of 1758 the same golden rule was laid down as that with which the Germans, seventy years previous, had taunted them, and the institution of slavery was categorically condemned. [5] Here they rested until 1775, when,

---

[4] " Colonial Records," I, 380–81.

[5] Thomas, 276; Whittier Intro. to Woolman, 16.

after a struggle of eighty-seven years, they decreed the exclusion of slaveholders from fellowship in the Society.

While in the councils of the State Church the freedom of Negroes was thus evolving, the legal status of Negroes of Pennsylvania was being laid.   Four bills were introduced in 1700 : one regulating slave marriages was lost ; the other three were passed, but the Act for the Trial of Negroes—a harsh measure providing death, castration and whipping for punishments, and forbidding the meeting together of more than four Negroes—was afterward disallowed by the Queen in Council.   The remaining acts became laws, and provided for a small duty on imported slaves and the regulation of trade with slaves and servants.[6]

In 1706 another act for the trial of Negroes was passed and allowed.   It differed but slightly from the Act of 1700 ; it provided that Negroes should be tried for crimes by two justices of the peace and a jury of six freeholders ; robbery and rape were punished by branding and exportation, homicide by death, and stealing by whipping ;[7] the meeting of Negroes without permission was prohibited.   Between this time and 1760 statutes were passed regulating the sale of liquor to slaves and the use of firearms by them ; and also the general regulative Act of 1726, "for the Better Regulation of Negroes in this Province."   This act was especially for the punishment of crime, the suppression of pauperism, the prevention of intermarriage, and the like— that is, for regulating the social and economic status of Negroes, free and enslaved.[8]

Meantime the number of Negroes in the colony continued to increase ; by 1720 there were between 2500 and 5000 Negroes in Pennsylvania ; they rapidly increased until there were a large number by 1750—some say 11,000

[6] See Appendix B.

[7] "Statutes-at-Large," Ch. 143, 881.   See Appendix B.

[8] "Statutes-at-Large," III, pp. 250, 254; IV, 59 ff.   See Appendix B.

or more—when they decreased by war and sale, so that the census of 1790 found 10,274 in the State.[9]

The slave duties form a pretty good indication of the increase of Negro population.[10] The duty in 1700 was from 6s. to 20s. This was increased, and in 1712, owing to the large importations and the turbulent actions of Negroes in neighboring States, a prohibitive duty of £20 was laid.[11] England, however, who was on the eve of signing the Assiento with Spain, soon disallowed this act and the duty was reduced to £5. The influx of Negroes after the English had signed the huge slave contract with Spain was so large that the Act of 1726 laid a restrictive duty of £10. For reasons not apparent, but possibly connected with fluctuations in the value of the currency, this duty was reduced to £2 in 1729, and seems to have remained at that figure until 1761.

The £10 duty was restored in 1761, and probably helped much to prevent importation, especially when we remember the work of the Quakers at this period. In 1773 a prohibitive duty of £20 was laid, and the Act of 1780 finally prohibited importation. After 1760 it is probable that the efforts of the Quakers to get rid of their slaves made the export slave trade much larger than the importation.

Very early in the history of the colony the presence of unpaid slaves for life greatly disturbed the economic condition of free laborers. While most of the white laborers were indentured servants the competition was not so much felt; when they became free laborers, however, and were joined by other laborers, the cry against slave competition was soon raised. The particular grievance was the hiring out of slave mechanics by masters; in 1708 the free white mechanics protested to the Legislature against this

---

[9] DuBois' "Slave Trade," p. 23, note. U. S. Census.
[10] See Appendix B. Cf. DuBois' "Slave Trade," *passim.*
[11] DuBois' "Slave Trade," p. 206.

custom,[12] and this was one of the causes of the Act of 1712 in all probability. When by 1722 the number of slaves had further increased, the whites again protested against the "employment of blacks," apparently including both free and slave. The Legislature endorsed this protest and declared that the custom of employing black laborers and mechanics was "dangerous and injurious to the republic." [13] Consequently the Act of 1726 declared the hiring of their time by Negro slaves to be illegal, and sought to restrict emancipation on the ground that "free negroes are an idle and slothful people," and easily become public burdens.[14]

As to the condition of the Negroes themselves we catch only glimpses here and there. Considering the times, the system of slavery was not harsh and the slaves received fair attention. There appears, however, to have been much trouble with them on account of stealing, some drunkenness and general disorder. The preamble of the Act of 1726 declares that "it too often happens that Negroes commit felonies and other heinous crimes," and that much pauperism arises from emancipation. This act facilitated punishment of such crimes by providing indemnification for a master if his slave suffered capital punishment. They were declared to be often "tumultuous" in 1693, to be found "cursing, gaming, swearing, and committing many other disorders" in 1732; in 1738 and 1741 they were also called "disorderly" in city ordinances.[15]

In general, we see among the slaves at this time the low condition of morals which we should expect in a barbarous people forced to labor in a strange land.

8. **Emancipation, 1760–1780.**—The years 1750–1760 mark the culmination of the slave system in Pennsylvania

---

[12] Scharf-Westcott's "History of Philadelphia," I, 200.
[13] Watson's "Annals," (Ed. 1850) I, 98.
[14] See Appendix B.
[15] Cf. Chapter XIII.

and the beginning of its decline.   By that time most
shrewd observers saw that the institution was an economic
failure, and were consequently more disposed than formerly
to listen to the earnest representations of the great anti-
slavery agitators of that period.   There were, to be sure,
strong vested interests still to be fought.   When the £10
duty act of 1761 was pending, the slave merchants of the
city, including many respectable names, vigorously protested ; " ever desirous to extend the Trade of this Province," they declared that they had " seen for some time
past the many inconveniencys the Inhabitants have suffered
for want of Labourers and Artificers," and had consequently " for some time encouraged the importation of
Negroes."   They prayed at the very least for delay in
passing this restrictive measure.   After debate and altercation with the governor the measure finally passed, indicating renewed strength and determination on the part of
the abolition party.[16]

Meantime voluntary emancipation increased.   Sandiford
emancipated his slaves in 1733, and there were by 1790 in
Philadelphia about one thousand black freedmen.   A school
for these and others was started in 1770 at the instance of
Benezet, and had at first twenty-two children in attendance.[17]   The war brought a broader and kindlier feeling
toward the Negroes ; before its end the Quakers had
ordered manumission,[18] and several attempts were made to
prohibit slavery by statute.   Finally, in 1780, the Act for
the Gradual Abolition of Slavery was passed.[19]   This act,
beginning with a strong condemnation of slavery, provided that no child thereafter born in Pennsylvania should
be a slave.   The children of slaves born after 1780 were to
be bond-servants until twenty-eight years of age—that is,

---

[16] " Colonial Records," VIII, 576; DuBois' " Slave Trade," p. 23.
[17] Cf. Pamphlet: " Sketch of the Schools for Blacks," also Chapter VIII.
[18] Cf. Thomas' "Attitude of Friends," etc., p. 272.
[19] Dallas' " Laws," I, 838, Ch. 881; DuBois' " Slave Trade," p. 225.

beginning with the year 1808 there was to be a series of emancipations. Side by side with this growth of emancipation sentiment went an increase in the custom of hiring out Negro slaves and servants, which increased the old competition with the whites. The slaves were owned in small lots, especially in Philadelphia, one or two to a family, and were used either as house servants or artisans. As a result they were encouraged to learn trades and seem to have had the larger share of the ordinary trades of the city in their hands. Many of the slaves in the better families became well-known characters—as Alice, who for forty years took the tolls at Dunk's Ferry; Virgil Warder, who once belonged to Thomas Penn, and Robert Venable, a man of some intelligence.[20]

9. The Rise of the Freedman, 1780–1820.—A careful study of the process and effect of emancipation in the different States of the Union would throw much light on our national experiment and its ensuing problems. Especially is this true of the experiment in Pennsylvania; to be sure, emancipation here was gradual and the number emancipated small in comparison with the population, and yet the main facts are similar: the freeing of ignorant slaves and giving them a chance, almost unaided from without, to make a way in the world. The first result was widespread poverty and idleness. This was followed, as the number of freedmen increased, by a rush to the city. Between 1790 and 1800 the Negro population of Philadelphia County increased from 2489 to 6880, or 176 per cent, against an increase of 43 per cent among the whites. The first result of this contact with city life was to stimulate the talented and aspiring freedmen; and this was the easier because the freedman had in Philadelphia at that time a secure economic foothold; he performed all kinds of domestic service, all common labor and much of the skilled labor. The group being thus secure in its daily

---

[20] Cf. Watson's "Annals" (Ed. 1850), I, 557, 101–103, 601, 602, 515.

bread needed only leadership to make some advance in general culture and social effectiveness. Some sporadic cases of talent occur, as Derham, the Negro physician, whom Dr. Benjamin Rush, in 1788, found "very learned."[21] Especially, however, to be noted are Richard Allen,[22] a former slave of the Chew family, and Absalom Jones,[23] a Delaware Negro. These two were real leaders and actually succeeded to a remarkable degree in organizing the freedmen for group action. Both had bought their own freedom and that of their families by hiring their time—Allen being a blacksmith by trade, and Jones also having a trade. When, in 1792, the terrible epidemic drove Philadelphians away so quickly that many did not remain to bury the dead, Jones and Allen quietly took the work in hand, spending some of their own funds and doing so well that they were publicly commended by Mayor Clarkson in 1794.[24]

The great work of these men, however, lay among their own race and arose from religious difficulties. As in other colonies, the process by which the Negro slaves learned the English tongue and were converted to Christianity is not clear. The subject of the moral instruction of slaves had early troubled Penn and he had urged Friends to provide meetings for them.[25] The newly organized Methodists soon attracted a number of the more intelligent, though the

---

[21] The *American Museum*, 1789, pp. 61–62.

[22] For life of Allen, see his "Autobiography," and Payne's "History of the A. M. E. Church."

[23] For life of Jones, see Douglass' "Episcopal Church of St. Thomas."

[24] The testimonial was dated January 23, 1794, and was as follows: "Having, during the prevalence of the late malignant disorder, had almost daily opportunities of seeing the conduct of Absalom Jones and Richard Allen, and the people employed by them to bury the dead, I, with cheerfulness give this testimony of my approbation of their proceedings as far as the same came under my notice. Their diligence, attention and decency of deportment, afforded me at the time much satisfaction.   William Clarkson, Mayor."

From Douglass' "St. Thomas' Church."

[25] See Thomas, p. 266.

masses seem at the end of the last century not to have been church-goers or Christians to any considerable extent. The small number that went to church were wont to worship at St. George's, Fourth and Vine; for years both free Negroes and slaves worshiped here and were made welcome. Soon, however, the church began to be alarmed at the increase in its black communicants which the immigration from the country was bringing, and attempted to force them into the gallery. The crisis came one Sunday morning during prayer when Jones and Allen, with a crowd of followers, refused to worship except in their accustomed places, and finally left the church in a body.[26]

This band immediately met together and on April 12, 1787, formed a curious sort of ethical and beneficial brotherhood called the Free African Society. How great a step this was, we of to-day scarcely realize; we must remind ourselves that it was the first wavering step of a people toward organized social life. This society was more than a mere club: Jones and Allen were its leaders and recognized chief officers; a certain parental discipline was exercised over its members and mutual financial aid given. The preamble of the articles of association says: "Whereas, Absalom Jones and Richard Allen, two men of the African Race, who for their religious life and conversation, have obtained a good report among men, these persons from a love to the people of their own complexion whom they beheld with sorrow, because of their irreligious and uncivilized state, often communed together upon this painful and important subject in order to form some kind of religious body; but there being too few to be found under the like concern, and those who were, differed in their religious sentiments; with these circumstances they labored for some time, till it was proposed after a serious communication of sentiments that a society should be formed without regard to religious tenets, provided the persons

---

[26] See Allen's "Autobiography," and Douglass' "St. Thomas."

lived an orderly and sober life, in order to support one another in sickness, and for the benefit of their widows and fatherless children."[27]

The society met first at private houses, then at the Friends' Negro school house. For a time they leaned toward Quakerism; each month three monitors were appointed to have oversight over the members; loose marriage customs were attacked by condemning cohabitation, expelling offenders and providing a simple Quaker-like marriage ceremony. A fifteen-minute pause for silent prayer opened the meetings. As the representative body of the free Negroes of the city, this society opened communication with free Negroes in Boston, Newport and other places. The Negro Union of Newport, R. I., proposed in 1788 a general exodus to Africa, but the Free African Society soberly replied: "With regard to the emigration to Africa you mention we have at present but little to communicate on that head, apprehending every pious man is a good citizen of the whole world." The society co-operated with the Abolition Society in studying the condition of the free blacks in 1790. At all times they seem to have taken good care of their sick and dead and helped the widows and orphans to some extent. Their methods of relief were simple: they agreed "for the benefit of each other to advance one-shilling in silver Pennsylvania currency a month; and after one year's subscription, from the dole hereof then to hand forth to the needy of the Society if any should require, the sum of three shillings and nine pence per week of the said money; provided the necessity is not brought on them by their own imprudence." In 1790 the society had £42 9s. 1d. on deposit in the Bank of North America, and had applied for a grant of the Potter's Field to be set aside as a burial ground for them, in a petition signed by Dr. Rush, Tench Coxe and others.

---

[27] Douglass' "St. Thomas."

It was, however, becoming clearer and clearer to the leaders that only a strong religious bond could keep this untrained group together. They would probably have become a sort of institutional church at first if the question of religious denomination had been settled among them; but it had not been, and for about six years the question was still pending. The tentative experiment in Quakerism had failed, being ill suited to the low condition of the rank and file of the society. Both Jones and Allen believed that Methodism was best suited to the needs of the Negro, but the majority of the society, still nursing the memory of St. George's, inclined toward the Episcopal church. Here came the parting of the ways : Jones was a slow introspective man, with a thirst for knowledge, with high aspirations for his people; Allen was a shrewd, quick, popular leader, positive and dogged and yet far-seeing in his knowledge of Negro character. Jones therefore acquiesced in the judgment of the majority, served and led them conscientiously and worthily, and eventually became the first Negro rector in the Episcopal church of America. About 1790 Allen and a few followers withdrew from the Free African Society, formed an independent Methodist church which first worshiped in his blacksmith's shop on Sixth near Lombard. Eventually this leader became the founder and first bishop of the African Methodist Episcopal Church of America—an organization which now has 500,000 members, and is by long odds the vastest and most remarkable product of American Negro civilization.[28]

Jones and the Free African Society took immediate steps to secure a church; a lot was bought at the corner of Fifth and Adelphi streets in February, 1792, and by strenuous effort a church was erected and dedicated on the seventeenth

---

[28] There is on the part of the A. M. E. Church a disposition to ignore Allen's withdrawal from the Free African Society, and to date the A. M. E. Church from the founding of that society, making it older than St. Thomas. This, however, is contrary to Allen's own statement in his " Autobiography." The point, however, is of little real consequence.

of July, 1794. This was the first Negro church in America, and known as the First African Church of St. Thomas ; in the vestibule of the church was written : "The people that walked in darkness have seen a great light." Bethel Church was erected by Allen and his followers in 1796, the same year that a similar movement in New York established the Zion Methodist Church. In 1794, too, the Methodists of St. George's, viewing with some chagrin the widespread withdrawal of Negroes from their body, established a mission at Camperdown, in the northeastern part of the city, which eventually became the present Zoar Church.

The general outlook for the Negroes at this period was encouraging, notwithstanding the low condition of the masses of the race. In 1788 Pennsylvania amended the Act of 1780, so as to prevent the internal and foreign slave trade, and correct kidnapping and other abuses that had arisen.[29] The convention which adopted the Constitution of 1790 had, in spite of opposition in the convention, refused to insert the word " white " in the qualifications for voters, and thus gave the right of suffrage to free Negro property holders ; a right which they held, and, in most counties of the State, exercised until 1837.[30] The general conference of Abolition Societies, held in Philadelphia in 1794, started an agitation which, when reinforced by the news of the Haytian revolt, resulted in the national statute of 1794, forbidding the export slave trade.[31] In 1799 and 1800 Absalom Jones led the Negroes to address a petition to the Legislature, praying for immediate abolition of slavery, and to Congress against the fugitive slave law, and asking prospective emancipation for all Negroes. This latter petition was presented by Congressman Waln, and created an uproar

---

[29] Carey & Bioren, Ch. 394. DuBois' " Slave Trade," p. 231.

[30] The constitution, as reported, had the word "white," but this was struck out at the instance of Gallatin. Cf. Ch. XVII.

[31] Cf. DuBois' " Slave Trade," Chapter VII.

in the House of Representatives; it was charged that
the petition was instigated by the Haytian revolutionists
and finally the Negroes were censured for certain parts of
the petition. [32]

The condition of the Negroes of the city in the last
decade of the eighteenth and the first two decades of the
nineteenth century, although without doubt bad, slowly
improved; an insurance society, in 1796, took the beneficial features of the old Free African Society. Some small
essays were made in business, mostly in small street stands,
near the wharves; and many were in the trades of all kinds.
Between 1800 and 1810 the city Negro population continued to increase, so that at the latter date there were
100,688 whites and 10,522 blacks in the city, the Negroes
thus forming the largest per cent of the population of the
city that they have ever attained. The free Negroes also
began to increase from the effect of the abolition law.
The school established in 1770 continued, and was endowed
by bequests from whites and Negroes. It had 414 pupils
by 1813. In this same year there were six Negro churches
and eleven benevolent societies. When the war broke out
many Philadelphia Negroes were engaged on land and sea.
Among these was James Forten—a fine character, expres-
sive of the best Negro development of the time. Born in
1766, and educated by Benezet, he " was a gentleman by
nature, easy in manner and able in intercourse; popular as
a man of trade or gentleman of the pave, and well received
by the gentry of lighter shade." [33] For years he conducted
a sail-making trade, employing both whites and Negroes.
In 1814 he, Jones, Allen and others were asked, in the
midst of the alarm felt at the approach of the British, to
raise colored troops. A meeting was called and 2500
volunteers secured, or three-fourths of the adult male

[32] "Annals of Congress," 6 Cong., I Sess., pp. 229–45. DuBois' "Slave
Trade," pp. 81–83.
[33] Quoted by W. C. Bolivar in Philadelphia *Tribune.*

population; they marched to Gray's Ferry and threw up fortifications. A battalion for service in the field was formed, but the war closed before they reached the front. [34]

The Negroes at this time held about $250,000 of city property, and on the whole showed great progress since 1780. At the same time there were many evidences of the effects of slavery. The first set of men emancipated by law were freed in 1808, and probably many entitled to freedom were held longer than the law allowed or sold out of the State. As late as 1794 some Quakers still held slaves, and the papers of the day commonly contain such advertisements, as :

"To be Sold for want of Employ, For a term of years, a smart active Negro boy, fifteen years of age. Enquire at Robert McGee's board yard, Vine street wharf." [35]

---

[34] Delany's "Colored People," p. 74.

[35] Dunlap's *American Daily Advertiser*, July 4, 1791. William White had a large commission-house on the wharves about this time. Considerable praise is given the Insurance Society of 1796 for its good management. Cf. "History of the Insurance Companies of North America." In 1817 the first convention of Free Negroes was held here, through the efforts of Jones and Forten.

CHAPTER IV.

10. Fugitives and Foreigners, 1820–1840.—Five social developments made the decades from 1820 to 1840 critical for the nation and for the Philadelphia Negroes; first, the impulse of the industrial revolution of the nineteenth century; second, the reaction and recovery succeeding the War of 1812; third, the rapid increase of foreign immigration; fourth, the increase of free Negroes and fugitive slaves, especially in Philadelphia; fifth, the rise of the Abolitionists and the slavery controversy.

Philadelphia was the natural gateway between the North and the South, and for a long time there passed through it a stream of free Negroes and fugitive slaves toward the North, and of recaptured Negroes and kidnapped colored persons toward the South. By 1820 the northward stream increased, occasioning bitterness on the part of the South, and leading to the Fugitive Slave Act of 1820, and the counter acts of Pennsylvania in 1826 and 1827.[1] During this time new installments of Pennsylvania freedmen, and especially their children, began to flock to Philadelphia. At the same time the stream of foreign immigration to this country began to swell, and by 1830 aggregated half a million souls annually. The result of these movements proved disastrous to the Philadelphia Negro; the better classes of them—the Joneses, Allens and Fortens—could not escape into the mass of white population and leave the new

---

[1] These laws were especially directed against kidnapping, and were designed to protect free Negroes. See Appendix B. The law of 1826 was declared unconstitutional in 1842 by the U. S. Supreme Court. See 16 Peters, 500 ff.

Negroes to fight out their battles with the foreigners. No distinction was drawn between Negroes, least of all by the new Southern families who now made Philadelphia their home and were not unnaturally stirred to unreasoning prejudice by the slavery agitation.

To this was added a fierce economic struggle, a renewal of the fight of the eighteenth century against Negro workmen. The new industries attracted the Irish, Germans and other immigrants ; Americans, too, were flocking to the city, and soon to natural race antipathies was added a determined effort to displace Negro labor—an effort which had the aroused prejudice of many of the better classes, and the poor quality of the new black immigrants to give it aid and comfort. To all this was soon added a problem of crime and poverty. Numerous complaints of petty thefts, house-breaking, and assaults on peaceable citizens were traced to certain classes of Negroes. In vain did the better class, led by men like Forten, protest by public meetings their condemnation of such crime [2];the tide had set against the Negro strongly, and the whole period from 1820 to 1840 became a time of retrogression for the mass of the race, and of discountenance and repression from the whites.

By 1830 the black population of the city and districts had increased to 15,624, an increase of 27 per cent for the decade 1820 to 1830, and of 48 per cent since 1810. Nevertheless, the growth of the city had far outstripped this ; by 1830 the county had nearly 175,000 whites, among whom was a rapidly increasing contingent of 5000 foreigners. So intense was the race antipathy among the lower classes, and so much countenance did it receive from the middle and upper class, that there began, in 1829, a series of riots directed chiefly against Negroes, which recurred frequently until about 1840, and did not wholly cease until

---

[2] A meeting of Negroes held in 1822, at the A. M. E. Church, denounced crime and Negro criminals.

after the war. These riots were occasioned by various
incidents, but the underlying cause was the same : the simul-
taneous influx of freedmen, fugitives and foreigners into
a large city, and the resulting prejudice, lawlessness, crime
and poverty. The agitation of the Abolitionists was the
match that lighted this fuel. In June and July, 1829, Mrs.
Fanny Wright Darusmont, a Scotch woman, gave a number of addresses in Philadelphia, in which she boldly
advocated the emancipation of the Negroes and something
very like social equality of the races. This created great
excitement throughout the city, and late in the fall the first
riot against the Negroes broke out, occasioned by some
personal quarrel.[3]

The Legislature had proposed to stop the further influx
of Southern Negroes by making free Negroes carry passes
and excluding all others ; the arrival of fugitives from the
Southampton massacre was the occasion of this attempt,
and it was with difficulty that the friends of the Negro pre-
vented its passage.[4]   Quakers hastened to advise against
the sending of fugitives to the State, " as the effects of such
a measure would probably be disastrous to the peace and
comfort of the whole colored population of Pennsylvania."
Edward Bettle declared in 1832 : " The public mind here
is more aroused even among respectable persons than it
has been for several years," and he feared that the laws of
1826 and 1827 would be repealed, " thus leaving kidnap-
pers free scope for their nefarious labors."[5]

In 1833 a demonstration took place against the Abolitionists, and in 1834 serious riots occurred. One night in
August a crowd of several hundred boys and men, armed

---

[3] Scharf-Westcott's " History of Philadelphia," I, 824. There was at
this time much lawlessness in the city which had no connection with the
presence of Negroes, and which led to rioting and disorder in general.
Cf. Price's " History of Consolidation."

[4] Southampton was the scene of the celebrated Nat Turner insurrection
of Negroes.

[5] Letter to Nathan Mendelhall, of North Carolina.

with clubs, marched down Seventh street to the Pennsylvania Hospital. They were joined by others, and all proceeded to some places of amusement where many Negroes were congregated, on South street, near Eighth. Here the rioting began, and four or five hundred people engaged in a free street fight. Buildings were torn down and inmates assaulted on Bedford and St. Mary streets and neighboring alleys, until at last the policemen and constables succeeded in quieting the tumult. The respite, however, was but temporary. The very next night the mob assembled again at Seventh and Bainbridge; they first wrecked a Negro church and a neighboring house, then attacked some twenty Negro dwellings; " great excesses are represented as having been committed by the mob, and one or two scenes of a most revolting character are said to have taken place." That the riots occurred by prearranged plan was shown by the signals—lights in windows—by which the houses of the whites were distinguished and those of the Negroes attacked and their inmates assaulted and beaten. Several persons were severely injured in this night's work and one Negro killed, before the mayor and authorities dispersed the rioters.

The next night the mob again assembled in another part of the city and tore down another Negro church. By this time the Negroes began to gather for self-defence, and about one hundred of them barricaded themselves in a building on Seventh street, below Lombard, where a howling mob of whites soon collected. The mayor induced the Negroes to withdraw, and the riot ended. In this three days' uprising thirty-one houses and two churches were destroyed and Stephen James " an honest, industrious colored man " killed.[6]

The town meeting of September 15 condemned the riots and voted to reimburse the sufferers, but also took occasion to condemn the impeding of justice by Negroes when any

---

[6] Hazard's " Register," XIV, 126-28, 200-203.

of their number was arrested, and also the noise made in Negro churches. The fires smouldered for about a year, but burst forth again on the occasion of the murder of his master by a Cuban slave, Juan. The lower classes were aroused and a mob quickly assembled at the corners of Sixth and Seventh and Lombard streets, and began the work of destruction and assault, until finally it ended by setting fire to a row of houses on Eighth street, and fighting off the firemen. The following night the mob met again and attacked a house on St. Mary street, where an armed body of Negroes had barricaded themselves. The mayor and recorder finally arrived here and after severely lecturing the Negroes (!) induced them to depart. The whole of the afternoon of that day black women and children fled from the city.[7]

Three years now passed without serious disturbance, although the lawless elements which had gained such a foothold were still troublesome. In 1838 two murders were committed by Negroes—one of whom was acknowledged to be a lunatic. At the burial of this one's victim, rioting again began, the mob assembling on Passyunk avenue and Fifth street and marching up Fifth. The same scenes were re-enacted but finally the mob was broken up.[8] Later the same year, on the dedication of Pennsylvania Hall, which was designed to be a centre of anti-slavery agitation, the mob, encouraged by the refusal of the mayor to furnish adequate police protection, burned the hall to the ground and the next night burned the Shelter for Colored Orphans at Thirteenth and Callowhill streets, and damaged Bethel Church, on Sixth street.[9]

The last riot of this series took place in 1842 when a mob devastated the district between Fifth and Eighth

---

[7] *Ibid.*, XVI. 35–38.

[8] Scharf-Westcott's " Philadelphia," I, 654–55.

[9] Price, " History of Consolidation," etc., Ch. VII.   The county eventually paid $22,658.27, with interest and costs, for the destruction of the hall.

streets, near Lombard street, assaulted and beat Negroes
and looted their homes, burned down a Negro hall and a
church; the following day the rioting extended to the section between South and Fitzwater streets and was finally
quelled by calling out the militia with artillery.[10]

While these riots were taking place a successful effort
was made to deprive free Negroes of the right of suffrage
which they had enjoyed nearly fifty years. In 1836 a case
came before the court of a Negro who had been denied
the right of voting. The court decided in a peculiar decision that free Negroes were not " freemen " in the lan-
guage of the constitution and, therefore that Negroes could
not vote.[11] The reform convention settled the matter by
inserting the word "white" in the qualifications for
election in the Constitution of 1837.[12] The Negroes protested earnestly by meetings and appeals. " We appeal to
you " said they, " from the decision of the ' Reform Convention,' which has stripped us of a right peaceably
enjoyed during forty-seven years under the constitution of
this commonwealth. We honor Pennsylvania and her
noble institutions too much to part with our birthright, as
her free citizens, without a struggle. To all her citizens
the right of suffrage is valuable in proportion as she is free;
but surely there are none who can so ill afford to spare it
as ourselves." Nevertheless the right was lost, for the
appeal fell on deaf ears.[13]

A curious comment on human nature is this change of
public opinion in Philadelphia between 1790 and 1837.
No one thing explains it—it arose from a combination of
circumstances. If, as in 1790, the new freedmen had been
given peace and quiet and abundant work to develop
sensible and aspiring leaders, the end would have been

---

[10] Scharf-Westcott, I, 660–61.

[11] Case of Fogg *vs.* Hobbs, 6 Watts, 553–560. See Chapter XII.

[12] See Chapter XII and Appendix B.

[13] Appeal of 40,000 citizens, etc., Philadelphia, 1838. Written chiefly
by the late Robert Purvis, son-in-law of James Forten.

different; but a mass of poverty-stricken, ignorant fugitives and ill-trained freedmen had rushed to the city, swarmed in the vile slums which the rapidly growing city furnished, and met in social and economic competition equally ignorant but more vigorous foreigners.   These foreigners outbid them at work, beat them on the streets, and were enabled to do this by the prejudice which Negro crime and the anti-slavery sentiment had aroused in the city.

Notwithstanding this the better class of Negroes never gave up. Their school increased in attendance; their churches and benevolent societies increased ; they held public meetings of protest and sympathy.   And twice, in 1831 and 1833, there assembled in the city a general convention of the free Negroes of the country, representing five to eight States, which, among other things, sought to interest philanthropists of the city in the establishment of a Negro industrial school.[14]   When the Legislature showed a disposition in 1832 to curtail the liberties of Negroes, the Negroes held a mass meeting and memorialized the lawmaking body and endeavored to show that all Negroes were not criminals and paupers; they declared that while the Negroes formed eight per cent of the population they furnished but four per cent of the paupers ; that by actually produced tax receipts they could show that Negroes held at least $350,000 of taxable property in the city.   Moreover, they said, "Notwithstanding the difficulty of getting places for our sons to learn mechanical trades, owing to the prejudices with which we have to contend, there are between four and five hundred people of color who follow mechanical employments."[15]   In 1837 the census of the Abolition Society claimed for the Negroes 1724 children in school, $309,626 of unencumbered property, 16 churches and 100 benevolent societies.

---

[14] See Minutes of Conventions; the school was to be situated in New Haven, but the New Haven authorities, by town meeting, protested so vehemently that the project had to be given up. Cf. also Hazard, V, 143.

[15] Hazard's "Register," IX, 361–62.

11. The Guild of the Caterers, 1840–1870.—The outlook for the Negro in Philadelphia about 1840 was not encouraging. The last of the first series of riots took place in 1842, and has been mentioned. The authorities were wakened to their duty by this last outbreak of barbarism, and for several years the spirit of lawlessness, which now extended far beyond the race question and seriously threatened the good name of the city, was kept within control. However, in 1849, a mob set upon a mulatto who had a white wife, at the corner of Sixth street and St. Mary's, and there ensued a pitched battle for a night and a day; firemen fought with firemen; the blacks, goaded to desperation, fought furiously; houses were burned and firearms used, with the result that three white men and one Negro were killed and twenty-five wounded persons taken to the hospital. The militia was twice called before the disturbance was quelled. These riots and the tide of prejudice and economic proscription drove so many Negroes from the city that the black population actually showed a decrease in the decade 1840–50. Worse than this, the good name of the Negroes in the city had been lost through the increased crime and the undeniably frightful condition of the Negro slums. The foreign element gained all the new employments which the growing industries of the State opened, and competed for the trades and common vocations. The outlook was certainly dark.

It was at this time that there arose to prominence and power as remarkable a trade guild as ever ruled in a mediæval city. It took complete leadership of the bewildered group of Negroes, and led them steadily on to a degree of affluence, culture and respect such as has probably never been surpassed in the history of the Negro in America. This was the guild of the caterers, and its masters include names which have been household words in the city for fifty years: Bogle, Augustin, Prosser, Dorsey, Jones and Minton. To realize just the character of this new economic development we must not forget the economic history of the slaves. At first they were wholly house servants or field hands. As city life in the colony became more important, some of the slaves acquired trades, and thus there arose a class of Negro artisans. So long as the pecuniary interests of a slaveholding class stood back of these artisans the protests of white mechanics had little effect; indeed it is probable that between 1790 and 1820 a very large portion, and perhaps most, of the artisans of Philadelphia were Negroes. Thereafter, however, the sharp competition of the foreigners and the demand for new sorts of skilled labor of which the Negro was ignorant, and was not allowed to learn, pushed the black artisans more and more to the wall. In 1837 only about 350 men out of a city population of 10,500 Negroes, pursued trades, or about one in every twenty adults.

The question, therefore, of obtaining a decent livelihood was a pressing one for the better class of Negroes. The masses of the race continued to depend upon domestic service, where they still had a practical monopoly, and upon common labor, where they had some competition from the Irish. To the more pushing and energetic Negroes only two courses were open: to enter into commercial life in some small way, or to develop certain lines of home service into a more independent and lucrative employment. In this latter way was the most striking advance made; the whole catering business, arising from an evolution shrewdly, persistently and tastefully directed, transformed the Negro cook and waiter into the public caterer and restaurateur, and raised a crowd of underpaid menials to become a set of self-reliant, original business men, who amassed fortunes for themselves and won general respect for their people.

The first prominent Negro caterer was Robert Bogle, who, early in the century, conducted an establishment on Eighth street, near Sansom. In his day he was one of the

best known characters of Philadelphia, and virtually created the business of catering in the city.[16] As the butler
or waiter in a private family arranged the meals and
attended the family on ordinary occasions, so the public
waiter came to serve different families in the same capacity
at larger and more elaborate functions; he was the butler
of the smart set, and his taste of hand and eye and palate
set the fashion of the day. This functionary filled a unique
place in a time when social circles were very exclusive,
and the millionaire and the French cook had not yet
arrived. Bogle's place was eventually taken by Peter
Augustin, a West Indian immigrant, who started a business
in 1818 which is still carried on. It was the Augustin
establishment that made Philadelphia catering famous all
over the country. The best families of the city, and the
most distinguished foreign guests, were served by this
caterer. Other Negroes soon began to crowd into the field
thus opened. The Prossers, father and son, were prominent
among these, perfecting restaurant catering and making
many famous dishes. Finally came the triumvirate Jones,
Dorsey and Minton, who ruled the fashionable world from
1845–1875. Of these Dorsey was the most unique character; with little education but great refinement of manner, he became a man of real weight in the community,
and associated with many eminent men. " He had the
sway of an imperial dictator. When a Democrat asked
his menial service he refused, because ' he could not wait
on a party of persons who were disloyal to the government,
and Lincoln '—pointing to the picture in his reception
rooms—' was the government.' " [17] Jones was Virginia

---

[16] Biddle's "Ode to Bogle," is a well-known squib; Bogle himself is
credited with considerable wit. " You are of the people who walk in
darkness," said a prominent clergyman to him once in a dimly lighted
hall. " But," replied Bogle, bowing to the distinguished gentleman, " I
have seen a great light."

[17] See in Philadelphia *Times*, October 17, 1896, the following notes by
" Megargee :" Dorsey was one of the triumvirate of colored caterers—the

born, and a man of great care and faithfulness. He catered
to families in Philadelphia, New Jersey and New York.[18]
Minton, the younger of the three, long had a restaurant at
Fourth and Chestnut, and became, as the others did, moderately wealthy.[19]

Such men wielded great personal influence, aided the
Abolition cause to no little degree, and made Philadelphia
noted for its cultivated and well-to-do Negro citizens.
Their conspicuous success opened opportunities for Negroes
in other lines. It was at this time that Stephen Smith
amassed a very large fortune as a lumber merchant, with
which he afterward handsomely endowed a home for aged

---

other two being Henry Jones and Henry Minton—who some years ago
might have been said to rule the social world of Philadelphia through its
stomach. Time was when lobster salad, chicken croquettes, deviled
crabs and terrapin composed the edible display at every big Philadelphia
gathering, and none of those dishes were thought to be perfectly prepared unless they came from the hands of one of the three men
named. Without making any invidious comparisons between those who
were such masters of the gastronomic art, it can fairly be said that outside of his kitchen, Thomas J. Dorsey outranked the others. Although
without schooling, he possessed a naturally refined instinct that led him
to surround himself with both men and things of an elevating character.
It was his proudest boast that at his table, in his Locust street residence,
there had sat Charles Sumner, William Lloyd Garrison, John W. Forney,
William D. Kelley and Fred Douglass. . . . Yet Thomas Dorsey had
been a slave; had been held in bondage by a Maryland planter. Nor did
he escape from his fetters until he had reached a man's estate. He fled
to this city, but was apprehended and returned to his master. During
his brief stay in Philadelphia, however, he made friends, and these raised
a fund of sufficient proportion to purchase his freedom. As a caterer he
quickly achieved both fame and fortune. His experience of the horrors
of slavery had instilled him with an undying reverence for those cham-
pions of his down-trodden race, the old-time Abolitionists. He took a
prominent part in all efforts to elevate his people, and in that way he
came in close contact with Sumner, Garrison, Forney and others.

[18] Henry Jones was in the catering business thirty years, and died
September 24, 1875, leaving a considerable estate.

[19] Henry Minton came from Nansemond County, Virginia, at the age
of nineteen, arriving in Philadelphia in 1830. He was first apprenticed
to a shoemaker, then went into a hotel as waiter. Finally he opened
dining rooms at Fourth and Chestnut. He died March 20, 1883.

and infirm Negroes. Whipper, Vidal and Purnell were associated with Smith at different times. Still and Bowers were coal merchants and Adger was in the furniture business. There were also some artists of ability : Bowser, who painted a portrait of Lincoln, and Douglass and Burr; Johnson, the leader of a famous colored band and a composer.[20]

During this time of effort, advance and assimilation the Negro population increased but slowly, for the economic struggle was too earnest for young and indiscriminate marriages, and immigrants had been frightened away by the riots. In 1840 there were 19,833 Negroes in the county, and ten years later, as has been noted, there were only 19,761. For the next decade there was a moderate increase to 22,185, when the war brought a slight decrease, leaving the Negro population 22,147 in 1870. Meantime the white population had increased by leaps and bounds :

POPULATION OF PHILADELPHIA COUNTY, 1840–1870.

Date.	Whites.	Negroes.
1840	238,204	19,833
1850	389,001	19,761
1860	543,344	22,185
1870	651,854	22,147

In 1810 the Negroes had formed nearly one-tenth of the total population of the city, but in 1870 they formed but little over one thirty-third, the lowest proportion ever reached in the history of Philadelphia.

The general social condition showed some signs of improvement from 1840 on. In 1847 there were 1940 Negro children in school ; the Negroes held, it was said, about $400,000 in real estate and had 19 churches and 106 benevolent societies. The mass of the race were still domestic servants—about 4000 of the 11,000 in the city

---

[20] This band was in great demand at social functions, and its leader received a trumpet from Queen Victoria.

proper being thus employed, a figure which probably meant a considerable majority of the adults. The remainder were chiefly employed as laborers, artisans, coachmen, expressmen and barbers.

The habitat of the Negro population changed somewhat in this period. About 1790 one-fourth of the Negroes lived between Vine and Market and east of Ninth ; one-half between Market and South, mostly in the alleys bounded by Lombard, Fifth, Eighth and South ; one-eighth lived below South, and one-eighth in the Northern Liberties. Many of these, of course, lived in white families. In 1837 a quarter of the Negroes were in white families, a little less than one-half were in the city limits centring at Sixth and Lombard or thereabouts ; a tenth lived in Moyamensing, a twentieth in the Northern Liberties, and the remaining part in Kensington and Spring Garden districts. The riots concentrated this population somewhat, and in 1847, of the 20,000 Negroes in the county, only 1300 lived north of Vine and east of Sixth. The rest were in the city proper, in Moyamensing and in Southwark. Moyamensing was the worst slum district : between South and Fitzwater and Fifth and Eighth there were crowded 302 families in narrow, filthy alleys. Here was concentrated the worst sort of depravity, poverty, crime and disease. The present slums at Seventh and Lombard are bad and dangerous, but they are decent compared with those of a half century ago. The Negroes furnished one-third of all the commitments for crime in 1837, and one-half in 1847.

Beginning with 1850 the improvement of the Negro was more rapid. The value of real estate held was estimated to have doubled between 1847 and 1856. The proportion of men in the trades remained stationary ; there were 2321 children in school. Toward the time of the outbreak of war the feeling toward the Negro in certain classes softened somewhat, and his staunch friends were enabled to open many benevolent institutions; in many ways a disposition to help them was manifested: the newspapers treated them with more respect, and they were not subject so frequently to personal insult on the street.

They were still kept off the street cars in spite of energetic protest. Indeed, not until 1867 was a law passed prohibiting this discrimination. Judicial decisions upheld the railways for a long time, and newspapers and public opinion supported them. When by Judge Allison's decision the attitude of the courts was changed, and damages granted an evicted Negro, the railway companies often side-tracked and left cars which colored passengers had entered. Separate cars were run for them on some lines, and in 1865 a public ballot on the cars was taken to decide the admission of Negroes. Naturally the conductors returned a large majority against any change. Finally, after public meetings, pamphlets and repeated agitation, the prospective enfranchisement of the freedmen gained what decency and common sense had long refused.[21]

Steps toward raising Negro troops in the city were taken in 1863, as soon as the efficiency of the Negro soldier had been proven. Several hundred prominent citizens petitioned the Secretary of War and were given permission to raise Negro regiments. The troops were to receive no bounties, but were to have $10 a month and rations. They were to rendezvous at Camp William Penn, Chelten Hills. A mass meeting was soon held attended by the prominent caterers, teachers and merchants, together with white citizens, at which Frederick Douglass, W. D. Kelley and Anna Dickinson spoke. Over $30,000 was raised in the city by subscription, and the first squad of soldiers went into camp June 26, 1863. By December, three

---

[21] See Spiers' "Street Railway System of Philadelphia," pp. 23–27; also unpublished MS. of Mr. Bernheimer, on file among the senior theses in the Wharton School of Finance and Economy, University of Pennsylvania.

regiments were full, and by the next February, five. The first three regiments, known as the Third, Sixth and Eighth United States Regiments of Colored Troops, went promptly to the front, the Third being before Fort Wagner when it fell. The other regiments followed as called, leaving still other Negroes anxious to enlist.[22]

After the war and emancipation great hopes were entertained by the Negroes for rapid advancement, and nowhere did they seem better founded than in Philadelphia. The generation then in its prime had lived down a most intense and bitter race feud and had gained the respect of the better class of whites. They started with renewed zeal, therefore, to hasten their social development.

12. **The Influx of the Freedmen, 1870–1896.**—The period opened stormily, on account of the political rights newly conferred on black voters. Philadelphia city politics have ever had a shady side, but when it seemed manifest that one political party, by the aid of Negro votes, was soon to oust the time-honored incumbents, all the lawless elements which bad city government for a half-century had nurtured naturally fought for the old régime. They found this the easier since the city toughs were largely Irish and hereditary enemies of the blacks. In the spring elections of 1871 there was so much disorder, and such poor police protection, that the United States marines were called on to preserve order.[23]

In the fall elections street disorders resulted in the cold-blooded assassination of several Negroes, among whom was an estimable young teacher, Octavius V. Catto. The murder of Catto came at a critical moment; to the Negroes it seemed a revival of the old slavery-time riots in the day when they were first tasting freedom; to the better classes of Philadelphia it revealed a serious state of barbarism and lawlessness in the second city of the land; to the politicians

---

[22] Pamphlet on "Enlistment of Negro Troops," Philadelphia Library.
[23] Cf. Scharf-Westcott, I, 837.

it furnished a text and example which was strikingly effective and which they did not hesitate to use. The result of all this was an outburst of indignation and sorrow, which was remarkable, and which showed a determined stand for law and order. The outward expression of this was a great mass meeting, attended by some of the best citizens, and a funeral for Catto which was perhaps the most imposing ever given to an American Negro.[24]

[24] The following account of an eye-witness, Mr. W. C. Bolivar, is from the Philadelphia *Tribune*, a Negro paper: "In the spring election preceding the murder of Octavius V. Catto, there was a good deal of rioting. It was at this election that the United States Marines were brought into play under the command of Col. James Forney. Their very presence had the salutary effect of preserving order. The handwriting of political disaster to the Democratic party was plainly noticed This galled 'the unterrified,' and much of the rancor was owing to the fact that the Negro vote would guarantee Republican supremacy beyond a doubt. Even then Catto had a narrow escape through a bullet shot at Michael Maher, an ardent Republican, whose place of business was at Eighth and Lombard streets. This assault was instigated by Dr. Gilbert, whose paid or coerced hirelings did his bidding. The Mayor, D. M. Fox, was a mild, easygoing Democrat, who seemed a puppet in the hands of astute conscienceless men. The night prior to the day in question, October 10, 1871, a colored man named Gordon was shot down in cold blood on Eighth street. The spirit of mobocracy filled the air, and the object of its spleen seemed to have been the colored men. A cigar store kept by Morris Brown, Jr., was the resort of the Pythian and Banneker members, and it was at this place on the night prior to the murder that Catto appeared among his old friends for the last time. When the hour arrived for home going, Catto went the near and dangerous way to his residence, 814 South street, and said as he left, 'I would not stultify my manhood by going to my home in a roundabout way.' When he reached his residence he found one of its dwellers had his hat taken from him at a point around the corner. He went out and into one of the worst places in the Fourth Ward and secured it.

"Intimidation and assault began with the opening of the polls. The first victim was Levi Bolden, a playfellow, as a boy, with the chronicler of these notes. Whenever they could conveniently catch a colored man they forthwith proceeded to assail him. Later in the day a crowd forced itself into Emeline street and battered in the brains of Isaac Chase, going into his home, wreaking their spite on this defenceless man, in the presence of his family. The police force was Democratic, and not only stood idly by, but gave practical support. They took pains to keep that part of the city not in the bailiwick of the rioters from knowing anything of

This incident, and the general expression of opinion after the war, showed a growing liberal spirit toward the

---

what was transpiring. Catto voted and went to school, but dismissed it after realizing the danger of keeping it open during the usual hours. Somewhere near 3 o'clock as he neared his dwelling, two or three men were seen to approach him from the rear, and one of them, supposed to have been either Frank Kelly or Reddy Dever, pulled out a pistol and pointed it at Catto. The aim of the man was sure, and Catto barely got around a street car before he fell. This occurred directly in front of a police station, into which he was carried. The news spread in every direction. The wildest excitement prevailed, and not only colored men, but those with the spirit of fair play, realized the gravity of the situation, with a divided sentiment as to whether they ought to make an assault on the Fourth Ward or take steps to preserve the peace. The latter prevailed, and the scenes of carnage, but a few hours back, when turbulence was supreme, settled down to an opposite state of almost painful calmness. The rioting during that day was in parts of the Fifth, Seventh and Fourth wards, whose boundary lines met. It must not be supposed that the colored people were passive when attacked, because the records show ' an eye for an eye and a tooth for a tooth,' in every instance. No pen is graphic enough to detail the horrors of that day. Each home was in sorrow, and strong men wept like children, when they realized how much had been lost in the untimely death of the gifted Catto.

" Men who had sat quietly unmindful of things not directly concerning themselves, were aroused to the gravity of the situation, wrought by the spirit of a mob, came out of their seclusion and took a stand for law and order. It was a righteous public sentiment that brought brute force to bay. The journals not only here, but the country over, with one voice condemned the lawless acts of October 10, 1871. Sympathetic public gatherings were held in many cities, with the keynote of condemnation as the only true one. Here in Philadelphia a meeting of citizens was held, from which grew the greater, held in National Hall, on Market street, below Thirteenth. The importance of this gathering is shown by a list its promoters. Samuel Perkins, Esq., called it to order, and the eminent Hon. Henry C. Carey presided. Among some of those in the list of vice-presidents were Hon. William M. Meredith, Gustavus S. Benson, Alex. Biddle, Joseph Harrison, George H. Stuart, J. Effingham Fell, George H. Boker, Morton McMichael, James L. Claghorn, F. C. and Benjamin H. Brewster, Thomas H. Powers, Hamilton Disston, William B. Mann, John W. Forney, John Price Wetherill, R. L. Ashhurst, William H. Kemble, William S. Stokley, Judge Mitchell, Generals Collis and Sickel, Congressmen Kelley, Harmer, Myers, Creely, O'Neill, Samuel H. Bell and hundreds more. These names represented the wealth, brains and moral excellence of this community. John Goforth, the eminent lawyer, read the resolutions, which were seconded in

Negro in Philadelphia. There was a disposition to grant him, within limits, a man's chance to make his way in the world ; he had apparently vindicated his right to this in war, and his ability for it in peace. Slowly, but surely, therefore, the community was disposed to throw off the trammels, brush away petty hindrances and to soften the harshness of race prejudice, at least enough to furnish the new citizen the legal safeguards of a citizen and the personal privileges of a man. By degrees the restrictions on personal liberty were relaxed ; the street cars, which for

---

speeches by Hon. William B. Mann, Robert Purvis, Isaiah C. Weirs, Rev. J. Walker Jackson, Gen. C. H. T. Collis and Hon. Alex. K. McClure. These all breathed the same spirit, the condemnation of mob law and a demand for equal and exact justice to all. The speech of Col. McClure stands out boldly among the greatest forensic efforts ever known to our city. His central thought was ' the unwritten law,' which made an impression beyond my power to convey. In the meanwhile, smaller meetings were held in all parts of the city to record their earnest protest against the brute force of the day before. That was the end of disorder in a large scale here. On the sixteenth of October the funeral occurred. The body lay in state at the armory of the First Regiment, Broad and Race streets, and was guarded by the military. Not since the funeral cortege of President Lincoln had there been one as large or as imposing in Philadelphia. Outside of the Third Brigade, N. G. P., detached commands from the First Division, and the military from New Jersey, there were civic organizations by the hundreds from Philadelphia, to say nothing of various bodies from Washington, Baltimore, Wilmington, New York and adjacent places. All the city offices were closed, beside many schools. City Councils attended in a body, the State Legislature was present, all the city employes marched in line, and personal friends came from far and near to testify their practical sympathy. The military was under the command of General Louis Wagner, and the civic bodies marshaled by Robert M. Adger. The pall-bearers were Lieutenant Colonel Ira D. Cliff, Majors John W. Simpson and James H. Grocker, Captains J. F. Needham and R. J. Burr, Lieutenants J. W. Diton, W. W. Morris and Dr. E. C. Howard, Major and Surgeon of the Twelfth Regiment. This is but a mere glance backward at the trying days of October, 1871, and is written to refresh the minds of men and women of that day, as well as to chronicle a bit of sad history that this generation may be informed. And so closed the career of a man of splendid equipment, rare force of character, whose life was so interwoven with all that was good about us, as to make it stand out in bold relief, as a pattern for those who have followed after.''

many years had sought by every species of proscription to get rid of colored passengers or carry them on the platform, were finally compelled by law to cancel such rules ; the railways and theatres rather tardily followed, and finally even the schools were thrown open to all.[25] A deep-rooted and determined prejudice still remained, but it showed signs of yielding.

It cannot be denied that the main results of the development of the Philadelphia Negro since the war have on the whole disappointed his well-wishers. They do not pretend that he has not made great advance in certain lines, or even that in general he is not better off to-day than formerly. They do not even profess to know just what his condition to-day is, and yet there is a widespread feeling that more might reasonably have been expected in the line of social and moral development than apparently has been accomplished. Not only do they feel that there is a lack of positive results, but the relative advance compared with the period just before the war is slow, if not an actual retrogression ; an abnormal and growing amount of crime and poverty can justly be charged to the Negro ; he is not a large taxpayer, holds no conspicuous place in the business world or the world of letters, and even as a working man seems to be losing ground. For these reasons those who, for one purpose and another, are anxiously watching the development of the American Negro desire to know first how far these general impressions are true, what the real condition of the Negro is and what movements would best be undertaken to improve the present situation. And this local problem is after all but a small manifestation of the larger and similar Negro problems throughout the land.

For such ends the investigation, the results of which are here presented, was undertaken. This is not the first time such a study has been attempted. In 1837, 1847 and 1856

---

[25] Cf. Appendix B.

studies were made by the Abolition Society and the Friends and much valuable data procured.[26] The United States censuses have also added to our general knowledge, and newspapers have often interested themselves in the matter. Unfortunately, however, the Friends' investigations are not altogether free from a suspicion of bias in favor of the Negro, the census reports are very general and newspaper articles necessarily hurried and inaccurate. This study seeks to cull judiciously from all these sources and others, and to add to them specially collected data for the years 1896 and 1897.

Before, however, we enter upon the consideration of this matter, we must bring to mind four characteristics of the period we are considering : (1) The growth of Philadelphia ; (2) the increase of the foreign population in the city; (3) the development of the large industry and increase of wealth, and (4) the coming in of the Southern freedmen's sons and daughters. Even Philadelphians hardly realize that the population of their staid old city has nearly doubled since the war, and that consequently it is not the same place, has not the same spirit, as formerly ; new men, new ideas, new ways of thinking and acting have gained some entrance ; life is larger, competition fiercer, and conditions of economic and social survival harder than formerly. Again, while there were perhaps 125,000 foreign born persons in the city in 1860, there are 260,000 now, not to

---

[26] See Appendix C. The inquiry of 1838 was by the Philadelphia Society for Promoting the Abolition of Slavery, and the report was in two parts, one a register of trades and one a general report of forty pages. The Society of Friends, or the Abolition Society, undertook the inquiry of 1849, and published a pamphlet of forty-four pages. There was also the same year a report on the health of colored convicts. A pamphlet by Edward Needles was also published in 1849, comparing the Negroes in 1837 and 1848. Benjamin C. Bacon, at the instance of the Abolition Society, made the inquiry in 1856, which was published that year. In 1859, a second edition was issued with criminal statistics. All these pamphlets may be consulted at the Library Company of Philadelphia, or the Ridgway branch.

mention the children of the former born here. These foreigners have come in to divide with native Americans the industrial opportunities of the city, and have thereby intensified competition. Thirdly, new methods of conducting business and industry are now rife : the little shop, the small trader, the house industry have given way to the department store, the organized company and the factory. Manufacturing of all kinds has increased by leaps and bounds in the city, and to-day employs three times as many men as in 1860, paying three hundred millions annually in wages; hacks and expressmen have turned into vast inter-urban businesses: restaurants have become palatial hotels—the whole face of business is being gradually transformed. Finally, into this rapid development have precipitated themselves during the last twenty years fifteen thousand immigrants, mostly from Maryland, Virginia and Carolina—untrained and poorly educated countrymen, rushing from the hovels of the country or the cottages of country towns, suddenly into the new, strange life of a great city to mingle with 25,000 of their race already there. What has been the result?

[Note.—There was a small riot in 1843 during the time of Mayor Swift. In 1832 began a series of literary societies—the Library Company, the Banneker Society, etc., —which did much good for many years. The first Negro newspaper of the city, the "Demosthenian Shield," appeared in 1840. Among men not already mentioned in this period should be noted the Rev. C. W. Gardner, Dr. J. Bias, the dentist, James McCrummell, and Sarah M. Douglass. All these were prominent Negroes of the day and had much influence. The artist, Robert Douglass, is the painter of a portrait of Fannie Kemble, which its Philadelphia owner to-day prefers to attribute to Thomas Dudley.]

CHAPTER V.

THE SIZE, AGE AND SEX OF THE NEGRO POPULATION.

13. The City for a Century.—The population of the county[1] of Philadelphia increased about twenty-fold from 1790 to 1890; starting with 50,000 whites and 2500 Negroes at the first census, it had at the time of the eleventh census, a million whites and 40,000 Negroes. Comparing the rate of increase of these two elements of the population we have:

RATES OF INCREASE OF NEGROES AND WHITES.

Decade from	Negroes.	Whites.	Decade from	Negroes.	Whites.
1790–1800 . .	176.42 %	42.92 %	1840–1850* . .	.36 %	63.30 %
1800–1810 . . .	52.93	35.55	1850–1860 . .	12.26	39.67
1810–1820 . . .	13.00	22.80	1860–1870* . .	.17	19.96
1820–1830 . . .	31.39	39.94	1870 1880 . .	43.13	25.08
1830–1840 . . .	27.07	37.54	1880–1890	24.20	23.42

* Decrease for Negroes.

The first two decades were years of rapid increase for the Negroes, their number rising from 2489 in 1790 to 10,552 in 1810. This was due to the incoming of the new freedmen and of servants with masters, all to some extent attracted by the social and industrial opportunities of the city. The white population during this period also increased largely, though not so rapidly as the Negroes, rising from

---

[1] The unit for study throughout this essay has been made the *county* of Philadelphia, and not the city, except where the city is especially mentioned. Since 1854, the city and county have been coterminous. Even before that the population of the "districts" was for our purposes an urban population, and a part of the group life of Philadelphia.

51,902 in 1790 to 100,688 in 1810. During the next decade the war had its influence on both races although it naturally had its greatest effect on the lower which increased only 13 per cent against an increase of 28.6 per cent among the Negroes of the country at large. This brought the Negro population of the county to 11,891, while the white population stood at 123,746. During the next two decades, 1820 to 1840, the Negro population rose to 19,833, by natural increase and immigration, while the white population, feeling the first effects of foreign immigration, increased to 238,204. For the next thirty years the continued foreign arrivals, added to natural growth, caused the white population to increase nearly three-fold, while the same cause combined with others allowed an increase of little more than 2000 persons among the Negroes, bringing the black population up to 22,147. In the last two decades the rush to cities on the part of both white and black has increased the former to 1,006,590 souls and the latter to 39,371. The following table gives the exact figures for each decade :

POPULATION OF PHILADELPHIA, 1790–1890.

Date.	Whites.		Negroes.		Total.	
	City.	County.	City.	County.	City.	County.
1790 . . .	. . .	51,902	. . .	2,489	28,552	54,391
1800	. . .	74,129	. . .	6,880	41,220	81,009
1810	. . .	100,688	. . .	10,552	53,722	111,240
1820	56,220	123,746	7,582	11,891	63,802	135,637
1830	. . .	173,173	. . .	15,624	80,462	188,797
1838	. . .	. . .	. . .	17,500	. . .	. . .
1840	83,158	238,204	10,507	19,833	93,665	258,037
1847	. . .	. . .	11,000?	20,240	. . .	. . .
1850	110,640	389,001	10,736	19,761	121,376	408,762
1856	. . .	. . .	. . .	. . .	. . .	. . .
1860	543,344		22,185		565,529	
1870	651,854		22,147		674,022*	
1880	815,362		31,699		847,170*	
1890	1,006,590		39,371		1,046,964*	

*These totals include Chinese, Indians, etc.

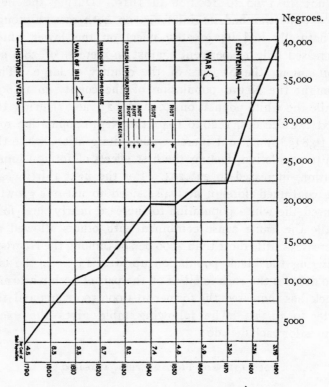

INCREASE OF THE NEGRO POPULATION IN PHILA-
DELPHIA FOR A CENTURY.

[NOTE.—Each horizontal line represents an increment of
2500 persons in population ; the upright lines represent the
decades. The broken diagonal shows the course of Negro
population, and the arrows above recall historic events previously referred to as influencing the increase of the
Negroes. At the base of the upright lines is a figure
giving the percentage which the Negro population formed
of the total population.]

The Negro has never formed a very large percent of the
population of the city, as this diagram shows:

PROPORTION OF NEGROES IN TOTAL POPULATION OF PHILADELPHIA.

A glance at these tables shows how much more sensitive
the lower classes of a population are to great social changes
than the rest of the group; prosperity brings abnormal
increase, adversity, abnormal decrease in mere numbers, not
to speak of other less easily measurable changes. Doubtless if we could divide the white population into social
strata, we would find some classes whose characteristics
corresponded in many respects to those of the Negro. Or
to view the matter from the opposite standpoint we have
here an opportunity of tracing the history and condition
of a social class which peculiar circumstances have kept
segregated and apart from the mass.

If we glance beyond Philadelphia and compare conditions as to increase of Negro population with the situation in the country at large we can make two interesting comparisons: the rate of increase in a large city compared with

that in the country at large; and the changes in the proportion of Negro inhabitants in the city and the United States.

INCREASE OF NEGROES IN THE UNITED STATES AND IN THE CITY
OF PHILADELPHIA COMPARED.

Decade.	Increase in		Census Year.	Percentage of Negroes in Total Population in	
	Phila-delphia.	United States.		Phila-delphia.	United States.
	%	%		%	%
1790–1800 . . .	176.42	32.33	1790	4.57	19.27
1800–1810 . . .	52.93	37.50	1800	8.49	18.88
1810–1820 . .	13.00	28.59	1810	9.45	19.03
1820–1830 . . .	31.39	31.44	1820	8.76	18.39
1830–1840 . . .	27.07	23.40	1830	8.27	18.10
1840–1850 . . .	.36*	26.63	1840	7.39	16.84
1850–1860 . . .	12.26	22.07	1850	4.83	15.69
1860–1870 . . .	.17*	9.86	1860	3.92	14.13
1870–1880 . . .	43.13	34.85	1870	3 28	12.66
1880–1890 . . .	24.20	13.51	1880	3.74	13.12
			1890	3.76	11.93

* Decrease.

A glance at the proportion of Negroes in Philadelphia
and in the United States shows how largely the Negro
problems are still problems of the country. (See diagram
of the proportion of Negroes in the total population of
Philadelphia and of the United States on opposite page.)

This is even more striking if we remember that Philadelphia ranks high in the absolute and relative number of
its Negro inhabitants. For the ten largest cities in the
United States we have:

TEN LARGEST CITIES IN THE UNITED STATES ARRANGED ACCORDING
TO NEGRO POPULATION.

Cities.	Negro Population.	Cities.	Proportion of Negroes to Total Population.
1. Baltimore	67,104	1. Baltimore	15.49%
2. Philadelphia . .	39.371	2. St. Louis	5.94
3. St. Louis	26,865	3. Philadelphia . .	3.76
4. New York . . .	23,601	4. Cincinnati . . .	3.72
5. Chicago	14,271	5. Boston	1.76
6. Cincinnati . . .	11,655	6. New York . . .	1.55
7. Brooklyn	10,287	7. Chicago	1.29
8. Boston	8,125	8. Brooklyn	1.27
9. Cleveland	2,989	9. Cleveland	1.14
10. San Francisco . .	1,847	10. San Francisco . .	.61

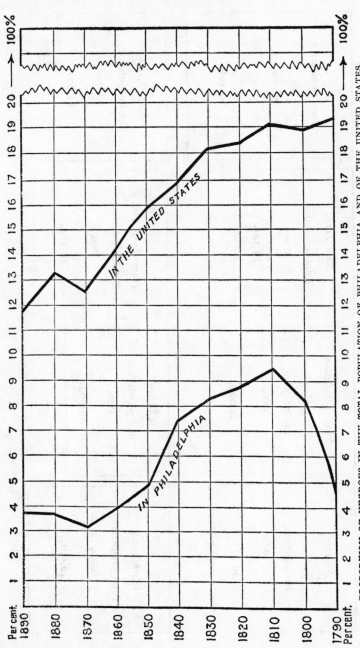

PROPORTION OF NEGROES IN THE TOTAL POPULATION OF PHILADELPHIA AND OF THE UNITED STATES.

Total population of Boston, 1820, **43,298.**

Norfolk, Va., Total population, 1890, **34,871.**

New York, Total population, 1790, **33,131.**

Harrisburg, Pa., Total population, 1890, **39,385.**

Total population of Philadelphia, 1800, **41,220.**

Chicago, Total population, 1850, **29,963.**

Negroes of Philadelphia, 1890, **39,371.**

Washington, Total population, 1850, **40,001.**

Of all the large cities in the United States, only three have a larger absolute Negro population than Philadelphia: Washington, New Orleans and Baltimore. We seldom realize that none of the great Southern cities, except the three mentioned, have a colored population approaching that of Philadelphia:

COLORED* POPULATION OF LARGE SOUTHERN CITIES.

Cities.	Colored Inhabitants.	Cities.	Colored Inhabitants.
Washington, D. C. . .	75,697	Nashville, Tenn. . .	29,395
New Orleans, La. . .	64,663	Memphis, Tenn. . .	28,729
Philadelphia, Pa. . .	40,374*	Louisville, Ky. . . .	28,672
Richmond, Va. . . .	32,354	Atlanta, Ga.	28,117
Charleston, S. C. . .	31,036	Savannah, Ga. . . .	22,978

*Includes Chinese, Japanese and civilized Indians, an insignificant number in these cases.

Taken by itself, the Negro population of Philadelphia is no insignificant group of men, as the foregoing diagrams show. (See page 52.)

In other words, we are studying a group of people the size of the capital of Pennsylvania in 1890, and as large as Philadelphia itself in 1800.

Scanning this population more carefully, the first thing that strikes one is the unusual excess of females. This fact, which is true of all Negro urban populations, has not often been noticed, and has not been given its true weight as a social phenomenon.[2] If we take the ten cities having the greatest Negro populations, we have this table:[3]

---

[2] My attention was first called to this fact by Professor Kelly Miller, of Howard University; cf. " Publications of American Negro Academy," No. 1. There is probably, in taking censuses, a larger percentage of omissions among males than among females; such omissions would, however, go but a small way toward explaining this excess of females.

[3] In a good many of the Eleventh Census tables, " Chinese, Japanese and civilized Indians," were very unwisely included in the total of the Colored, making an error to be allowed for when one studies the Negro. In most cases the discrepancy can be ignored. In this case this fact but serves to decrease the excess of females, as these other groups have an excess of males. The city of Philadelphia has 1003 Chinese, Japanese

COLORED* POPULATION OF TEN CITIES BY SEX.

Cities.	Males.	Females.
Washington	33,831	41,866
New Orleans	28,936	35,727
Baltimore	29,165	38,131
Philadelphia	18,960	21,414
Richmond, Va.	14,216	18,138
Nashville	13,334	16,061
Memphis	13,333	15,396
Charleston, S. C.	14,187	16,849
St. Louis	13,247	13,819
Louisville, Ky.	13,348	15,324
Total	192,557	232,725
Proportion	1,000	1208.5

* Includes Chinese, Japanese and civilized Indians—an element that can be ignored, being small.

This is a very marked excess and has far-reaching effects. In Philadelphia this excess can be traced back some years :

PHILADELPHIA NEGROES BY SEX. [4]

County of Philadelphia.				City of Philadelphia.			
Year.	Males.	Females.	Number Females to 1000 Males.	Year.	Males.	Females.	Number Females to 1000 Males.
1820 . .	5,220	6,671	1,091	1820 . .	3,156	4,426	1,383
1838 . .	6,896	9,146	1,326	1838 . .	3,772	5,304	1,395
1840 . .	8,316	11,515	1,387	1840 . .	3,986	6,521	1,630
1850 . .				1850 . .	8,435	11,326	1,348
1890 . .				1890 . .	18,960	21,414	1,127

The cause of this excess is easy to explain. From the beginning the industrial opportunities of Negro women in

and Indians. The figures for the whole United States show that this excess of females is probably confined to cities :

NEGROES ACCORDING TO SEX.

SECTION.	MALES.	FEMALES.
United States	3,725,561	3,744,479
North Atlantic	133,277	136,629
South Atlantic	1,613,769	1,648,921
North Central	222,384	208,728
South Central	1,739,565	1,739,686
Western	16,566	10,515

[4] Figures for other years have not been found.

cities have been far greater than those of men, through their large employment in domestic service. At the same time the restriction of employments open to Negroes, which perhaps reached a climax in 1830–1840, and which still plays a great part, has served to limit the number of men. The proportion, therefore, of men to women is a rough index of the industrial opportunities of the Negro. At first there was a large amount of work for all, and the Negro servants and laborers and artisans poured into the city. This lasted up until about 1820, and at that time we find the number of the sexes approaching equality in the county, although naturally more unequal in the city proper. In the next two decades the opportunities for work were greatly restricted for the men, while at the same time, through the growth of the city, the demand for female servants increased, so that in 1840 we have about seven women to every five men in the county, and sixteen to every five in the city. Industrial opportunities for men then gradually increased largely through the growth of the city, the development of new callings for Negroes and the increased demand for male servants in public and private. Nevertheless the disproportion still indicates an unhealthy condition, and its effects are seen in a large percent of illegitimate births, and an unhealthy tone in much of the social intercourse among the middle class of the Negro population.[5]

Looking now at the age structure of the Negroes, we notice the disproportionate number of young persons, that is, women between eighteen and thirty and men between twenty and thirty-five. The colored population of Philadelphia contains an abnormal number of young untrained persons at the most impressionable age; at the age when,

---

[5] In social gatherings, in the churches, etc., men are always at a premium, and this very often leads to lowering the standard of admission to certain circles, and often gives one the impression that the social level of the women is higher than the level of the men.

as statistics of the world show, the most crime is committed, when sexual excess is more frequent, and when there has not been developed fully the feeling of responsibility and personal worth. This excess is more striking in recent years than formerly, although full statistics are not available :

Proportion of Population.	1848.	1880.	1890.*
Under 5 years	14.7	9.8	7.8
Under 15 years	33.6	. . .	22.5
15 to 50 years	41.8	. . .	63.6†
Over 50 years	9.9	. . .	6.1‡

*Including Chinese, Japanese and Indians.   † 15 to 55.   ‡ Over 55.

This table is too meagre to be conclusive, but it is probable that while the age structure of the Negro urban population in 1848 was about normal, it has greatly changed in recent years. Detailed statistics for 1890 make this plainer :

NEGROES* OF PHILADELPHIA BY SEX AND AGE, 1890.

Ages.	Males.	Per Cent.	Females.	Per Cent.	Total.
Under 1	400	2.1	369	1.7	769
1 to 4	1,121	5.9	1,264	5.9	2,385
5 to 9	1,458	7.7	1,515	7.1	2,973
10 to 14	1,409	7.5	1,567	7.4	2,976
15 to 19	2,455	7.7	2,123	9.9	3,578
20 to 24	2,408	12.9	3,133	14.8	5,541
25 to 29	1,521	13.5	2,774	13.1	5,295
30 to 34	2,034	10.9	2,046	9.6	4,080
35 to 44	3,375	18.0	3,139	14.8	6,514
45 to 54	1,645	8.7	1,783	8.4	3,428
55 to 64	581	3.1	799	3.9	1,380
65 and over	376	2.0	726	3.4	1,102
Unknown	177	. .	176	. .	353
Total	18,960	100.0	21,414	100.0	40,374

*Includes 1003 Chinese, Japanese and Indians.

Comparing this with the age structure of other groups we have this table :[6]

---

[6] The age groupings in these tables are necessarily unsatisfactory on account of the vagaries of the census.

Age.	Negroes of Philad'a.	Negroes U. S.	England.	France.	Germany.	United States.
Under 10 .	15.31	28.22	23.9	17.5	24.2	24.29
10 to 20 . .	16.37	25.19	21.3	17.4	20.7	21.70
20 to 30 . .	27.08	17.40	17.02	16.3	16.2	18.24
30 and over	41.24	29.19	37.6	48.8	38.9	35.77

In few large cities does the age structure approach the abnormal condition here presented ; the most obvious comparison would be with the age structure of the whites of Philadelphia, for 1890, which may be thus represented :

We find then in Philadelphia a steadily and, in recent years, rapidly growing Negro population, in itself as large as a good-sized city, and characterized by an excessive number of females and of young persons.

14. **The Seventh Ward, 1896.**—We shall now make a more intensive study of the Negro population, confining ourselves to one typical ward for the year 1896. Of the nearly forty thousand Negroes in Philadelphia in 1890, a little less than a fourth lived in the Seventh Ward, and over half in this and the adjoining Fourth, Fifth and Eighth Wards :

Ward.	Negroes.	Whites.
Seventh	8,861	21,177
Eighth	3,011	13,940
Fourth	2,573	17,792
Fifth	2,335	14,619

The distribution of Negroes in the other wards may be seen by the accompanying map. (See opposite page.)

The Seventh Ward starts from the historic centre of Negro settlement in the city, South Seventh street and Lombard, and includes the long narrow strip, beginning at South Seventh and extending west, with South and Spruce streets as boundaries, as far as the Schuylkill River. The colored population of this ward numbered 3621 in 1860, 4616 in 1870, and 8861 in 1890. It is a thickly populated district of varying character ; north of it is the residence and business section of the city ; south of it a middle class and workingmen's residence section ; at the east end it joins Negro, Italian and Jewish slums ; at the west end, the wharves of the river and an industrial section separating it from the grounds of the University of Pennsylvania and the residence section of West Philadelphia.

Starting at Seventh street and walking along Lombard, let us glance at the general character of the ward. Pausing a moment at the corner of Seventh and Lombard, we can at a glance view the worst Negro slums of the city. The houses are mostly brick, some wood, not very old, and in general uncared for rather than dilapidated. The blocks between Eighth, Pine, Sixth and South have for many decades been the centre of Negro population. Here the riots of the thirties took place, and here once was a depth of poverty and degradation almost unbelievable. Even to-day there are many evidences of degradation,

WARDS OF PHILADELPHIA, WITH NEGRO POPULATION, 1890.

although the signs of idleness, shiftlessness, dissoluteness and crime are more conspicuous than those of poverty.

The alleys[7] near, as Ratcliffe street, Middle alley, Brown's court, Barclay street, etc., are haunts of noted criminals, male and female, of gamblers and prostitutes, and at the same time of many poverty-stricken people, decent but not energetic. There is an abundance of political clubs, and nearly all the houses are practically lodging houses, with a miscellaneous and shifting population. The corners, night and day, are filled with Negro loafers—able-bodied young men and women, all cheerful, some with good-natured, open faces, some with traces of crime and excess, a few pinched with poverty. They are mostly gamblers, thieves and prostitutes, and few have fixed and steady occupation of any kind. Some are stevedores, porters, laborers and laundresses. On its face this slum is noisy and dissipated, but not brutal, although now and then highway robberies and murderous assaults in other parts of the city are traced to its denizens. Nevertheless the stranger can usually walk about here day and night with little fear of being molested, if he be not too inquisitive.[8]

Passing up Lombard, beyond Eighth, the atmosphere suddenly changes, because these next two blocks have few alleys and the residences are good-sized and pleasant. Here some of the best Negro families of the ward live. Some are wealthy in a small way, nearly all are Philadelphia born, and they represent an early wave of emigration from the old slum section.[9] To the south, on Rodman

---

[7] "In the Fifth Ward only there are 171 small streets and courts; Fourth Ward, 88. Between Fifth and Sixth, South and Lombard streets, 15 courts and alleys." "First Annual Report College Settlement Kitchen." p. 6.

[8] In a residence of eleven months in the centre of the slums, I never was once accosted or insulted. The ladies of the College Settlement report similar experience. I have seen, however, some strangers here roughly handled.

[9] It is often asked why do so many Negroes persist in living in the slums. The answer is, they do not; the slum is continually scaling off emigrants for other sections, and receiving new accretions from without. Thus the efforts for social betterment put forth here have often their best

The Seventh Ward of Philadelphia

The Distribution of Negro Inhabitants Throughout the Ward, and their social condition

Grade 3: The Poor.

Grade 2: The Working People — Fair to Comfortable.

Grade 1: The "Middle Classes" and those above.

Residences of Whites, Stores, Public Buildings, etc.

(continued)

Grade 1: The "Middle Classes" and those above.

Residences of Whites, Stores, Public Buildings, etc.

(continued)

SPRUCE

PL.

PINE

LOMBARD

EIGHTEENTH

SEVENTEENTH

COMPROMISE ST

ST.

COOKE ST.

BRADFORD

VASEY ST

ST

ST

HELMUTH ST.

RICHARD ST

BURTON

CARVER

	Grade 4: Vicious and Criminal Classes.
	Grade 3: The Poor.
	Grade 2: The Working People — Fair to Comfortable.

Grade 1: The "Middle Classes" and those above.

Residences of Whites, Stores, Public Buildings, etc.

(continued)

SPRUCE

BROAD

PINE ST

LOMBARD ST

RODMAN

Grade 4: Vicious and Criminal Classes.

Grade 3: The Poor.

Grade 2: The Working People — Fair to Comfortable.

Grade 1: The "Middle Classes" and those above.

Residences of Whites, Stores, Public Buildings, etc.

(continued)

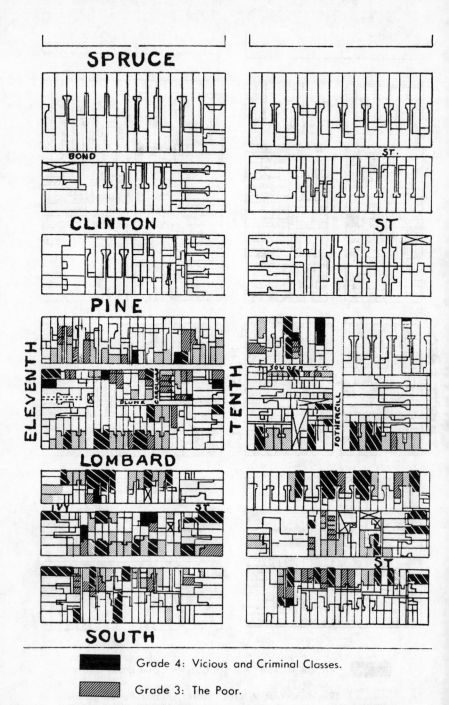

SPRUCE

BOND ST.

CLINTON ST

PINE

ELEVENTH

TENTH

SOUDER ST.

BLUME

FOTHERGILL

LOMBARD

IVY ST

ST

SOUTH

Grade 4: Vicious and Criminal Classes.

Grade 3: The Poor.

Grade 2: The Working People – Fair to Comfortable.

Grade 1: The "Middle Classes" and those above.

Residences of Whites, Stores, Public Buildings, etc.

street, are families of the same character. North of
Pine and below Eleventh there are practically no Negro
residences. Beyond Tenth street, and as far as Broad
street, the Negro population is large and varied in character. On small streets like Barclay and its extension below
Tenth—Souder, on Ivy, Rodman, Salem, Heins, Isemin-
ger, Ralston, etc., is a curious mingling of respectable
working people and some of a better class, with recent
immigrations of the semi-criminal class from the slums.
On the larger streets, like Lombard and Juniper, there live
many respectable colored families—native Philadelphians,
Virginians and other Southerners, with a fringe of more
questionable families. Beyond Broad, as far as Sixteenth,
the good character of the Negro population is maintained
except in one or two back streets.[10] From Sixteenth to
Eighteenth, intermingled with some estimable families, is
a dangerous criminal class. They are not the low, open
idlers of Seventh and Lombard, but rather the graduates of
that school : shrewd and sleek politicians, gamblers and
confidence men, with a class of well-dressed and partially
undetected prostitutes. This class is not easily differentiated and located, but it seems to centre at Seventeenth
and Lombard. Several large gambling houses are near
here, although more recently one has moved below Broad,
indicating a reshifting of the criminal centre. The whole
community was an earlier immigration from Seventh and
Lombard. North of Lombard, above Seventeenth, including Lombard street itself, above Eighteenth, is one of the
best Negro residence sections of the city, centring about
Addison street. Some undesirable elements have crept in
even here, especially since the Christian League attempted to

---

results elsewhere, since the beneficiaries move away and others fill their
places. There is, of course, a permanent nucleus of inhabitants, and
these, in some cases, are really respectable and decent people. The
forces that keep such a class in the slums are discussed further on.

[10] Gulielma street, for instance, is a notorious nest for bad characters,
with only one or two respectable families.

clear out the Fifth Ward slums,[11] but still it remains a centre of quiet, respectable families, who own their own homes and live well. The Negro population practically stops at Twenty-second street, although a few Negroes live beyond.

We can thus see that the Seventh Ward presents an epitome of nearly all the Negro problems ; that every class is represented, and varying conditions of life. Nevertheless one must naturally be careful not to draw too broad conclusions from a single ward in one city. There is no proof that the proportion between the good and the bad here is normal, even for the race in Philadelphia ; that the social problems affecting Negroes in large Northern cities are presented here in most of their aspects seems credible, but that certain of those aspects are distorted and exaggerated by local peculiarities is also not to be doubted.

In the fall of 1896 a house-to-house visitation was made to all the Negro families of this ward. The visitor went in person to each residence and called for the head of the family. The housewife usually responded, the husband now and then, and sometimes an older daughter or other member of the family. The fact that the University was making an investigation of this character was known and discussed in the ward, but its exact scope and character was not known. The mere announcement of the purpose secured, in all but about twelve cases,[12] immediate admission. Seated then in the parlor, kitchen, or living room,

---

[11] The almost universal and unsolicited testimony of better class Negroes was that the attempted clearing out of the slums of the Fifth Ward acted disastrously upon them; the prostitutes and gamblers emigrated to respectable Negro residence districts, and real estate agents, on the theory that all Negroes belong to the same general class, rented them houses. Streets like Rodman and Juniper were nearly ruined, and property which the thrifty Negroes had bought here greatly depreciated. It is not well to clean a cess-pool until one knows where the refuse can be disposed of without general harm.

[12] The majority of these were brothels. A few, however, were homes of respectable people who resented the investigation as unwarranted and unnecessary.

the visitor began the questioning, using his discretion as to the order in which they were put, and omitting or adding questions as the circumstances suggested. Now and then the purpose of a particular query was explained, and usually the object of the whole inquiry indicated. General discussions often arose as to the condition of the Negroes, which were instructive. From ten minutes to an hour was spent in each home, the average time being fifteen to twenty-five minutes.

Usually the answers were prompt and candid, and gave no suspicion of previous preparation. In some cases there was evident falsification or evasion. In such cases the visitor made free use of his best judgment and either inserted no answer at all, or one which seemed approximately true. In some cases the families visited were not at home, and a second or third visit was paid. In other cases, and especially in the case of the large class of lodgers, the testimony of landlords and neighbors often had to be taken.

No one can make an inquiry of this sort and not be painfully conscious of a large margin of error from omissions, errors of judgment and deliberate deception. Of such errors this study has, without doubt, its full share. Only one fact was peculiarly favorable and that is the proverbial good nature and candor of the Negro. With a more cautious and suspicious people much less success could have been obtained. Naturally some questions were answered better than others ; the chief difficulty arising in regard to the questions of age and income. The ages given for people forty and over have a large margin of error, owing to ignorance of the real birthday. The question of income was naturally a delicate one, and often had to be gotten at indirectly. The yearly income, as a round sum, was seldom asked for ; rather the daily or weekly wages taken and the time employed during the year.

On December 1, 1896, there were in the Seventh Ward of Philadelphia 9675 Negroes; 4501 males and 5174

females.   This total includes all persons of Negro descent,
and thirty-three intermarried whites.[13]   It does not include

NEGRO POPULATION OF SEVENTH WARD.

Age.	Male.	Female.
Under 10	570	641
10 to 19	483	675
20 to 29	1,276	1,444
30 to 39	1,046	1,084
40 to 49	553	632
50 to 59	298	331
60 to 69	114	155
70 and over	41	96
Age unknown	120	116
Total	4,501	5,174
Grand total 9,675		

residents of the ward then in prisons or in almshouses.
There were a considerable number of omissions among the
loafers and criminals without homes, the class of lodgers
and the club-house habitués.   These were mostly males,
and their inclusion would somewhat affect the division by
sexes, although probably not to a great extent.[14]   The
increase of the Negro population in this ward for six and a
half years is 814, or at the rate of 14.13 per cent per decade.
This is perhaps somewhat smaller than that for the population of the city at large, for the Seventh Ward is crowded and
overflowing into other wards.   Possibly the present Negro
population of the city is between 43,000 and 45,000.   At
all events it is probable that the crest of the tide of immigration is passed, and that the increase for the decade 1890
–1900 will not be nearly as large as the 24 per cent of the
decade 1880–1890.

---

[13] Twenty-nine women and four men.   The question of race intermarriage is discussed in Chapter XIV.

[14] There may have been some duplication in the counting of servant
girls who do not lodge where they work.   Special pains was taken to
count them only where they lodge, but there must have been some
errors. Again, the Seventh Ward has a very large number of lodgers; some of
these form a sort of floating population, and here were omissions; some
were forgotten by landladies and others purposely omitted.

The division by sex indicates still a very large and, it would seem, growing excess of women. The return shows 1150 females to every 1000 males. Possibly through the omission of men and the unavoidable duplication of some servants lodging away from their place of service, the disproportion of the sexes is exaggerated. At any rate it is great, and if growing, may be an indication of increased restriction in the employments open to Negro men since 1880 or even since 1890.

The age structure also presents abnormal features.[15] Comparing the age structure with that of the large cities of Germany, we have:

Age.	Negroes of Philadelphia.	Large Cities of Germany.
Under 20	25.1	39.3
20 to 40	51.3	37.2
Over 40	23.6	23.5

Comparing it with the Whites and Negroes in the city in 1890, we have:

Age.	Negroes of Philadelphia, 1896, Seventh Ward.	Negroes* of Philadelphia, 1890.	Native Whites of Philadelphia, 1890.
Under 10	12.8%	15.31%	24.6%
10 to 20	12.3	16.37	19.5
20 to 30	28.7	27.08	18.5
30 and over	46.2	41.24	37.4

*Includes 1003 Chinese, Japanese and Indians.

As was noticed in the whole city in 1890, so here is even more striking evidence of the preponderance of young people at an age when sudden introduction to city life is apt to be dangerous, and of an abnormal excess of females.

[15] There is a wide margin of error in the matter of Negroes' ages, especially of those above fifty; even of those from thirty-five to fifty, the age is often unrecorded and is a matter of memory, and poor memory at that. Much pains was taken during the canvass to correct errors and to throw out obviously incorrect answers. The error in the ages under forty is probably not large enough to invalidate the general conclusions; those under thirty are as correct as is general in such statistics, although the

CHAPTER VI.

CONJUGAL CONDITION.

15. The Seventh Ward.—The conjugal condition of the Negroes above fifteen years of age living in the Seventh Ward is as follows :[1]

Conjugal Condition.	Males.	Per Cent.	Females.	Per Cent.
Single	1,482	41.4	1,240	30.5
Married	1,876	52.5	1,918	47.1
Widowed	200	} 6.1	841	} 22.4
Permanently separated	18		66	
Total	3,576	100.0	4,065	100.0
Unknown	125	. . .	179	. . .
Under 15	800	. . .	930	. . .
Total population	4,501	. . .	5,174	. . .

For a people comparatively low in the scale of civilization there is a large proportion of single men—more than in Great Britain, France or Germany ; the number of married women, too, is small, while the large number of widowed and separated indicates widespread and early breaking

ages of children under ten is liable to err a year or so from the truth. Many women have probably understated their ages and somewhat swelled the period of the thirties as against the forties. The ages over fifty have a large element of error.

[1] There are many sources of error in these returns: it was found that widows usually at first answered the question " Are you married?" in the negative, and the truth had to be ascertained by a second question; unfortunate women and questionable characters generally reported themselves as married; divorced or separated persons called themselves widowed. Such of these errors as were made through misapprehension, were often corrected by additional questions; in case of designed deception the answer was naturally thrown out if the deception was detected, which of course happened in few cases. The net result of these errors is difficult to ascertain: certainly they increase the apparent number of the truly widowed to some extent at the expense of the single and married.

up of family life.[2]   The number of single women is probably lessened by unfortunate girls, and increased somewhat by deserted wives who report themselves as single. The number of deserted wives, however, allowing for false reports, is astoundingly large and presents many intricate problems. A very large part of charity given to Negroes is asked for this reason. The causes of desertion are partly laxity in morals and partly the difficulty of supporting a family.

The lax moral habits of the slave régime still show themselves in a large amount of cohabitation without marriage.   In the slum districts there are many such families, which remain together years and are in effect common law marriages. Some of these connections are broken by whim or desire, although in many cases they are permanent unions.

The economic difficulties arise continually among young waiters and servant girls ; away from home and oppressed by the peculiar lonesomeness of a great city, they form chance acquaintances here and there, thoughtlessly marry and soon find that the husband's income cannot alone support a family ; then comes a struggle which generally results in the wife's turning laundress, but often results in desertion or voluntary separation.

The great number of widows is noticeable. The conditions of life for men are much harder than for women and they have consequently a much higher death rate. Unacknowledged desertion and separation also increases this total. Then, too, a large number of these widows are

---

[2] The number of actually divorced persons among the Negroes is naturally insignificant; on the other hand the permanent separations are large in number and an attempt has been made to count them. They do not exactly correspond to the divorce column of ordinary statistics and therefore take something from the married column. The number of widowed is probably exaggerated somewhat, but even allowing for errors, the true figure is high. The markedly higher death rate for males has much to do with this. Cf. Chapter X.

simply unmarried mothers and thus represent the unchastity of a large number of women.[3]

The result of this large number of homes without husbands is to increase the burden of charity and benevolence, and also on account of their poor home life to increase crime. Here is a wide field for social regeneration.

Separating the sexes by age periods according to conjugal condition we have these tables :

MALES.

Conjugal Condition.	15–19.	20–29.	30–39.	40–49.	50–59.	60–69.	70 and over.	Unk. Age.
Single	250	783	298	90	23	6	2	20
Married	2	474	681	396	212	79	17	15
Widowed . .	. .	7	43	53	42	30	21	4
Separated . .	. .	3	9	5	1	. .	. .	. .

FEMALES.

Conjugal Condition.	15–19.	20–29.	30–39.	40–49.	50–59.	60–69	70 and over.	Unk. Age.
Single	337	559	222	68	32	9	3	10
Married	35	754	633	326	110	34	4	22
Widowed	. .	47	192	217	179	111	88	9
Separated . .	. .	23	22	12	5	1	1	2

When we remember that in slavery-time slaves usually began to cohabit at an early age, these figures indicate the sudden and somewhat disastrous application of the preventive check to population through the economic stress of life in large cities. Negro girls no longer marry in their 'teens as their mothers and grandmothers did. Of those in the twenties over 40 per cent are still unmarried, and of those in the thirties 21 per cent. So sudden a change in marriage customs means grave dangers, as shown by the fact that forty-five of the married couples under forty were permanently separated and 239 women were widowed.

---

[3] Unfortunately Philadelphia has no reliable registration of births, and the illegitimate birth rate of Negroes cannot be ascertained. This is probably high judging from other conditions.

If we reduce the general conjugal condition to per cents,
we have this table:

MEN.

Conjugal Condition.	15-40.	%	40-60.	%	Over 60.	%
Single	1,333	52.2	113	13.7	8	5.1
Married	1,157	45.3	608	73.9	96	62.0
Widowed	50	} 2.5	95	} 12.4	51	32.9
Separated	12		6			
Total	2,552	100	822	100	155	100

Here it is plain that although a large per cent of men
under forty marry there is nevertheless a number who wait
until they are settled in life and have a competence. With
the mass of Negroes, however, the waiting past the fortieth
year means simply increased caution about marriage; or,
if they are widowers, about remarriage.   Consequently
while, for instance, in Germany 84.8 per cent of the men
from forty to sixty are married, among the Negroes of this
ward less than 74 per cent are married.   At the same time
there are indications of a large number of broken marriage
ties.   Of the men under forty the bulk marry late, that is
in the thirties:

Conjugal Condition.	20-29.	30-39.
Single	61.8%	29%
Married	37.4	66
Widowed	} .8	5
Separated		
Total	100%	100%

Turning now to the women, we have a table in which

Conjugal Condition.	15-40. Number.	Per Cent.	40-60. Number.	Per Cent.	Over 60. Number.	Per Cent.
Single	1,118	39.6	100	10.5	12	4.9
Married . . .	1,422	50.3	436	46.0	38	15.0
Widowed . . .	239	} 10.1	396	} 43.5	199	} 80.1
Separated . . .	45		17		2	
Total	2,824	100	949	100	251	100

the noticeable feature is the extraordinary number of widowed and separated persons, indicating economic stress, a high death rate and lax morality. Such are the social results of a large excess of young women in a city where young men cannot afford to marry. Of the women below forty, we have this tabulation :

Conjugal Condition.	15–19.	20–29.	30–39.
Single	90.6%	40.4%	20.8
Married	9.4	54.5	59.2
Widowed . . . . }	.0	5.1	20.0
Separated . . . . }			

The comparatively large number of separations is here to be noticed, and the fact that over a fifth of the women between thirty and forty are unmarried and 40 per cent are without husbands.

From all these statistics, making some allowance for the small number of persons counted and the peculiar conditions of the ward, we may conclude :

1. That a tendency to much later marriage than under the slave system is revolutionizing the Negro family and incidentally leading to much irregularity.

2. There is nevertheless still the temptation for young men and women under forty to enter into matrimony before their economic condition warrants it.

3. Among persons over forty there is a marked tendency to single life.

4. The very large number of the widowed and separated points to grave physical, economic and moral disorder.

16. The City.—The census of 1890 showed that the conjugal condition of Negroes in the city was as follows :

Conjugal Condition.	Males over 15		Females over 15	
	Number.	Per Cent.	Number	Per Cent.
Single	6,047	44.0	6,267	37.8
Married	7,042	51.3	7,154	42.5
Widowed	603	4.4	3,078	18.6
Divorced	15	.3	35	1.1
Total	13,707	100	16,534	100

Similar statistics for native whites with native parents for the city, are:

Conjugal Condition.	Males over 15.	Females over 15.
Single	43.2%	38.0%
Married	52.0	49.0
Widowed	4.5	13.7
Divorced	.3	.3
Total	100%	100%

These figures, although six years earlier, for the most part confirm the statistics of the Seventh Ward, except in the statistics of separation. In this respect the returns for the Seventh Ward are probably more reliable, as the census counted only actually divorced persons. The largest discrepancy is in the percentage of single females; this probably comes from the fact that outside the Seventh Ward the single servant girls form a large part of the Negro population. On the whole it is noticeable that the conjugal condition of the Negroes approaches so nearly that of the whites, when the economic and social history of the two groups has been so strikingly different.

These statistics are the best measurements of the condition and tendencies of the Negro home which we have, and although they are crude and difficult in some cases rightly to interpret, yet they shed much light on the problem. First it must be remembered that the Negro home and the stable marriage state is for the mass of the colored people of the country and for a large per cent of those of Philadelphia, a new social institution. The strictly guarded savage home life of Africa, which with all its shortcomings protected womanhood, was broken up completely by the slave ship, and the promiscuous herding of the West Indian plantation put in its stead. From this evolved the Virginia plantation where the double row of little slave cabins were but parts of a communistic paternalism centring in the Big House which was the real centre of the family life. Even in Pennsylvania where the plantation system never was developed the slave family was dependent in morals as well as work upon the master. With emancipation the Negro family was first made independent and with the migration to cities we see for the first time the thoroughly independent Negro family. On the whole it is a more successful institution than we had a right to expect, even though the Negro has had a couple of centuries of contact with some phases of the monogamic ideal.[4] The great weakness of the Negro family is still lack of respect for the marriage bond, inconsiderate entrance into it, and bad household economy and family government. Sexual looseness then arises as a secondary consequence, bringing adultery and prostitution in its train. And these results come largely from the postponement of marriage among the young. Such are the fruits of sudden social revolution.[5]

---

[4] And, to tell the truth, contact with some very unsavory phases of it.

[5] There can be no doubt but what sexual looseness is to-day the prevailing sin of the mass of the Negro population, and that its prevalence can be traced to bad home life in most cases. Children are allowed on the street night and day unattended; loose talk is often indulged in; the sin is seldom if ever denounced in the churches. The same freedom is allowed the poorly trained colored girl as the white girl who has come through a strict home, and the result is that the colored girl more often falls. Nothing but strict home life can avail in such cases. Of course there is much to be said in palliation: the Negress is not respected by men as white girls are, and consequently has no such general social protection; as a servant, maid, etc., she has peculiar temptations; especially the whole tendency of the situation of the Negro is to kill his self-respect which is the greatest safeguard of female chastity.

CHAPTER VII.

SOURCES OF THE NEGRO POPULATION.

17. The Seventh Ward.—We have seen that there is in Philadelphia a large population of Negroes, largely young unmarried folks with a disproportionate number of women. The question now arises, whence came these people? How far are they native Philadelphians, and how far immigrants, and if the latter, how long have they been here? Much depends on the answer to these questions; no conclusions as to the effects of Northern city conditions on Negroes, as to the effects of long, close contact with modern culture, as to the general question of social and economic survival on the part of this race, can be intelligently answered until we know how long these people have been under the influence of given conditions, and how they were trained before they came.[1]

It is often tacitly assumed that the Negroes of Philadelphia are one homogeneous mass, and that the slums of the Fifth Ward, for instance, are one of the results of long contact with Philadelphia city life on the part of this mass. There is just enough truth and falsehood in such an assumption to make it dangerously misleading. The slums of Seventh and Lombard streets are largely the results of the contact of the Negro with city life, but the Negro in question is a changing variable quantity and has felt city

---

[1] The chief source of error in the returns as to birthplace are the answers of those who do not desire to report their birthplace as in the South. Naturally there is considerable social distinction between recently arrived Southerners and old Philadelphians; consequently the tendency is to give a Northern birthplace. For this reason it is probable that even a smaller number than the few reported were really born in the city.

influences for periods varying in different persons from one day to seventy years. A generalization then that includes a North Carolina boy who has migrated to the city for work and has been here for a couple of months, in the same class with a descendant of several generations of Philadelphia Negroes, is apt to make serious mistakes. The first lad may deserve to be pitied if he falls into dissipation and crime, the second ought perhaps to be condemned severely. In other words our judgment of the thousands of Negroes of this city must be in all cases considerably modified by a knowledge of their previous history and antecedents.

Of the 9675 Negroes in the Seventh Ward, 9138 gave returns as to their birthplace. Of these, there were born :

In Philadelphia . . . . 2939 or 32.1 per cent.
In Pennsylvania, outside of Philadelphia . 526 or 6.0 "
In the New England and Middle States . 485 or 5.3 "
In the South . . . . 4980 or 54.3 "
In the West and in foreign lands . . . . 208 or 2.3 "

That is to say, less than one-third of the Negroes living in this ward were born here, and over one-half were born in the South. Separating them by sex and giving their birthplaces more in detail, we have :

BIRTHPLACE OF NEGROES, SEVENTH WARD.

Born in	Males	Females.	Total.
Philadelphia	1,307	1,632	2,939
Pennsylvania, outside of Philadelphia . .	231	295	526
Virginia	939	1,012	1,951
Maryland	550	794	1,344
Delaware	168	296	464
New Jersey	141	190	331
District of Columbia	146	165	311
Other parts, and undesignated parts, of the South	528	382	910
Other New England and Middle States .	62	92	154
Western States	28	27	55
Foreign countries	110	43	153
Unknown	291	246	537
Total	4,501	5,174	9,675

This means that a study of the Philadelphia Negroes would properly begin in Virginia or Maryland and that only a portion have had the opportunity of being reared amid the advantages of a great city. To study this even more minutely let us divide the population according to age periods:

BIRTHPLACE BY AGE PERIODS.

Birthplace.	0–9.	10–20.	21–30.	31–40.	Over 40.	Un-known.	Total.
Philadelphia	1,004	737	502	289	396	11	2,939
Pennsylvania	8	52	185	110	168	3	526
Virginia, Maryland, New Jersey, Delaware, District of Columbia	137	432	1,564	1,150	1,090	28	4,401
South in general . . .	20	79	375	259	175	2	910
North	11	12	45	36	48	2	154
West.	10	9	12	18	6	0	55
Foreign lands	2	2	63	43	42	1	153
Unknown	19	19	142	105	63	189	537
Total	1,211	1,342	2,888	2,010	1,988	236	9,675

That the Negro immigration to the city is not an influx of whole families is shown by the fact that 83 per cent of the children under ten were born in Philadelphia. Of the youth from ten to twenty about one-half were born in the city. The great influx comes in the years from twenty-one to thirty, for of these but 17 per cent were born in the city; of the men and women born between 1856 and 1865, that is, in war time, about one-seventh were born in the city; of the freedmen, that is those born before 1856, a larger portion, one-fifth, were born in Philadelphia. The wave of immigration may therefore be thus plotted:

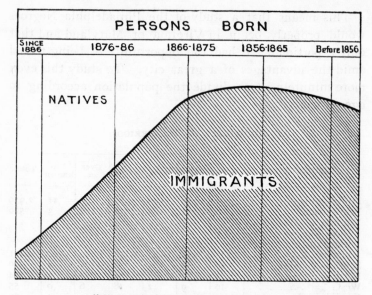

PERSONS   BORN

| SINCE 1886 | 1876-86 | 1866-1875 | 1856-1865 | Before 1856 |

NATIVES

IMMIGRANTS

THE WAVE OF NEGRO IMMIGRATION.

The square represents the Negro population of the Seventh Ward, divided into segments according to age by the upright lines; the shaded portions show the proportion of immigrants.

Further detailed information as to birthplace is given in the next table.   (See pages 77 and 78.)

Much of the immigration to Philadelphia is indirect; Negroes come from country districts to small towns; then go to larger towns; eventually they drift to Norfolk, Va., or to Richmond. Next they come to Washington, and finally settle in Baltimore or Philadelphia.[2] The training they receive from such wanderings is not apt to improve young persons greatly, and the custom has undoubtedly helped to swell the numbers of a large migratory criminal class who are often looked upon as the product of particular cities, when, as a matter of fact, they are the offscourings of

---

[2] Compare "The Negroes of Farmville: A Social Study," in *Bulletin* of U. S. Labor Bureau, January, 1898.

PHILADELPHIA—NEGROES OF SEVENTH WARD, 1896.

BIRTHPLACE—MALES BY FIVE AGE PERIODS.

Section	Place.	0–9.	10–20.	21–30.	31–40.	Over 40.	Un-known.
City.	Philadelphia	486	337	208	123	151	2
State.	Pennsylvania . .	5	20	92	49	64	1
Neighboring States.	New Jersey	10	14	31	42	44	0
	Maryland	20	48	164	137	176	5
	Virginia	19	48	420	268	178	6
	District of Columbia .	6	13	55	50	22	0
	Delaware	2	12	40	42	71	1
South.	North Carolina	5	21	97	63	35	0
	South Carolina	0	5	22	16	11	1
	Georgia	0	0	14	5	10	0
	Florida	1	1	11	5	1	0
	Alabama	0	0	2	0	4	0
	Mississippi	0	0	0	2	0	0
	Louisiana	0	0	4	1	1	0
	West Virginia	0	1	13	3	4	0
	Kentucky	0	1	2	4	3	0
	Tennessee	0	0	9	3	2	0
	Missouri	0	0	0	0	2	0
	Texas	0	0	1	2	0	0
	"South"	1	5	55	50	29	0
New England and Middle States.	Massachusetts	1	2	7	1	4	0
	Connecticut	2	0	1	1	2	0
	New York	1	4	8	5	15	0
	Rhode Island	0	2	1	3	0	0
	Maine	0	0	1	1	0	0
West.	Minnesota	1	0	0	0	0	0
	Nebraska	0	1	0	0	0	0
	Ohio	0	4	4	5	3	0
	Michigan	0	1	0	0	0	0
	Illinois	0	0	2	2	0	0
	California	0	0	0	1	0	0
	"West"	0	0	0	2	2	0
Foreign Countries.	West Indies	0	0	37	30	24	0
	Canada	2	0	1	1	3	0
	Africa	0	0	3	1	0	0
	Portugal	0	0	2	0	0	0
	Mexico	0	0	1	0	0	0
	East Indies	0	0	0	1	0	0
	Nova Scotia	0	0	0	1	0	0
	South America	0	0	0	2	1	0
?	Unknown	8	7	87	56	25	108

PHILADELPHIA—NEGROES OF SEVENTH WARD, 1896.

BIRTHPLACE—FEMALES BY FIVE AGE PERIODS.

Section	Place.	0–9.	10–20.	21–30.	31–40.	Over 40.	Un-known.
City.	Philadelphia	518	400	294	166	245	9
State.	Pennsylvania	3	32	93	61	104	2
Neighboring States.	New Jersey	15	19	44	52	58	2
	Maryland	16	92	254	217	211	4
	Virginia	35	129	431	242	169	6
	District of Columbia .	13	31	69	29	22	1
	Delaware	1	26	56	71	139	3
South.	North Carolina	8	31	66	32	32	0
	South Carolina	1	4	8	12	11	0
	Georgia	2	3	12	4	3	0
	Florida	0	1	5	1	0	1
	Alabama	0	0	6	0	0	0
	Mississippi	0	3	1	3	1	0
	Louisiana	0	0	1	2	2	0
	West Virginia . . .	0	1	7	9	1	0
	Kentucky	0	0	3	1	1	0
	Tennessee	0	0	1	2	4	0
	Missouri	0	0	1	2	2	0
	Texas	0	0	0	1	0	0
	Arkansas	0	0	1	0	0	0
	" South "	2	3	33	36	16	0
New England and Middle States.	Massachusetts	2	0	5	4	3	0
	Connecticut	1	0	4	2	10	1
	New York	4	4	17	15	9	1
	Rhode Island	0	0	1	4	2	0
	Maine	0	0	0	0	3	0
West.	Minnesota	2	0	0	0	0	0
	Ohio	0	1	6	7	1	0
	Michigan	3	0	0	1	0	0
	Delaware	4	1	0	0	0	0
	Kansas	0	1	0	0	0	0
Foreign Countries.	West Indies	0	0	7	1	6	0
	Canada	0	0	3	3	5	0
	South America	0	0	1	0	0	0
	Cuba	0	0	1	0	0	0
	Europe*	0	2	7	3	3	1
?	Unknown	11	12	55	49	38	81

* Intermarried whites.

country districts, sharpened and prepared for crime by the
slums of many cities through which they have passed.

Besides these, there is the large and well-intentioned class who are seeking to better their lot and are attracted by the larger life of the city.

Much light, therefore, will be thrown on the question of migration if we take the Negro immigrants as a class and inquire how long they have lived in the city ; we can separate the immigrants into four classes, corresponding to the waves of immigration : first, the ante-bellum immigrants, resident thirty-five years or more ; second, the refugees of war time and the period following, resident twenty-one to thirty-four years ; third, the laborers and sightseers of the time of the Centennial, resident ten to twenty years ; fourth, the recent immigration, which may be divided into those resident from five to nine years, from one to four years, and those who have been in the city less than a year.   Of 5337 immigrants,[3] the following classes may be made :

Arrived since December 1.	Resident.	Number.	Per cent.	Per cent.	
	Years.				
1895	Under 1	293	5.5	} 28.7	} 53.2
1892	1 to 4	1,242	23.2		
1887	5 to 9	1,308	24.5	} 45.9	
1875	10 to 20	1,143	21.4		} 46.8
1862	21 to 34	1,040	19.4	} 25.4	
Before 1860 . . .	35 and over.	311	6.0		
Before 1896 . .	. . . . .	5,337	100	100	100

Thus we see that the majority of the present immigrants arrived since 1887, and nearly 30 per cent since 1892. Carrying out the division by age periods, we have :

---

[3] In the case of lodgers not at home and sometimes of members of families answers could not be obtained to this question.   There were in all 862 persons born outside the city from whom answers were not obtained.

Age. Years Resident.	0–9.	10–20.	21–30.	31–40.	Over 40.	Un- known.
Under 1 year	40	56	113	60	22	3
1 to 4 years	77	181	648	239	94	3
5 to 9 years	48	139	603	355	157	6
10 to 20 years	0	103	343	449	238	10
21 to 34 years	0	0	107	334	595	4
35 years and over . .	0	0	0	17	294	0
Total	165	479	1,814	1,454	1,400	26

This table simply confirms the testimony of others as to
the recent immigration of young people. Without doubt
these statistics of immigration considerably understate the
truth ; strong social considerations lead many Negroes to
give their birthplace as Philadelphia when, as a matter of
fact, it may be elsewhere. We may then safely conclude
that less than a third of the Negroes in the city were born
here, and of the others less than a quarter have been resident twenty years or more. So that half the Negro population can not in any sense be said to be a product of the
city, but rather represents raw material, whose transforma-
tion forms a pressing series of social problems. Of course,
not all immigrants are undesirable material, nor are the
native Negroes all creditable to the city ; on the contrary,
many of the best specimens of Negroes both past and
present were not born in the city,[4] while some of the most
baffling problems arise as to the young people of native
families. Nevertheless, as a whole, it is true that the
average of culture and wealth and social efficiency is far
lower among immigrants than natives, and that this gives
rise to the gravest of the Negro problems.

18. **The City.**—The available figures for the past are not
many nor altogether reliable, yet it seems probable that
the per cent of immigrants to-day is as large as at any
previous time and perhaps larger. In 1848, 57.3 per cent
of 15,532 Negroes were natives of the State, and the

---

[4] Absalom Jones, Dorsey, Minton, Henry Jones and Augustin were
none of them natives of Philadelphia.

remaining 42.7 per cent immigrants. In 1890 we have only figures for the whole State, which show that 45 per cent of the Negroes were immigrants mainly from Virginia, Maryland, Delaware, New Jersey, North Carolina, etc.[5] For Philadelphia the percentage would probably be higher.

The new immigrants usually settle in pretty well-defined localities in or near the slums, and thus get the worst possible introduction to city life. In 1848, five thousand of the 6600 immigrants lived in the narrow and filthy alleys of the city and Moyamensing. To-day they are to be found partly in the slums and partly in those small streets with old houses, where there is a dangerous intermingling of good and bad elements fatal to growing children and unwholesome for adults. Such streets may be found in the Seventh Ward, between Tenth and Juniper streets, in parts of the Third and Fourth wards and in the Fourteenth and Fifteenth wards. This mingling swells the apparent size of many slum districts, and at the same time screens the real criminals. Investigators are often surprised in the worst districts to see red-handed criminals and good-hearted, hard-working, honest people living side by side in apparent harmony. Even when the new immigrants seek better districts, their low standard of living and careless appearance make them unwelcome to the better class of blacks and to the great mass of whites. Thus they find themselves

---

[5] Chinese, Japanese and Indians are included in these tables. The exact figures are:

Negro population of Pennsylvania	107,626
Of these, born in Pennsylvania	58,681
Virginia	19,873
Maryland	12,202
Delaware	4,851
New Jersey	1,786
New York	891
North Carolina	1,362
District Columbia	1,131
Unknown	1,804

hemmed in between the slums and the decent sections, and they easily drift into the happy-go-lucky life of the lowest classes and rear young criminals for our jails. On the whole, then, the sociological effect of the immigration of Negroes is the same as that of illiterate foreigners to this country, save that in this case the brunt of the burden of illiteracy, laziness and inefficiency has been, by reason of peculiar social conditions, put largely upon the shoulders of a group which is least prepared to bear it.

CHAPTER VIII.

EDUCATION AND ILLITERACY.

19. The History of Negro Education.—Anthony Benezet and the Friends of Philadelphia have the honor of first recognizing the fact that the welfare of the State demands the education of Negro children. On the twenty-sixth of January, 1770, at the Philadelphia Monthly Meeting of Friends, the general situation of the Negroes, and especially the free Negroes, was discussed. On motion of one, probably Benezet, it was decided that instruction ought to be provided for Negro children.[1] A committee was appointed, and on February 30 this committee proposed " that a committee of seven Friends be nominated by the Monthly Meeting, who shall be authorized to employ a schoolmistress of prudent and exemplary conduct, to teach not more at one time than thirty children in the first rudiments of school learning, and in sewing and knitting. That the admission of scholars into the said school be entrusted to the said committee, giving to the children of free Negroes and Mulattoes the preference, and the opportunity of being taught clear of expense to their parents." A subscription of £100 (about $266.67) was recommended for this purpose. This report was adopted, and the school opened June 28, 1770, with twenty-two colored children in attendance. In September the pupils had increased to thirty-six, and a teacher in sewing and knitting was employed. Afterward those who could were required to pay a sum, varying from seven shillings sixpence to ten shillings per quarter, for tuition. The following

---

[1] This account is mainly from the pamphlet: "A Brief Sketch of the Schools for Black People," etc. Philadelphia, 1867.

year a school-house was built on Walnut street, below Fourth—a one-story brick building, 32 by 18 feet.

From 1770 to 1775 two hundred and fifty children and grown persons were instructed. Interest, however, began to wane, possibly under the war-cloud, and in 1775 but five Negro children were in attendance and some white children were admitted. Soon, however, the parents were aroused, and we find forty Negroes and six whites attending.

After the war Benezet took charge of the school and held it in his house at Third and Chestnut. At his death, in 1784, he left a part of his estate to " hire and employ a religious-minded person or persons to teach a number of Negro, Mulatto or Indian children, to read, write, arithmetic, plain accounts, needle-work, etc." Other bequests were received, including one from a Negro, Thomas Shirley, and from this fund the schools, afterward known as the Raspberry street schools, were conducted for many years, and a small school is still maintained. In the early part of the century sixty to eighty scholars attended the school, and a night school was opened. In 1844 a lot on Raspberry street was purchased, and a school-house erected. Here, from 1844 to 1866, eight thousand pupils in all were instructed.

Public schools for Negroes were not established until about 1822, when the Bird school, now known as the James Forten, was opened on Sixth street, above Lombard ; in 1830 an unclassified school in West Philadelphia was begun, and in 1833 the Coates street school, now known as the Vaux school, on Coates street (now called Fairmount Avenue), near Fifth, was established. Other schools were opened at Frankford in 1839, at Paschalville in 1841, on Corn street in 1849, and at Holmesburg in 1854. In 1838 the Negro school statistics were as follows :

NEGRO SCHOOL STATISTICS, 1838.

Schools.	Pupils Enrolled.	Average Attendance.
9 free schools	1,116	713
3 schools, partly free	226	125
3 pay schools, white teachers	102	89
10 pay schools, colored teachers	288	260
25 schools	1,732	1,187

Total children of school age . . . . 3,025.

Ten years later school facilities had greatly increased:

NEGRO SCHOOL STATISTICS, 1847.

Schools.	Pupils Enrolled.
Public Grammar School, Lombard street	463
Abolition Society Infant School, Lombard street	70
Public Primary School, Gaskill street	226
Raspberry Street School	155
Public Primary School, Brown street	113
Adelphi School, Wager street	166
Shiloh Baptist Church Infant School, Clifton and Cedar Sts.	207
Bedford Street School	32
Moral Reform School	81
Public School, Oak street, West Philadelphia	12
At undesignated public schools	67
At twenty private schools	296
Total	1,888
At work and apprenticed	504
At home and unaccounted for	2,074
Total Negro children	4,466

This would seem to indicate a smaller percentage of children in school than in the last decade—a natural outcome of the period of depression through which the Negroes had just passed.

In 1850 the United States census reported 3498 adults who could neither read nor write, among the Negroes of the city. The adult population at that time must have been about 8000. There were 2176 children in school. In 1856 we have another set of detailed statistics :

Schools.	Total Enrolment.	Average Attendance.
Public schools	1,031	821
Charity schools	748	491
Benevolent and reformatory schools	211	. .
Private schools	331	. .
Total	2,321	. .

Children from 8 to 18 not in school . . . . 1,620.

The schools by this time had increased in number. There were the following public schools :

Schools and Situations.	Number Teachers.	Enrolment.	Average Attendance
Bird, Sixth above Lombard street, Boys' Department, Grammar School . . .	4	228	208
Bird, Sixth above Lombard street, Girls' Department, Grammar School	4	252	293
Bird, Sixth above Lombard street, Primary Department	3	183	150
Robert Vaux, Coates street, unclassified .	2	136	93
West Philadelphia, Oak street, unclassified	2	97	78
Corn street, unclassified	1	47	32
Frankford, unclassified	1	31	25
Holmesburg, unclassified	1	25	19
Banneker, Paschalville, unclassified . . .	1	32	15
Total	19	1,031	913

The public schools seemed to have been largely manned by colored teachers, and were for a long time less efficient than the charity schools. The grammar schools at one time, about 1844, were about to be given up, but were saved, and in 1856 were doing fairly well. The charity schools were as follows :

Schools.	Teachers.	Enrolment.	Av. Attendance.
Institute for Colored Youth, Lombard St. .	2	31	26
Raspberry St. schools, Boys' Department	2	90	64
Raspberry St. schools, Girls' Department	2	79	53
Adelphi, Wager Street, Girls' Department	2	70	42
Adelphi, Wager street, Infants' Department	2	95	61
Sheppard, Randolph street	2	60	40
School at the House of Industry	3	100	75
School for Destitute, Lombard street . .	1	73	45
Infant School, South and Clifton streets .	3	150	85
House of Refuge School	3	119	111
Orphans' Shelter School, Thirteenth street	2	73	73
Home for Colored Children, Girard avenue	1	19	19
Total	25	959	694

Of the above schools, the House of Refuge, Orphans' Shelter, House of Industry, and Home for Colored Children were schools connected with benevolent and reformatory institutions. The Raspberry school was that founded by Benezet. The Institute for Colored Youth was founded by Richard Humphreys, a West Indian ex-slaveholder, who lived in Philadelphia. On his death, in 1832, he bequeathed the sum of $10,000 to the Friends, to found an institution, "having for its object the benevolent design of instructing the descendants of the African race in school learning, in the various branches of the mechanic arts and trades, and in agriculture, in order to prepare, fit and qualify them to act as teachers." The Institute was acccordingly founded in 1837, chartered in 1842, and upon receiving further gifts was temporarily located on Lombard street. In 1866 additional sums were raised, and the Institute located on Bainbridge street, above Ninth, where it is still conducted.

There were in 1856 the following private schools :

Grade.	Schools.	Enrollment.
For high school work	1	30
For grammar school work	2	30
For common branches	10	271
Total	13	331

There were also two night schools, with an attendance of 150 or more.

The percentage of illiteracy in the city was still large. Bacon's investigation showed that of 9021 adults over twenty years of age, 45½ per cent were wholly illiterate, 16½ per cent could read and write and 19 per cent could "read, write and cipher." Detailed statistics for each ward are given in the next table :

ILLITERACY OF PHILADELPHIA NEGROES, 1854–6.

Ward.	Total Adults over 20 Years of Age.	Of these there can Read, Write and Cipher.	Read and Write.	Read.	Totally Illiterate.
I	223	25	23	47	128
2	349	36	54	76	183
3	275	60	48	68	99
4	1,427	262	199	273	693
5	1,818	350	285	310	873
6	151	21	25	34	71
7	1,867	431	337	311	788
8	969	204	192	199	374
9	76	20	16	19	21
10	208	40	39	42	87
11	37	2	11	5	19
12	234	53	35	42	104
13	69	15	12	15	27
14	233	34	46	66	87
15	157	20	26	29	82
16	82	17	12	13	40
17	70	13	8	11	38
18	4	1	1	0	2
19	114	6	20	18	70
20	99	22	12	15	50
21	2	0	0	1	1
22	36	7	4	7	18
23	249	30	43	48	128
24	252	41	34	37	140
Total	9,001	1,710	1,482	1,686	4,123

Separate schools for black and white were maintained from the beginning, barring the slight mixing in the early Quaker schools. Not only were the common schools separate, but there were no public high schools for Negroes, professional schools were closed to them, and within the memory of living men the University of Pennsylvania not only refused to admit Negroes as students, but even as listeners in the lecture halls.[2]   Not until 1881 was a law passed declaring it "unlawful for any school director, superintendent or teacher to make any distinction whatever on account of, or by reason of, the race or color of any pupil or scholar who may be in attendance upon, or seeking admission to, any public or common school maintained

---

[2] Within a few years a Negro had to fight his way through a prominent dental college in the city.

wholly or in part under the school laws of this commonwealth." This enactment was for some time evaded, and
even now some discrimination is practiced quietly in the
matter of admission and transfers. There are also schools
still attended solely by Negro pupils and taught by
Negro teachers, although, of course, the children are at
liberty to go elsewhere if they choose. They are kept
largely through a feeling of loyalty to Negro teachers.
In spite of the fact that several Negroes have been graduated with high marks at the Normal School, and in at
least one case " passed one of the best examinations for a
supervising principal's certificate that has been accomplished in Philadelphia by any teacher,"[3] yet no Negro
has been appointed to a permanent position outside the
few colored schools.

20. **The Present Condition.**—There were, in 1896,
5930 Negro children in the public schools of the city,
against 6150 in 1895 and 6262 in 1897. Confining ourselves simply to the Seventh Ward, we find the total population of legal school age—six to thirteen in Pennsylvania—
was 862 in 1896, of whom 740, or 85.8 per cent, were
reported as attending school at some time during the year.
Of the persons five to twenty years of age about 48 per
cent were in school. Statistics by age and sex are in the
next table.[4] (See page 90.)

Some difference is to be noted between the sexes : Of
the children six to thirteen years of age, 85 per cent of the
boys and nearly 86 per cent of the girls are in school ; of
the youth fourteen to twenty, 20 per cent of the boys and
21 per cent of the girls are in school. The boys stop
school pretty suddenly at sixteen, the girls at seventeen.

---

[3] Philadelphia *Ledger*, August 13, 1897.
[4] The chief error in the school returns arises from irregularity in
attendance. Those reported in school were there sometime during the
year, and possibly off and on during the whole year, but many were not
steady attendants.

Nearly 11 per cent of the children in school were in attendance less than the full term;[5] of these attending the whole term there is much irregularity through absences and tardiness. On the whole, therefore, the effective school attendance is less than appears at first sight.

SCHOOL POPULATION AND ATTENDANCE (1896–97) BY AGE.
Negroes of the Seventh Ward.

Age.	Males.		Females.	
	School Population.	School Attendance.	School Population.	School Attendance.
Kindergarten { 4 years .	67	5	66	6
age { 5 years .	46	11	51	19
Total of Kindergarten age	113	16	117	25
Pennsylvania legal school age. { 6 years .	50	28	56	35
7 years .	48	40	59	45
8 years .	53	48	67	59
9 years .	54	50	51	50
10 years .	49	44	57	52
11 years .	39	38	58	55
12 years .	45	39	62	56
13 years .	53	46	61	55
Total of legal school age	391	333	471	407
Youth above legal school age, and under voting age. { 14 years .	45	35	52	36
15 years .	39	22	52	24
16 years .	53	24	71	31
17 years .	50	6	87	19
18 years .	55	4	80	4
19 years .	56	2	91	1
20 years .	67	0	122	2
Total youth . . 14–20	365	93	555	117
Total children . 5–20 (Usual school age.)	802	437	1077	543

The question of illiteracy is a difficult one to have answered without actual tests, especially when the people questioned have some motives for appearing less ignorant than they actually are. The figures for the Seventh Ward, therefore, undoubtedly understate the illiteracy somewhat; nevertheless the error is not probably large enough to

---

[5] Of 647 school children 62 were in school less than nine months—some less than three. Probably many more than this did not attend the full term.

deprive the figures of considerable value, and compared with statistics taken in a similar manner they are probably of average reliability.[6] Of 8464 Negroes in the Seventh Ward the returns show that 12.17 per cent are totally illiterate. Comparing this with previous years we have :

1850 44   per cent.   1890 18   per cent.
1856 . . . . . 45½   "   1896 (7th Ward) 12.17   "   [7]
1870 22   "

The large number of young people in the Seventh Ward probably brings the average of illiteracy below the level of the whole city.   Why this is so may be seen if we take the illiteracy of four age-classes :

Age.	Read and Write.	Read.[1]	Illiterate.
Youth, 10 to 20 years of age	94%	2%	4%
Men and women, 21 to 30 years of age . .	90	6	4
Men and women, 31 to 40 years of age .	77	6	17
Men and women, over 40 years of age . .	61	10	29

The same difference is plain if we take the returns of the census of 1890 for the colored population of the whole city :

Age.	Illiterate Males.	Illiterate Females.	Total Illiterates.
10 to 19	138	216	354
20 to 34	836	1,096	1,932
35 to 44	1,098	1,571	2,669
45 and over	334	775	1,109
Total (including those of unknown age)	2,450	3,719	6,169
	Males.	Females.	Colored Persons.
Population over 10	15,981	18,266	34,247
Per cent of total illiteracy	15%	21%	18%

[6] As has before been noted, the Negroes are less apt to deceive deliberately than some other peoples.   The ability to read, however, is a point of pride with them, and especial pains was taken in the canvass to avoid error; often two or more questions on the point were asked.   Nevertheless all depended in the main on voluntary answers.

[7] This looks small and yet it probably approximates the truth.   My general impression from talking with several thousand Negroes in the Seventh Ward is that the percentage of total illiteracy is small among them.

Separating those in the Seventh Ward by sex, we have this table, showing a total illiteracy of 10 per cent among the males and 17 per cent among the females :

ILLITERACY BY SEX AND BY AGE PERIODS.—SEVENTH WARD.

Sex—Ages.	Males.					Females.				
	Total.	Read and Write.	Read.	Wholly Illiterate.	Unknown.	Total.	Read and Write.	Read.	Wholly Illiterate.	Unknown.
Youth, 10 to 20 years .	550	514	10	13	13	792	730	16	38	8
Post-bellum men, (born since 1865), 21 to 30 years	1,396	1,229	45	61	61	1,492	1,283	55	116	38
Men of war time (born between 1855 and 1866), 31 to 40 years	978	784	40	111	43	1,032	697	84	211	40
Freedmen (born before 1856), over 40 years	887	625	63	181	18	1,101	558	136	381	26
Of unknown age . .	120	12	1	3	104	116	24	2	4	86
Total	3,931	3,164	159	369	230	4,533	3,292	293	750	198

Granting that those reporting themselves as able to read should in most cases be included under the illiterate, and that therefore the rate of illiteracy in the Seventh Ward is about 18 per cent, and perhaps 20 per cent for the city, nevertheless the rate is, all things considered, low and places the Philadelphia Negroes in a position not much worse than that of the total population of Belgium (15.9 per cent), so far as actual illiterates are concerned.[8]

[8]The Seventh Special Report of the United States Commissioner of Labor enables us to make some comparison of the illiteracy of the foreign and Negro populations of the City:

Nationalities.	Persons able to Read and Write.		Illiterates.		Comparison of Illiteracy.
Italians, 1894	1396	36.37 p. c.	2442	63.63 p.c.	
Russians, 1894 . . .	1128	58.08 "	814	41.92 "	
Poles, 1894	838	59.73 "	565	40.27 "	
Hungarians, 1894 .	314	69.16 "	140	30.84 "	
Irish, 1894	541	74.21 "	188	25.79 "	
Negroes, 7th W., 1896	6893	81.44 "	1571	18.56 "	
Germans, 1894 . . .	451	85.26 "	78	14.74 "	

The foreigners here reported include all those living in certain parts of the Third and Fourth Wards of Philadelphia. They are largely recent immigrants. The Russians and Poles are mostly Jews.—ISABEL EATON.

The degree of education of those who can read and write can only be indicated in general terms. The majority have only a partial common school education from the country schools of the South or the primary grades of the city; a considerable number have taken grammar school work; a very few have entered the high schools and there have been from fifty to one hundred graduates from colleges and professional schools since the war. Exact figures as to the proportion of students taking higher courses are not easily obtained.

In the Catto School, 1867–96, 11 per cent of those entering the primary grade were promoted to the grammar school; less than 1 per cent of those entering the primary grade of the Vaux School were promoted to the High School. Of those graduating from the course at the Institute for Colored Youth, 8 per cent have taken a college or professional course.[9] Thus it appears that of 1000 colored children entering the primary grade 110 go to the grammar school, ten to the high school and one to college or to a professional school. The basis of induction here is, however, too small for many conclusions.[10]

At present there are in the Seventh Ward thirteen schools for children of all races and sixty-four teachers, with school property valued at $214,382. The schools are : one combined grammar and secondary, three secondary, one combined secondary and primary, four primary and four kindergartens.

In the city the following are the public schools chiefly attended by Negroes :

---

[9] Data furnished by two principals of colored schools. At present (1897) there are 58 Negro students in the following schools: Central High, Girls' Normal, Girls' High, Central Manual Training and North East Manual Training; or about one per cent of the total school enrollment.

[10] Probably the percentage of children promoted from primary to grammar grades in this case is unusually small.

Coulter street, Twenty-second Section . . 45 boys, 39 girls, all colored.
J. E. Hill, Germantown . . . . 84 " 89 " "
Robert Vaux, Wood street . . . . 67 " 74 " "
O. V. Catto, Lombard street . . . . . . 140 " 150 " "
Wilmot, Meadow and Cherry streets . . 48 " 47 " "
James Miller, Forty-second and Ludlow sts., 24 " 13 " "
J. S. Ramsey, Quince and Pine streets . . 243 " 253 " nearly all
colored.

All the teachers are colored except those in the Ramsey
and Miller schools, who are all white. There are a few
colored kindergarten teachers in various sections, and large
numbers of colored children go to other schools beside
those designated. Many of the colored schools have a high
reputation for efficient work.[11] There is, theoretically,
no discrimination in night schools and some Negroes
go to white schools; for the most part, however, the
Negroes are in the following night schools:

PHILADELPHIA COLORED NIGHT SCHOOLS, 1895.

Name of School.	No. Registered at Beginning of Term.	No. Registered at End of Term.	Average Attendance.	Average per Cent Present during Term.	Pupils under 15 Years.	Pupils 15-20 Years.	Pupils 21-29 Years.	Pupils 30-40 Years.	Pupils 40-50 Years.	Pupils over 50 Years.	Average Age.
O. V. Catto	60	175	69	64	17	47	49	32	25	5	27
Vaux	18	71	25	59	1	12	23	16	9	0	28
Park Avenue	35	95	51	62	14	34	40	3	4	0	21
J. E. Hill	30	112	40	64	4	47	40	11	6	4	24
West Philadelphia .	50	94	38	49	3	14	39	32	6	0	27
Coulter street . . .	48	88	47	68	5	48	24	11	0	0	20
Total night schools of city – white and colored	8957	2208	8352	67	6172	11,963	2844	625	183	44	18

[11] The following report from a member of the Committee on Schools of
the City Councils is taken from the Philadelphia *Ledger*, December 2,
1896: On the matter of the needs of the colored population in connection
with the schools, Mr. Meehan had to say: " Young women of the colored
race are qualifying themselves for public school teachers by taking the
regular course through our Normal School. No matter how well
qualified they may be to teach, directors do not elect them to positions in
the schools. It is taken for granted that only white teachers shall be
placed in charge of white children. The colored Normal School graduates might be given a chance by appointments in the centre of some
colored population, so that colored people might support their own
teachers if so disposed, as they support their own ministers in their

The Institute for Colored Youth is still a popular and useful institution. It gives grammar and high school courses. In 1890, by the efforts of both white and colored friends,[12] an industrial department, with eleven teachers, was added. Among the men trained here are Octavius V. Catto, Jacob C. White, Jr., who was for thirty-five years principal of the Vaux School, two ex-ministers from the United States to Haiti, and the young colored physician who recently broke twenty-five years record in the excellence of his examination before the State Board. Under Mr. White, mentioned above, Mr. Henry Tanner, the artist recently honored by the French government, was graduated from the Vaux School.

Considering this testimony as a whole, it seems certain that the Negro problem in Philadelphia is no longer, in the main, a problem of sheer ignorance ; to be sure, there is still a very large totally illiterate class of perhaps 6000 persons over ten years of age ; then, too, the other 24,000 are not in any sense of the word educated as a mass ; most of them can read and write fairly well, but few have a training beyond this. The leading classes among them are mostly grammar school graduates, and a college bred person is very exceptional. Thus the problem of education is still large and pressing ; and yet considering their ignorance in the light of history and present experience, it must be acknowledged that there are other social problems connected with this people more pressing than that of education ; that a fair degree of persistence in present methods will settle in time the question of ignorance, but other social questions are by no means so near solution.

The only difficulties in the matter of education are carelessness in school attendance, and poverty which keeps

---

separate colored churches. The good result of this arrangement is shown by the experience in the Twenty-second Section, where there are two schools with seven colored teachers, ranking among the most popular in the section.''

[12] Negroes in the city raised $2000 toward this.

children out of school. The former is a matter for the colored people to settle themselves, and is one to which their attention needs to be called. While much has been done, yet it cannot be said that Negroes have fully grasped their great school advantages in the city by keeping their younger children regularly in school, and from this remissness much harm has sprung.

CHAPTER IX.

THE OCCUPATIONS OF NEGROES.

21. The Question of Earning a Living.—For a group of freedmen the question of economic survival is the most pressing of all questions; the problem as to how, under the circumstances of modern life, any group of people can earn a decent living, so as to maintain their standard of life, is not always easy to answer. But when the question is complicated by the fact that the group has a low degree of efficiency on account of previous training; is in competition with well-trained, eager and often ruthless competitors; is more or less handicapped by a somewhat indefinite but existent and wide-reaching discrimination; and, finally, is seeking not merely to maintain a standard of living but steadily to raise it to a higher plane—such a situation presents baffling problems to the sociologist and philanthropist.

And yet this is the situation of the Negro in Philadelphia; he is trying to better his condition; is seeking to rise; for this end his first need is work of a character to engage his best talents, and remunerative enough for him to support a home and train up his children well. The competition in a large city is fierce, and it is difficult for any poor people to succeed. The Negro, however, has two especial difficulties: his training as a slave and freedman has not been such as make the average of the race as efficient and reliable workmen as the average native American or as many foreign immigrants. The Negro is, as a rule, willing, honest and good-natured; but he is also, as a rule, careless, unreliable and unsteady. This is without doubt to be expected in a people who for generations have

been trained to shirk work ; but an historical excuse
counts for little in the whirl and battle of bread-winning.
Of course, there are large exceptions to this average rule ;
there are many Negroes who are as bright, talented and
reliable as any class of workmen, and who in untrammeled
competition would soon rise high in the economic scale,
and thus by the law of the survival of the fittest we should
soon have left at the bottom those inefficient and lazy
drones who did not deserve a better fate.   However, in the
realm of social phenomena the law of survival is greatly
modified by human choice, wish, whim and prejudice.
And consequently one never knows when one sees a social
outcast how far this failure to survive is due to the defi-
ciencies of the individual, and how far to the accidents or
injustice of his environment.   This is especially the case
with the Negro.   Every one knows that in a city like
Philadelphia a Negro does not have the same chance to
exercise his ability or secure work according to his talents
as a white man.   Just how far this is so we shall discuss
later ; now it is sufficient to say in general that the sorts
of work open to Negroes are not only restricted by their
own lack of training but also by discrimination against
them on account of their race ; that their economic rise is
not only hindered by their present poverty, but also by a
widespread inclination to shut against them many doors of
advancement open to the talented and efficient of other
races.

What has thus far been the result of this complicated
situation?   What do the mass of the Negroes of the city
at present do for a living, and how successful are they in
those lines?   And in so far as they are successful, what
have they accomplished, and where they are inefficient in
their present sphere of work, what is the cause and remedy?   These are the questions before us, and we proceed
to answer the first in this chapter, taking the occupations
of the Negroes of the Seventh Ward first, then of the city

in a general way, and finally saying a word as to the past.

22. Occupations in the Seventh Ward.—Of the 257 boys between the ages of ten and twenty, who were regularly at work in 1896, 39 per cent were porters and errand boys; 25.5 per cent were servants; 16 per cent were common laborers, and 19 per cent had miscellaneous employment. The occupations in detail are as follows:[1]

```
Total population, males 10 to 20  . . . . 651
Engaged in gainful occupations  . . . . 257
                                         ════

Porters and errand boys . . . . . . . 100     39.0 per cent.
Servants . . . . . . . . . . . . . 66         25.5    "
Common laborers . . . . . . . . . . 40        16.0    "
Teamsters  . . . . . . . . . . . .  7
Apprentices. . . . . . . . . . . .  6
Bootblacks . . . . . . . . . . . .  6
Drivers . . . . . . . . . . . . .  5
Newsboys. . . . . . . . . . . . .  5
Peddlers . . . . . . . . . . . . .  4
Typesetters . . . . . . . . . . . .  3
Actors . . . . . . . . . . . . . .  2
Bricklayers . . . . . . . . . . . .  2
Hostlers . . . . . . . . . . . . .  2
Typewriters . . . . . . . . . . . .  2
Barber, bartender, bookbinder, factory
   hand, rubber-worker, sailor, shoe-
   maker—one each . . . . . . . .  7
                                   ──  51     19.5    "

                                   257    100   per cent.
```

---

[1] The returns as to occupations are on the whole reliable. There was in the first place little room for deception, since the occupations of Negroes are so limited that a false or indefinite answer was easily revealed by a little judicious probing; moreover there was little disposition to deceive, for the Negroes are very anxious to have their limited opportunities for employment known; thus the motives of pride and complaint balanced each other fairly well. Some error of course remains: the number of servants and day workers is slightly understated; the number of caterers and men with trades is somewhat exaggerated by the answers of men with two occupations: *e. g.*, a waiter with a small side business of catering returns himself as caterer; a carpenter who gets little work and makes his living largely as a laborer is sometimes returned as a carpenter, etc. In the main the errors are small and of little consequence.

Of the men twenty-one years of age and over, there were in gainful occupations, the following :

In the learned professions	61	2.0 per cent.
Conducting business on their own account	207	6.5 "
In the skilled trades	236	7.0 "
Clerks, etc.	159	5.0 "
Laborers, better class	602	
Laborers, common class	852	
	— 1454	45.0 "
Servants	1079	34.0 "
Miscellaneous	11	.5 "
	3207	100 per cent.

Total male population, 21 and over . . . . . 3850.[2]

---

[2] A more detailed list of the occupations of male Negroes, twenty-one years of age and over, living in the Seventh Ward in 1896, is as follows:

Entrepreneurs.

Caterers	65	Employment Agents	3
Hucksters	37	Lodging House Keepers	3
Proprietors Hotels and Restaurants	22	Proprietors of Pool Rooms	3
Merchants: Fuel and Notions	22	Real Estate Agencies	3
Proprietors of Barber Shops	15	Job Printers	3
Expressmen owning outfit	14	Builder and Contractor	1
Merchants, Cigar Stores	7	Sub-landlord	1
Merchants, Grocery Stores	4	Milk Dealer	1
Proprietors of Undertaking Establishments	2	Publisher	1
			——
			207

In Learned Professions.

Clergymen	22	Dentists	3
Students	17	Editors	1
Teachers	7		——
Physicians	6		61
Lawyers	5		

In the Skilled Trades.

Barbers	64	Apprentice	1
Cigar Makers	39	Boilermaker	1
Shoemakers	18	Blacksmith	1
Stationary Engineers	13	China Repairer	1
Bricklayers	11	Cooper	1
Printers	10	Cabinetmaker	1

This shows that three-fourths of the male Negroes ten years of age and over in gainful occupations are laborers and servants, while the remaining fourth is equally divided into three parts : one to the trades, one to small business

Painters	10	Dyer	1
Upholsterers	7	Furniture Polisher	1
Carpenters	6	Gold Beater	1
Bakers	4	Kalsominer	1
Tailors	4	Locksmith	1
Undertakers	4	Laundryman (steam)	1
Brickmakers	3	Paper Hanger	1
Framemakers	3	Roofer	1
Plasterers	3	Tinsmith	1
Rubber Workers	3	Wicker Worker	1
Stone Cutters	3	Horse Trainer	1
Bookbinders	2	Chemist	1
Candy Makers	2	Florist	1
Chiropodists	2	Pilot	1
Ice Carvers	2		—
Photographers	2		236

Clerks, Semi-Professional and Responsible Workers.

Messengers	33	Policemen	5
Stewards	31	Sextons	4
Musicians	20	Shipping Clerks	3
Clerks	18	Dancing Masters	3
Agents	15	Inspector in Factory	1
Clerks in Public Service	8	Cashier	1
Managers and Foremen	6		—
Actors	6		159
Bartenders	5		

Servants.

Domestics	582	Nurses	2
Hotel Help	457		—
Public Waiters	38		1079

Laborers (Select Class).

Stevedores	164	China Packers	14
Teamsters	134	Watchmen	14
Janitors	94	Drivers	12
Hod Carriers	79	Oyster Openers	4
Hostlers	44		—
Elevator Men	22		602
Sailors	21		

enterprises, and one to professional men, clerks and miscellaneous employments.

Turning now to the females, ten to twenty years of age,
we have:

Housewives	38	4.5	per cent.
At work [3]	289	36.5	"
At school	333	42.0	"
At home, unoccupied, etc.	133	17.0	"
	—	—	
Total female population 10–20	793	100	per cent.

Of the 289 at work there were:

In domestic service	211	73.0	per cent.
Doing day's work	32	11.0	"
Dressmakers and seamstresses	16	5.5	"
Servants in public places	12	4.3	"
Apprentices	6		
Musicians	4		
Teachers	3		
Clerks	2		
Actresses	2		
Hairdressers	1		
	— 18	6.2	"
	289	100	per cent.

Taking the occupations of women twenty-one years of
age and over, we have:

Domestic servants	1262	37.0	per cent.
Housewives and day laborers	937	27.0	"
Housewives	568	17.0	"
Day laborers, maids, etc.	297	9.0	"

Laborers (Ordinary).

Common Laborers	493	Casual Laborers	12
Porters	274	Miscellaneous Laborers	4
Laborers for City	47		—
Bootblacks	22		852

Miscellaneous.

Rag Pickers	6	Prize Fighter	1
"Politicians"	2		—
Root Doctors	2		11

[3] This includes 12 housewives who also work.

In skilled trades   221   6.0 per cent.
Conducting businesses   63   2.0   "
Clerks, etc.   40   1.0   "
Learned professions   37   1.0   "

                                        3425   100 per cent.
Total female population 21 and over . . . . . 3740. [4]

Leaving out housewives who do no outside work and scheduling all women over twenty-one who have gainful occupations, we have:

---

[4] A more detailed list of the occupations of female Negroes, twenty-one years of age and over, living in the Seventh Ward in 1896, is as follows:

Entrepreneurs.

Caterers	18	Undertakers	3
Restaurant Keepers	17	Child-Nursery Keepers	3
Merchants	17		—
Employment Agents	5		63

Learned Professions.

Teachers	22	Students	7
Trained Nurses	8		—
			37

Skilled Trades.

Dressmakers	204	Manicure	1
Hairdressers	6	Barber	1
Milliners	3	Typesetter	1
Shrouders of Dead	4		—
Apprentice	1		221

Clerks, Semi-Professional and Responsible Workers.

Musicians	12	Matrons	2
Clerks	10	Actress	1
Stewardesses	4	Missionary	1
Housekeepers	4		—
Agents	3		40
Stenographers	3		

Laborers, etc.

Housewives and Day Workers .	937	Janitresses	22
Day Workers	128	Factory Employe	1
Public Cooks	72	Office Maids	12
Seamstresses	48		—
Waitresses in Restaurants, etc.	14		1234

Servants.

Domestic Servants 1262

Professions 37
Working on own account 63
In trades 221
Clerks and agents, etc. 40
Day workers, janitresses, seamstresses, cooks, etc. 1234
Servants 1262

                                                        2857

The following tables gather up all these statistics and give full returns with distinctions of age and sex :

OCCUPATIONS—FEMALES, TEN YEARS OF AGE AND OVER. SEVENTH WARD, 1896.

Occupations.	10 Years.	11 Years.	12 Years.	13 Years.	14 Years.	15 Years.	16 Years.	17 Years.	18 Years.	19 Years.	20 Years.	21-30 Years.	31-40 Years.	Over 40 Years.	Unknown Age.	Total.	
																10-20 Years.	21 and over and Unk.
At school	52	55	56	55	36	24	31	19	4	1	2	5	1	0	1	335	7
At home	5	3	5	3	9	16	16	23	22	13	8	. . .	. . .	. . .	. . .	. . .	. . .
Housewives	0	0	0	0	0	0	1	3	4	11	19	246	128	187	7	38	568
Housewives and day workers	0	0	0	0	0	1	0	1	1	4	5	255	329	344	9	12	937
Day workers	0	0	1	0	0	0	1	3	6	5	4	54	24	46	4	20	128
Domestic service	0	0	0	3	7	11	22	28	33	43	64	661	347	240	14	211	1262
Apprentice to trade	0	0	0	0	0	0	0	4	1	0	1	0	1	0	0	6	1
Janitresses	0	0	0	0	0	0	0	0	0	1	0	7	7	8	0	1	22
Public waitresses	0	0	0	0	0	0	0	1	1	2	1	12	1	0	1	5	14
Office and public maids	0	0	0	0	0	0	0	0	1	0	1	3	5	4	0	2	12
Public cooks	0	0	0	0	0	0	0	0	2	1	1	17	28	27	0	4	72
Musicians	0	0	0	0	0	0	0	2	0	2	0	5	6	1	0	4	12
Hairdressers	0	0	0	0	0	0	0	0	0	0	1	0	1	5	0	1	6
Seamstresses	0	0	0	0	0	0	0	0	0	1	5	23	12	13	0	6	48
Dressmakers	0	0	0	0	0	0	0	0	4	3	3	78	68	57	1	10	204
Actress	0	0	0	0	0	0	0	1	0	0	1	1	0	0	0	2	1
Teachers	0	0	0	0	0	0	0	0	0	1	2	12	6	4	0	3	22
Clerks	0	0	0	0	0	0	0	0	0	1	1	6	4	0	0	2	10
Restaurant keepers	0	0	0	0	0	0	0	0	0	0	0	5	8	4	0	0	17
Milliners	0	0	0	0	0	0	0	0	0	0	0	1	1	1	0	0	3
Nursery keepers	0	0	0	0	0	0	0	0	0	0	0	0	1	2	0	0	3
Trained nurses	0	0	0	0	0	0	0	0	0	0	0	3	0	4	1	0	8
Agents (beneficial soc.)	0	0	0	0	0	0	0	0	0	0	0	3	0	0	0	0	3
Cateresses	0	0	0	0	0	0	0	0	0	0	0	2	8	8	0	0	18
Shrouders of dead	0	0	0	0	0	0	0	0	0	0	0	0	0	4	0	0	4
Stenographers	0	0	0	0	0	0	0	0	0	0	0	1	2	0	0	0	3
Factory employee	0	0	0	0	0	0	0	0	0	0	0	1	0	0	0	0	1
Matron (of Home)	0	0	0	0	0	0	0	0	0	0	0	0	1	1	0	0	2
Manicure	0	0	0	0	0	0	0	0	0	0	0	1	0	0	0	0	1
Merchants—Cigar store	0	0	0	0	0	0	0	0	0	0	0	1	1	0	0	0	2
Groceries	0	0	0	0	0	0	0	0	0	0	0	0	2	2	0	0	4
Notions, etc.	0	0	0	0	0	0	0	0	0	0	0	0	3	4	0	0	7
Fuel	0	0	0	0	0	0	0	0	0	0	0	0	1	2	0	0	3
Hardware	0	0	0	0	0	0	0	0	0	0	0	0	0	1	0	0	1
Barber	0	0	0	0	0	0	0	0	0	0	0	0	1	0	0	0	1
Undertakers	0	0	0	0	0	0	0	0	0	0	0	0	1	2	0	0	3
Stewardesses	0	0	0	0	0	0	0	0	0	0	0	0	2	2	0	0	4
Missionary	0	0	0	0	0	0	0	0	0	0	0	0	1	0	0	0	1
Prop. Employment Ag.	0	0	0	0	0	0	0	0	0	0	0	0	3	2	0	0	5
Typesetters	0	0	0	0	0	0	0	0	0	0	0	0	1	0	1	0	
Housekeepers	0	0	0	0	0	0	0	0	0	0	0	0	2	1	0	0	3
Prostitutes	0	0	0	0	0	0	0	2	1	2	3	51	26	11	12	8	100

OCCUPATIONS—MALES, TEN TO TWENTY-ONE YEARS OF AGE.
SEVENTH WARD, 1896.

Occupations.	10 Years.	11 Years.	12 Years.	13 Years.	14 Years.	15 Years.	16 Years.	17 Years.	18 Years.	19 Years.	20 Years.	Total.
Total boys at given age	49	39	45	53	45	39	53	50	55	56	67	463
Total in school	44	38	39	46	35	22	24	6	4	2	0	178
Total at home	5	1	1	2	5	4	11	3	0	2	0	28
Actors	0	0	0	0	0	0	0	0	1	0	1	2
Apprentices to trades	0	0	0	0	0	0	0	1	3	1	1	6
Barber	0	0	0	0	0	0	0	0	0	1	0	1
Bartender	0	0	0	0	0	0	0	0	0	1	0	1
Bookbinder	0	0	0	0	0	0	0	1	0	0	0	1
Bootblacks	0	0	0	0	0	1	1	2	1	1	0	6
Bricklayer	0	0	0	0	0	0	0	0	0	2	0	2
Drivers for Doctors	0	0	0	0	0	0	0	1	0	3	1	5
Errand-boys	0	0	2	2	4	5	6	6	5	1	2	33
Factory laborer	0	0	0	0	0	0	0	0	0	1	0	1
Hostlers	0	0	0	0	0	0	0	1	0	1	0	2
Laborers	0	0	0	1	0	0	1	3	12	12	11	40
Newsboys	0	0	1	0	0	1	2	0	0	1	0	5
Peddlers	0	0	0	0	0	0	1	0	1	1	1	4
Printers	0	0	0	0	0	0	0	0	1	1	1	3
Porters	0	0	1	0	1	4	5	10	15	11	20	67
Rubber worker	0	0	0	0	0	0	0	0	0	1	0	1
Sailor	0	0	0	0	0	0	0	1	0	0	0	1
Service (domestic)	0	0	1	2	0	0	1	11	7	7	18	47
Service (public)	0	0	0	0	0	1	1	1	3	5	8	19
Shoemakers	0	0	0	0	0	0	0	0	0	0	1	1
Teamsters	0	0	0	0	0	1	0	2	2	0	2	7
Typewriters	0	0	0	0	0	0	0	1	0	1	0	2

OCCUPATIONS—MALES, TWENTY-ONE YEARS AND OVER.
SEVENTH WARD, 1896.

Occupations.	21–30 Years.	31–40 Years.	41 and over.	Unk. Age.	Total.
Actors	4	2	. .	. .	6
Agents (ins. societies and drummers)	6	3	6	. .	15
Apprentice to trade	1	. .	. .	. .	1
Barbers	28	21	15	. .	64
Bartenders	2	3	. .	. .	5
Bellmen	32	10	1	. .	43
Bookbinders	1	1	. .	. .	2
Bootblacks	15	6	1	. .	22
Bricklayers	. .	7	4	. .	11
Brickmakers	2	. .	1	. .	3
Builder and contractor	1	. .	. .	. .	1
Bakers	. .	1	3	. .	4
Boiler-maker	. .	1	. .	. .	1
Blacksmith and wheelwright	. .	. .	1	. .	1
Chiropodists	. .	1	1	. .	2
China repairer	. .	. .	1	. .	1
Compounder of liquors	. .	1	. .	. .	1
Cooper	. .	1	. .	. .	1
Carpenter (ship)	. .	1	. .	. .	1
Carpenters	1	2	2	. .	5
Cashier	. .	1	. .	. .	1

OCCUPATIONS—Continued.

Occupations.	21–30 Years.	31–40 Years.	41 and over.	Unk. Age.	Total.
Cabinet-maker	1	..	..	..	1
Candy-makers	1	1	..	..	2
Caterers	11	18	36	..	65
Chemist	1	..	..	..	1
Cigar-makers	17	17	4	1	39
Clerks	7	4	7	..	18
Clerks (in public service)	3	1	4	..	8
Clerks (shipping)	1	2	..	..	3
Conductor (railroad)*	..	1	..	..	1
Dairymen	..	2	..	..	2
Dancing-masters	1	2	..	..	3
Drivers (for doctor)	10	1	1	..	12
Dyer	..	..	1	..	1
Errand boys	2	..	..	.	2
Engineers (stationary)	7	4	2	..	13
Elevator men	16	5	1	..	22
Editor	1	..	..	..	1
Florist	..	1	..	..	1
Frame-makers	2	..	1	..	3
Furniture polisher	1	..	.	..	1
Gold beater	..	..	1	..	1
Gamblers	4	3	1	8	16
Hucksters	12	15	10	..	37
Hostlers	21	12	11	..	44
Hod carriers	27	23	29	..	79
Inspector of furniture	..	1	..	..	1
Ice carvers	1	1	..	..	2
Janitors	29	20	45	..	94
Kalsominer	..	..	1	..	1
Lodging-house keepers	..	..	3	..	3
Landlord	..	.	1	..	1
Locksmith	..	1	..	..	1
Laborers (casual)	1	4	7	..	12
(soap factory)	2	..	..	..	2
(furnace-setters)	2	..	..	..	2
(on buildings)	3	4	..	..	7
(brickyard)	19	7	7	..	32
(on streets)	33	10	4	..	37
(general)	149	120	120	21	410
(farm)	2	1	..	..	3
(water works and gas, etc.)	9	9	28	1	47
Laundrymen	0	1	1	..	2
Managers and foremen	3	2	1	..	6
Messengers	9	10	12	2	33
Musicians	10	7	3	..	20
Manufacturers	..	..	1	..	1
Nurses	1	1	..	..	2
Oyster openers	2	2	..	..	4
Packers (china)	5	4	5	..	14
Painters	3	4	3	..	10
Paper-hanger	3	..	.	..	23
Porters	135	77	60	2	74

*Intermarried white man.

OCCUPATIONS—Continued.

Occupations.	21–30 Years.	31–40 Years.	41 and over.	Unk. Age.	Total.
Politicians	1	1	..	..	2
Photographers	1	1	..	..	2
Plasterers	..	3	..	..	3
Printers	6	1	2	..	9
Proprietors—Hotels and restaurants	6	6	10	..	22
Express business	3	4	7	..	14
Printing office	3	1	..	..	4
Cigar store	1	6	..	..	7
Milk-dealing	1	..	..	..	1
Store, notions and fuel,	3	9	10	..	22
Grocery	1	1	2	..	4
Employment agency	1	1	1	..	3
Barber shop	..	5	10	..	15
Newspaper	..	1	..	..	1
Pool-room	..	2	1	..	3
Professions—Teachers	1	3	3	..	7
Lawyers	2	2	1	..	5
Clergymen	4	8	10	..	22
Physicians	2	1	3	..	6
Dentists	..	1	2	..	3
Policemen	..	5	..	..	5
Pilot	..	..	1	..	1
Prize fighter	..	1	..	..	1
Rubber workers	2	..	1	..	3
Roofer	1	..	..	..	1
Rag pickers	2	..	4	..	6
Real estate agents	..	1	2	..	3
Root doctors	1	..	1	..	2
Service—Domestic	288	161	123	10	582
Hotel and restaurants, etc.	205	126	72	11	414
Public waiters (with caterers)	9	15	13	1	38
Stewards	8	14	9	..	31
Students	13	4	..	..	17
Sailors	14	3	3	1	21
Sextons	1	1	2	..	4
Shoemakers	4	1	13	..	18
Stevedores	64	60	40	..	164
Stone-cutters	1	1	1	..	3
Tinsmith	..	1	..	..	1
Trainer (horses)	..	1	..	..	1
Tailors	1	3	..	..	4
Teamsters	63	38	32	1	134
Upholsterers	2	1	4	..	7
Undertakers	4	1	1	..	6
Watchmen	1	4	9	..	14
Wicker-worker	..	1	..	..	1

Let us now glance at the occupations as a whole : of the 9675 Negroes in the Seventh Ward, 1212 are children nine years of age or less. Of the remaining 8463 there are :

At work 6,610
In school 609
Housewives 568
Known criminals 116
Unoccupied, at home, defective, unknown, etc. 550

                                                    ———
                                                    8,463

The 6610 at work are distributed as follows:

Professions 101
Working on own account 268
In trades 492
Clerks, semi-professional and responsible workers 216
Laborers (select) 778
Laborers (ordinary) 2,111
Servants 2,644

                                                    ———
                                                    6,610

We can grasp the true meaning of these figures only by comparing the distribution of occupations among the Negroes with that of the total population of the city; for this purpose we must redistribute the occupations according to the simpler, but in many respects unsatisfactory, divisions of the United States census. We then have:

	Whole Population of Philadelphia, 1890.		Negroes of Seventh Ward, 1896.	
	Number.	Per Cent.	Number.	Per Cent.
Total population over 10	847,283	. .	8,463	. .
Number in gainful occupations . . .	466,791	. .	6,611	. .
Per cent in gainful occupations . . .	55.1	. .	78	. .
Engaged in agriculture	6,497	1.5	11	.2
Engaged in professional service . . .	19,438	4.2	130*	2.0
Engaged in domestic and personal service	106,129	22.7	4,889	74.3
Engaged in trade and transportation	115,462	24.7	1,006	15.3
Engaged in manufacturing and mechanical industries	219,265	46.9	541	8.2

*Omitting 24 students 21 years of age and over.

Illustrated graphically, this is:

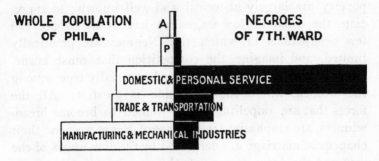

WHOLE POPULATION OF PHILA.

NEGROES OF 7TH. WARD

DOMESTIC & PERSONAL SERVICE

TRADE & TRANSPORTATION

MANUFACTURING & MECHANICAL INDUSTRIES

Comparing the whole population with the Negroes of the Seventh Ward by sex, we have:

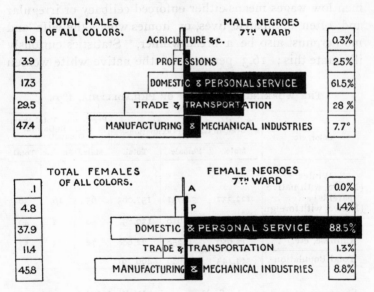

TOTAL MALES OF ALL COLORS.		MALE NEGROES 7TH WARD
1.9	AGRICULTURE &c.	0.3%
3.9	PROFESSIONS	2.5%
17.3	DOMESTIC & PERSONAL SERVICE	61.5%
29.5	TRADE & TRANSPORTATION	28 %
47.4	MANUFACTURING & MECHANICAL INDUSTRIES	7.7°

TOTAL FEMALES OF ALL COLORS.		FEMALE NEGROES 7TH WARD
.1		0.0%
4.8		1.4%
37.9	DOMESTIC & PERSONAL SERVICE	88.5%
11.4	TRADE & TRANSPORTATION	1.3%
45.8	MANUFACTURING & MECHANICAL INDUSTRIES	8.8%

In these statistics and tables we have first to notice the large proportion of these people who work for a living; taking the population ten years of age and over, and we have 78 per cent for the Negroes of the Seventh Ward, and 55.1 per cent for the whole city, white and colored. This is an indication of an absence of accumulated wealth, arising from poverty and low wages; the general causes of poverty are largely historical and well known; to appreciate the cause of low wages, we have only to see the few occupations to which the Negroes are practically limited, and imagine the competition that must ensue. This is true among the men, and especially true among the women, where the limitation is greatest. All the forces that are impelling white women to become bread-winners, are emphasized in the case of Negro women : their chances of marriage are decreased by the low wages of the men and the large excess of their own sex in the great cities; they must work, and if there are few chances open they must suffer from competition in wages. Among the men low wages means either enforced celibacy or irregular and often dissipated lives, or homes where the wife and mother must also be a bread-winner. Statistics curiously illustrate this; 16.3 per cent of the native white women

THE WORKING POPULATION OF PHILADELPHIA, 1890.

Color, etc.	Number, Ten Years of Age and over, in Gainful Occupations.			Per Cent of Total Population in Gainful Occupations.		
	Male.	Female.	Total.	Male.	Female	Total.
Whites. (Native, with native parents)	122,332	34,731	157,063	65	16	38
(Native, with foreign parents)	91,280	39,618	130,898	58	24	40
Colored (Negro and Chinese, etc.) . .	13,650	9,258	22,908	72	43	57
Total Population .	344,143	122,648	466,791	. .	. .	. .

of native parents and of all ages, in Philadelphia are bread-winners;[5] their occupations are restricted, and there is great competition; yet among Negro women, where the

---

[5] A better comparison here would be made by finding the percentages of the population above 10 years of age; statistics unfortunately are not available for this.

restriction in occupation reaches its greatest limit, nevertheless 43 per cent are bread-winners, and their wages are at the lowest point in all cases save in some lines of domestic service where custom holds them at certain figures; even here, however, the tendency is downward.

The causes of this peculiar restriction in employment of Negroes are twofold: first, the lack of training and experience among Negroes; second, the prejudice of the whites. The first is to be expected in some degree, although undoubtedly carelessness and culpable inefficiency have played their part. The second cause will be discussed at length, later. One point, however, needs mention: the peculiar distribution of employments among whites and Negroes makes the great middle class of white people seldom, if ever, brought into contact with Negroes—may not this be a cause as well as an effect of prejudice?

Another noticeable fact is the absence of child-labor; this is not voluntary on the part of the Negroes, but due to restricted opportunity; there is really very little that Negro children may do. Their chief employment, therefore, is found in helping about the house while the mother is at work. Thus those children scheduled as at home represent child-labor in many cases.

23. Occupations in the City.—Turning from the more detailed study of the Seventh Ward, let us glance in a general way over the occupations of Negroes in the city at large.

The Professions.—The learned professions are represented among Negroes by clergymen, teachers, physicians, lawyers and dentists, in the order named. Practically all Negroes go to their own churches, where they have, save in a very few cases, clergymen of their own race. There are not less than sixty Negro ministers in the city (possibly a hundred) mostly Methodists and Baptists, with three or four Presbyterians and two Episcopalians. The Presbyterian and Episcopalian clergymen are well trained and educated men

in nearly every case. The ministers of the African Methodists vary ; those in charge of the larger churches are all men
of striking personality, with genius for leadership and
organization in some lines, and in some cases, though not
in all, they are well-educated men. Practically none of
them are illiterate. The Baptist ministers are not on the
whole so well trained as the Methodists, although some
are well-educated.

Taken on the average the Negro ministers of the city are
good representatives of the masses of the Negroes. They
are largely chosen by the masses, must cater to their
tastes, and must in every way be men whom the rank and
file of the race like and understand. Sometimes a strong
personality, like the late Theodore Miller, will take a
church and lift it to a high level ; usually the minister
rather follows than leads, and indicates public opinion
among his people rather than forms it. The Baptist minister is the elected chairman of a pure democracy, who, if
he can command a large enough following, becomes a
virtual dictator ; he thus has the chance to be a wise leader
or a demagogue, or, as in many cases, a little of both. The
Methodist minister is the appointed steward of a large corporation, of which his particular church is a small part.
His success depends upon the way in which he conducts
this church : his financial success, his efforts to increase
church membership and his personal popularity. The
result is that the colored Methodist minister is generally a
wide-awake business man, with something of the politician
in his make-up, who is sometimes an inspiring and valuable
leader of men; in other cases he may develop into a loud
but wily talker, who induces the mass of Negroes to put
into fine church edifices money which ought to go to charity
or business enterprise.

Ministers receive from $250 a year, in small missions, to
$1500 in three or four of the largest churches. The aver-
age would be between $600 and $1000.

Next to the clergymen come the teachers, of whom there are about forty in the city :

School.	Princi-pals.	Assistant Teachers	Kinder-gartners.	Indus'l teachers.
Institute for Colored Youth	2	7	0	2
O. V. Catto	1	6	2	0
Vaux	1	3	0	0
J. E. Hill	1	3	1	0
Coulter street	1	1	0	0
Wilmot	1	1	0	0
House of Industry	0	4	0	0
James Forten	0	0	2	0
Berean Church	0	0	1	0
Total	7	25	6	2

These teachers are in nearly every case well equipped and have made good records. Save in the kindergartens, or in one or more temporary cases, they teach Negro children exclusively. The public school teachers receive the same pay as the white teachers.[6]

The Negro physician is to-day just beginning to reap the reward of a long series of attempts and failures. At first thought it would seem natural for Negroes to patronize Negro merchants, lawyers and physicians, from a sense of pride and as a protest against race feeling among whites. When, however, we come to think further, we can see many hindrances. If a child is sick, the father wants a good physician ; he knows plenty of good white physicians ; he knows nothing of the skill of the black doctor, for the black doctor has had no opportunity to exercise his skill. Consequently for many years the colored physician had to sit idly by and see the 40,000 Negroes healed principally by white practitioners. To-day this has largely changed, and principally through the efforts of the younger class of doctors, who have spared no pains to equip themselves at the best schools of the country. The result is that fully half the Negroes employ Negro physicians, and to a small extent these physicians practice among the whites. There

---

[6] This has been the case only in comparatively recent times.

are still many of the old class of root doctors and patent medicine quacks with a lucrative trade among Negroes.[7] Of reputable Negro physicians there are in the city about fifteen, graduated as follows :

University of Pennsylvania	5
Hahnemann (Homeopathic)	2
Women's Medical	2
Medico-Chirurgical	1
Harvard	1
University of Michigan	1
Howard	2
	14

Seven of these have good-sized practice, running from $1500 a year to $3000 or more. Five others have practically just commenced to get practice and are doing fairly well. The other two have outside work and have a limited practice. There are many medical students in the city, and this field is the most attractive open to the Negro among the learned professions.

In contrast to the fair success of the Negro in medicine is his partial failure in law. There are at present about ten practicing Negro lawyers in the city, graduated as follows :

Howard	3
University of Pennsylvania	4
Unknown	3

Two of these are fairly successful practitioners—well versed in law, with some experience, and a small but steady practice. Three others are with difficulty earning a living at criminal practice in police cases ; and the rest are having little or no practice. This failure of most Negro lawyers is not in all cases due to lack of ability and push on their part. Its principal cause is that the Negroes furnish little lucrative law business, and a Negro lawyer will seldom be employed by whites. Moreover, while the work of a physician is largely private, depending on individual skill,

---

[7] Negroes also buy immense quantities of patent medicines, etc.

a lawyer must have co-operation from fellow lawyers and respect and influence in court; thus prejudice or discrimination of any kind is especially felt in this profession. For these reasons Negro lawyers are for the most part confined to petty criminal practice and seldom get a chance to show their ability.

There are three Negro dentists, two being graduated from first-class institutions and enjoying good practice.

On the whole, the professional class of Negroes is creditable to the race. The teachers and physicians would bear comparison with any race ; the ranks of the clergy are overcrowded and they present all degrees, from excellent and well-trained spiritual guides to blatant demagogues ; the lawyers have little chance to show themselves.

The Entrepreneur—The number of individual undertakers of business enterprise among Negroes is small but growing. Let us first take the Seventh Ward alone and glance over the field. There are in this ward twenty-three establishments for meals and other entertainment, varying from a small one-room restaurant to a twenty-room hotel ; some of these on Lombard and South streets have capacious dining-rooms with twenty or more tables ; some are little dark places with two or three dubious looking stands. In length of establishment they vary : eight had in 1896 been running a year or less ; four, two years ; two, three years ; four, from four to eight years. They represent investments varying from $40 to $1500, and employ beside the proprietors between fifty and one hundred persons according to the season.

There are in the Seventh Ward twenty-three barber-shops varying from two months to forty years in length of establishment ; eight are from three to five years old, five over ten years old. They employ beside the proprietors from twenty to forty journeymen more or less regularly. A shop represents an investment varying from $50 to $250 or more. The Negro as a barber is rapidly losing ground

in the city. It is difficult to say why this has occurred, but
there are several contributory reasons : first the calling was
for so long an almost exclusively Negro calling that it
came in for a degree of the contempt and ridicule poured
on Negroes in general ; it therefore grew very unpopular
among Negroes, and apprentices became very scarce. To-
day one would have to look a long time among young and
aspiring Negroes to find one who would willingly become
a barber—it smacks perhaps a little too much of domestic
service, and is a thing to fall back upon but not to aspire
to. In the second place the business became unpopular
with Negroes because it compels them to draw a color line.
No first-class Negro barber would dare shave his own
brother in his shop in Philadelphia on account of the color
prejudice. This is peculiarly galling and has led to much
criticism and unpopularity for certain leading barbers
among their own people. These two reasons led to a lack
of interest and enterprise in the business for a long time
and it needed but one movement to hasten the collapse,
that is, competition. The competition of German and
Italian barbers furnished the last and most potent reason
for the withdrawal of the Negro ; they were skilled workmen, while skilled Negro barbers were becoming scarce ;
they cut down the customary prices and some of them
found business co-operation and encouragement which
Negroes could not hope for. For these reasons the business
is slipping from the Negro. This is undoubtedly a calamity
and unless the Negro in spite of sentiment awakens in
time he will find a lucrative employment gone and nothing
in its place. Already a white labor union movement is
beginning to crowd the Negro, to ask for legislation which
will strike him most forcibly and in other ways to bring
organized endeavor to bear upon disorganized apathy.

The Seventh Ward has thirteen small Negro grocery
stores. They are mostly new ventures, eight being less
than a year old ; four, one to five years old, and one fifteen

years old. Two are co-operative enterprises but have had
no great success. All of these stores with two or three
exceptions are really experiments and most of them will
soon go to the wall and their places be taken by others.
The six smaller shops represent investments of $25 to
$50; two have $50 and $100 invested; three between $100
and $200, and one from $500 to $1000. The ambition of
the middle class of Negroes lies in this direction and their
endeavors are laudable. In another age of industrial
development they would have already constituted themselves a growing class of small tradesmen; but to-day the
department store and stock-company make the competition
too great for people with so little commercial training and
instinct. Nevertheless the number of Negro groceries will
undoubtedly grow considerably in the next decade.

Next come fourteen cigar stores representing a total
investment of $1000 to $1500 mostly in sums of $25, $50
and $100. These stores have been established as follows:
one year or less, six; two years, four; three to sixteen years,
four. They sell cigars and tobacco, and daily papers; some
also rent bicycles, or have a boot-blacking stand or pool
room attached. One of the proprietors conducts, beside his
cigar store, three barber shops and a restaurant, and
employs twenty people. Some of these stores are finely
equipped. This business is new for Negroes and growing;
a few women have ventured into it, and thus in some cases
it furnishes a side occupation for wives.

There are four candy and notion shops established
respectively five months, six months, one year and three
years, and each representing an investment of $10 to $100.
They are in most cases in the hands of women and do a
small business. There are also numberless places for selling
fuel of all kinds, of which about thirteen rise to the dignity
of shops. They represent small investments.

Three retail liquor shops and one bottling establishment
are conducted by colored people, representing considerable

investments. Two of the saloons are old and well conducted, and financially successful. The other saloon and
the bottling establishment are not very successful.

Four large employment agencies and some smaller ones
are situated in the ward. They conduct lodging houses
and in some cases boarding houses in connection. One
is sixteen years old; all hire clerks. Their business
is to act as agents for persons desiring servants, and
to guide unemployed persons to situations; for this
they charge a percentage or fixed sum out of the wages.
They also often serve as homes for unemployed servants,
giving them board and lodging, sometimes on credit.
Their work is thus useful and lucrative when properly
conducted as in two or three establishments. In one
or two others, however, there is some suspicion of unfair
dealing; servants are attracted from the South by catchy
advertisements and personal letters, only to find themselves
eventually penniless and out of work in a large city.[8]
Questionable acquaintanceships are also made at the
agencies at times, which lead to ruin. These agencies
need strict regulation.

There are four undertaking establishments, two of which
are conducted by women. They represent investments of
$1000–$10,000 and two of them do a business which probably aggregates $8000 or more annually in each case. They
are all old establishments—six to thirty-three years—and in
no branch of business, save one, has the Negro evinced so
much push, taste and enterprise. Two of the establishments will, in equipment, compare favorably with the
white businesses in the city; indeed, in fair competition
they have gained the great bulk of Negro and some white
patronage from white competitors.

Three bakeries, established two and three years respect-

---

[8] In Norfolk, Va., I once saw the advertisement on a street sign calling
for colored "clerks, saleswomen, stenographers," etc., for Northern
cities!

ively are having moderate success. Six printing offices established, one, six months, the others four to seven years, do job work on small presses; two publish weekly papers. These shops are fairly successful and get considerable work from the colored people. One dressmaker has a shop with $150 invested; another runs a dressmaking school.

Four upholsterers have shops, old and well established, and all do a good business ; in two cases the business amounts to two to five thousand a year. One sells antique furniture also.

There are a large number of caterers in the ward—eighty-three[9] in all. Most of these, however, do a small business, and in some cases have other work also for at least a part of the year. Of the principal caterers there are about ten, of whom the *doyen* was the late Andrew F. Stevens. [10] These ten caterers do a large business, amounting in some cases probably to $3000 to $5000 a year. They have a small co-operative store on Thirteenth street, with a considerable stock of dishes, and such things as olives, pickles, etc. This is conducted by a manager and has one hundred or more members. There is also a caterers' association, which is really a trades union. Its club room serves as a clearing house for business and the employment of waiters. This has been running ten years. The catering business presents many interesting phases to the economist and sociologist. Undoubtedly the pre-eminence of Negroes in this business has declined since the Augustins, Jones and Dorsey passed. Negro caterers are still prominent, but they do not by any means dominate the field, as then. The chief reason for this is the change that has come over American

---

[9] This total includes a large number of men and women who do some private catering, but for the most part work under other caterers; strictly a large part of them are waiters rather than caterers.

[10] Mr. Stevens died in 1898—he was an honest, reliable, business man—of pleasant address, and universally respected. He was easily the successor of Dorsey, Jones and Minton in the catering business.

fashionable society in the last twenty-five years, and the application of large capital to the catering business. Philadelphia society is no longer a local affair, but receives its cue as to propriety and fashion from New York, London and Paris; consequently the local caterers can no longer dictate fashion for any single American city; more than this, demands have so risen with increasing wealth that catering establishments like Delmonico's, which would keep in the front rank, represent a large investment of capital—investments far beyond the power of the local Negro caterers of Philadelphia. Thus we find a large business built up by talent and tact, meeting with changed social conditions; the business must therefore change too. It is the old development from the small to the large industry, from the house-industry to the concentrated industry, from the private dining room to the palatial hotel. If the Negro caterers of Philadelphia had been white, some of them would have been put in charge of a large hotel, or would have become co-partners in some large restaurant business, for which capitalists furnished funds. For such business co-operation, however, the time was not ripe, and perhaps only a few of the best Negro caterers would have been capable of entering into it with success. As it was, the change in fashion and mode of business changed the methods of the Negro caterers and their clientele. They began to serve the middle class instead of the rich and exclusive, their prices had to become more reasonable, and their efforts to excel had consequently fewer incentives. Moreover, they now came into sharp competition with a class of small white caterers, who, if they were worse cooks, were better trained in the tricks of the trade. Then, too, with this new and large clientele that personal relationship between the caterer and those served was broken up, and a larger place for color prejudice was made.

It is thus plain that a curious economic revolution in one industry has gone on during twenty-nine years, not

unaccompanied by grave social problems. In this case the
Negro has emerged in better condition and has shown more
capacity for hand-to-hand economic encounter than, for
instance, in the barbering business. Yet he has not emerged
unscathed; in every such battle, when a Negro is fighting
for an economic advantage, there is ever a widespread
feeling among all his neighbors that it is inexpedient to
allow this class to became wealthy or even well-to-do.
Consequently the battle always becomes an *Athanasius
contra mundum*, where almost unconsciously the whole
countenance and aid of the community is thrown against
the Negro.

The three Negro cemetery companies of the city have
their headquarters in the Seventh Ward. They arose from
the curious prejudice of the whites against allowing
Negroes to be buried near their dead. The companies
hold valuable property and are fairly well conducted. [11]
There are several expressmen in the ward owning their
own outfits; one has been established twenty-five years;
he has three or four wagons and hires four or five men
regularly. There was in 1896 a hardware and furniture
business forty-seven years old, on South street, but the
proprietor, Robert Adger, has since died. [12]   There are

---

[11] When the caterer Henry Jones died his funeral procession was
actually turned back from the cemetery by the refusal of the authorities
of Mt. Moriah Cemetery to allow him interment there; he had before his
death bought and paid for a lot in the cemetery and the Supreme Court
eventually confirmed his title. To-day this absurd prejudice is not so
strong and Negroes own lots in the Episcopal Cemetery of St. James the
Less and in perhaps one other.

[12] The following clipping from the Philadelphia *Ledger*, November 2,
1896, illustrates a typical life:

"Robert Adger, a colored Abolitionist, died on Saturday, at his home,
835 South street. He was born a slave, in Charleston, S. C., in 1813.
His mother, who was born in New York, went to South Carolina about
1810, with some of her relatives, and while there was detained as a slave.

"When his master died, Mr. Adger, together with his mother and other
members of the family, were sold at auction, but, through the assistance

several bicycle shops, a flourishing milk, butter and egg store, a china repairing shop, of long standing; a hair goods store, a rubber goods repairing shop, seventeen years old; a second-hand stove store and two patent medicine shops.

To test the accuracy of these statistics and to note changes, a second visit was made in this ward in 1897, with this result :

NEGRO BUSINESS ESTABLISHMENTS, SEVENTH WARD, 1896–97.

Business.	1896 (Dec.)	1897 (Oct.)
Restaurants	23	39
Barber shops	23	24
Grocery stores.	13	11
Cigar stores	14	11
Candy and notions.	4	2
Shoemaker shops	8	13
Upholsterers	4	4
Liquor saloons	3	2
Undertakers	4	4
Newspapers	2	1
Drug store	0	1
Patent medicine stores	2	2
Printing offices	4	4

Such small businesses represent the efforts of a class of poor people to save capital.[13] They are all alike hindered by three great drawbacks : First, the Negro never was trained for business and can get no training now ; it is very seldom that a Negro boy or girl can on any terms get a

---

of friends, legal proceedings were instituted, and their release finally secured. Mr. Adger then came to this city about 1845, and secured a position as a waiter in the old Merchants' Hotel. Later he was employed as a nurse, and while working in that capacity, saved enough money to start in the furniture business on South street, above Eighth, which he continued to conduct with success until his death. Mr. Adger always took an active interest in the welfare of the people of his race.''

[13] One enterprising capitalist hires and sub-rents eight different houses with furnished apartments, paying $1944 annually in rent; he has a bicycle shop which brings in $1000 a year for an expense of about $330. He also owns a barber shop which brings in about $1000 a year; one-half the gross receipts of this he pays to a foreman, who pays his journeymen barbers; the owner pays for rent and material. " If I had an education,'' he said, " I could get on better."

position in a store or other business establishment where he can learn the technique of the work or general business methods. Second, Negro merchants are so rare that it is natural for customers, both white and colored, to take it for granted that their business is poorly conducted without giving it a trial.[14] Third, the Negroes are unused to co-operation with their own people and the process of learning it is long and tedious. Hitherto, their economic activities have been directed almost entirely to the satisfaction of wants of the upper classes of white people, and, too, of personal and household wants ; they are just beginning to realize that within their own group there is a vast field for development in economic activity. The 40,000 Negroes of Philadelphia need food, clothes, shoes, hats and furniture; these by proper thrift they see ought to be in part supplied by themselves, and the little business ventures we have noticed are attempts in this direction. These attempts would, however, be vastly more successful in another economic age. To-day, as before noted, the application of large capital to the retail business, the gathering of workmen into factories, the wonderful success of trained talent in catering to the whims and taste of customers almost precludes the effective competition of the small store. Thus the economic condition of the day militates largely against the Negro ; it requires more skill and experience to run a small store than formerly and the large store and factory are virtually closed to him on any terms.

Turning now to the other wards of the city let us notice some of the chief business ventures of the Negroes. This list is by no means exhaustive, but it is representative :

---

[14] Several storekeepers have had white persons enter the store, look at the proprietors and say " Oh! I—er—made a mistake," and go out.

Ward.	Character of Business.	No. Establishments.
Second.	Harness shop	1
Third.	Grocery stores	3
	Barber shop	1
Fourth.	Barber shops	5
	Second-hand clothing	1
	Second-hand furniture	1
	Coal and wood shops	4
	Newspaper	1
	Restaurants	10
	Hair goods and dressmaking	1
	Expressmen	5
	Decorating and paper-hanging	1
	Job printer	1
	Shoe repair shops	3
	Candy store (manufacture)	1
	Cigar stores	2
	Crockery store	1
	Second-hand stoves	1
Fifth.	Barber shops	7
	Pool-room	1
	Shoeblacking shop	1
	Restaurants	8
	Undertaker	1
	Fuel and notions	2
	Cigar store	1
	Publishing house (books and papers) . . .	1
	Blacksmith and wheelwright	1
Eighth.	Florist	1
	Watch repairer	1
	Newspaper and job printing	1
	Undertaker	1
	Hotel and liquor saloon	1
	Barber shops	9
	Upholsterers	2
	Rag warehouse	1
	Restaurants	5
	Fuel and newspaper shop	1
	Grocery store	1
	Cigar stores	2
	Employment bureau	1
	Hair dresser for ladies	1
Fourteenth.	Barber	1
	Grocery store	1
	Upholsterer	1
	Dealer in mineral water	1
	Second-hand furniture store	1
	Fuel and candy store	1
	Restaurants	2
Twentieth.	Tailor shop	1
	Shoe-repairing shop	1
	Barber shops	2

Ward.	Character of Business.	No. Establishments.
Twenty-seventh.	Real estate agent	I
	Meat dealer (wholesale)	I
Fifteenth and Twenty-ninth.	Carpet cleaning works	I
	Meat and provisions	I
	Barber shops and various small establishments	20
Twenty-sixth and Thirtieth.	Second-hand stoves	I
	Cigar store	I
	Barber shops	2
	Expressman	I
	Second-hand furniture	I
	Upholsterer	I
	Grocery store	I
	Milk and ice shop	I
	Job printing	I
	Restaurant	I
Twenty-second.	Restaurant and lodging house	I
	Grocery stores	2
	Barbers	2
	Upholsterer	I
	Expressman	I
	Steam laundry	I

The most important omissions here are barber shops, on account of the large number, caterers, because their headquarters are mainly in private houses, and many small stores which are easily overlooked and which quickly come and disappear. Some of the businesses are large and important : Three or four caterers do a business of several thousand dollars per year; the well-known Chestnut street florist does a flourishing and well conducted business ;[15] the undertaker in the Eighth Ward and the real estate dealer in the Twenty-seventh are unusually successful in their lines. The crockery store in the Fourth Ward is neat and tasty. The three largest enterprises are the provision and wholesale meat businesses in the Fifteenth Ward, and the carpet cleaning works. It is reported that the business of each of these approaches $10,000 a year.

---

[15] Here was a case where some persons sought to drive an enterprising and talented Negro out of business simply because he was colored. A Chestnut street property owner made a special effort to give him a start and now he conducts a business of which no merchant need be ashamed.

There are five weekly newspapers and a quarterly magazine published in the city by Negroes. Two of the papers are denominational organs for churches; another paper is the official organ of the Odd Fellows; the fourth and fifth are local news sheets. The quarterly is published by the A. M. E. Church. These papers are fairly successful, and are considerably read and reflect the general public opinion pretty well. Most of them have been very weak editorially, though there are some signs of improvement, especially in the case of the quarterly. The publishing house does a business of $15,000 a year.

The Trades.—The practical exclusion of the Negro from the trades and industries of a great city like Philadelphia is a situation by no means easy to explain. It is often said simply: the foreigners and trades unions have crowded Negroes out on account of race prejudice and left employers and philanthropists helpless in the matter. This is not strictly true. What the trades unions and white workmen have done is to seize an economic advantage plainly offered them. This opportunity arose from three causes: Here was a mass of black workmen of whom very few were by previous training fitted to become the mechanics and artisans of a new industrial development; here, too, were an increasing mass of foreigners and native Americans who were unusually well fitted to take part in the new industries; finally, most people were willing and many eager that Negroes should be kept as menial servants rather than develop into industrial factors. This was the situation, and here was the opportunity for the white workmen; they were by previous training better workmen on the average than Negroes; they were stronger numerically and the result was that every new industrial enterprise started in the city took white workmen. Soon the white workmen were strong enough to go a step further than this and practically prohibit Negroes from entering trades under any circumstances; this affected not only new

enterprises, but also old trades like carpentering, masonry,
plastering and the like. The supply of Negroes for such
trades could not keep pace with the extraordinary growth
of the city and a large number of white workmen entered
the field. They immediately combined against Negroes
primarily to raise wages; the standard of living of the
Negroes lets them accept low wages, and, conversely, long
necessity of accepting the meagre wages offered have made
a low standard of living. Thus partially by taking
advantage of race prejudice, partially by greater economic
efficiency and partially by the endeavor to maintain and
raise wages, white workmen have not only monopolized
the new industrial opportunities of an age which has
transformed Philadelphia from a colonial town to a world-
city, but have also been enabled to take from the Negro
workman the opportunities he already enjoyed in certain
lines of work.

If now a benevolent despot had seen the development,
he would immediately have sought to remedy the real
weakness of the Negro's position, *i. e.*, his lack of training; and he would have swept away any discrimination
that compelled men to support as criminals those who
might support themselves as workmen.

He would have made special effort to train Negro boys
for industrial life and given them a chance to compete on
equal terms with the best white workmen; arguing that
in the long run this would be best for all concerned, since
by raising the skill and standard of living of the Negroes
he would make them effective workmen and competitors who
would maintain a decent level of wages. He would have
sternly suppressed organized or covert opposition to Negro
workmen.

There was, however, no benevolent despot, no philanthropist, no far-seeing captain of industry to prevent the
Negro from losing even the skill he had learned or to inspire
him by opportunities to learn more. As the older Negroes

with trades dropped off, there was little to induce younger men to succeed them. On the contrary special effort was made not to train Negroes for industry or to allow them to enter on such a career. Consequently they gradually slipped out of industrial life until in 1890 when the Negroes formed 4 per cent of the population, only 1.1 per cent of 134,709 men in the principal trades of the city were Negroes; of 46,200 women in these trades 1.3 per cent were Negroes; or taking men and women together, 2160 or 1.19 per cent of all were Negroes. This does not, however, tell the whole story, for of this 2160, the barbers, brickmakers, and dressmakers formed 1434. In the Seventh Ward the number in the trades is much larger than the proportion in the city, but here again they are confined to a few trades—barbers, dressmakers, cigarmakers and shoemakers.

How now has this exclusion been maintained? In some cases by the actual inclusion of the word "white" among qualifications for entrance into certain trade unions. More often, however, by leaving the matter of color entirely to local bodies, who make no general rule, but invariably fail to admit a colored applicant except under pressing circumstances. This is the most workable system and is adopted by nearly all trade unions. In sections where Negro labor in certain trades is competent and considerable, the trades union welcomes them, as in Western Pennsylvania among miners and iron-workers, and in Philadelphia among cigarmakers; but whenever there is a trade where good Negro workmen are comparatively scarce each union steadfastly refuses to admit Negroes, and relies on color prejudice to keep up the barrier. Thus the carpenters, masons, painters, iron-workers, etc., have succeeded in keeping out nearly all Negro workmen by simply declining to work with non-union men and refusing to let colored men join the union. Sometimes, in time of strikes, the unions are compelled in self-defence not only to allow Negroes to join but to solicit them; this happened, for instance, in the stone-cutters' strike some years ago.

To repeat, then, the real motives back of this exclusion are plain : a large part is simple race prejudice, always strong in working classes and intensified by the peculiar history of the Negro in this country. Another part, however, and possibly a more potent part, is the natural spirit of monopoly and the desire to keep up wages. So long as a cry against " Irish " or " foreigners " was able to marshal race prejudice in the service of those who desired to keep those people out of some employments, that cry was sedulously used. So to-day the workmen plainly see that a large amount of competition can be shut off by taking advantage of public opinion and drawing the color line. Moreover, in this there is one thoroughly justifiable consideration that plays a great part : namely, the Negroes are used to low wages—can live on them, and consequently would fight less fiercely than most whites against reduction.

The employers in this matter are not altogether blameless. Their objects in conducting business are not, of course, wholly philanthropic, and yet, as a class, they represent the best average intelligence and morality of the community. A firm stand by some of them for common human right might save the city something in taxes for the suppression of crime and vice. There came some time since to the Midvale Steel Works a manager whom many dubbed a "crank ;" he had a theory that Negroes and whites could work together as mechanics without friction or trouble.[16] In spite of some protest he put his theory into practice, and to-day any one can see Negro mechanics working in the same gangs with white mechanics without disturbance. A few other cases on a smaller scale

---

[16] The large steel manufactory known as the "Midvale Steel Works " is located at Nicetown, near Germantown, in Philadelphia County. This

have occurred throughout the city. In general, however, the black mechanic who seeks work from a mill owner, or a contractor, or a capitalist is told : "I have no feeling in the matter, but my men will not work with you." Without doubt, in many cases, the employer is really powerless; in many other cases he is not powerless, but is willing to appear so.

The Negroes of the city who have trades either give them up and hire out as waiters or laborers, or they become job workmen and floating hands, catching a bit of carpentering here or a little brick-work or plastering there at reduced wages. Undoubtedly much blame can rightly be laid at the door of Negroes for submitting rather tamely to this organized opposition. If they would meet organization with organization and excellence of work by excellence,

---

establishment was visited by the writer, and the manager of the establishment interviewed as to the success of the experiment made by him in employing Negroes as workmen along with whites.

About 1200 men are employed altogether, and fully 200 of these are Negroes. About 40 per cent of the whole number of employes are American-born, but generally of Irish, English or German parentage. The remaining 43 per cent are foreign-born, chiefly English, Irish and German, with a few Swedes.

"Our object in putting Negroes on the force," said the manager, " was twofold. First, we believed them to be good workmen ; secondly, we thought they could be used to get over one difficulty we had experienced at Midvale, namely, the clannish spirit of the workmen and a tendency to form cliques. In steel manufacture much of the work is done with large tools run by gangs of men; the work was crippled by the different foremen trying always to have the men in their gang all of their own nationality. The English foreman of a hammer gang, for instance, would want only Englishmen, and the Irish Catholics only Irishmen. This was not good for the works, nor did it promote friendliness among the workmen. So we began bringing in Negroes and placing them on different gangs, and at the same time we distributed the other nationalities. Now our gangs have, say, one Negro, one or two Americans, an Englishman, etc. The result has been favorable both for the men and for the works. Things run smoothly, and the output is noticeably greater."

The manager was especially questioned about the grade of work done by Negroes and their efficiency as skilled workmen. He said:

they could do much to win standing in the industries of the cities. This is to-day hard to begin, but it is worth the trying, and the Industrial Department of the Institute for Colored Youth, which the Negroes themselves helped equip, is a step in this direction.

Clerks, Semi-professional and Responsible Workers.— Under this head has been grouped a miscellaneous mass of occupations : clerks in public and private service, stewards, messengers, musicians, agents, managers and foremen, actors, policemen, etc., *i. e.*, that class of persons whose position demands a degree of attainment in education, reliability, talent or skill. Here the number of Negroes is small, but they are nearly as well represented as in trades—an indication of a rather abnormal development. Of 46,393 men in this class of occupations in the city (*i. e.*, policemen, watchmen, agents, commercial travelers, bankers

---

"They do all the grades of work done by the white workmen. Some of this work is of such a nature that it had been supposed that only very intelligent English and American workmen could be trusted with it. We have 100 colored men doing that skilled work now, and they do it as well as any of the others."

As to wages, the manager said no discrimination was made between Negroes and whites. They start as laborers at $1.20 a day and " we try to treat them as individuals, not as a herd; they know that good work gives them a chance for better work and better pay. Thus their ambition is aroused; yesterday, for instance, four Negroes saved a furnace worth $30,000. The furnace was full of molten steel, which had become clogged, so that it could not be gotten out in the usual way. A number of powerful men were required to open the side of the furnace. Four colored men volunteered and saved the steel."

With regard to the relations between white and black workmen the manager said: " We have had no trouble at all. The unions generally hold potential strikes over their employers' heads to keep the Negro out of employment. There has, however, been no strike in this establishment for seventeen years, and Negroes have been employed for the last seven years."

Finally the manager declared that according to his belief the Negro workman does not have half a. chance to show his ability. " He does good work and betters his condition when he has any inducement to do so."   ISABEL EATON.

and brokers, bookkeepers, clerks and salesmen, and bar-
keepers) 327, or seven-tenths of 1 per cent were Negroes ;
if we add to this stewards, messengers, musicians, and
clerks in government service, they form about 1 per cent of
those in the city. Nearly all the clerks and salesmen are to
be found in Negro stores, although there are a few exceptions.

CLERKS, SEMI-PROFESSIONAL AND RESPONSIBLE WORKERS IN
PHILADELPHIA, 1890.

Occupation.	Total.	Negroes.
Watchmen, policemen and detectives	4,113	62
Bartenders	1,683	32
Agents and collectors	5,049	38
Bankers, brokers, etc.	2,072	6
Bookkeepers, clerks, etc.	23,057	130
Salesmen	10,419	38
Total	46,393	326

There are about sixty colored policemen on the force at
present, and the general impression seems to be that they
make good average officers. They were first appointed to
the police force by Mayor King in 1884. At first there
was violent opposition, which would have been listened to
had it not been for political complications. The Negro
policemen are put on duty mostly in or near the chief
Negro settlements and no one of them has yet been promoted from the ranks. The number of Negroes in
government service is as follows :

Municipal departments 11
Custom House 1
Post-office 17
Navy yard 1

Beside these there are a number of messengers and
ordinary laborers. In many cases these clerks have made
very excellent records, as in the case of the discount clerk
in the tax office, who has held his position for many years,
and is perhaps the most efficient clerk in the office ; or

again the Negro postmaster and employes in the post-
office at Wanamaker's store who have been unusually
successful in administrating the second largest sub-station
in the city.   In a few cases certain Negroes have received
office through political influence and have been plainly
unfitted for their work.

There are a few clerks in responsible positions—one
employed by the Pennsylvania railway company, another
in a bank.   Such cases, however, are rare.

Laborers.—The great mass of the men and a large percentage of the women are manual laborers—*i. e.*, teamsters,
janitors, stevedores, hod-carriers, hostlers, elevator-men,
sailors, china-packers and night-watchmen.   Their wages
are usually:

Teamsters . . . . . $1 to $1.50 a day.
Janitors , ... $30 to $60 a month.
Stevedores . . . . . 20c. to 30c. an hour (irregular employment).
Hod-carriers . . . . $1.50 to $2.50 a day (employed according to season).
Hostlers . . . . . . $16 to $30 a month.
Elevator-men . . . $16 to $25 a month.

Besides these there are the ordinary porters, errand
boys, newsboys and day-laborers, whose earnings vary
considerably, but usually are too small to support a family
without much help from wife and children.   Stevedores,
hod-carriers and day-laborers are especially liable to
irregular employment, which makes life hard for them
sometimes.   The mass of the men are, save in the lower
grades, given average wages and meet their greatest difficulty in securing work.   The competition in ordinary
laboring work is severe in so crowded a city.   The women
day-laborers are, on the whole, poorly paid, and meet fierce
competition in laundry work and cleaning.

The most noticeable thing about the Negro laborers as
a whole is their uneven quality.   There are some first-
class, capable and willing workers, who have held their
positions for years and give perfect satisfaction.   On the

other hand, there are numbers of inefficient and unintelligent laborers on whom employers cannot rely and who are below average American labor in ability. This unevenness arises from two causes: the different training of the various groups of Negroes composing the city population; some are the descendants of generations of free Negroes; some of trained house-servants, long in close contact with their masters' families; others are the sons of field-hands, untouched and untrained by contact with civilized institutions: all this vast difference in preparation shows vast differences in results. The second reason lies in the increased competition within the group, and the growing lack of incentive to good work, owing to the difficulty of escaping from manual toil into higher and better paid callings; the higher classes of white labor are continually being incorporated into the skilled trades, or clerical workers, or other higher grades of labor. Sometimes this happens with Negroes but not often. The first-class ditcher can seldom become foreman of a gang; the hod-carrier can seldom become a mason; the porter cannot have much hope of being a clerk, or the elevator-boy of becoming a salesman. Consequently we find the ranks of the laborers among Negroes filled to an unusual extent with disappointed men, with men who have lost the incentive to excel, and have become chronic grumblers and complainers, spreading this spirit further than it would naturally go. At the same time this shutting of the natural outlet for ability means an increase of competition for ordinary work.

Without doubt there is not in Philadelphia enough work of the kind that the mass of Negroes can and may do, to employ at fair wages the laborers who at present desire work. The result of this must, of course, be disastrous, and give rise to many loafers, criminals, and casual laborers. The situation is further complicated by the fact that in seasons when work is more plentiful, temporary immigrations from the South swell the number of laborers abnormally; every spring the tide of immigration sets in, consisting of brickmakers, teamsters, asphalt-workers, common laborers, etc., who work during the summer in the city and return to the cheaper living of Virginia and Maryland for the winter. This makes the competition in summer close for Philadelphians, and often brings actual distress in winter. A pressing duty is to see that the opportunities for work in the city are not misrepresented, and to relieve congestion in some avenues by opening others to Negro labor. Nor would this be a boon simply for Negroes: the excessive competition of Negroes in certain lines of work makes more suffering for their white competitors than if that competition were less intense in places and spread over a larger area. White hod-carriers and porters suffer greatly from competition, while other branches of labor are artificially protected—an economic injustice which might be remedied.

Another custom that works much harm to all classes and colors of laborers is the custom of working exclusively white or exclusively colored gangs of workmen. It is unjust to the Negro because it virtually closes the greater part of the field of labor against him, since his numbers are small compared with the population of the city, and it is harder for him to gather gangs than for the whites. It is, however, a fruitful cause of injustice to white laborers; for the contractor who gets a gang of Negroes to work, has a temptation to force down wages which he seldom resists or cares to resist. He knows that the standard of living of the Negroes is low, and their chances for employment limited. He therefore takes on a gang of Negroes, lowers wages, and then if whites wish to regain their places, they must accept the lower wages. The white laborers then blame the Negroes for bringing down wages—a charge with just enough truth in it to intensify existing prejudices. If laborers on ordinary jobs were hired regardless

of color and according to efficiency, no doubt both white
and black labor would gain, and the employer would not
in the long run lose much.

Servants.—Probably over one-fourth of the domestic
servants of Philadelphia are Negroes, and conversely
nearly one-third of the Negroes in the city are servants.
This makes the Negro a central problem in any careful
study of domestic service, and domestic service a large
part of the Negro problems. The matter thus is so
important that it has been made the subject of a special
study appended to this work. A few general considerations only will be advanced here.

So long as entrance into domestic service involves a loss
of all social standing and consideration, so long will domestic service be a social problem. The problem may vary in
character with different countries and times, but there will
always be some maladjustment in social relations when any
considerable part of a population is required to get its support in a manner which the other part despises, or affects
to despise. In the United States the problem is complicated by the fact that for years domestic service was performed by slaves, and afterward, up till to-day, largely by
black freedmen—thus adding a despised race to a despised
calling. Even when white servants increased in number
they were composed of white foreigners, with but a small
proportion of native Americans. Thus by long experience
the United States has come to associate domestic service
with some inferiority in race or training.

The effect of this attitude on the character of the service
rendered, and the relation of mistress and maid, has been
only too evident, and has in late years engaged the attention of some students and many reformers. These have
pointed out how necessary and worthy a work the domestic
performs, or could perform, if properly trained; that the
health, happiness and efficiency of thousands of homes,
which are training the future leaders of the republic, depend

largely on their domestic service. This is true, and yet the remedy for present ills is not clear until we recognize how far removed the present commercial method of hiring a servant in market is from that which obtained at the time when the daughters of the family, or of the neighbor's family, helped in the housework. In other words, the industrial revolution of the century has affected domestic service along with other sorts of labor, by separating employer and employed into distinct classes. With the Negro the effect of this was not apparent so long as slavery lasted ; the house servant remained an integral part of the master's family, with rights and duties. When emancipation broke this relation there went forth to hire a number of trained black servants, who were welcomed South and North; they liked their work, they knew no other kind, they understood it, and they made ideal servants. In Philadelphia twenty or thirty years ago there were plenty of this class of Negro servants and a few are still left.

A generation has, however, greatly altered the face of affairs. There were in the city, in 1890, 42,795 servants, and of these 10,235 were Negroes. Who are these Negroes ? No longer members of Virginia households trained for domestic work, but principally young people who were using domestic service as a stepping-stone to something else ; who worked as servants simply because they could get nothing else to do ; who had received no training in service because they never expected to make it their life-calling. They, in common with their white fellow citizens, despised domestic service as a relic of slavery, and they longed to get other work as their fathers had longed to be free. In getting other work, however, they were not successful, partly on account of lack of ability, partly on account of the strong race prejudice against them. Consequently to-day the ranks of Negro servants, and that means largely the ranks of domestic service in general in Philadelphia, have received all those whom the harsh competition of a great city has pushed down, all whom a relentless color proscription has turned back from other chosen vocations ; half-trained teachers and poorly equipped students who have not succeeded; carpenters and masons who may not work at their trades ; girls with common school training, eager for the hard work but respectable standing of shop girls and factory hands, and proscribed by their color—in fact, all those young people who, by natural evolution in the case of the whites, would have stepped a grade higher than their fathers and mothers in the social scale, have in the case of the post-bellum generation of Negroes been largely forced back into the great mass of the listless and incompetent to earn bread and butter by menial service.

And they resent it ; they are often discontented and bitter, easily offended and without interest in their work. Their attitude and complaint increases the discontent of their fellows who have little ability, and probably could not rise in the world if they might. And, above all, both the disappointed and the incompetents are alike ignorant of domestic service in nearly all its branches, and in this respect are a great contrast to the older set of Negro servants.

Under such circumstances the first far-sighted movement would have been to open such avenues of work and employment to young Negroes that only those best fitted for domestic work would enter service. Of course this is difficult to do even for the whites, and yet it is still the boast of America that, within certain limits, talent can choose the best calling for its exercise. Not so with Negro youth. On the contrary, the field for exercising their talent and ambition is, broadly speaking, confined to the dining room, kitchen and street. If now competition had drained off the talented and aspiring into other avenues, and eased the competition in this one vocation, then there would have been room for a second movement, namely, for training schools, which would fit the mass of Negro and white domestic servants for their complicated and important duties. Such a twin movement—the diversification of Negro industry and the serious training of domestic servants—would do two things: it would take the ban from the calling of domestic service by ceasing to make "Negro" and "servant" synonymous terms. This would make it possible for both whites and blacks to enter more freely into service without a fatal and disheartening loss of self-respect; secondly, it would furnish trained servants—a sad necessity to-day, as any housekeeper can testify.

Such a movement did not, however, take place, but, on the contrary, another movement. English trained servants, the more docile Swedes and better paid white servants were brought in to displace Negro servants. One has but to notice the coachmen on the driveways, or the butlers on Rittenhouse Square, or the nursemaids in Fairmount Park, to see how largely white servants have displaced Negroes. How has this displacement been brought about? First, by getting better trained and more willing servants; secondly, by paying servants higher wages. The Swedish and American servants, in most cases, know more of domestic service than the post-bellum generation of Negroes, and certainly as a class they are far more reconciled to their lot. In the higher branches of domestic service—cooks, butlers and coachmen—the process has been to substitute a man at $50 to $75 a month for one at $30 to $40, and naturally again the result has been gratifying, because a better class of men are attracted by the wages; thus the waiters at the new large hotels are not merely white, but better paid, and undoubtedly ought to render better service. In these ways without doubt domestic service has in some respects improved in the city by a partial substitution of better trained, better paid and more contented white servants for poorly trained, discontented, and in the case of waiters, butlers and coachmen, poorly paid Negroes.

Moreover, the substitution has not met with active opposition or economic resistance on the part of the Negroes, because fully one-half of those in domestic service would be only too glad to get other work of any kind.

What now has been the result of these economic changes? The result has undoubtedly been the increase of crime, pauperism and idleness among Negroes : because while they are being to some extent displaced as servants, no corresponding opening for employment in other lines has been made. How long can such a process continue? How long can a community pursue such a contradictory economic policy— first confining a large portion of its population to a pursuit which public opinion persists in looking down upon ; then displacing them even there by better trained and better paid competitors. Manifestly such a course is bound to make that portion of the community a burden on the public ; to debauch its women, pauperize its men, and ruin its homes ; it makes the one central question of the Seventh Ward, not imperative social betterments, raising of the standard of home life, taking advantage of the civilizing institutions of the great city—on the contrary, it makes it a sheer question of bread and butter and the maintenance of a standard of living above that of the Virginia plantation.

Nor has the whole group failed in every case to answer this question : the foregoing statistics show how, slowly and under many discouragements, diversification of employments is taking place among the black population. This, however, is the brighter side and represents the efforts of that determined class among all people that surmount eventually nearly all obstacles. The spirit of the age however looks to-day not to the best and most energetic, but to those on the edge, those who will become effective members of society only when properly encouraged. The great mass of the Negroes naturally belong to this class and when we turn to the darker side of the picture and study the disease, poverty and crime of the Negro population, then we realize that the question of employment for Negroes is the most pressing of the day and that the starting point is domestic service which still remains their peculiar province. First then as before said the object of social reform should be so to diversify Negro employments as to afford proper escape from menial employment for the talented few, and so as to allow the mass some choice in their lifework : this would be not only for the sake of Negro development, but for the sake of a great human industry which must continue to suffer as long as the odium of race is added to a disposition to look down upon the employment under any circumstances ; the next movement ought to be to train servants—not toward servility and toadying, but in problems of health and hygiene, in proper cleaning and cooking, and in matters of etiquette and good form.

To this must be added such arousing of the public conscience as shall lead people to recognize more keenly than now the responsibility of the family toward its servants—to remember that they are constituent members of the family group and as such have rights and privileges as well as duties. To-day in Philadelphia the tendency is the other way. Thousands of servants no longer lodge where they work but are free at night to wander at will, to hire lodgings in suspicious houses, to consort with paramours, and thus to bring moral and physical disease to their place of work. A reform is imperatively needed, and here, as in most of the Negro problems, a proper reform will benefit white and black alike—the employer as well as the employed.

24. **History of the Occupations of Negroes.**—There early arose in the colony of Pennsylvania the custom of hiring out slaves, especially mechanics and skilled workmen. This very soon roused the ire of the free white workmen, and in 1708 and 1722 we find them petitioning the legislature against the practice, and receiving some encouragement therefrom. As long, however, as an influential class of slaveholders had a direct financial interest

in black mechanics they saw to it that neither law nor prejudice hindered Negroes from working. Thus before and after the Revolution there were mechanics as well as servants among the Negroes. The proportion of servants, however, was naturally very large. We have no figures until 1820, when of, the 7582 Negroes in the city, 2585 or 34 per cent were servants; in 1840, 27 per cent were servants. Some of these servants represented families, so that the proportion of those dependent on domestic service was larger even than the percentage indicated. In 1896 in the Seventh Ward the per cent of servants, using the same method of computation,was 27.3 per cent.

Of those not servants, the Negroes themselves declared in 1832, that "notwithstanding the difficulty of getting places for our sons as apprentices to learn mechanical trades, owing to the prejudices with which we have to contend, there are between four and five hundred people of color in the city and suburbs who follow mechanical employments." In 1838 the investigator of the Abolition Society found 997 of the 17,500 Negroes in the county who had learned trades, although only a part of these (perhaps 350) actually worked at their trades at that time. The rest, outside the servants and men with trades, were manual laborers. Many of these mechanics were afterward driven from the city by the mobs.

In 1848 another study of the Negroes found the distribution of the Negroes as follows:

Of 3358 men, twenty-one years of age and over:

Laborers	1581
Waiters, cooks, etc.	557
Mechanics	286
Coachmen, carters, etc.	276
Sailors, etc.	240
Shopkeepers, traders, etc.	166
Barbers	156
Various occupations	96
	3358

Of 4249 women, twenty-one years and over there were:

Washerwomen	1970
Seamstresses	486
Day workers	786
In trades	213
Housewives	290
Servants (living at home)	156
Cooks	173
Rag pickers	103
Various occupations	72
	4249

Of both sexes five to twenty years of age there were:

School children	1940
Unaccounted for	1200
At home	484
Helpless	33
Working at home	274
Servants	354
Laborers	253
Sweeps	12
Porters	18
Apprentices	230
	4798

Besides these there were in white families 3716 servants.
Just how accurate the statistics of 1847 were it is now
difficult to say, probably there was some exaggeration from
the well-meant effort of the friends of the Negro to show
the best side.   Nevertheless it seems as though the diver-
sity of employments at this time was considerable, although
of course under such heads as " shopkeepers and traders "
street stands more often than stores were meant.

In 1856 the inquiry appears to have been more exhaustive and careful, and the number of Negroes with trades
had increased to 1637—including barbers and dressmakers.
Even here, however, some uncertainty enters, for " less than
two-thirds of those who have trades follow them.   A few
of the remainder pursue other avocations from choice, but
the greater number are compelled to abandon their trades

on account of the unrelenting prejudice against their color." The following table gives these returns:

OCCUPATION OF PHILADELPHIA NEGROES, 1856.

Mechanical Trades.

Dressmakers	588
Barbers	248
Shoemakers	112
Shirt and dressmakers	70
Brickmakers	53
Carpenters	49
Milliners and dressmakers	45
Tailors	49
Tanners and curriers	24
Blacksmiths	22
Cabinetmakers	20
Weavers	16
Pastry cooks	10
Plasterers	14
Sailmakers	12
113 other trades with one to nine in each	305
	1637

In the light of such historical testimony it seems certain that the industrial condition of the Negro in the last century has undergone great vicissitudes, although it is difficult sometimes to trace them. A diagram something like this would possibly best represent the historical development for a century:

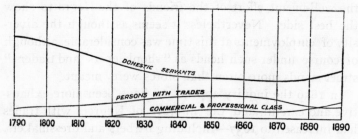

Such a diagram must of course be based largely upon conjecture, but it represents as nearly as the data allow the proportionate—not the absolute—extent to which the Negroes of the city are represented in certain pursuits.

In the half century 1840 to 1890 the proportion of
Negroes who are domestic servants has not greatly changed ;
the mass of the remainder are still laborers ; their opportunities for employment have been restricted by three
causes : competition, industrial change, color prejudice.
The competition has come in later years from the phenomenal growth of cities and the consequent hardening of
conditions of life ; the Negro has especially felt this change
because of all the elements of our urban population he is
least prepared by previous training for rough, keen competition ; the industrial changes since and just before the
emancipation of the slaves have had a great influence on
their development, to which little notice has hitherto been
given.   In the industrial history of nations the change
from agriculture to manufacturing and trade has been a
long, delicate process : first came house industries—spinning and weaving and the like ; then the market with its
simple processes of barter and sale ; then the permanent
stall or shop, and at last the small retail store.   In our day
this small retail store is in process of evolution to something larger and more comprehensive.   When we look at
this development and see how suddenly the American city
Negro has been snatched from agriculture to the centres of
trade and manufactures, it should not surprise us to learn
that he has not as yet succeeded in finding a permanent place
in that vast system of industrial co-operation.   Apart from
all questions of race, his problem in this respect is greater
than the problem of the white country boy or the European
peasant immigrant, because his previous industrial condition
was worse than theirs and less calculated to develop the
power of self-adjustment, self-reliance and co-operation.
All these considerations are further complicated by the fact
that the industrial condition of the Negro cannot be considered apart from the great fact of race prejudice—indefinite and shadowy as that phrase may be.   It is certain
that, while industrial co-operation among the groups of a

great city population is very difficult under ordinary circumstances, that here it is rendered more difficult and in
some respects almost impossible by the fact that nineteen-
twentieths of the population have in many cases refused
to co-operate with the other twentieth, even when the
co-operation means life to the latter and great advantage to
the former.   In other words, one of the great postulates of
the science of economics—that men will seek their
economic advantage—is in this case untrue, because in many
cases men will not do this if it involves association, even
in a casual and business way, with Negroes.   And this
fact must be taken account of in all judgments as to the
Negro's economic progress.

CHAPTER X.

25. The Interpretation of Statistics.—The characteristic signs which usually accompany a low civilization are a high birth rate and a high death rate; or, in other words, early marriages and neglect of the laws of physical health. This fact, which has often been illustrated by statistical research, has not yet been fully apprehended by the general public because they have long been used to hearing more or less true tales of the remarkable health and longevity of barbarous peoples. For this reason the recent statistical research which reveals the large death rate among American Negroes is open to very general misapprehension. It is a remarkable phenomenon which throws much light on the Negro problems and suggests some obvious solutions. On the other hand, it does not prove, as most seem to think, a vast recent change in the condition of the Negro. Reliable data as to the physical health of the Negro in slavery are entirely wanting; and yet, judging from the horrors of the middle passage, the decimation on the West Indian plantations, and the bad sanitary condition of the Negro quarters on most Southern plantations, there must have been an immense death rate among slaves, notwithstanding all reports as to endurance, physical strength and phenomenal longevity. Just how emancipation has affected this death rate is not clear; the rush to cities, where the surroundings are unhealthful, has had a bad effect, although this migration on a large scale is so recent that its full effect is not yet apparent; on the other hand, the better care of children and improvement in home life has also had some favorable effect. On the whole, then, we must remember that reliable statistics as to Negro health are but recent in date and that as yet no important conclusions can be arrived at as to historic changes or tendencies. One thing we must of course expect to find, and that is a much higher death rate at present among Negroes than among whites : this is one measure of the difference in their social advancement. They have in the past lived under vastly different conditions and they still live under different conditions : to assume that, in discussing the inhabitants of Philadelphia, one is discussing people living under the same conditions of life, is to assume what is not true. Broadly speaking, the Negroes as a class dwell in the most unhealthful parts of the city and in the worst houses in those parts ; which is of course simply saying that the part of the population having a large degree of poverty, ignorance and general social degradation is usually to be found in the worst portions of our great cities.

Therefore, in considering the health statistics of the Negroes, we seek first to know their absolute condition, rather than their relative status ; we want to know what their death rate is, how it has varied and is varying and what its tendencies seem to be ; with these facts fixed we must then ask, What is the meaning of a death rate like that of the Negroes of Philadelphia? Is it, compared with with other races, large, moderate or small ; and in the case of nations or groups with similar death rates, What has been the tendency and outcome? Finally, we must compare the death rate of the Negroes with that of the communities in which they live and thus roughly measure the social difference between these neighboring groups ; we must endeavor also to eliminate, so far as possible, from the problem disturbing elements which would make a difference in health among people of the same social advancement. Only in this way can we intelligently interpret statistics of Negro health.

Here, too, we have to remember that the collection of statistics, even in Philadelphia, is by no means perfect.

The death returns are to be relied upon, but the returns of births are wide of the true condition ; the statistics of causes of death are also faulty.

26. The Statistics of the City.—The mortality of Negroes in Philadelphia, according to the best reports, has been as follows :[1]

Date.	Average Annual Deaths per 1000 Negroes.
1820–1830	47.6
1830–1840	32.5
1884–1890	31.25*
1891–1896	28.02†

* Including still-births ; excluding still-births, 29.52.

† Including still-births and assuming the average Negro population, 1891–1896, at the low figure of 41,500.[2] For this period, excluding still-births, 25.41.

The average annual death rate, 1884 to 1890, in the wards having over 1000 Negro inhabitants, was as follows :

Ward.	Negro Population.	Death Rate per 1000, excluding Still-births, 1884–90
Fourth	2,573	43.38
Fifth	2,335	48.46
Seventh	8,861	30.54
Eighth	3,011	29.25
Fourteenth	1,379	22.38
Fifteenth	1,751	20.18
Twentieth	1,333	18.64
Twenty-second	1,798	15.91
Twenty-third	1,026	18.67
Twenty-sixth	1,375	18.15
Twenty-seventh	2,077	39.86
Twenty-ninth	1,476	19.09
Thirtieth	1,789	21.74
Twenty-fourth and Thirty-fourth	2,003	35.11
City	39,371	29.52

[1] The earlier figures are from Dr. Emerson's reports, in the "Condition," etc., of the Negro, 1838, and from the pamphlet, "Health of Convicts." All the tables, 1884 to 1890, are from Dr. John Billings' report in the Eleventh Census. Later reports are compiled from the City Health Reports, 1890 to 1896.

[2] This figure is conjectural, as the real Negro population is unknown. Estimated according to the rate of increase from 1880 to 1890, the average annual population would have been 42,229 ; I think this is too high, as the rate of increase has been lower in this decade.

Separating the deaths by the sex of the deceased, we have :

Total death rate of Negroes, 1890, (still-births
        included) . . . . 32.42 per 1000.
For Negro males . . . . 36.02   "
For Negro females . . . . 29.23   "

Separating by age, we have :

Total death rate, 1890 (still-births included)
        all ages . . . . 32.42 per 1000.
Under fifteen . . . .   69.24   "
Fifteen to twenty . . . . 13.61   "
Twenty to twenty-five . . . .   14.50   "
Twenty-five to thirty-five . . . . 15.21   "
Thirty-five to forty-five . . . . 17.16   "
Forty-five to fifty-five . . . . 29.41   "
Fifty-five to sixty-five . . . .   40.09   "
Sixty-five and over . . . . 116.49   "

The large infant mortality is shown by the average annual rate of 171.44 (including still-births), for children under five years of age, during the years 1884 to 1890.

These statistics are very instructive. Compared with modern nations the death rate of Philadelphia Negroes is high, but not extraordinarily so : Hungary (33.7), Austria (30.6), and Italy (28.6), had in the years 1871–90 a larger average than the Negroes in 1891–96, and some of these lands surpass the rate of 1884–90. Many things combine to cause the high Negro death rate : poor heredity, neglect of infants, bad dwellings and poor food. On the other hand the age classification of city Negroes with its excess of females and of young people of twenty to thirty-five years of age, must serve to keep the death rate lower than its rate would be under normal circumstances. The influence of bad sanitary surroundings is strikingly illustrated in the enormous death rate of the Fifth Ward—the worst Negro slum in the city, and the worst part of the city in respect to sanitation. On the other hand the low death rate of the Thirtieth Ward illustrates the influences of good houses and clean streets in a district where the better class of Negroes have recently migrated.

The marked excess of the male death rate points to a great difference in the social condition of the sexes in the city, as it far exceeds the ordinary disparity; as, *e. g.*, in Germany where the rates are, males 28.6, females 25.3.[3] The young girls who come to the city have practically no chance for work except domestic service. This branch of work, however, has the great advantage of being healthful; the servant has usually a good dwelling, good food and proper clothing. The boy, on the contrary, usually has to live in a bad part of the city, on poorly prepared or irregular food and is more exposed to the weather. Moreover, his chances of securing any work at all are much smaller than the girls'. Consequently the female death rate is but 81 per cent of the male rate.

When we turn to the statistics of death according to age, we immediately see that, as is usual in such cases, the high death rate is caused by an excessive infant mortality, which ranks very high compared with other groups.

The chief diseases to which Negroes fall victims are :[4]

Disease.	Death Rate per 100,000, 1890.
Consumption	532.52
Diseases of the nervous system	388.86
Pneumonia	356.67
Heart disease and dropsy	257.59
Still-births	203.10
Diarrheal diseases	193.19
Diseases of the urinary organs	133.75
Accidents and injuries	99.07
Typhoid fever	91.64

For the period, 1891–1896, the average annual rate was as follows :

[3] This and other comparisons are mostly taken from Mayo-Smith, "Statistics and Sociology."

[4] For death rate, 1884–1890, Cf. below, p. 159.

Disease.	Death Rate per 100,000, 1891–1896.
Consumption	426.50
Diseases of the nervous system	307.63
Pneumonia	290.76
Heart disease and dropsy	172.69
Still and premature births	210.12
Typhoid fever	44.98

The strikingly excessive rate here is that of consumption, which is the most fatal disease for Negroes. Bad ventilation, lack of outdoor life for women and children, poor protection against dampness and cold are undoubtedly the chief causes of this excessive death rate. To this must be added some hereditary predisposition, the influence of climate, and the lack of nearly all measures to prevent the spread of the disease.

We find thus a group of people with a high, but not unusual, death rate, which rate has been gradually decreasing, if statistics are reliable, for seventy-five years. This death rate is due principally to infantile mortality and consumption, and these are caused chiefly by conditions of life and poor hereditary physique.

How now does this group compare with the condition of the mass of the community with which it comes in daily contact? Comparing the death rates of whites and Negroes, we have:

Date.	Whites.	Negroes.
1820–1830	. . .	47.6
1830–1840	23.7	32.5
1884–1890 *	22.69	31.25
1891–1896 †	21.20‡	25.41§

* Including still-births.

† Excluding still-births.

‡ Assuming white population, 1891–96, has increased in the same ratio as 1880–90, and that it averaged 1,056,985 in these years.

§ Assuming that the mean Negro population was 41,500.

This shows a considerable difference in death rates, amounting to nearly 10 per cent in 1884–1890, and to 4 per cent by the estimated rates of 1891–1896. If the estimate of population on which the latter rate is based is correct, then the difference in death rate is not larger than would be expected from different conditions of life.[5]

The absolute number of deaths (excluding still-births) has been as follows :

Year.	Whites.	Negroes.
1891	22,384	983
1892	23,233	1,072
1893	22,621	1,034
1894	21,960	1,030
1895	22,645	1,151
1896	22,903	1,079

Comparing the death rate by wards we have this table :

POPULATION AND DEATH RATE, PHILADELPHIA, 1884-90.

Wards.	Population, 1890.		Death Rate per 1000, excluding Still-births.	
	White.	Colored.	White.	Colored.
First	53,057	794	22.08	33.07
Second	31,016	522	23.93	24.21
Third	19,043	861	23.91	21.71
Fourth	17,792	2,573	29.98	43.38
Fifth	14,619	2,335	25.67	48.46
Sixth	8,574	125	24.30	49.77
Seventh	21,177	8,861	24.30	30.54
Eighth	13,940	3,011	24.26	29 25
Ninth	9,284	497	25.40	22 32
Tenth	20,495	798	19.88	14.51
Eleventh	12,931	11	28.31	500.00
Twelfth	13,821	338	21.57	44.85

[5] The official figures of the Board of Health give no estimate of the Negro death-rate alone. They give the following death rate for the city including both whites and blacks, and excluding still-births:

Year.	Total Number of Deaths.	Death rate per 1000 of Population.
1891	23,367	21.85
1892	24,305	22.25
1893	23,655	21.20
1894	22,680	19.90
1895	23,796	20.44
1896	23,982	20.17

Average death rate for the six years, **20.97**; by my calculation, the rate for the whole population would be **21.63**.

POPULATION AND DEATH RATE, 1884–90—*Continued.*

Wards.	Population, 1890.		Death Rate per 1000, excluding Still-births.	
	White.	Colored.	White.	Colored.
Thirteenth	17,362	539	20.67	28.76
Fourteenth	19,339	1,379	21.47	22.38
Fifteenth	50,954	1,751	20.08	20.18
Sixteenth	16,973	104	28.04	46.38
Seventeenth	19,412	124	28.89	64.95
Eighteenth	29,142	1	24.42	90.91
Nineteenth	55,249	275	23.73	51.33
Twentieth	43,127	1,333	20.77	18.64
Twenty-first	26,800	93	19.45	56.78
Twenty-second	43,512	1,798	17.77	15.91
Twenty-third	34,255	1,026	18.50	18.67
Twenty-fourth	41,600	930	17.95	35.11
Twenty-fifth	35,677	260	24.29	33.33
Twenty-sixth	60,722	1,375	19.48	18.15
Twenty-seventh	30,712	2,077	31.91	39.86
Twenty-eighth	45,727	644	15.56	15.96
Twenty-ninth	53,261	1,476	20.19	19.09
Thirtieth	28,808	1,789	22.12	21.74
Thirty-first	32,944	16	21.46	57.47
Thirty-second	29,662	382	14.61	13.66
Thirty-third	32,975	190	13.07	18.63
Thirty-fourth	22,628	1,073	*	*
Whole city	1,006,590	39,371	21.54	29.52

*Death rate included in that of the Twenty-fourth ward.

From this table we may make some interesting comparisons ; take first the worst wards :

Ward.	Whites.	Negroes.*
Fourth	29.98	43.38
Fifth	25 67	48.46
Seventh	24.30	30.54
Eighth	24.26	29.25

* Total Negro population, 16,780.

In all these wards there is a large Negro population comprising a considerable per cent of new immigrants ; and
these wards contain the worst slum districts and most unsanitary dwellings of the city. However, there are in
these same wards peculiar circumstances which decrease
the death rate of the whites : First, in the Fourth and
Fifth wards a large number of foreign immigrants whose

death rate, on account of the absence of old people and
children, is small; and of Jews whose death rate is, on
account of their fine family life, also small; secondly, in the
Seventh and Eighth wards there are, as all Philadelphians
know, large sections inhabited by the best people of the
city, with a death rate below the average.

Taking another set of wards, we have :

Ward.	Whites.	Negroes.*
Fourteenth	21.47	22.38
Fifteenth	20.08	20.18
Twenty-sixth	19.48	18.15
Twenty-seventh	31.91	39.86
Thirtieth	22.12	21.74

* Total Negro population, 8,371.

Here we have quite a different tale. These are the
wards where the best Negro families have been renting
and buying homes in the last ten years, in order to escape
from the crowded downtown wards. The Thirtieth and
Twenty-sixth wards are the best sections; the statistics of
the Fourteenth and Fifteenth wards show the same thing
although their validity is somewhat vitiated by the large
number of Negro servants there in the prime of life.

A last set of wards is as follows :

Ward.	Whites.	Negroes.*
Twentieth	20.77	18.64
Twenty-second	17.77	15.91
Twenty-third	18 50	18.67
Twenty-eighth	15.56	15.96
Twenty-ninth	20.19	19.09

* Total Negro population, 6,277.

In most of these some exceptional circumstances make
the Negro death rate abnormally low. Generally this
arises from the fact that these are white residential wards
and the Negro population is largely composed of servants.
These, as has been before noted, have a small death rate
because of their ages, and then too, when they are sick

they go home to die in the Seventh Ward, or to the hospitals in the Twenty-seventh and other wards.

These tables would seem to adduce considerable proof that the Negro death rate is largely a matter of condition of living.

When we look at the comparative deaths of the races, by sex, we see that the forces operating among Negroes to make a disparity between the death rates of men and women are largely absent among the whites.

Sex.	White.	Negro.	Total.
Male	23.85	36.02	24.30
Female	20.79	29.23	21.12

(1890, including still-births.)

The age structure reveals partially the character of the great differences in death rate between the races. (See page 157.)

DEATH RATE OF PHILADELPHIA BY AGE PERIODS, FOR 1890.

(STILL-BIRTHS INCLUDED)
■ NEGROES □ WHITES

NUMBER OF DEATHS IN PHILADELPHIA, BY AGES, 1884–1890.

Ward.	Color'd Population.	WHITE							NEGRO						
		All Ages.	Deaths in Six Years at Certain Ages.						All Ages.	Deaths in Six Years at Certain Ages.					
			Under 5.	5-15.	15-25.	25-65.	Over65.	Unknown.		Under 5.	5-15.	15-25.	25-65.	Over 65.	Un-kn'n.
Seventh	8,861	3,225	1,044	139	215	1,148	625	54	1,753	765	95	128	582	165	18
Eighth	3,011	2,191	498	76	168	855	533	61	584	241	33	51	193	59	7
Fourth	2,573	3,346	1,624	164	191	993	338	36	700	336	42	43	216	58	5
Fifth	2,335	2,338	900	81	151	885	320	21	720	265	32	62	285	69	5
Twenty-seventh	2,077	5,425	2,165	148	291	1,785	951	85	477	156	19	60	168	62	12
Twenty-fourth and Thirty-fourth	2,003	6,519	2,549	366	468	1,966	1,094	76	399	147	19	26	77	125	5
Twenty-second	1,798	4,373	1,535	177	338	1,294	94	89	170	84	14	14	41	12	5
Thirtieth	1,789	3,911	1,423	195	313	1,331	591	58	248	118	13	25	74	17	1
Fifteenth	1,751	6,256	2,214	265	458	2,205	1,034	80	214	71	18	39	66	17	3
Twenty-ninth	1,476	6,217	2,200	339	440	2,044	1,120	74	170	86	21	21	44	10	0
Fourteenth	1,379	2,670	931	116	183	875	530	35	203	109	9	16	47	17	5
Twenty-sixth	1,375	6,337	2,957	358	421	1,856	678	67	138	55	9	11	43	19	1
Twentieth	1,333	5,585	1,912	236	416	1,852	1,056	63	159	70	15	13	48	9	4
Twenty-third	1,026	3,603	1,251	208	260	1,128	730	26	110	46	6	9	32	13	4
Third	861	2,836	1,366	138	151	879	339	33	120	53	5	12	42	8	0
Tenth	798	2,614	869	114	163	948	539	41	95	42	2	4	38	4	1
First	794	6,916	3,187	390	463	2,014	789	73	162	75	9	8	49	15	0
Twenty-eighth	644	3,553	1,522	193	221	1,012	557	48	52	27	5	14	11	4	2
Thirteenth	539	2,277	869	90	130	723	446	19	105	56	1	3	33	9	0
Second	522	4,580	1,970	212	357	1,413	572	56	86	37	5	3	21	13	1
Total	39,371	127,556	51,479	6,096	8,787	40,497	19,170	1,527	7,322	3,125	390	624	2,328	768	87

DEATH RATE IN PHILADELPHIA, 1890, BY EIGHT AGE PERIODS.

Color.	All Ages.	Under 15.	15–20.	20–25.	25–35.	35–45.	45–55.	55–65.	65 and Over.
Total whites	22.28	34.89	6.17	8.81	10.85	13.60	18.98	31.56	88.88
Total male whites	23.85	37.22	6.49	10.12	11.28	15.30	20.85	36.44	93.51
Total female whites	20.79	32.51	5.89	7.64	10.43	11.91	17.20	27.42	85.35
Total Negroes	32.42	69.24	13.61	14.50	15.21	17.16	29.41	40.09	116.49
Total male Negroes	36.02	75.81	15.01	19.75	14.12	20.52	33.67	47.70	155.26
Total female Negroes. . . .	29.23	63.12	12.66	10.46	16.24	13.55	25.48	34.57	96.47
Native whites	22.80	36.84	6.20	8.64	10.74	12.55	17.85	29.61	89.23
Native white males	24.43	39.37	6.34	9.65	10.95	13.73	19.44	34.04	98.66
Native white females . . .	21.25	34.25	6.07	7.70	10.55	11.43	16.35	25.82	82.78

For children under five, including still-births, we find
these average annual death rates, 1884–1890 :

Race.	City.	Seventh Ward.
Native white	94.00	111.04
Negro	171.44	188.82
Total population	94.79	132.63

Nothing shows more plainly the poor home life of the
Negroes than these figures. A comparison of the differences in death rate from various diseases will complete the
picture :

DEATH RATE PER 100,000 FROM SPECIFIED DISEASES, 1890.
For Whole City.

Disease.	Negro.	White.
Consumption	532.52	269.42
Pneumonia	356.67	180.31
Diarrheal diseases	193.19	151.40
Diseases of the nervous system	388.86	302.01
Diphtheria and croup	44.58	82.06
Diseases of the urinary system	133.75	60.81
Heart disease and dropsy	257.59	157.16
Cancer and tumor	37.15	56.63
Disease of the liver	12.38	27.82
Malarial fever	7.43	5.66
Typhoid fever	91.64	72.82
Still-births	203.10	135.61
Suicides	3.20	12.99
Other accidents and injuries	99.07	78.78

AVERAGE ANNUAL DEATH RATE OF PHILADELPHIA, 1884–1890, PER
EACH 100,000 OF POPULATION.

For Specified Diseases.

Causes.	Total.	Whites.			Negro.
		Total.	Native.	Foreign.	
All causes	2303.43	2269.19	2562.31	1470.26	3124.81
Scarlet fever	26.18	26.86	35.84	2.39	9.82
Typhoid fever. . . .	69.35	69.65	73.10	60.25	62.31
Malarial fever	7.21	7.19	8.22	4.37	7.68
Diphtheria	50.48	51.48	69.30	2.92	26.46
Croup	47.82	49.03	66.41	1.66	18.78
Diarrheal diseases . .	156.11	155.30	196.16	43.94	195.40
Consumption	297.87	287.06	299.29	253.72	557.36
Pneumonia	164.17	158.77	174.79	115.13	293.62
Measles.	10.67	10.67	14.37	.60	10.67
Whooping-cough . .	11.39	10.69	14.52	.27	28.17
Cancer and tumor . .	54.73	55.17	48.15	74.30	44.38
Heart disease and dropsy	146.27	142.10	37.44	154.83	246.25
Childbirth and puerperal diseases . .	10.06	9.98	9.61	11.00	11.95
Diseases of liver . .	27.58	28.32	24.70	38.18	9.82
nervous system	318.83	315.86	373.38	159.07	390.07
urinary organs	74.90	73.44	72.54	75.89	110.11
Old age.	46.08	45.99	37.13	70.12	48.23
Still-births . . .	117.68	115.38	157.72	. . . .	172.84
All other causes . . .	656.01	646.23	743.50	381.10	890.67
Unknown.	10.02	10.02	10.19	9.54	10.24

The Negroes exceed the white death rate largely in consumption, pneumonia, diseases of the urinary system, heart disease and dropsy, and in still-births ; they exceed moderately in diarrheal diseases, diseases of the nervous system, malarial and typhoid fevers. The white death rate exceeds that of Negroes for diphtheria and croup, cancer and tumor, diseases of the liver, and deaths from suicide.

We have side by side and in intimate relationship in a large city two groups of people, who as a mass differ considerably from each other in physical health ; the difference is not so great as to preclude hopes of final adjustment ; probably certain social classes of the larger group are in no better health than the mass of the smaller group. So too there are without doubt classes in the smaller group whose physical condition is equal to, or superior to the average of the larger group. Particularly with regard to consumption it must be remembered that Negroes are not the first people who have been claimed as its peculiar victims; the Irish were once thought to be doomed by that disease—but that was when Irishmen were unpopular.

Nevertheless, so long as any considerable part of the population of an organized community is, in its mode of life and physical efficiency distinctly and noticeably below the average, the community must suffer. The suffering part furnishes less than its quota of workers, more than its quota of the helpless and dependent and consequently becomes to an extent a burden on the community. This is the situation of the Negroes of Philadelphia to-day : because of their physical health they receive a larger portion of charity, spend a larger proportion of their earnings for physicians and medicine, throw on the community a larger number of helpless widows and orphans than either they or the city can afford. Why is this? Primarily it is because the Negroes are as a mass ignorant of the laws of health. One has but to visit a Seventh Ward church on Sunday night and see an audience of 1500 sit two and three hours in the foul atmosphere of a closely shut auditorium to realize that long formed habits of life explain much of Negro consumption and pneumonia ; again the Negroes live in unsanitary dwellings, partly by their own fault, partly on account of the difficulty of securing decent houses by reason of race prejudice. If one goes through the streets of the Seventh Ward and picks out those streets and houses which, on account of their poor condition, lack of repair, absence of conveniences and limited share of air and light, contain the worst dwellings, one finds that the great majority of such streets and houses are occupied by Negroes. In some cases it is the Negroes' fault that the houses are so bad ; but in very many cases landlords refuse to repair and refit for Negro tenants because they know that there are few

dwellings which Negroes can hire, and they will not therefore be apt to leave a fair house on account of damp walls
or poor sewer connections. Of modern conveniences
Negro dwellings have few. Of the 2441 families of the
Seventh Ward only 14 per cent had water closets and baths,
and many of these were in poor condition. In a city of
yards, 20 per cent of the families had no private yard
and consequently no private outhouses.

Again, in habits of personal cleanliness and taking proper
food and exercise, the colored people are woefully defi-
cient. The Southern field-hand was hardly supposed to
wash himself regularly, and the house servants were none
too clean. Habits thus learned have lingered, and a gospel
of soap and water needs now to be preached. Negroes are
commonly supposed to eat rather more than necessary. And
this perhaps is partially true. The trouble is more in the
quality of the food than its quantity, in the wasteful method
of its preparation, and in the irregularity in eating.[6] For instance, one family of three living in the depth of dirt and
poverty on a crime-stricken street spent for their daily food :

	Cents.
Milk, for child	4
One pound pork chops	10
One loaf bread	5
	19

When we imagine this pork fried in grease and eaten
with baker's bread, taken late in the afternoon or at bed-
time, what can we expect of such a family? Moreover,
the tendency of the classes who are just struggling out of
extreme poverty is to stint themselves for food in order to
have better looking homes ; thus the rent in too many
cases eats up physical nourishment.

Finally, the number of Negroes who go with insufficient
clothing is large. One of the commonest causes of

---

[6] Cf. Atwater & Woods:"Dietary Studies with reference to the Food
of the Negro in Alabama." (Bulletin No. 38, U. S. Dept. of Agriculture),
p. 21, and *passim.*

consumption and respiratory disease is migration from the warmer South to a Northern city without change in manner of dress. The neglect to change clothing after becoming damp with rain is a custom dating back to slavery time.

These are a few obvious matters of habit and manner of life which account for much of the poor health of Negroes. Further than this, when in poor health the neglect to take proper medical advice, or to follow it when given, leads to much harm. Often at the hospital a case is treated and temporary relief given, the patient being directed to return after a stated time. More often with Negroes than with whites, the patient does not return until he is worse off than at first. To this must be added a superstitious fear of hospitals prevalent among the lower classes of all people, but especially among Negroes. This must have some foundation in the roughness or brusqueness of manner prevalent in many hospitals, and the lack of a tender spirit of sympathy with the unfortunate patients. At any rate, many a Negro would almost rather die than trust himself to a hospital.

We must remember that all these bad habits and surroundings are not simply matters of the present generation, but that many generations of unhealthy bodies have bequeathed to the present generation impaired vitality and hereditary tendency to disease. This at first seems to be contradicted by the reputed robustness of older generations of blacks, which was certainly true to a degree. There cannot, however, be much doubt, when former social conditions are studied, but that hereditary disease plays a large part in the low vitality of Negroes to-day, and the health of the past has to some extent been exaggerated. All these considerations should lead to concerted efforts to root out disease. The city itself has much to do in this respect. For so large and progressive a city its general system of drainage is very bad ; its water is wretched, and in many other respects the city and the whole State are "woefully and discreditably behind almost all the other States in Christendom."[7] The main movement for reform must come from the Negroes themselves, and should start with a crusade for fresh air, cleanliness, healthfully located homes and proper food. All this might not settle the question of Negro health, but it would be a long step toward it.

The most difficult social problem in the matter of Negro health is the peculiar attitude of the nation toward the well-being of the race. There have, for instance, been few other cases in the history of civilized peoples where human suffering has been viewed with such peculiar indifference. Nearly the whole nation seemed delighted with the discredited census of 1870 because it was thought to show that the Negroes were dying off rapidly, and the country would soon be well rid of them. So, recently, when attention has been called to the high death rate of this race, there is a disposition among many to conclude that the rate is abnormal and unprecedented, and that, since the race is doomed to early extinction, there is little left to do but to moralize on inferior species.

Now the fact is, as every student of statistics knows, that considering the present advancement of the masses of the Negroes, the death rate is not higher than one would expect; moreover there is not a civilized nation to-day which has not in the last two centuries presented a death rate which equaled or surpassed that of this race. That the Negro death rate at present is anything that threatens the extinction of the race is either the bugbear of the untrained, or the wish of the timid.

What the Negro death rate indicates is how far this race is behind the great vigorous, cultivated race about it. It should then act as a spur for increased effort and sound upbuilding, and not as an excuse for passive indifference, or increased discrimination.

---

[7] Dr. Dudley Pemberton before the State Homeopathic Medical Society.—Philadelphia *Ledger*, October 1, 1896.

CHAPTER XI.

THE NEGRO FAMILY.

27. The Size of the Family.—There were in the Seventh Ward, in 1896, 7751 members of families (including 171 persons living alone), and 1924 single lodgers.[1] The average size of the family, without lodgers and boarders, was 3.18.

FAMILIES ACCORDING TO SIZE.

Number in Family.	Number of Families.	Per Cent of Different Size Families.	Members of Families.
One	171	7.0	171
Two	1,031	42.2	2,062
Three	470		1,410
Four	327		1,308
Five	183	44.3	915
Six	106		636
Seven	76		532
Eight	28		224
Nine	25	5.8	225
Ten	13		130
Eleven	2		22
Twelve	4		48
Thirteen	3	0.7	39
Fourteen	1		14
Fifteen	1		15
Total	2,441	100	7,751
Lodgers	. . .	. . .	1,924
Total population	. . .	. . .	9,675
Average size real family	. . .	. . .	3.18
Average size of family, including single lodgers			3.96
Average size of census family	. . .	. . .	5.08

With the whole population of the ward included, the average size was about four, and counting married and

---

[1] Families who were lodging—and there were many—were counted as families, not as lodgers. They were mostly young couples with one or no children. The lodgers were not counted with the families because of their large numbers, and the shifting of many of them from month to month.

single lodgers as part of the renting family, the average size is about five.[2] In any case the smallness of the families is remarkable, and is probably due to local causes in the ward, to the general situation in the city and to development in the race at large. The Seventh Ward is a ward of lodgers and casual sojourners; newly married couples settle down here until they are compelled, by the appearance of children, to move into homes of their own, and these in later years are being chosen in the Twenty-sixth, Thirtieth and Thirty-sixth wards, and up-town. Some couples leave their families in the South with grandmothers and live in lodgings here, returning to Virginia or Maryland only temporarily in summer or winter; a good many men come here from elsewhere, live as lodgers and support families in the country; then, too, childless couples often work out, the woman at service and the man lodging in this ward; the woman joins her husband once or twice a week, but does not lodge regularly there, and so is not a resident of the ward; such are the local conditions that affect greatly the size of families.[3]

The size of families in cities is nearly always smaller than elsewhere, and the Negro family follows this rule; late marriages among them undoubtedly act as a check to population; moreover, the economic stress is so great that only the small family can survive; the large families are either kept from coming to the city or move away, or, as is most common, send the breadwinners to the city while they stay in the country. It is of course but

---

[2] This figure is obtained by dividing the total population of the ward by the number of homes directly rented, viz., 1675. There is an error here arising from the fact that some sub-renting families are really lodgers and should be counted with the census family, while others are partially separate families and some wholly separate. This error cannot be eliminated.

[3] The excessive infant mortality also has its influence on the average size of families. Cf. Chapter X. Whether infanticide or fœticide is prevalent to any extent there are no means of knowing. Once in a while such a case finds its way to the courts.

conjecture to say how far these causes are working among the general Negro population of the country; but considering that the whole race has to-day begun its great battle for economic survival, and that few of the better class, male or female, can expect to get married early in life, it is fair to expect that for several decades to come the average size of the Negro family will decrease until economic well-being can keep pace with the demands of a rising standard of living; and that then we shall have another era of good-sized though not very large Negro families.[4]

As has before been intimated, the difficulty of earning income enough to afford to marry, has had its ill effects on the sexual morality of city Negroes, especially, too, since their hereditary training in this respect has been lax. It is, therefore, fair to conclude that a number of the families of two are simply more or less permanent cohabitations; and that a large number of families are centres of irregular sexual intercourse. Observation in the ward bears out this conclusion, and shows that fifty-eight of the families of two were certainly unmarried persons.

The result of all these causes is shown in the following table, although the comparison is not strictly allowable; the real family of the Negroes is compared with the census family of other groups, and this exaggerates the proportion of the smaller families among the Negroes:

Number in Family.	Negroes Seventh Ward.	Whole Population of City.	Brookl'n, N. Y.	United States.
	%	%	%	%
One	7.0	1.91	2.71	3.63
Two	42.2	. . .	. . .	. . .
Two to six	86.5	74.67	78.37	73.33
Seven to ten	5.8	21.09	17.53	20.97
Eleven and over	0.7	2.33	1.39	2.07

[4] During the last ten years I have been bidden to a dozen or more weddings among the better class of Negroes. In no case was the bridegroom under 30, or the bride under 20. In most cases the man was about 35, and the woman 25 or more.

Further comparison with France may be made : [5]

Number in Family.	Negroes Seventh Ward.	France.
One	7.0	14.0
Two to three	61.5	41.3
Four to five	20.9	29.8
Six or more	10.6	14.5

Making allowance for the errors of this comparison, it nevertheless seems true that the conditions of family life in the ward are abnormal and characterized by an unusually large number of families of two persons.

There are no statistics for the Negro families of the whole city such as would serve to eliminate the local peculiarities of the Seventh Ward. General observation would indicate in the Fifth and Eighth wards similar conditions to the Seventh. In most of the other wards conditions are different, and in all probability vary widely from these crowded central wards. Nevertheless, throughout all of them large families are not the rule, the number of bachelors and lodgers is considerable, and there is some cohabitation, although this is, in the city at large, much less prevalent than in the Seventh Ward. It would seem, therefore, that the indications of our study of conjugal

---

[5] The figures relative to other groups of city Negroes as collected by the conference at Atlanta University are as follows:

FAMILIES OF	ATLANTA, GA.	NASHVILLE, TENN.	CAMBRIDGE, MASS.	OTHER CITIES.	ALL GROUPS.
1	6.79	2.04	5.10	4.69	4.75
2	20.06	17.89	25.51	17.91	19.17
2–6	79.63	82.10	83.68	78.04	79.85
7–10	13.58	15.45	11.22	17.06	15.22
11 and Over.	0	.41	0	.21	.18

These figures apply to only 1137 families in the above named and other cities. Cf. " U. S. Bulletin of Labor," May, 1897.

condition were here emphasized, and that the Negro urban
home has commenced a revolution which will either purify
and raise it or more thoroughly debauch it than now ; and
that the determining factor is economic opportunity.   The
full picture of this change demands statistics of births and
marriages from year to year.   These unfortunately are not
so registered as to be even partially reliable.   Both the
birth and marriage rate, however, are in all probability
steadily decreasing.[6]   The death rate also comes in here
as a factor, not only by reason of the great infant mortality
but also on account of the excessive death rate of the men.
In all this one catches a faint glimpse of the intricacy and
far-reaching influence of the Negro problems.

   28. Incomes.—The economic problem of the Negroes
of the city has been repeatedly referred to.   We now come
directly to the question, What do Negroes earn?   In a
year about what is the income of an average family?
Such a question is difficult to answer with anything like
accuracy.   Only returns based on actual written accounts
would furnish thoroughly reliable statistics ; such accounts
cannot be had in this case.   The few that keep accounts
would in many cases naturally be unwilling to produce
them.   On the other hand, the great mass of people in the

---

[6] The birth rate for the city is given in official returns as follows:

   1894. Total for city: males, 16,185; females, 14,552.   Negroes: males,
536; females, 476.

   1895. Total for city: males, 15,618; females, 14,220.   Negroes: males,
568; females, 524.

   1896. Total for city: males, 15,534; females, 14,219.   Negroes: males,
572; females 514.

   Average per year for whites, 29,013.

   Average per year for Negroes, 1,063.

   White birth rate, 27.2 per thousand.

   Negro birth rate, 25.1 per thousand.

   Assuming white population as 1,066,985.

   Assuming Negro population as 41,500.

   The Department of Health declares these returns considerably below
the truth, and the omissions among Negroes are of course large.   Nevertheless, the Negro birth rate in Philadelphia is probably not high.

lower walks of life scarcely know how much they earn in a year. The tables here presented, therefore, must be regarded simply as careful estimates. These estimates are based on three or more of the following items: (1) The statement of the family as to their earnings. Some of the better class gave a general estimate of their average yearly income; most gave the wages earned per week or month at their usual occupation. (2) The occupations followed by the several members of the family; (3) the time lost from work in the last year or the time usually lost; (4) the apparent circumstances of the family judging from the appearance of the home and inmates, the rent paid, the presence of lodgers, etc.

In most cases the first item was given the greatest weight in settling the matter, but was modified by the others; in other cases, however, either this statement could not be obtained or was vague, and in a few instances evidently false. In such circumstances the second item was decisive: the occupations followed by the mass of Negroes are paid according to a pretty well-known scale of prices; a hotel waiter's income could be pretty accurately fixed without further data. The third item was important in many occupations; stevedores, for instance, receive generally twenty cents per hour; nevertheless, few if any earn $600 a year, because they lose much time between ships and in winter. Finally, as a general corrective to deception or inadvertence the circumstances of home life as seen by the investigator on his visit, the rent paid—an item which could be pretty accurately ascertained—the number of lodgers, the occupation of the housewife and children—all these items served to confirm or throw doubt on the conclusions indicated by the other data, and were given some weight in the final judgment.

Thus it can easily be seen that these returns may contain, and probably do contain, considerable error. On the one hand they cannot be as accurate as returns based on income tax reports, and on the other hand they are probably more reliable than data founded solely on the bare statements of those asked. The personal judgment of the investigator enters into the determination of the figures to a larger extent than is desirable, and yet it has been limited as carefully as the nature of the inquiry permitted.[7]

The income according to size of family is indicated in the next table. From this, making the standard a family of five,

INCOMES, ACCORDING TO SIZE OF FAMILY IN SEVENTH WARD, 1896.

Amount of Income per Year.	Size of Family.											Total Number of Families.
	1.	2.	3.	4.	5.	6.	7.	8.	9.	10.	11 to 15.	
$ 50	7	5	1	.	.	.	1	.	.	.	.	14
100	22	18	2	2	1	.	.	.	.	.	.	45
150	31	69	19	4	6	4	.	.	.	.	.	133
200	23	105	35	12	8	4	.	.	.	.	.	187
250	32	95	46	26	7	1	5	2	.	.	.	214
300	10	108	49	33	9	3	1	.	.	.	.	213
350	9	121	46	30	11	10	2	1	.	.	.	230
400	4	95	39	34	22	9	6	.	.	.	.	209
450	1	79	40	26	14	7	3	1	1	.	.	172
500	7	115	47	37	26	17	1	3	2	.	1	256
550	.	23	12	8	4	4	1	0	3	.	.	55
600	1	17	14	8	7	3	3	.	1	.	.	54
650	1	45	26	27	11	7	4	2	1	.	1	125
700	.	10	16	12	9	5	6	3	2	.	.	63
750	3	23	19	16	13	7	9	3	1	.	.	94
800	.	7	7	7	3	2	2	1	.	1	1	31
850	.	3	2	1	3	1	4	2	2	.	.	18
900	.	5	4	8	3	3	5	9	1	1	1	40
1000–1200	.	1	1	1	4	.	.	.	1	3	1	12
1200–1500	1	3	10	3	5	7	6	2	5	3	1	46
1500 and over	2	6	10	12	6	5	10	3	2	4	5	65
Unknown	15	67	17	6	2	2	1	.	.	.	.	110
Unknown	of unknown size											55

and making some allowance for larger and smaller families, we can conclude that 19 per cent of the Negro families in the Seventh Ward earn five dollars and less per week on the average; 48 per cent earn between $5 and $10 ; 26 per

---

[7] There were many families who were undoubtedly tempted to exaggerate their income so as to appear better off than they were; others, on the contrary, understated their resources. In most cases, however, the testimony so far as it went appeared to be candid and honest.

cent, $10–$15, and 8 per cent over $15 per week. Tabulating this we have :

AVERAGE EARNINGS PER WK	No. OF FAMILIES	%	COMPARISON.	
$5 & LESS	420 { 192	8.9	VERY POOR	
	228	9.6	POOR	
$5–10	1088	47.8	FAIR	
$10–15	581	25.5	COMFORTABLE	
$15–20	91	4.	GOOD CIRCUMSTANCES	
$20 & OVER	96	4.2	WELL-TO-DO	
TOTAL	2276	100.00%		

It is difficult to compare this with other groups because of the varying meaning of the terms poor, well-to-do, and the like.   Nevertheless, a comparison with Booth's diagram of London will, if not carried too far, be interesting: [8]

POVERTY IN LONDON AND AMONG THE NEGROES OF THE SEVENTH
WARD OF PHILADELPHIA.

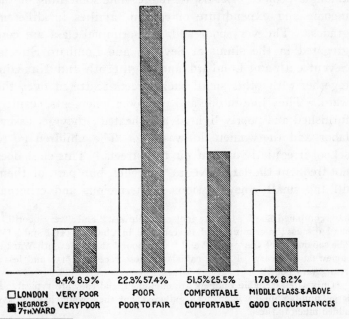

8.4% 8.9%	22.3% 57.4%	51.5% 25.5%	17.8% 8.2%
□LONDON VERY POOR	VERY POOR	COMFORTABLE	MIDDLE CLASS & ABOVE
■NEGROES VERY POOR	7TH.WARD	POOR TO FAIR	COMFORTABLE	GOOD CIRCUMSTANCES

[8] Cf. Booth's " Life and Labor of the People," II, 21.   In this case I

The chief difficulty of this comparison lies in the distribution of the population between the "poor" and "comfortable;" probably the former class among the Negroes is here somewhat exaggerated. At any rate, the division between these two grades is in the Seventh Ward much less stable than in London since their economic status is less fixed. In good times perhaps 50 per cent of the Negroes could well be designated comfortable, but in time of financial stress vast numbers of this class fall below the line into the poor and go to swell the number of paupers, and in many cases of criminals. Indeed this whole division into incomes of different classes is, among the Negroes, much less stable than among the whites, just as it used to be less stable among the whites of fifty years ago than it is among those of to-day.

The whole division into "poor," "comfortable" and "well-to-do" depends primarily on the standard of living among a people. Let us, therefore, note something of the income and expenditure of certain families in different grades.[9] The very poor and semi-criminal class are congregated in the slums at Seventh and Lombard Streets, Seventeenth and Lombard, and Eighteenth and Naudain, together with other small back streets scattered over the ward. They live in one-and two-room tenements, scantily furnished and poorly lighted and heated; they get casual labor, and the women do washing. The children go to school irregularly or loaf on the streets. This class does not frequent the large Negro churches, but part of them fill the small noisy missions. The vicious and criminal

have combined Booth's two lower classes, "lowest" and "very poor." I shall discuss the criminal and lowest class in Chapters XIII and XIV. The separation of the "poor" and "very poor" in the Seventh Ward is somewhat arbitrary. I have called all those receiving $150 and less a year "very poor."

[9] Only a few reliable budgets are subjoined, and they are typical. A large number might have been gathered, but they would hardly have added much to these.

portion do not usually go to church. Those of this class
who are poor but decent are next-door neighbors usually
to pronounced criminals and prostitutes. The income and
expenditure of some of these families follow.

Family No. 1 lives in one of the worst streets of the
ward, surrounded by thieves and prostitutes. There are
three persons in the family: a woman of thirty-four, with
a son of sixteen and a second husband of twenty-six. Both
the husband and son are out of work, the former being a
waiter and the latter a bootblack. They live in one filthy
room, twelve feet by fourteen, scantily furnished and
poorly ventilated. The woman works at service and
receives about three dollars a week. They pay twelve dollars a month for three rooms, and sub-rent two of them to
other families, which makes their rent about three dollars.

Their food costs them about $1.00 a week and the fuel
56 cents a week during the winter. Their expenditure for
other items is varying and indefinite; beer, however,
comes in for something. Their whole expenditure is
probably $125-$150 a year, of which the woman earns at
least $100.

Family No. 2 has a yearly budget as follows for two
persons :

Rent, @ $4 a month	$48.00
Food—Bread, pork, tea, etc., @ $1.44 a week . . .	74.88
Fuel, 20-47 cents a week	16.60
	$139.48

Other items would bring this up to about $150 to $175.
Family No. 3, consisting of one person, reports the following budget, not including rent :

Food	$30.00
Fuel	15.00
Clothing	10.00
Amusements	1.50
Sickness, etc	10.00
Other purposes	15.00
Total, per year	$81.50

The rent of such a family would not exceed $40, making the total expenditure about $121.50.

Family No. 4—four persons—man and wife and two babies, living in one room, spend as follows :

Rent, @ $3 a month		$36.00
Food—Weekly: milk	$0.28	
pork	.70	
bread	.35	
	1.33	69.16
Fuel, 20-98 cents a week		18.00
		$123.16

The man has work one and one-half weeks in the month as a wire fence maker, when regularly employed, which is about half the time. The rest of the time he takes care of the babies while his wife works at service. The last two families seem respectable, but unfortunate. The other two are doubtful.

The " poor " are a degree above these cases ; they are composed of the inefficient, unfortunate and improvident, and just manage to get enough to eat, a little to wear, and shelter. A specimen family is composed of six persons— man and wife, a widowed daughter, two grandsons of thirteen and eleven, and a nephew of twenty-eight. They live in three rooms, with poor furniture and of fair cleanliness. The father and nephew are laborers, often out of work. The mother does day's work and the daughter is at service. They spend for :

Rent—$8 per month	$ 96.00
Food—$2.16 a week	112.32
Fuel—50-84 cents a week . . . . ·	31.20
	$239.52

Clothing, etc., will bring this total to $250-$275. This is an honest family, belonging to one of the large Baptist churches.

Family No. 5, a mother and child, expends for

Food	$ 96.00
Fuel	30.00
Clothing	30.00
Amusements	10.00
Sickness	15.00
Other purposes	25.00
Total	$206.00

To this must be added house-rent, bringing the total to $250 or $275.

We next come to the great hard-working laboring class —the 47 per cent of the population which is, on the whole, most truly representative of the mass. They live in houses with three to six rooms, nearly always well furnished; they spend considerable for food and dress, and for churches and beneficial societies. They are honest and good-natured for the most part, but are not used to large responsibility.

No. 6, a family of three from this class—man, wife and seventeen-year-old son—earn and spend as follows:

INCOME.

Man—hod-carrier and laborer, $1.25–$2.00 a day— casual — averages $3.00 a week $150.00

Wife—washerwoman, Oct. to Mch., earns $5.00 to $6.00 a week, rest of year $1.50–$2.00, average, $3.50, 180.00

Son—porter in office building, $2.50 per week and board 6 days 125.00

$455.00

EXPENSE.

Rent, $22.00 a month, of which $14.00 is repaid by lodgers—net rent, $8.00　$96.00

Food—$3.50–$4.00 a week　190.00

Fuel 35.00

$321.00

Clothing and all other purposes, and savings . . . 134.00

$455.00

This family occupies a seven-room house, but rents out three of the rooms to lodgers. They have a nicely furnished parlor.

Three other families of the same class follow :

No. 7. Expenditure for one year, $338 (not including rent).   Number in family, adults 2, chidren 2.

Food	$110.00
Fuel	40.00
Clothing	50.00
Amusements	35.00
Sickness	40.00
Other purposes	63.00

No. 8. Expenditure for One Year, $520.00.

Number in Family, Adults 3, Children 2.

Expenditure for	Weekly.	Monthly.	Yearly.	Expenditure for	Weekly.	Monthly.	Yearly.
Rent	. . . .	$16.00	$192.00	Amusements . . .	. . . .	. . . .	$2.00
Food	$4.00	16.00	192.00	Sickness and d'th	. . . .	. . . .	10.00
Fuel	. . . .	. . . .	34.00	All other purposes	. . . .	. . . .	30.00
Clothing	. . . .	. . . .	60.00				

No. 9. Expenditure for One Year, About $600.00.

Number in Family, Adults 2, Children 7.

Expenditure for	Weekly.	Monthly.	Yearly.	Expenditure for	Weekly.	Monthly.	Yearly.
Rent	. . . .	. . . .	$200.00	Clothing	. . . .	5.00	60.00
Food	$5.00	$20.00	240.00	All other purposes	. . . .	. . . .	$28.00
Fuel	1.50	6.00	72.00				

Three other budgets are appended, representing a still better class :

No. 10.

Total income, $840.00.

Rent	$192.00
Food	260.00
Fuel	50.00
Clothing	25.00
Amusements	15.00
	$542.00

This is a small family—mother and daughter—who are evidently saving money.   The daughter is a teacher.

No. 11. Total expenditure, exclusive of rent, $683.

Food $378.00
Fuel 45.00
Clothing 100.00
Amusements 20.00
Sickness 50.00
Other purposes 90.00

There are four adults and three children in this family.
No. 12. Total expenditure, exclusive of rent, $805.

Food $420.00
Fuel 60.00
Clothing 150.00
Amusements 20.00
Sickness 5.00
Travel, and other purposes 150.00

This is one of the best families in the city; they keep
one servant. There are three adults and two children in
the family.

The class to which these last families belong is often
lost sight of in discussing the Negro. It is the germ of a
great middle class, but in general its members are curiously
hampered by the fact that, being shut off from the world
about them, they are the aristocracy of their own people,
with all the responsibilities of an aristocracy, and yet they,
on the one hand, are not prepared for this rôle, and their
own masses are not used to looking to them for leadership.
As a class they feel strongly the centrifugal forces of class
repulsion among their own people, and, indeed, are compelled to feel it in sheer self-defence. They do not relish
being mistaken for servants; they shrink from the free and
easy worship of most of the Negro churches, and they
shrink from all such display and publicity as will expose
them to the veiled insult and depreciation which the
masses suffer. Consequently this class, which ought to
lead, refuses to head any race movement on the plea that
thus they draw the very color line against which they
protest. On the other hand their ability to stand

apart, refusing on the one hand all responsibility for the masses of the Negroes and on the other hand seeking no recognition from the outside world, which is not willingly accorded—their opportunity to take such a stand is hindered by their small economic resources. Even more than the rest of the race they feel the difficulty of getting on in the world by reason of their small opportunities for remunerative and respectable work. On the other hand their position as the richest of their race—though their riches are insignificant compared with their white neighbors— makes unusual social demands upon them. A white Philadelphian with $1500 a year can call himself poor and live simply. A Negro with $1500 a year ranks with the richest of his race and must usually spend more in proportion than his white neighbor in rent, dress and entertainment.

In every class thus reviewed there comes to the front a central problem of expenditure. Probably few poor nations waste more money by thoughtless and unreasonable expenditure than the American Negro, and especially those living in large cities like Philadelphia. First, they waste much money in poor food and in unhealthful methods of cooking. The meat bill of the average Negro family would surprise a French or German peasant or even an Englishman. The crowds that line Lombard street on Sundays are dressed far beyond their means ; much money is wasted in extravagantly furnished parlors, dining-rooms, guest chambers and other visible parts of the homes. Thousands of dollars are annually wasted in excessive rents, in doubtful " societies " of all kinds and descriptions, in amusements of various kinds, and in miscellaneous ornaments and gewgaws. All this is a natural heritage of a slave system, but it is not the less a matter of serious import to a people in such economic stress as Negroes now are. The Negro has much to learn of the Jew and Italian, as to living within his means and saving every penny from excessive and wasteful expenditures.

29. Property.—We must next inquire what part of these
incomes have been turned into real property. Philadelphia
keeps no separate account of her white and Negro real
estate owners and it is very difficult to get reliable data on
the subject. Even the house-to-house inquiry could but
approximate the truth on account of the number of houses
owned by Negroes but rented out through white real estate
agents. From the returns it appears that 123 of the 2441
families in the Seventh Ward or 5.3 per cent own property
in that ward; seventy-four other families own property
outside the ward, making in all 197 or 8 per cent of the
families who are property holders. It is possible that
omissions may raise this total to 10 per cent. The total
value of this property is partly conjectural but a careful
estimate would place it at about $1,000,000, or 4½ per
cent of the valuation of a ward where the Negroes form
42 per cent of the population.

Two estimates for the whole city represent the holdings
of the well-to-do Negroes, that is, those having $10,000
and more of property, as follows : [10]

From $ 10,000 to $ 15,000	27
" 15,000 to 25,000	10
" 25,000 to 50,000	11
" 50,000 to 100,000	4
" 100,000 to 500,000	1
	53

In all, these persons represent an ownership of at least
$1,500,000. The other property holders can only be
estimated ; the total ownership of property by Philadelphia
Negroes must be at least five millions, not including

---

[10] These estimates are by lifelong residents of Philadelphia, who have
had unusual opportunity of knowing the men of whom they speak. One
says, "I have . . . prepared an estimate which I herein enclose. I
have endeavored to be as conservative as possible. There are, doubtless,
several omitted because they are not known, or if known are not now
thought of; but I believe the estimate is approximately correct."

church property. Comparing this with estimates in the past, we have : [11]

1821, real estate, assessed value, $112,464; real value, $281,162
1832, " " . . . . " " 357,000
1838, " " . . . . " " 322,532
1848, " " . . . . " " 531,809
1855, real and personal estate . . . . . . " " 2,685,693
1898, " " " " . . . . . . " " 5,000,000

In 1849 the returns of the investigation showed that 7.4 per cent of the Negroes in the county owned property, and 5.5 per cent in the city proper, compared with 5.3 per

[11] The figures for 1821 are from assessors' reports, quoted in the investigation of 1838. The figures for 1832 are from a memorial to the Legislature, in which the Negroes say that by reference to the receipts of taxpayers which were "actually produced," they paid at least $2500 in taxes, and had also $100,000 in church property. From this the inquiry of 1838 estimates that they owned $357,000 outside church property. The same study estimates the property of Negroes in 1838 as follows:

	Real Estate (true value).	Personal Property.
City	$241,962	$505,322
Northern Liberties	26,700	35,539
Kensington	2,255	3,825
Spring Garden	5,935	21,570
Southwark	15,355	26,848
Moyamensing	30,325	74,755
	$322,532	$667,859
Encumbrances	12,906	
	$309,626	

The report says: "This amount must, of course, be received as only an approximation of the truth." Fifteen church edifices, a cemetery and hall are not included in the above. "Condition," etc., 1838. pp. 7, 8.

The investigation in 1847–48, gave the following results:

	Value Real Estate.	Encumbrances.
City	$368,842	$78,421
Spring Garden	27,150	11,050
Northern Liberties	40,675	13,440
Southwark	31,544	5,915
Moyamensing	51,973	20,216
West Philadelphia	11,625	1,400
	$531,809	$130,442

cent in the Seventh Ward to-day. In this comparison,
however, we must consider the enormous increase in the
value of Philadelphia real estate.

This property was distributed as follows:

	WHOLE NUM-BER HEADS OF FAMILIES.	OWNERS OF REAL ESTATE.	PER CENT.
City	2562	141	5.5
Spring Garden	272	44	16.1
Northern Liberties	202	23	11.3
Southwark	287	30	10.4
Moyamensing	866	52	6.0
West Philadelphia	73	25	34.4
	4262	315	7.4

The occupations of the 315 freeholders was as follows:

78 laborers.
49 traders.
41 mechanics.
35 coachmen and hackmen.
28 waiters.
20 barbers.
11 professional men.
53 females.

315

The personal property was as follows:

AMOUNT.	CITY.	SPRING GARDEN.	NORTHERN LIBERTIES.	SOUTHWARK.	MOYAMENSING	WEST PHILADELPHIA	TOTAL.
Under $25.	570	66	62		259	5	
$25–$50.	772	79	102		160	16	
$50–$100.	404	38	63		134	9	
$100–$500.	650	19	83	102	291	42	
$500–$20,000.	156		5	2	5	1	
No Estate.	6				15		
Total personal property.	$455,620	$9,562	$34,044	$30,402	$90,553	$12,065	$632,246
Average.	$178.63	$47.33	$108.07	$105.30	$106.63	$151.57	$147.52

"Statistical Inquiry," etc., p. 15.

Taking the heads of the 123 families known to live in the Seventh Ward and to own real estate we find that they were born as follows:

Philadelphia	41	= 41 = 33⅓ per cent.
Pennsylvania	7 ⎫	
Maryland	22 ⎪	
Virginia	21 ⎪	
South	13 ⎬ 82 = 66⅔ per cent.	
Delaware and New Jersey	8 ⎪	
Other parts of United States and	⎪	
abroad	7 ⎪	
Unknown	4 ⎭	

$$123$$

A comparison between 1838 and 1848 was made by Needles' " Progress," etc., pp. 8, 9.

	1837.	1847.	Increase.
Real estate, less incumbrances .	$309,626	$401,362	$91,736
House and water rents	161,482	200,697	39,225
Taxes	3,253	6,308	3,056

The Inquiry of 1856, pp. 15, 16, declares that the previous year the Negroes owned:

Real and personal property (true value)	$2,685,693.00
Taxes paid -	9,766.42
House, water and ground rent	396,782.27

A detailed estimate for 1897 gives the following:

Value of Estate.	Number of Estates.	Total.
$250,000–$500,000	1 . . . = . .	$350,000
100,000	1 . . . = . .	100,000
80,000	1 . . . = . .	80,000
75,000	1 . . . = . .	75,000
60,000	1 . . . = . .	60,000
40,000	4 . . . = . .	160,000
35,000	3 . . . = . .	105,000
30,000	4 . . . = . .	120,000
20,000	10 . . . = . .	200,000
15,000	11 . . . = . .	165,000
10,000	16 . . . = . .	160,000
	52	$1,575,000

The total of $1,575,000 is the estimated wealth of the well-to-do.

This estimate is as reliable as can be obtained, and is probably not far from the real facts.

The eighty-two not born in Philadelphia have lived there
as follows :

Over 2 and under 10 years 5
10 to 14 years 7
15 to 19 "　　. 7
20 to 24 "　　. 14
25 to 29 "　　. 8
30 to 34 "　　. 8
35 to 39 "　　. 16
40 to 44 "　　. 4
45 to 49 "　　. 3
50 to 54 "　　. 3
60 years and over 3
Unknown 4
　　　　　　　　　　　　　　　　　　　　　　—
　　　　　　　　　　　　　　　　　　　　　　82

Nineteen have lived less than twenty years in the city
and fifty-nine, twenty years or more.

The occupations of the 123 property owners were as
follows :

Caterers	22	Hotel keepers and restaurateurs	3
Waiters	12	Cooks	2
Porters and Janitors	10	Undertakers	2
Housewives	9	School-teachers	2
Laundresses	8	Barbers	2
Mechanics	7	Physicians	2
Coachmen	6	Shrouder of dead	1
Clerks in public service	4	Newspaper publisher	1
Drivers and teamsters	4	Real estate dealer	1
Upholsterers	3	Sexton	1
Employment agents	3	No occupation	3
Merchants	3	Unknown	2
Stewards	3		—
Ministers	3		123
Hod-carriers and laborers	2		
Policemen and watchmen	2		

This shows that the real estate owners are either Philadelphia born or old residents and that the mass of them
are caterers and house servants, with a sprinkling of those
representing the newer employments as clerks in public
service, merchants, and the like.

Of these one hundred and twenty-three families

62 own the houses they occupy.

20 own the houses they occupy, and also other real estate in
the city.

7 own the houses they occupy, own other real estate in the
city, and also own real estate elsewhere.

5 own homes outside the city, and other real estate elsewhere.

22 own real estate in the city.

7 own real estate in the city and elsewhere also.

In other words, 89 own homes in the city, and 34 own
real estate somewhere.

Returns from forty of these holders indicate a total holding of $250,000, or if we add in one large estate, $650,000.
Other less definite but fairly reliable returns raise the total
ownership of property in the Seventh Ward to $1,000,000
or more. Sixty-three of the seventy-four owning property
outside the city report $49,010 in real estate.[12] In none
of these returns has there been any account of the mortgage indebtedness taken, nor is there any means of ascer-
taining this debt.[13]

On the whole the statistics show comparatively few
Negro property holders in Philadelphia. In a city where
the percentage of home owners is unusually large, over 94
per cent of the Negroes appear from the imperfect returns
available to be renters. There are several reasons for this:
first, the Negroes distrust all saving institutions since
the fatal collapse of the Freedmen's Bank; secondly, they
have difficulty in buying homes in decent neighborhoods;
thirdly, the rising price of real estate, and the falling off of
wage and industrial opportunity for the Negro must be
taken into account. Finally a curious effect of color

---

[12] There is more property than this owned, but only the answers that
seemed reliable and definite were recorded. Most of this property is in
the country districts of the South.

[13] Many efforts were made to get official data on the matter of property,
but the authorities had no way of even approximately distinguishing the
races.

prejudice, to be discussed later, has had enormous influence
in concentrating Negro population in localities where it was
hard to buy homes.   All these are cogent reasons, and yet
they are not enough to excuse the Negroes from not buying
much more property than they have.   Much of the money
that should have gone into homes has gone into costly
church edifices, dues to societies, dress and entertainment.
If the Negroes had bought little homes as persistently as
they have worked to develop a church and secret society
system, and had invested more of their earnings in savings-
banks and less in clothes they would be in a far better
condition to demand industrial opportunity than they are
to-day.

This does not mean that the Negro is lazy or a spend-
thrift; it simply means misdirected energies which cause
the Negro people yearly to waste thousands of dollars in
rents and live in poor homes when they might with proper
foresight do much better.

There are some signs of awakening to this fact among
the Negroes. Lately they are just beginning to understand
and profit by the Building and Loan Associations.   Forty-
one families in the Seventh Ward, or about 2 per cent,
belong now to such associations and the number is increasing.   Outside the Seventh Ward as large and probably a
larger percentage belong to co-operative home-buying
societies. The peculiar phenomenon among the colored
people, however, is the wide development of beneficial and
secret orders. Three hundred and six families, or 17 per
cent of the Negroes of the ward, are reported as belonging
to beneficial societies and probably 25 per cent or more
actually belong. Beside these there are the petty insurance
societies, to which 1021 families or 42 per cent belong.
In more prosperous times this membership may reach 50 or
60 per cent or a total of at least 4000 men, women and
children. The beneficial and secret societies, being organizations of Negroes, will be spoken of later. The petty

insurance societies are for the most part conducted by whites. Some of these are reliable enterprises, and by careful management and honest dealing do something to encourage the saving spirit among the Negroes. It is doubtful, however, if they form the best kind of incentive, and probably they stand in the way of the savings-bank and building association. Only a few deserve this qualified approval. The large majority are little better than licensed gambling operations; it is a disgrace that a great municipality allows them to prey upon the people in the manner they do.[14] They usually rest on no sound business principles; they take any and all risks, generally without medical examination and depend on lapses in payments and bold cheating to make money. Even the best conducted of these societies have to depend on the unreturned contributions of persons who cannot keep up their payments, to make both ends meet.

There were in 1897 thirty-one insurance societies doing business in the Seventh Ward. The following table gives the weekly premiums required for sick and death benefits in one society:

RATES AND DEATH BENEFITS.
Weekly Dues for Benefits Payable at Death only.

Age.	$100 Benefit.	$200 Benefit.
12–15	$0.04	$0.07
15–25	.05	.09
25–30	.06	.11
30–35	.07	.13
35–40	.08	.15
40–45	.10	.18
45–50	.12	.23
50–53	.14	.26
53–55	.15	.28
55–58	.18	.35
58–60	.20	.39

[14] For an account of a partial investigation of this subject and some attempts at reform, see "Report of Citizens' Permanent Relief Committee, etc., 1893-4," pp. 31, ff. Cf. Also the work of the Star Kitchen at Seventh and Lombard streets, Philadelphia.

This is at the rate of $46.80 to $52 for a $1000 life policy at the age of 43, which can be had in regular companies for about $35. The excess represents the expense of collection and the gambler's risk.

SICKNESS AND ACCIDENT BENEFITS.
Weekly Dues for Specified Sums per Week.

Age next Birthday.	$4.00.	$5.00.	$6.00.	$7.00.	$8.00.	$10.00.
12–20	.10	.13	.16	.19	.22	.25
20–25	.11	.14	.17	.20	-23	.26
25–30	.12	.15	.18	.21	.24	.27
30–35	.14	.17	.20	.23	.26	.29
35–40	.15	.18	.21	.24	.27	.30
40–43	.17	.20	.23	.26	.29	.32
43–45	.18	.21	.24	.27	.30	.33
45–48	.19	.22	.25	.28	.31	.34
48–50	.20	.23	.26	.29	.32	.35
50–53	.22	.25	.28	.31	.34	.37
53–55	.23	.26	.29	.32	.35	.38
55–58	.24	.27	.30	.33	.37	.41
58–60	.28	.31	.34	.37	.41	.44

Children—Age, 2 to 11 years.

Amount payable to children after their certificates have been issued for the following periods:

Three months, one-third; six months, one-half; nine months, three-fourths; one year, full amount.

Death benefits, $40.

Weekly dues, 5 cents.

Upon payment of 10 cents weekly dues, children from six to eleven years will be paid weekly sick benefits of $2.50.

Membership fee for children, 50 cents.

Membership fee for adults, $1.

Into these companies a large part of the income of many families goes. For instance, let us examine the expenditures of certain actual families for such insurance, remembering that the total income of these families is in most cases $20 to $40 a month.

Monthly.

1. A family of 2 adults and 2 children (stevedore) . . $3.29
2. A family of 2 adults have for 10 years paid 1.00
3. A family of 4 adults 2.20
4. A family of 4 adults 2.40
5. A family of 1 adult and 1 child 2.00
6. A family of 4 adults 1.84

Monthly.

7. A family of 1 adult $2.57
8. A family of 2 adults (waiter) 2.20
9. A family of 2 adults (servant) 1.50
10. A family of 5 adults and 2 children (laborer) . . . 3.00
11. A family of 2 adults and 3 children (stevedore) . . 1.44
12. A family of 9 adults and 1 child 5.00
13. A family of 8 adults and 4 children 4.20
14. A family of 9 adults 4.43
15. A family of 2 adults 2.50
16. A family of 2 adults (stevedore) 3.00
17. A family of 2 adults (stevedore) 3.00
18. A family of 10 adults 8.50
19. A family of 2 adults, 1 child (stevedore) 5.00
20. A family of 5 adults, 1 child 5.00
21. A family of 3 adults 3.90
22. A family of 4 adults, 1 child (laborer) 5.00
23. A family of 2 adults, 3 children (waiter) 4.60

It is impossible to get accurate returns as to the total amount spent by the Negroes of the Seventh Ward for insurance in such societies, but answers to questions on this point indicate a total expenditure of approximately $25,000 annually. For this enormous outlay something comes back in the benefits, but probably much less than half. The method of conducting these societies puts a premium on dishonesty and misrepresentation and a tax on honesty and health. A certain class of the insured get sick regularly and draw benefits and are winked at by the societies as a paying advertisement on the street. Their honest neighbors on the other hand will struggle on and work for years, paying regularly—in some cases five, ten and fifteen or more years in various societies—only to be cheated out of their insurance by rascally agents, or conniving home offices, or their own failure at the last moment to keep up payments. Of course the sum involved is too small, and the cheated persons too unknown and lowly to lead to litigation. Let us take some examples :[15]

---

[15] Once in a while the affairs of one of these companies are revealed to the public, as for instance, the following noted in the Public *Ledger*,

1. This family lost $100 paid in for insurance, by final lapse in payments. The woman was sixty years old, and poor.

2. This family belonged to the ———— society ten years and paid $12 a year. Finally fell seven days in arrears with payments, and was dropped. Had received $65 in benefits.

3. This family had paid in $50; was one day behind and was dropped.

4. This family had a woman insured for $2.50 a week, and $50 at death. She received no sick benefits at all,

---

October 20, 1896. The company became bankrupt, and its affairs were found hopelessly involved.

" This was the scheme, according to the former agent and some of the certificate holders. Upon the payment of ten cents a week for seven years, the subscriber was promised $100, to be paid at the end of the seventh year. In a year ten cents a week would amount to $5.20; in seven years to $36.40. The Keystone Investment Company promised to give $100 for $36.40.

" Later the assessment was raised to fifteen cents a week. This would amount in seven years to $54.60, for which sum $100 was promised in return. Some few of the certificate holders paid twenty cents a week, it is said. This, in seven years, would amount to $72.80, for which sum, according to the agreement, the certificate holder was to be paid $100.

" Just how many subscribers the company had it is impossible to learn from the officers. A gentleman, who has a store next door to the company's office, said yesterday that a great many people went there each week to pay their assessments. They appeared to be poor people, he said. There were a great many Negroes among them, and some of them, he said, came from New Jersey.

" The concern started in business in 1891, and has always occupied its present quarters, which are very unpretentious, by the way, for a financial company of any standing. A lady residing on Girard avenue, east of Hanover street, yesterday related her experience with the company as follows:

" 'I invested in certificates for my mother and my little daughter, paying fifteen cents a week on each. The agreement was that each was to receive $100 at the end of seven years. I have been paying for my little girl nearly three years, and for my mother nearly two years. It will be two years next Christmas. The payments were made regularly. On both certificates I have paid in about $35.' "

and only $20 at death. They said: "We stint ourselves of our victuals to keep up and then lose it all."

5. A family who put $75 into a society and lost it all.

6. A mother was in the ———— society two years. When she was taken sick, she sent her child to notify them; they took no notice of this on the ground that the notification by a child was not legal, and paid her nothing.

7. This man was a member of the ———— society fifteen years, and his wife seven years; paid in $354 in all and drew out $90 in benefits; the society then "discovered" that the man belonged to the G. A. R., and dropped him and kept the money.

8. This man belonged to a society seven years, at $1.30 per month; received $20 in benefits and lost the rest through a lapse in payments.

9. This family belonged to different societies eight years and lost all the money invested.

10. This person was a member of a society some time, when the collector absconded with the money, and the society refused to bear the responsibility.

11. The mother had paid $54.60 to a society for a death benefit, but at her death the society paid nothing.

12. The society collapsed and this person lost $75.

13. This family invested $1.23 a month with a society for thirteen years in order to receive $200 endowment. This was at the rate of $73.80 annually for a $1000 policy!

14. This man has paid in $88 so far, and has never received sick or other benefits.

15. This woman had belonged to a society for years and was once taken sick just before the agent called. When he came he was asked to return, as the sick woman was asleep. He did not return, and when a claim for sick benefits was made, it was denied on the ground that the woman had not paid her dues when the agent called.

In many other cases the matter of age is made a loophole for cheating; numbers of the Negroes do not know

their exact ages ; in such cases the insurance agent will
suggest an age, usually below the evident truth, and insert
it in the policy ; if the insured dies the physician guesses
at another age nearer the truth, and inserts it in the death
certificate. Thereupon the insurance company points to
the discrepancy, alleges an attempt to deceive on the part
of the insured, and either refuses to pay any of the policy
or generally offers to compound for a half or a third of the
amount promised. This is perhaps the most common form
of cheating outside the failure to account for the payments
of lapsed members. In some cases the home office pays
the death claim, and the local office or agent cheats the
insured.

Without doubt such societies meet outrageous attempts
at deception on the part of the insured ; and yet since their
methods of business put a premium on this sort of cheating they can hardly complain. The whole business is
nothing more than gambling, where one set of sharpers bet
against another set, and the honest hard-working but
ignorant toilers pay the bill.[16] With all the harm that
open policy-playing and other sorts of gambling do, it is to
be doubted if their effects on character are more deleterious
than this form of insurance business. The Negroes by the
crime of the Freedmen's Bank have been long prejudiced
against banks, and this business encourages their aversion
to the slow, sure methods of saving. If the colored people
are ever to learn " forehandedness," in place of the slip-
shod chance methods of living, the savings-bank must
soon replace the insurance society ; and that they could
support savings-banks in abundance is shown by the fact

---

[16] As before noted, I am aware that a few of these societies do not
wholly deserve this sweeping condemnation, and that all of them are
defended by certain short-sighted persons as encouraging savings. My
observation convinces me, however, of the substantial truth of my conclusions. Of course, all this has nothing to do with the legitimate life
insurance business.

that they annually invest between $75,000 and $100,000 in insurance societies in the city of Philadelphia.

It is not generally known how lucrative a business the exploitation of the Negro in various lines has become. In ornaments, clothes, entertainments, books and investment schemes, the shrewd and unscrupulous have a broad field of work, and it is being industriously cultivated, especially by whites and to some extent by certain classes of Negroes. Instead then of a struggling people being met by aid in the direction of their greatest weakness, they are surrounded by agencies which tend to make them more wasteful and dependent on chance than they are now. One has only to watch the pawn-brokers' shops on Saturday night in winter to see how largely Negroes support them; and it is but a step from the insurance society to the pawnshop and thence to the policy shop.

30. Family Life.—Among the masses of the Negro people in America the monogamic home is comparatively a new institution, not more than two or three generations old. The Africans were taken from polygamy and transplanted into a plantation where the home life was protected only by the caprice of the master, and practically unregulated polygamy and polyandry was the result, on the plantations of the West Indies. In States like Pennsylvania the marriage institution among slaves was early established and maintained. Consequently one meets among the Philadelphia Negroes the result of both systems—the looseness of plantation life and the strictness of Quaker teaching. Among the lowest class of recent immigrants and other unfortunates there is much sexual promiscuity and the absence of a real home life. Actual prostitution for gain is not as widespread as would at first thought seem natural. On the other hand, there are two widespread systems among the lowest classes, viz., temporary cohabitation and the support of men. Cohabitation of a more or less permanent character is a direct offshoot

of the plantation life and is practiced considerably ; in
distinctly slum districts, like that at Seventh and Lombard, from 10 to 25 per cent of the unions are of this
nature. Some of them are simply common-law marriages
and are practically never broken. Others are compacts,
which last for two to ten years ; others for some months ;
in most of these cases the women are not prostitutes, but
rather ignorant and loose. In such cases there is, of course,
little home life, rather a sort of neighborhood life, center-
ing in the alleys and on the sidewalks, where the children
are educated. Of the great mass of Negroes this class
forms a very small percentage and is absolutely without social standing. They are the dregs which indicate
the former history and the dangerous tendencies of the
masses. The system of supporting men is one common
among the prostitutes of all countries, and widespread
among the Negro women of the town. Two little colored
girls walking along South street stopped before a gaudy
pair of men's shoes displayed in a shop window, and one
said : " That's the kind of shoes I'd buy my fellow ! " The
remark fixed their life history ; they were from among the
prostitutes of Middle Alley, or Ratcliffe street, or some
similar resort, where each woman supports some man from
the results of her gains. The majority of the well-dressed
loafers whom one sees on Locust street near Ninth, on Lombard near Seventh and Seventeenth, on Twelfth near Kater,
and in other such localities, are supported by prostitutes and
political largesse, and spend their time in gambling. They
are absolutely without home life, and form the most dangerous class in the community, both for crime and political
corruption.

Leaving the slums and coming to the great mass of the
Negro population we see undoubted effort has been made
to establish homes. Two great hindrances, however, cause
much mischief : the low wages of men and the high rents.
The low wages of men make it necessary for mothers to

work and in numbers of cases to work away from home several days in the week. This leaves the children without guidance or restraint for the better part of the day—a thing disastrous to manners and morals. To this must be added the result of high rents, namely, the lodging system. Whoever wishes to live in the centre of Negro population, near the great churches and near work, must pay high rent for a decent house. This rent the average Negro family cannot afford, and to get the house they sub-rent a part to lodgers. As a a consequence, 38 per cent of the homes of the Seventh Ward have unknown strangers admitted freely into their doors. The result is, on the whole, pernicious, especially where there are growing children. Moreover, the tiny Philadelphia houses are ill suited to a lodging system. The lodgers are often waiters, who are at home between meals, at the very hours when the housewife is off at work, and growing daughters are thus left unprotected. In some cases, though this is less often, servant girls and other female lodgers are taken. In such ways the privacy and intimacy of home life is destroyed, and elements of danger and demoralization admitted. Many families see this and refuse to take lodgers, and move where they can afford the rent without help. This involves more deprivations to a socially ostracized race like the Negro than to whites, since it often means hostile neighbors or no social intercourse. If a number of Negroes settle together, the real estate agents dump undesirable elements among them, which some enthusiastic association has driven from the slums.

There are a large number of waiters, porters and servant girls in the city who naturally have no home life and are exposed to peculiar temptations. The church is the rallying place of the best class of these young people, and it attempts to furnish their amusements. Loafing and promenading the streets is the only other entertainment most of these young folks have. They form a serious problem, to which the lodging system is the only attempted answer, and that a dangerous one. Homes and clubs properly conducted ought to be opened for them. A Young Men's Christian Association which would not degenerate into an endless prayer meeting might meet the wants of the young men.

The home life of the middle laboring class lacks many of the pleasant features of good homes. Traces of plantation customs still persist, and there is a widespread custom of seeking amusement outside the home; thus the home becomes a place for a hurried meal now and then, and lodging. Only on Sundays does the general gathering in the front room, the visits and leisurely dinner, smack of proper home life. Nevertheless, the spirit of home life is steadily growing. Nearly all the housewives deplore the lodging system and the work that keeps them away from home; and there is a widespread desire to remedy these evils and the other evil which is akin to them, the allowing of children and young women to be out unattended at night.

In the better class families there is a pleasant family life of distinctly Quaker characteristics. One can go into such homes in the Seventh Ward and find all the quiet comfort and simple good-hearted fare that one would expect among well-bred people. In some cases the homes are lavishly furnished, in others they are homely and old-fashioned. Even in the best homes, however, there is easily detected a tendency to let the communal church and society life trespass upon the home. There are fewer strictly family gatherings than would be desirable, fewer simple neighborhood gatherings and visits; in their place are the church teas, the hall concerts, or the elaborate parties given by the richer and more ostentatious. These things are of no particular moment to the circle of families involved, but they set an example to the masses which may be misleading. The mass of the Negro people must be taught sacredly to

guard the home, to make it the centre of social life and
moral guardianship. This it is largely among the best
class of Negroes, but it might be made even more conspicuously so than it is. Such emphasis undoubtedly
means the decreased influence of the Negro church, and
that is a desirable thing.

On the whole, the Negro has few family festivals; birth-
days are not often noticed, Christmas is a time of church
and general entertainments, Thanksgiving is coming to be
widely celebrated, but here again in churches as much as
in homes. The home was destroyed by slavery, struggled
up after emancipation, and is again not exactly threatened,
but neglected in the life of city Negroes. Herein lies food
for thought.

CHAPTER XII.

THE ORGANIZED LIFE OF NEGROES.

31. History of the Negro Church in Philadelphia.—
We have already followed the history of the rise of the
Free African Society, which was the beginning of the
Negro Church in the North.[1] We often forget that the
rise of a church organization among Negroes was a curious
phenomenon. The church really represented all that was
left of African tribal life, and was the sole expression of
the organized efforts of the slaves. It was natural that
any movement among freedmen should centre about their
religious life, the sole remaining element of their former
tribal system. Consequently when, led by two strong men,
they left the white Methodist Church, they were naturally
unable to form any democratic moral reform association;
they must be led and guided, and this guidance must have
the religious sanction that tribal government always has.
Consequently Jones and Allen, the leaders of the Free
African Society, as early as 1791 began regular religious
exercises, and at the close of the eighteenth century there
were three Negro churches in the city, two of which were
independent.[2]

---

[1] Cf. Chapter III.

[2] St. Thomas', Bethel and Zoar. The history of Zoar is of interest. It
"extends over a period of one hundred years, being as it is an offspring
of St. George's Church, Fourth and Vine streets, the first Methodist
Episcopal church to be established in this country, and in whose edifice
the first American Conference of that denomination was held. Zoar
Church had its origin in 1794, when members of St. George's Church
established a mission in what was then known as Campingtown, now
known as Fourth and Brown streets, at which place its first chapel was
built. There it remained until 1883, when economic and sociological

St. Thomas' Church has had a most interesting history. It early declared its purpose "of advancing our friends in a true knowledge of God, of true religion, and of the ways and means to restore our long lost race to the dignity of men and of Christians." [3] The church offered itself to the Protestant Episcopal Church and was accepted on condition that they take no part in the government of the general church. Their leader, Absalom Jones, was ordained deacon and priest, and took charge of the church. In 1804 the church established a day school which lasted until 1816. [4] In 1849 St. Thomas' began a series of attempts to gain full recognition in the Church by a demand for delegates to the Church gatherings. The Assembly first declared that it was not expedient to allow Negroes to take part. To this the vestry returned a dignified answer, asserting that "expediency is no plea against the violation of the great principles of charity, mercy, justice and truth." Not until 1864 was the Negro body received into full fellowship with the Church. In the century and more of its existence St. Thomas' has always represented a high grade of intelligence, and to-day it still represents the most cultured and wealthiest of the Negro population and the Philadelphia born residents. Its membership has conse-

---

causes made necessary the selection of a new site. The city had grown, and industries of a character in which the Negroes were not interested had developed in the neighborhood, and, as the colored people were rapidly moving to a different section of the city, it was decided that the church should follow, and the old building was sold. Through the liberality of Colonel Joseph M. Bennett a brick building was erected on Melon street, above Twelfth.

"Since then the congregation has steadily increased in numbers, until in August of this year it was found necessary to enlarge the edifice. The corner-stone of the new front was laid two months ago. The present membership of the church is about 550."—*Public Ledger*, November 15, 1897.

[3] See Douglass' "Annals of St. Thomas'."

[4] It was then turned into a private school and supported largely by an English educational fund.

quently always been small, being 246 in 1794, 427 in 1795, 105 in 1860, and 391 in 1897.[5]

The growth of Bethel Church, founded by Richard Allen, on South Sixth Street, has been so phenomenal that it belongs to the history of the nation rather than to any one city. From a weekly gathering which met in Allen's blacksmith shop on Sixth near Lombard, grew a large church edifice; other churches were formed under the same general plan, and Allen, as overseer of them, finally took the title of bishop and ordained other bishops. The Church, under the name of African Methodist Episcopal, grew and spread until in 1890 the organization had 452,725 members, 2481 churches and $6,468,280 worth of property.[6]

By 1813[7] there were in Philadelphia six Negro churches with the following membership : [8]

St. Thomas', P. E.	560
Bethel, A. M. E.	1272
Zoar, M. E.	80
Union, A. M. E.	74
Baptist, Race and Vine Streets	80
Presbyterian	300
	2366

The Presbyterian Church had been founded by two Negro missionaries, father and son, named Gloucester, in 1807.[9] The Baptist Church was founded in 1809. The inquiry of 1838 gives these statistics of churches:

---

[5] St. Thomas' has suffered often among Negroes from the opprobrium of being "aristocratic," and is to-day by no means a popular church among the masses. Perhaps there is some justice in this charge, but the church has nevertheless always been foremost in good work and has many public spirited Negroes on its rolls.

[6] Cf. U. S. Census, Statistics of Churches, 1890.

[7] In 1809 the leading Negro churches formed a " Society for Suppressing Vice and Immorality," which received the endorsement of Chief Justice Tilghman, Benjamin Franklin, Jacob Rush, and others.

[8] " Condition of Negroes, 1838," pp. 39–40.

[9] Cf. Robert Jones' "Fifty years in Central Church." John Gloucester began preaching in 1807 at Seventh and Bainbridge.

Denomination.	No. Churches.	Members.	Annual Expenses.	Value of Property.	Incumbrance.
Episcopalian	1	100	$1,000	$36,000	. . .
Lutheran	1	10	120	3,000	$1,000
Methodist	8	2,860	2,100	50,800	5,100
Presbyterian	2	325	1,500	20,000	1,000
Baptist	4	700	1,300	4,200	. . .
Total	16	3,995	$6,020	$114,000	$7,100

Three more churches were added in the next ten years, and then a reaction followed.[10] By 1867 there were in all probability nearly twenty churches, of which we have statistics of seventeen :[11]

STATISTICS OF NEGRO CHURCHES, 1867.

Name.	Founded.	Number of Members.	Value of Property.	Pastors' Salary.
P. E.—				
St. Thomas'	1792	. .	. . .	. . .
Methodist—				
Bethel	1794	1,100	$50,000	$600
Union	1827	467	40,000	850
Wesley	1817	464	21,000	700
Zoar	1794	400	12,000	. . .
John Wesley	1844	42	3,000	No regular salary.
Little Wesley	1821	310	11,000	500
Pisgah	1831	116	4,600	430
Zion City Mission . . .	1858	90	4,500	. . .
Little Union	1837	200	. . .	. . .
Baptist—				
First Baptist	1809	360	5,000	. . .
Union Baptist	. .	400	7,000	600
Shiloh	1842	405	16,000	600
Oak Street	1827	137	. . .	. . .
Presbyterian—				
First Presbyterian	1807	200	8,000	. . .
Second Presbyterian . . .	1824	. .	. . .	. . .
Central Presbyterian . . .	1844	240	16,000	. . .

Since the war the growth of Negro churches has been by bounds, there being twenty-five churches and missions in 1880, and fifty-five in 1897.

---

[10] In 1847 there were 19 churches; 12 of these had 3974 members; 11 of the edifices cost $67,000. "Statistical Inquiry," 1848, pp. 29, 30.

In 1854 there were 19 churches reported and 1677 Sunday-school scholars. Bacon, 1856.

[11] See Inquiry of 1867.

So phenomenal a growth as this here outlined means more than the establishment of many places of worship. The Negro is, to be sure, a religious creature—most primitive folk are—but his rapid and even extraordinary founding of churches is not due to this fact alone, but is rather a measure of his development, an indication of the increasing intricacy of his social life and the consequent multiplication of the organ which is the function of his group life—the church. To understand this let us inquire into the function of the Negro church.

32. The Function of the Negro Church.—The Negro church is the peculiar and characteristic product of the transplanted African, and deserves especial study. As a social group the Negro church may be said to have antedated the Negro family on American soil; as such it has preserved, on the one hand, many functions of tribal organization, and on the other hand, many of the family functions. Its tribal functions are shown in its religious activity, its social authority and general guiding and co-ordinating work; its family functions are shown by the fact that the church is a centre of social life and intercourse; acts as newspaper and intelligence bureau, is the centre of amusements—indeed, is the world in which the Negro moves and acts. So far-reaching are these functions of the church that its organization is almost political. In Bethel Church, for instance, the mother African Methodist Episcopal Church of America, we have the following officials and organizations :

The Bishop of the District	
The Presiding Elder	} Executive.
The Pastor	
The Board of Trustees	Executive Council.
General Church Meeting	Legislative.
The Board of Stewards	
The Board of Stewardesses	} Financial Board.
The Junior Stewardesses	
The Sunday School Organization . . .	Educational System.
Ladies' Auxiliary, Volunteer Guild, etc.	Tax Collectors.

Ushers' Association	Police.
Class Leaders	
Local Preachers . . . . }	Sheriffs and Magistrates.
Choir	Music and Amusement.
Allen Guards	Militia.
Missionary Societies	Social Reformers.
Beneficial and Semi-Secret Societies, etc.	Corporations.

Or to put it differently, here we have a mayor, appointed from without, with great administrative and legislative powers, although well limited by long and zealously cherished custom ; he acts conjointly with a select council, the trustees, a board of finance, composed of stewards and stewardesses, a common council of committees and, occasionally, of all church members. The various functions of the church are carried out by societies and organizations. The form of government varies, but is generally some form of democracy closely guarded by custom and tempered by possible and not infrequent secession.

The functions of such churches in order of present emphasis are :

1. The raising of the annual budget.
2. The maintenance of membership.
3. Social intercourse and amusements.
4. The setting of moral standards.
5. Promotion of general intelligence.
6. Efforts for social betterment.

1. The annual budget is of first importance, because the life of the organization depends upon it. The amount of expenditure is not very accurately determined beforehand, although its main items do not vary much. There is the pastor's salary, the maintenance of the building, light and heat, the wages of a janitor, contributions to various church objects, and the like, to which must be usually added the interest on some debt. The sum thus required varies in Philadelphia from $200 to $5000. A small part of this is raised by a direct tax on each member. Besides this, voluntary contributions by members,

roughly gauged according to ability, are expected, and a strong public opinion usually compels payment. Another large source of revenue is the collection after the sermons on Sunday, when, amid the reading of notices and a subdued hum of social intercourse, a stream of givers walk to the pulpit and place in the hands of the trustee or steward in charge a contribution, varying from a cent to a dollar or more. To this must be added the steady revenue from entertainments, suppers, socials, fairs, and the like. In this way the Negro churches of Philadelphia raise nearly $100,000 a year. They hold in real estate $900,000 worth of property, and are thus no insignificant element in the economics of the city.

2. Extraordinary methods are used and efforts made to maintain and increase the membership of the various churches. To be a popular church with large membership means ample revenues, large social influence and a leadership among the colored people unequaled in power and effectiveness. Consequently people are attracted to the church by sermons, by music and by entertainments; finally, every year a revival is held, at which considerable numbers of young people are converted. All this is done in perfect sincerity and without much thought of merely increasing membership, and yet every small church strives to be large by these means and every large church to maintain itself or grow larger. The churches thus vary from a dozen to a thousand members.

3. Without wholly conscious effort the Negro church has become a centre of social intercourse to a degree unknown in white churches even in the country. The various churches, too, represent social classes. At St. Thomas' one looks for the well-to-do Philadelphians, largely descendants of favorite mulatto house servants, and consequently well-bred and educated, but rather cold and reserved to strangers or newcomers; at Central Presbyterian one sees the older, simpler set of respectable Philadelphians

with distinctly Quaker characteristics—pleasant but conservative; at Bethel may be seen the best of the great laboring class—steady, honest people, well dressed and well fed, with church and family traditions; at Wesley will be found the new arrivals, the sight-seers and the strangers to the city—hearty and easy-going people, who welcome all comers and ask few questions; at Union Baptist one may look for the Virginia servant girls and their young men; and so on throughout the city. Each church forms its own social circle, and not many stray beyond its bounds. Introductions into that circle come through the church, and thus the stranger becomes known. All sorts of entertainments and amusements are furnished by the churches: concerts, suppers, socials, fairs, literary exercises and debates, cantatas, plays, excursions, picnics, surprise parties, celebrations. Every holiday is the occasion of some special entertainment by some club, society or committee of the church; Thursday afternoons and evenings, when the servant girls are free, are always sure to have some sort of entertainment. Sometimes these exercises are free, sometimes an admission fee is charged, sometimes refreshments or articles are on sale. The favorite entertainment is a concert with solo singing, instrumental music, reciting, and the like. Many performers make a living by appearing at these entertainments in various cities, and often they are persons of training and ability, although not always. So frequent are these and other church exercises that there are few Negro churches which are not open four to seven nights in a week and sometimes one or two afternoons in addition.

Perhaps the pleasantest and most interesting social intercourse takes place on Sunday; the weary week's work is done, the people have slept late and had a good breakfast, and sally forth to church well dressed and complacent. The usual hour of the morning service is eleven, but people stream in until after twelve. The sermon is usually short and stirring, but in the larger churches elicits little

esponse other than an "Amen" or two. After the sermon
the social features begin ; notices on the various meetings
of the week are read, people talk with each other in subdued tones, take their contributions to the altar, and lin-
ger in the aisles and corridors long after dismission to laugh
and chat until one or two o'clock. Then they go home
to good dinners. Sometimes there is some special three
o'clock service, but usually nothing save Sunday school,
until night. Then comes the chief meeting of the day ;
probably ten thousand Negroes gather every Sunday night
in their churches. There is much music, much preaching,
some short addresses ; many strangers are there to be
looked at ; many beaus bring out their belles, and those
who do not gather in crowds at the church door and escort
the young women home. The crowds are usually well
behaved and respectable, though rather more jolly than
comports with a puritan idea of church services.

In this way the social life of the Negro centres in his
church—baptism, wedding and burial, gossip and court-
ship, friendship and intrigue—all lie in these walls. What
wonder that this central club house tends to become more
and more luxuriously furnished, costly in appointment
and easy of access !

4. It must not be inferred from all this that the
Negro is hypocritical or irreligious. His church is, to be
sure, a social institution first, and religious afterwards, but
nevertheless, its religious activity is wide and sincere. In
direct moral teaching and in setting moral standards for
the people, however, the church is timid, and naturally so,
for its constitution is democracy tempered by custom.
Negro preachers are often condemned for poor leadership
and empty sermons, and it is said that men with so
much power and influence could make striking moral reforms. This is but partially true. The congregation does
not follow the moral precepts of the preacher, but rather
the preacher follows the standard of his flock, and only

exceptional men dare seek to change this. And here it must be remembered that the Negro preacher is primarily an executive officer, rather than a spiritual guide. If one goes into any great Negro church and hears the sermon and views the audience, one would say: either the sermon is far below the calibre of the audience, or the people are less sensible than they look; the former explanation is usually true. The preacher is sure to be a man of executive ability, a leader of men, a shrewd and affable president of a large and intricate corporation. In addition to this he may be, and usually is, a striking elocutionist; he may also be a man of integrity, learning, and deep spiritual earnestness; but these last three are sometimes all lacking, and the last two in many cases. Some signs of advance are here manifest: no minister of notoriously immoral life, or even of bad reputation, could hold a large church in Philadelphia without eventual revolt. Most of the present pastors are decent, respectable men; there are perhaps one or two exceptions to this, but the exceptions are doubtful, rather than notorious. On the whole then, the average Negro preacher in this city is a shrewd manager, a respectable man, a good talker, a pleasant companion, but neither learned nor spiritual, nor a reformer.

The moral standards are therefore set by the congregations, and vary from church to church in some degree. There has been a slow working toward a literal obeying of the puritan and ascetic standard of morals which Methodism imposed on the freedmen; but condition and temperament have modified these. The grosser forms of immorality, together with theatre-going and dancing, are specifically denounced; nevertheless, the precepts against specific amusements are often violated by church members. The cleft between denominations is still wide, especially between Methodists and Baptists. The sermons are usually kept within the safe ground of a mild Calvinism, with much insistence on Salvation, Grace, Fallen Humanity and the like.

The chief function of these churches in morals is to conserve old standards and create about them a public opinion which shall deter the offender. And in this the Negro churches are peculiarly successful, although naturally the standards conserved are not as high as they should be.

5. The Negro churches were the birthplaces of Negro schools and of all agencies which seek to promote the intelligence of the masses ; and even to-day no agency serves to disseminate news or information so quickly and effectively among Negroes as the church. The lyceum and lecture here still maintain a feeble but persistent existence, and church newspapers and books are circulated widely. Night schools and kindergartens are still held in connection with churches, and all Negro celebrities, from a bishop to a poet like Dunbar, are introduced to Negro audiences from the pulpits.

6. Consequently all movements for social betterment are apt to centre in the churches. Beneficial societies in endless number are formed here ; secret societies keep in touch ; co-operative and building associations have lately sprung up ; the minister often acts as an employment agent ; considerable charitable and relief work is done and special meetings held to aid special projects.[12] The race problem in all its phases is continually being discussed, and, indeed, from this forum many a youth goes forth inspired to work.

Such are some of the functions of the Negro church, and a study of them indicates how largely this organization has come to be an expression of the organized life of Negroes in a great city.

33. **The Present Condition of the Churches.**—The 2441 families of the Seventh Ward were distributed among the various denominations, in 1896, as follows :

---

[12] Cf. Publications of Atlanta University No. 3, "Efforts of American Negroes for Social Betterment."

Families.

Methodists 842
Baptists 577
Episcopalians 156
Presbyterians 74
Catholic 69
Shakers 2
Unconnected and unknown 721
                                              ———
                                              2441

Probably half of the "unconnected and unknown" habitually attend church.

In the city at large the Methodists have a decided majority, followed by the Baptists, and further behind, the Episcopalians. Starting with the Methodists, we find three bodies : the African Methodist Episcopal, founded by Allen, the A. M. E. Zion, which sprung from a secession of Negroes from white churches in New York in the eighteenth century ; and the M. E. Church, consisting of colored churches belonging to the white Methodist Church, like Zoar.

The A. M. E. Church is the largest body and had, in 1897, fourteen churches and missions in the city, with a total membership of 3210, and thirteen church edifices, seating 6117 persons. These churches collected during the year, $27,074.13. Their property is valued at $202,229 on which there is a mortgage indebtedness of $30,000 to $50,000. Detailed statistics are given in the table on the next page.

These churches are pretty well organized, and are conducted with vim and enthusiasm. This arises largely from their system. Their bishops have been in some instances men of piety and ability like the late Daniel A. Payne. In other cases they have fallen far below this standard; but they have always been men of great influence, and had a genius for leadership—else they would not have been bishops. They have large powers of appointment and removal in the case of pastors, and thus each

A. M. E. Churches in Philadelphia, 1897.

Name of Church.	Number of Members.	No. of Societies: Missionary.	No. of Societies: Church Auxiliary.	Parsonage.	Seating Capacity.	General Church Support.	Local Church Expenses.	Pastor's Salary.	Missionary and Educational.	Charity.	Total Income.	Value of Church Property.	Indebtedness.
Bethel	1,104	1	21	1	1,500	$924.00	$1,560.00 (?)	$1,500.00	$137.45	$435.87	$4,557.32	$94,000.00	(?)
Murray Chapel	170	2	3	.	350	233.00	697.94	700.00	23.97	50.00	1,704.91	5,000.00	$137.00
Zion Mission	128	1	1	.	350	139.00	481.97	653.49	35.54	50.00	1,360.92	7,000.00	1,093.25
Germantown	119	2	2	.	450	156.87	1,685.26	1,000.00	39.83	41.18	2,913.14	14,500.00	7,400.00
Frankford	127	1	3	1	400	142.50	500.00 (?)	600.00	39.50	15.00	1,297.00	15,000.00	1,869.46
Darby	44	1	1	1	300	86.65	300.07	270.00	18.12	2.26	677.00	3,329.00	203.95
Allen Chapel	378	1	4	.	550	312.82	750.00 (?)	974.75	53.25	132.60	2,213.42	15,000.00	3,651.00
Disney	22	1	4	.	200	35.75	129.36	122.05	8.75	8.75	300.91	2,400.00	904.00
York	48	.	2	.	317	166.50	524.20	600.00	55.40	12.00	1,790.60	6,000.00	2,700.00
Tioga	.	.	.	.	.	10.33	182.42	286.05	.	.	478.80	.	.
Payne	25	.	1	.	200	20.13	583.68	47.62	1.25	8.38	661.46	.	.
Union	674	1	5	.	1,000	502.88	2,471.81	1,400.00	93.20	135.00	4,602.89	3,000.00	2,454.00
Mt. Pisgah	315	2	5	1	500	391.85	793.38	1,000.00	79.00	465.67	3,749.90	25,000.00	8,038.62
Morris Brown	46	2	2	1	.	74.75	287.58	265.62	8.93	8.88	645.86	12,000.00	7,162.00
Total	3,210	15	54	5	6,117	$3,137.03	$14,665.47	$9,368.58	$594.19	$1,358.84	$27,074.13	$202,229.00	$35,613.28

pastor, working under the eye of an inspiring chief, strains every nerve to make his church a successful organization. The bishop is aided by several presiding elders, who are traveling inspectors and preachers, and give advice as to appointments. This system results in great unity and power; the purely spiritual aims of the church, to be sure, suffer somewhat, but after all this peculiar organism is more than a church, it is a government of men.

The headquarters of the A. M. E. Church are in Philadelphia. Their publishing house, at Seventh and Pine, publishes a weekly paper and a quarterly review, besides some books, such as hymnals, church disciplines, short treatises, leaflets and the like. The receipts of this establishment in 1897 were $16,058.26, and its expenditures $14,119.15. Its total outfit and property is valued at $45,513.64, with an indebtedness of $14,513.64.

An episcopal residence for the bishop of the district has recently been purchased on Belmont avenue. The Philadelphia Conference disbursed from the general church funds in 1897, $985 to superannuated ministers, and $375 to widows of ministers. Two or three women missionaries visited the sick during the year and some committees of the Ladies' Mission Society worked to secure orphans' homes.[13] Thus throughout the work of this church there

---

[13] An account of the present state of the A. M. E. Church from its own lips is interesting, in spite of its somewhat turgid rhetoric. The following is taken from the minutes of Philadelphia Conference, 1897:

REPORT ON STATE OF THE CHURCH.

"To the Bishop and Conference: We your Committee on State of the Church beg leave to submit the following:

"Every truly devoted African Methodist is intensely interested in the condition of the church that was handed down to us as a precious heirloom from the hands of a God-fearing, self-sacrificing ancestry; the church that Allen planted in Philadelphia, a little over a century ago has enjoyed a marvelous development. Its grand march through the procession of a hundred years has been characterized by a series of brilliant

is much evidence of enthusiasm and persistent progress.[14]
There are three churches in the city representing the
A. M. E. Zion connection. They are:

Wesley . . . . Fifteenth and Lombard Sts.
Mount Zion . . . . Fifty-fifth above Market St.
Union . . . . Ninth St. and Girard Ave.

---

successes, completely refuting the foul calumnies cast against it and
overcoming every obstacle that endeavored to impede its onward march,
giving the strongest evidence that God was in the midst of her; she
should not be moved.

"From the humble beginnings in the little blacksmith shop, at Sixth
and Lombard streets, Philadelphia, the Connection has grown until we
have now fifty-five annual conferences, beside mission fields, with over
four thousand churches, the same number of itinerant preachers, near six
hundred thousand communicants, one and a half million adherents, with
six regularly organized and well-manned departments, each doing a
magnificent work along special lines, the whole under the immediate
supervision of eleven bishops, each with a marked individuality and all
laboring together for the further development and perpetuity of the
church. In this the Mother Conference of the Connection, we have
every reason to be grateful to Almighty God for the signal blessings He
has so graciously poured out upon us. The spiritual benedictions have
been many. In response to earnest effort and faithful prayers by both
pastors and congregations, nearly two thousand persons have professed
faith in Christ, during this conference year. Five thousand dollars have
been given by the membership and friends of the Connectional interests
to carry on the machinery of the church, besides liberal contributions for
the cause of missions, education, the Sunday-school Union and Church
Extension Departments, and beside all this, the presiding elder and
pastors have been made to feel that the people are perfectly willing to do
what they can to maintain the preaching of the word, that tends to
elevate mankind and glorify God.

"The local interests have not been neglected; new churches have been
built, parsonages erected, church mortgages have been reduced, auxiliary
societies to give everybody in the church a chance to work for God and
humanity, have been more extensively organized than ever before.

"The danger signal that we see here and there cropping out, which
is calculated to bring discredit upon the Church of Christ, is the unholy
ambition for place and power. The means ofttimes used to bring about
the desired results, cause the blush of shame to tinge the brow of

[14] Cf., *e. g.*, the account of the founding of new missions in the minutes
of the Philadelphia Conference, 1896.

No detailed statistics of these churches are available ;
the last two are small , the first is one of the largest and

Christian manhood. God always has and always will select those He
designs to use as the leaders of his Church.

"Political methods that are in too many instances resorted to, are contrary to the teaching and spirit of the Gospel of Christ. Fitness and
sobriety will always be found in the lead.

"Through mistaken sympathy we find that several incompetent men
have found their way into the ministerial ranks; men who can neither
manage the financial nor spiritual interests of any church or bring success
along any line, who are continuously on the wing from one conference to
the other. The time has come when the strictest scrutiny must be exercised as to purpose and fitness of candidates, and if admitted and found
to be continuous failures, Christian charity demands that they be given
an opportunity to seek a calling where they can make more success than
in the ministry. These danger signals that flash up now and then must
be observed and everything contrary to the teachings of God's word and
the spirit of the discipline weeded out. The church owes a debt of
gratitude to the fathers who have always remained loyal and true; who
labored persistently and well for the upbuilding of the connection, that
they can never repay.

"Particular care should be taken that no honorable aged minister of
our great Church should be allowed to suffer for the necessaries of life.
We especially commend to the consideration of every minister the
Ministers' Aid Association, which is now almost ready to be organized,
the object of which is to help assuage the grief and dry the tears of those
who have been left widowed and fatherless.

"Our Publication Department is making heroic efforts for the larger
circulation of our denominational papers and literature generally. These
efforts ought to be, and must needs be heartily seconded by the Church.
Lord Bacon says: 'Talking makes a ready man, writing an exact man,
but reading makes a full man.' We want our people at large to be brim-
ful of information relative to the growth of the church, the progress of
the race, the upbuilding of humanity and the glory of God.

"Our missionary work must not be allowed to retrograde. The banner
that Allen raised must not be allowed to trail, but must go forward until
the swarthy sons of Ham everywhere shall gaze with a longing and
loving look upon the escutcheon that has emblazoned on it, as its motto:
'The Fatherhood of God and the Brotherhood of man,' and the
glorious truth flashing over the whole world that Jesus Christ died to
redeem the universal family of mankind. Disasters and misfortunes
may come to us, but strong men never quail before adversities. The
clouds of to-day may be succeeded by the sunshine of to-morrow."

most popular in the city ; the pastor receives $1500 a year
and the total income of the church is between $4000 and
$5000.   It does considerable charitable work among its
aged members, and supports a large sick and death benefit
society.   Its property is worth at least $25,000.

Two other Methodist churches of different denominations are : Grace U. A. M. E., Lombard street, above Fifteenth ; St. Matthew Methodist Protestant, Fifty-eighth
and Vine streets.   Both these churches are small, although
the first has a valuable piece of property.

The Methodist Episcopal Church has six organizations
in the city among the Negroes ; they own church property
valued at $53,700, have a total membership of 1202, and an
income of $16,394 in 1897.   Of this total income, $1235,
or 7½ per cent, was given for benevolent enterprises.
These churches are quiet and well conducted, and although
not among the most popular churches, have nevertheless
a membership of old and respected citizens.

COLORED M. E. CHURCHES IN PHILADELPHIA, 1897.

Church.	Members.	Salary, etc., of Pastor.	Contributions to Presiding Elders and Bishops.	Value of Church.	Value of Parsonage.	Building and Improvements during Year.	Paid on Indebtedness.	Present Indebtedness.	Current Expenses.	Benevolent Collections.
Bainbridge Street	354	$1312	$151	$20,000	...	$190	$601	$4,433	$1274	$326
Frankford	72	720	35	1,500	...	15	146	130	155	87
Germantown . .	165	828	72	4,000	...	. . . .	400	1,000	270	177
Haven	72	440	39	3,400	...	24	. . .	3,836	277	25
Waterloo Street .	31	221	27	800	...	450	50	90	22	37
Zoar	508	1270	220	20,000	$4000	3522	2171	5,800	257	583
Total	1202	$4791	544	$49,700	$4000	$4201	$3368	$15,289	$2255	$1235

There were in 1896 seventeen Baptist churches in Philadelphia, holding property valued at more than $300,000,
having six thousand members, and an annual income of,
probably, $30,000 to $35,000.   One of the largest churches
has in the last five years raised between $17,000 and
$18,000.

COLORED BAPTIST CHURCHES OF PHILADELPHIA, 1896.

Church.	Member-ship.	Value of Property.	Expended in Missions, Local and Foreign.	Annual Income.
Monumental	435	$30,000	$7.00	. . .
Cherry Street	800	50,000	. . .	. . .
Union	1,020	50,000	58.10	. . .
St. Paul	422	25,000	1.00	. . .
Ebenezer	189	12,000	3.36	. . .
Macedonia	76	1,000	3.00	. . .
Bethsaida	78	. . .	. . .	. . .
Haddington	50	. . .	. . .	. . .
Germantown	305	24,800	. . .	. . .
Grace	57	2,000	5.50	. . .
Shiloh	1,000	50,000	. . .	$3,600
Holy Trinity	287	10,000	3.00	. . .
Second, Nicetown	164	2,000	9.73	. . .
Zion	700	40,000	. . .	. . .
Providence	. .	. . .	. . .	. . .
Cherry Street Mission	. .	. . .	. . .	. . .
Tabernacle	. .	. . .	. . .	. . .
Total	5,583	$296,800		. . .

The Baptists are strong in Philadelphia, and own many large and attractive churches, such as, for instance, the Union Baptist Church, on Twelfth street ; Zion Baptist, in the northern part of the city ; Monumental, in West Philadelphia, and the staid and respectable Cherry Street Church. These churches as a rule have large membership. They are, however, quite different in spirit and methods from the Methodists ; they lack organization, and are not so well managed as business institutions. Consequently statistics of their work are very hard to obtain, and indeed in many cases do not even exist for individual churches. On the other hand, the Baptists are peculiarly clannish and loyal to their organization, keep their pastors a long time, and thus each church gains an individuality not noticed in Methodist churches. If the pastor is a strong, upright character, his influence for good is marked. At the same time, the Baptists have in their ranks a larger percentage of illiteracy than probably any other church, and it is often possible for an inferior man to hold a large church for years and allow it to stagnate and retrograde. The Baptist policy is extreme democracy applied to church affairs, and no wonder that this often results in a pernicious dictatorship. While many of the Baptist pastors of Philadelphia are men of ability and education, the general average is below that of the other churches—a fact due principally to the ease with which one can enter the Baptist ministry.[15] These churches support a small publishing house in the city, which issues a weekly paper. They do some charitable work, but not much.[16]

There are three Presbyterian churches in the city:

Name.	Members.	Value of Property.	Annual Income.	
Berean	98	$75,000	$1,135	Parsonage.
Central	430	50,000	1,800	Parsonage.
First African	105	25,000	1,538	

Central Church is the oldest of these churches and has an interesting history. It represents a withdrawal from the First African Presbyterian Church in 1844. The congregation first worshiped at Eighth and Carpenter streets,

[15] Baptists themselves recognize this. One of the speakers in a recent association meeting, as reported by the press, "deprecated the spirit shown by some churches in spreading their differences to their detriment as church members, and in the eyes of their white brethren; and he recommended that unworthy brethren from other States, who sought an asylum of rest here, be not admitted to local pulpits except in cases where the ministers so applying are personally known or vouched for by a resident pastor. The custom of recognizing as preachers men incapable of doing good work in the pulpit, who were ordained in the South after they had failed in the North, was also condemned, and the President declared that the times demand a ministry that is able to preach. The practice of licensing incapable brethren for the ministry, simply to please them, was also looked upon with disfavor, and it was recommended that applicants for ordination be required to show at least ability to read intelligently the Word of God or a hymn."

[16] One movement deserves notice—the Woman's Auxiliary Society. It consists of five circles, representing a like number of colored Baptist churches in this city, viz., the Cherry Street, Holy Trinity, Union, Nicetown and Germantown, and does general missionary work.

and in 1845 purchased a lot at Ninth and Lombard, where they still meet in a quiet and respectable house of worship. Their 430 members include some of the oldest and most respectable Negro families of the city. Probably if the white Presbyterians had given more encouragement to Negroes, this denomination would have absorbed the best elements of the colored population; they seem, however, to have shown some desire to be rid of the blacks, or at least not to increase their Negro membership in Philadelphia to any great extent. Central Church is more nearly a simple religious organization than most churches; it listens to able sermons, but does little outside its own doors.[17]

Berean Church is the work of one man and is an institutional church. It was formerly a mission of Central Church and now owns a fine piece of property bought by donations contributed by whites and Negroes, but chiefly by the former. The conception of the work and its carrying out, however, is due to Negroes. This church conducts a successful Building and Loan Association, a kindergarten,

---

[17] See, Jones' "Fifty Years in Central Street Church," etc. The system and order in this church is remarkable. Each year a careful printed report of receipts and expenditures is made. The following is an abstract of the report for 1891:

Receipts.

Finance Committee	$977.39	
Pew Rents	709.75	
Legacy	760.77	
Other Receipts	329.54	
		$2777.45

Expenditures.

Pastor's Salary	$1000.00	
Other Salaries	476.00	
Repayment of Loan	409.00	
Interest on Mortgage	60.96	
Donations to General Church	31.57	
General Expenses, etc.	759.23	
		$2736.76
Balance		$ 40.69

a medical dispensary and a seaside home, beside the numerous church societies. Probably no church in the city, except the Episcopal Church of the Crucifixion, is doing so much for the social betterment of the Negro.[18] The First African is the oldest colored church of this denomination in the city.

The Episcopal Church has, for Negro congregations, two independent churches, two churches dependent on white parishes, and four missions and Sunday schools. Statistics of three of these are given in the table on page 218.

The Episcopal churches receive more outside help than others and also do more general mission and rescue work. They hold $150,000 worth of property, have 900–1000 members and an annual income of $7000 to $8000. They represent all grades of the colored population. The oldest of the churches is St. Thomas! Next comes the Church of the Crucifixion, over fifty years old and perhaps the most effective church organization in the city for benevolent and rescue work. It has been built up virtually by one Negro, a man of sincerity and culture, and of peculiar energy. This church carries on regular church work at Bainbridge and Eighth and at two branch missions; it helps in the Fresh Air Fund, has an ice mission, a vacation school of thirty-five children, and a parish visitor. It makes an especial feature of good music with its vested choir. One or two courses of University Extension lectures are held here each year, and there is a large beneficial and insurance society in active operation, and a Home for the Homeless on Lombard street. This church especially reaches after a class of neglected poor whom the other colored churches shun or forget and for whom there is little fellowship in white churches. The rector says of this work :

---

[18] For history and detailed account of this work see Anderson's " Presbyterianism and the Negro."

COLORED PROTESTANT EPISCOPAL CHURCHES IN PHILADELPHIA*, 1897.

	Church.	Members.	Rectors and Assistants	Church Societies.	Offerings of Church		Total Income.	Expenditures.							Total Expense.	Value Real and Personal Estate.	Encumbrances.	Endowment.
					For Parish.	Purposes Outside of Parish.		Salary of Rector.	Current Expense.	Poor.	Total Parochial Expenses.	Diocesan.	General Missions, etc.				
Independent.	Crucifixion and One Mission.	310	2	9	$437.58	$879.40	$2995.93	$1200	$2477.98	$73	$2632.98	$35.00	$101.37	$2769.35	$45,000	. . . .	$11,000
Independent.	St. Thomas'. .	391	1	9	1457.90	10.00	2347.53	. . .	2008.00	70	2475.81	. . . .	. . . .	2582.98	60,000	$5388.73	. . . .
Independent.	St. Michael and All Angels .	90	1	9	227.08	6.67	1270.79	760	1381.89	. . .	1411.89	6.50	. . . .	1420.56	25,000	1200.00	. . . .

* Besides these, there are the following Churches, from which statistics were not obtained : St. Mark's, Zion Sunday school, St. Faith's Mission, and St. Simon's Chapel. The first is supported mainly by a white parish, and has a new building ; the second and third are small Missions ; the fourth is a promising outgrowth of the Church of the Crucifixion.

" As I look back over nearly twenty years of labor in one parish, I see a great deal to be devoutly thankful for. Here are people struggling from the beginning of one year to another, without ever having what can be called the necessaries of life. God alone knows what a real struggle life is to them. Many of them must always be 'moving on,' because they cannot pay the rent or meet other obligations.

" I have just visited a family of four, mother and three children. The mother is too sick to work. The eldest girl will work when she can find something to do. But the rent is due, and there is not a cent in the house. This is but a sample. How can such people support a church of their own? To many such, religion often becomes doubly comforting. They seize eagerly on the promises of a life where these earthly distresses will be forever absent.

" If the other half only knew how this half is living—how hard and dreary, and often hopeless, life is—the members of the more favored half would gladly help to do all they could to have the gospel freely preached to those whose lives are so devoid of earthly comforts.

" Twenty or thirty thousand dollars (and that is not much), safely invested, would enable the parish to do a work that ought to be done and yet is not being done at present. The poor could then have the gospel preached to them in a way that it is not now being preached."

The Catholic church has in the last decade made great progress in its work among Negroes and is determined to do much in the future. Its chief hold upon the colored people is its comparative lack of discrimination. There is one Catholic church in the city designed especially for Negro work—St. Peter Clavers at Twelfth and Lombard— formerly a Presbyterian church; recently a parish house has been added. The priest in charge estimates that 400 or 500 Negroes regularly attend Catholic churches in various parts of the city. The Mary Drexel Home for Colored Orphans is a Catholic institution near the city which is doing much work. The Catholic church can do more than any other agency in humanizing the intense prejudice of many of the working class against the Negro, and signs of this influence are manifest in some quarters.

We have thus somewhat in detail reviewed the work of the chief churches. There are beside these continually springing up and dying a host of little noisy missions which represent the older and more demonstrative worship. A description of one applies to nearly all; take for instance one in the slums of the Fifth Ward:

"The tablet in the gable of this little church bears the date 1837. For sixty years it has stood and done its work in the narrow lane. What its history has been all this time it is difficult to find out, for no records are on hand, and no one is here to tell the tale.

"The few last months of the old order was something like this: It was in the hands of a Negro congregation. Several visits were paid to the church, and generally a dozen people were found there. After a discourse by a very illiterate preacher, hymns were sung, having many repetitions of senseless sentiment and exciting cadences. It took about an hour to work up the congregation to a fervor aimed at. When this was reached a remarkable scene presented itself. The whole congregation pressed forward to an open space before the pulpit, and formed a ring. The most excitable of their number entered the ring, and with clapping of hands and contortions led the devotions. Those forming the ring joined in the clapping of hands and wild and loud singing, frequently springing into the air, and shouting loudly. As the devotions proceeded, most of the worshipers took off their coats and vests and hung them on pegs on the wall. This continued for hours, until all were completely exhausted, and some had fainted and been stowed away on benches or the pulpit platform.   This was the order of things at the close of sixty years' history. * * * When this congregation vacated the church, they did so stealthily, under cover of darkness, removed furniture not their own, including the pulpit, and left bills unpaid." [19]

There are dozens of such little missions in various parts of Philadelphia, led by wandering preachers.   They are survivals of the methods of worship in Africa and the West Indies.   In some of the larger churches noise and excitement attend the services, especially at the time of revival or in prayer meetings.   For the most part, however, these customs are dying away.

To recapitulate, we have in Philadelphia fifty-five Negro churches with 12,845 members owning $907,729 worth of property with an annual income of at least $94,968.   And these represent the organized efforts of the race better than any other organizations.   Second to them however come the secret and benevolent societies, which we now consider.

34. Secret and Beneficial Societies, and Co-operative Business.—The art of organization is the one hardest for the freedman to learn, and the Negro shows his greatest deficiency here;   whatever success he has had has been shown most conspicuously in his church organizations, where the religious bond greatly facilitated union.   In other organizations where the bond was weaker his success has been less.   From early times the precarious economic condition of the free Negroes led to many mutual aid organizations.   They were very simple in form: an initiation fee of small amount was required, and small regular payments;   in case of sickness, a weekly stipend was paid, and in case of death the members were assessed to pay for the funeral and help the widow.   Confined to a few members, all personally known to each other, such societies

[19] Rev. Charles Daniel, in the *Nazarene*.   The writer hardly does justice to the weird witchery of those hymns sung thus rudely.

were successful from the beginning. We hear of them in the eighteenth century, and by 1838 there were 100 such small groups, with 7448 members, in the city. They paid in $18,851, gave $14,172 in benefits, and had $10,023 on hand. Ten years later about eight thousand members belonged to 106 such societies. Seventy-six of these had a total membership of 5187. They contributed usually 25 cents to 37½ cents a month; the sick received $1.50 to $3.00 a week, and death benefits of $10.00 to $20.00 were allowed. The income of these seventy-six societies was $16,814.23; 681 families were assisted.[20]

These societies have since been superceded to some extent by other organizations; they are still so numerous, however, that it is impractical to catalogue all of them; there are probably several hundred of various kinds in the city.

To these were early added the secret societies, which naturally had great attraction for Negroes. A Boston lodge of black Masons received a charter direct from England, and independent orders of Odd Fellows, Knights of Pythias, etc., grew up. During the time that Negroes were shut out of the public libraries there were many literary associations with libraries. These have now disappeared. Outside the churches the most important organizations among Negroes to-day are: Secret societies, beneficial societies, insurance societies, cemeteries, building and loan associations, labor unions, homes of various sorts and political clubs. The most powerful and flourishing secret order is that of the Odd Fellows, which has two hundred thousand members among American Negroes. In Philadelphia there are 19 lodges with a total membership of 1188, and $46,000 worth of property. Detailed statistics are in the next table: [21]

---

[20] Cf. report of inquiries in above years.

[21] From Report of Fourth Annual Meeting of the District Grand Lodge of Pennsylvania, G. U. of O. F., 1896.

COLORED ODD FELLOWS' LODGES IN PHILADELPHIA, 1896.

Name.	Organized.	Members.	Sick Benefit to Members.	Death Benefit.	Widows Relieved.	Widows Buried.	Orphans Buried.	Amount paid for Sick.	Amount paid for Funerals.	Amount paid Widows.	Amount paid in Charity.	Whole Amount Paid out.	Amount Invested.	Value of Property.	Balance in Fund.	Total Property, Funds, etc.
Unity	1844	121	.	.	2	.	.	$291.85	$25.00	$6.80	$10.00	$627.07	$763.75	$660.00	$42.97	$2547.61
Good Samaritan	1864	80	3	1	.	.	.	104.00	85.00	.	.	307.96	712.99	113.85	18.66	845.50
Fraternal	1864	88	7	.	.	.	.	84.00	.	.	28.36	249.42	452.50	250.00	820.84	1,522.34
Phœnix	1846	98	3	.	.	.	.	98.50	121.00	.	5.00	419.65	1420.30	100.00	163.11	1,620.30
Covenant	1847	77	5	1	1	.	2	214.00	160.00	7.50	6.00	547.50	450.00	550.00	86.00	1,036.50
Friendship	1847	24	.	1	.	.	1	43.50	.	.	.	98.93	.	200.00	5.00	205.00
Carthagenian	1848	113	15	.	1	.	.	272.00	70.00	5.00	16.00	798.19	2362.50	583.65	2281.25	5,227.40
Mt. Olive	1848	70	5	1	1	.	.	109.00	.	.	12.00	383.51	62.50	600.00	587.39	1,633.40
Good Hope	1855	46	7	1	.	3	.	36.00	10.00	15.00	.	348.44	248.00	1,500.00	60.72	1,809.82
Mt. Lebanon	1857	36	4	.	.	.	.	22.20	149.50	10.00	.	245.32	50.00	20,000.00	50.00	150.00
Equity	1867	173	3	1	.	.	.	134.55	175.00	25.00	.	415.99	200.00	2,500.00	100.00	28,300.00
St. Albans	1875	31	6	1	1	.	.	6.20	30.00	.	.	78.95	.	.	25.00	275.00
Keystone	1873	15	1	.	1	.	.	.	20.00	4.00	10.00	.	.	50.00	4.00	4.00
Gideon	1875	17	2	.	.	.	.	56.00	40.00	8.00	3.50	144.00	.	75.00	10.00	60.00
Beth Eden	1876	31	1	1	.	.	.	54.00	13.00	10.00	.	133.05	.	350.00	20.00	95.00
Philadelphia	1886	36	2	1	.	.	.	32.00	40.00	.	.	181.06	.	.	5.24	355.24
Pennsylvania	1889	.	2	.	.	.	.	.	.	5.00	10.00	.	.	.	.	.
John Rhodes	1891	15	.	.	1	.	.	.	20.00	.	.	15.00	10.00	33.00	40.00	40.00
Quaker City	1892	96	10	.	.	.	.	220.18	.	.	.	417.00	.	.	67.00	100.00
Total	.	1167	75	7	8	3	3	$1777.98	$958.50	$96.30	$100.86	$5381.04	$6732.54	$27,615.50	$4387.18	$45,827.11

This order owns two halls in the city worth perhaps $40,000. One is occupied by the officers of the Grand Lodge, which employs several salaried officials and clerks. The order conducts a newspaper called the *Odd Fellows' Journal.*

There are 19 lodges of Masons in the city, 6 chapters, 5 commanderies, 3 of the Scottish Rite, and 1 drill corp. The Masons are not so well organized and conducted as the Odd Fellows, and detailed statistics of their lodges are not available. They own two halls worth at least $50,000, and probably distribute not less than $3000 to $4000 annually in benefits.

Beside these chief secret orders there are numerous others, such as the American Protestant Association, which has many members, the Knights of Pythias, the Galilean Fishermen, the various female orders attached to these, and a number of others. It is almost impossible to get accurate statistics of all these orders, and any estimate of their economic activity is liable to considerable error. However, from general observation and the available figures, it seems fairly certain that at least four thousand Negroes belong to secret orders, and that these orders annually collect at least $25,000, part of which is paid out in sick and death benefits, and part invested. The real estate, personal property and funds of these orders amount to no less than $125,000.

The function of the secret society is partly social intercourse and partly insurance. They furnish pastime from the monotony of work, a field for ambition and intrigue, a chance for parade, and insurance against misfortune. Next to the church they are the most popular organizations among Negroes.

Of the beneficial societies we have already spoken in general. A detailed account of a few of the larger and more typical organizations will now suffice. The Quaker City Association is a sick and death benefit society, seven

years old, which confines its membership to native Philadelphians. It has 280 members and distributes $1400 to
$1500 annually. The Sons and Daughters of Delaware
is over fifty years old. It has 106 members, and owns
$3000 worth of real estate. The Fraternal Association
was founded in 1861 ; it has 86 members, and distributes
about $300 a year. It "was formed for the purpose of
relieving the wants and distresses of each other in the
time of affliction and death, and for the furtherance of
such benevolent views and objects as would tend to establish and maintain a permanent and friendly intercourse
among them in their social relations in life." The Sons
of St. Thomas was founded in 1823 and was originally
confined to members of St. Thomas' Church. It was
formerly a large organization, but now has 80 members,
and paid out in 1896, $416 in relief. It has $1500 invested
in government bonds. In addition to these there is the
Old Men's Association, the Female Cox Association, the
Sons and Daughters of Moses, and a large number of other
small societies.

There is arising also a considerable number of insurance societies, differing from the beneficial in being conducted by directors. The best of these are the Crucifixion
connected with the Church of the Crucifixion, and the
Avery, connected with Wesley A. M. E. Z. Church ; both
have a large membership and are well conducted. Nearly
every church is beginning to organize one or more such
societies, some of which in times past have met disaster
by bad management. The True Reformers of Virginia, the
most remarkable Negro beneficial organization yet started,
has several branches here. Beside these there are numberless minor societies, as the Alpha Relief, Knights and
Ladies of St. Paul, the National Co-operative Society, Colored Women's Protective Association, Loyal Beneficial, etc.
Some of these are honest efforts and some are swindling
imitations of the pernicious white petty insurance societies.

There are three building and loan associations conducted by Negroes. Some of the directors in one are white, all the others are colored. The oldest association is the Century, established October 26, 1886. Its board of directors is composed of teachers, upholsterers, clerks, restaurant keepers and undertakers, and it has had marked success. Its income for 1897 was about $7000. It has $25,000 in loans outstanding.

The Berean Building and Loan Association was established in 1888 in connection with Berean Presbyterian Church; 13 of the 19 officers and directors are colored. Its income for 1896 was nearly $30,000, and it had $60,000 in loans; 43 homes have been bought through this association.[22]

The Pioneer Association is composed entirely of Negroes, the directors being caterers, merchants and upholsterers. It was founded in 1888 and has an office on Pine street. Its receipts in 1897 were $9000, and it had about $20,000 in loans. Nine homes are at present being bought in this association.

There are arising some loan associations to replace the pawn-shops and usurers to some extent. The Small Loan Association, for instance, was founded in 1891, and has the following report for 1898:

Shares sold	$1144.00
Assessments on shares	114.40
Repaid loans	4537.50
Interest	417.06
Cash in treasury	275.54
Dividends paid	222.67
Loans made	4626.75
Expenses	82.02

The Conservative is a similar organization, consisting of ten members.

---

[22] This association has issued a valuable little pamphlet called "Helpful Hints on Home," which it distributes. This explains the object and methods of building and loan associations.

This account has attempted to touch only the chief and characteristic organizations, and makes no pretensions to completeness. It shows, however, how intimately bound together the Negroes of Philadelphia are. These associations are largely experiments, and as such, are continually reaching out to new fields. The latest ventures are toward labor unions, co-operative stores and newspapers. There are the following labor unions, among others : The Caterers' Club, the Private Waiters' Association, the Coachmen's Association, the Hotel Brotherhood (of waiters), the Cigar-makers' Union (white and colored), the Hod-Carriers' Union, the Barbers' Union, etc.

Of the Caterers' Club we have already heard.[23] The Private Waiters' Association is an old beneficial order with well-to-do members. The private waiter is really a skilled workman of high order, and used to be well paid. Next to the guild of caterers he ranked as high as any class of Negro workmen before the war—indeed the caterer was but a private waiter further developed. Consequently this labor union is still jealous and exclusive and contains some members long retired from active work. The Coachmen's Association is a similar society; both these organizations have a considerable membership, and make sick and death benefits and social gatherings a feature. The Hotel Brotherhood is a new society of hotel waiters and is conducted by young men on the lines of the regular trades unions, with which it is more or less affiliated in many cities. It has some relief features and considerable social life. It strives to open and keep open work for colored waiters and often arranges to divide territory with whites, or to prevent one set from supplanting the other. The Cigar-makers' Union is a regular trades union with both white and Negro members. It is the only union in Philadelphia where Negroes are largely represented. No friction

---

[23] See *supra*, p. 119 ff.

is apparent. The Hod-Carriers' Union is large and of considerable age but does not seem to be very active. A League of Colored Mechanics was formed in 1897 but did not accomplish anything. There was before the war a league of this sort which flourished, and there undoubtedly will be attempts of this sort in the future until a union is effected.[24]

The two co-operative grocery stores, and the caterers' supply store have been mentioned.[25] There was a dubious attempt in 1896 to organize a co-operative tin-ware store which has not yet been successful.[26]

With all this effort and movement it is natural that the Negroes should want some means of communication. This they have in the following periodicals conducted wholly by Negroes :

---

[24] The College Settlement was interested in this organization, but the movement was evidently premature.

[25] See *supra*, p. 117 and p. 119.

[26] An interesting advertisement of this venture is appended; it is a curious mixture of business, exhortation and simplicity. The present state of the enterprise is not known :

" NOTICE TO ALL.

"WE CALL YOUR ATTENTION

"To THIS WORK.

"THE UNION TIN-WARE MANUFACTURING CO.

" Is now at work, chartered under the laws of the States of New Jersey and Pennsylvania.

" The purpose of said Company is to manufacture everything in the TIN-WARE LINE that the law allows, and to sell stock all over the United States of America; and put in members enough in every city to open a Union Tin-Ware Store, and if the promoter finds that he has not enough members in a city to open a Tin-Ware Store, then he shall open it with money from the factory. SHARES are $10.00, they can be paid on installment plan; and you do not have any monthly dues to pay, but on the 20th of every December or whenever the Stockholders appoint the time, the dividend will be declared.

" We will make this one of the grandest organizations ever witnessed by the Race, if you lend us your aid. This Store will contain Groceries, Dry Goods and Tin-Ware, and you can do your dealing at your own store. This factory will give you work, and learn you a trade."

A. M. E. Church *Review*, quarterly, 8vo, about ninety-five pages.

Christian Recorder, eight-page weekly newspaper. (Both these are organs of the A. M. E. Church.)

Baptist *Christian Banner*, four-page weekly newspaper. (Organ of the Baptists.)

Odd Fellows' *Journal*, eight-page weekly newspaper. (Organ of Odd Fellows.)

Weekly *Tribune*, eight-page weekly newspaper, seventeen years established.

The *Astonisher*, eight-page weekly newspaper (Germantown).

The *Standard-Echo*, four-page weekly newspaper (since suspended).

The *Tribune* is the chief news sheet and is filled generally with social notes of all kinds, and news of movements among Negroes over the country. Its editorials are usually of little value chiefly because it does not employ a responsible editor. It is in many ways however an interesting paper and represents pluck and perseverance on the part of its publisher. The *Astonisher* and *Standard Echo* are news sheets. The first is bright but crude. The *Recorder*, *Banner* and *Journal* are chiefly filled with columns of heavy church and lodge news. The *Review* has had an interesting history and is probably the best Negro periodical of the sort published; it is often weighted down by the requirements of church politics, and compelled to publish some trash written by aspiring candidates for office; but with all this it has much solid matter and indicates the trend of thought among Negroes to some extent. It has greatly improved in the last few years. Many Negro newspapers from other cities circulate here and widen the feeling of community among the colored people of the city.

One other kind of organization has not yet been mentioned, the political clubs, of which there are probably fifty in the city. They will be considered in another chapter.

35. Institutions.—The chief Negro institutions of the city are: The Home for Aged and Infirmed Colored Persons, the Douglass Hospital and Training School, the Woman's Exchange and Girls' Home, three cemetery companies, the Home for the Homeless, the special schools, as the Institute for Colored Youth, the House of Industry, Raspberry street schools and Jones's school for girls, the Y. M. C. A., and University Extension Centre.

The Home for the Aged, situated at the corner of Girard and Belmont avenues, was founded by a Negro lumber merchant, Steven Smith, and is conducted by whites and Negroes. It is one of the best institutions of the kind; its property is valued at $400,000, and it has an annual income of $20,000. It has sheltered 558 old people since its foundation in 1864.

The Douglass Memorial Hospital and Training School is a curious example of the difficult position of Negroes: for years nearly every hospital in Philadelphia has sought to exclude Negro women from the course in nurse-training, and no Negro physician could have the advantage of hospital practice. This led to a movement for a Negro hospital; such a movement however was condemned by the whites as an unnecessary addition to a bewildering number of charitable institutions; by many of the best Negroes as a concession to prejudice and a drawing of the color line. Nevertheless the promoters insisted that colored nurses were efficient and needed training, that colored physicians needed a hospital, and that colored patients wished one. Consequently the Douglass Hospital has been established and its success seems to warrant the effort.[27]

---

[27] Since the opening of the hospital colored nurses have had less trouble in white institutions, and one colored physician has been

The total income for the year 1895–96 was $4,656.31; sixty-one patients were treated during the year, and thirty-two operations performed; 987 out-patients were treated. The first class of nurses was graduated in 1897.

The Woman's Exchange and Girls' Home is conducted by the principal of the Institute for Colored Youth at 756 South Twelfth street. The exchange is open at stated times during the week, and various articles are on sale. Cheap lodging and board is furnished for a few school girls and working girls. So far the work of the exchange has been limited but it is slowly growing, and is certainly a most deserving venture.[28]

The exclusion of Negroes from cemeteries has, as before mentioned, led to the organization of three cemetery companies, two of which are nearly fifty years old. The Olive holds eight acres of property in the Twenty-fourth Ward, claimed to be worth $100,000. It has 900 lot owners; the Lebanon holds land in the Thirty-sixth Ward, worth at least $75,000. The Merion is a new company which owns twenty-one acres in Montgomery County, worth perhaps $30,000. These companies are in the main well-conducted, although the affairs of one are just now somewhat entangled.

The Home for the Homeless is a refuge and home for the aged connected with the Church of the Crucifixion.

---

appointed intern in a large hospital. Dr. N. F. Mossell was chiefly instrumental in founding the Douglass Hospital.

[28] In connection with this work, Bethel Church often holds small receptions for servant girls on their days off, when refreshments are served and a pleasant time is spent. The following is a note of a similar enterprise at another church : "The members of the Berean Union have opened a ' Y ' parlor, where young colored girls employed as domestics can spend their Thursday afternoon both pleasantly and profitably. The parlor is open from 4 until 10 p. m., every Thursday, and members of the Union are present to welcome them. A light supper is served for ten cents. The evening is spent in literary exercises and social talk. The parlor is in the Berean Church, South College avenue, near Twentieth street."

It is supported largely by whites but not entirely. It has an income of about $500. During 1896, 1108 lodgings were furnished to ninety women, 8384 meals given to inmates, 2705 to temporary lodgers, 2078 to transients, and 812 to invalids.

The schools have all been mentioned before. The Young Men's Christian Association has had a checkered history, chiefly as it would seem from the wrong policy pursued ; there is in the city a grave and dangerous lack of proper places of amusement and recreation for young men. To fill this need a properly conducted Young Men's Christian Association, with books and newspapers, baths, bowling alleys and billiard tables, conversation rooms and short, interesting religious services is demanded ; it would cost far less than it now costs the courts to punish the petty misdemeanors of young men who do not know how to amuse themselves. Instead of such an institution however the Colored Y. M. C. A. has been virtually an attempt to add another church to the numberless colored churches of the city, with endless prayer-meetings and loud gospel hymns, in dingy and uninviting quarters. Consequently the institution is now temporarily suspended. It had accomplished some good work by its night schools, and social meetings.

Since the organization of the Bainbridge Street University Extension Centre, May 10, 1895, lectures have been delivered at the Church of the Crucifixion, Eighth and Bainbridge streets, by Rev. W. Hudson Shaw, on English History; by Thomas Whitney Surette, on the Development of Music; by Henry W. Elson, on American History, and by Hilaire Belloc, on Napoleon. Each of these lecturers, except Mr. Belloc, has given a course of six lectures on the subject stated, and classes have been held in connection with each course. The attendance has been above the average as compared with other Centres in the city.

Beside these efforts there are various embryonic institutions : A day nursery in the Seventh Ward by the Woman's Missionary Society, a large organization which does much charitable work ; an industrial school near the city, etc. There are, too, many institutions conducted by whites for the benefit of Negroes, which will be mentioned in another place.

Much of the need for separate Negro institutions has in the last decade disappeared, by reason of the opening of the doors of the public institutions to colored people. There are many Negroes who on this account strongly oppose efforts which they fear will tend to delay further progress in these lines. On the other hand, thoughtful men see that invaluable training and discipline is coming to the race through these institutions and organizations, and they encourage the formation of them.

36. The Experiment of Organization.—Looking back over the field which we have thus reviewed—the churches, societies, unions, attempts at business co-operation, institutions and newspapers—it is apparent that the largest hope for the ultimate rise of the Negro lies in this mastery of the art of social organized life. To be sure, compared with his neighbors, he has as yet advanced but a short distance ; we are apt to condemn this lack of unity, the absence of carefully planned and laboriously executed effort among these people, as a voluntary omission—a bit of carelessness. It is far more than this, it is lack of social education, of group training, and the lack can only be supplied by a long, slow process of growth. And the chief value of the organizations studied is that they are evidences of growth. Of actual accomplishment they have, to be sure, something to show, but nothing to boast of inordinately. The churches are far from ideal associations for fostering the higher life—rather they combine too often intrigue, extravagance and show, with all their work, saving and charity ; their secret societies are often diverted from their better ends by scheming and dishonest officers, and by the temptation of tinsel and braggadocio ; their beneficial associations, along with all their good work, have an unenviable record of business inefficiency and internal dissension.   And yet all these and the other agencies have accomplished much, and their greatest accomplishment is stimulation of effort to further and more effective organization among a disorganized and headless host. All this world of co-operation and subordination into which the white child is in most cases born is, we must not forget, new to the slave's sons. They have been compelled to organize before they knew the meaning of organization ; to co-operate with those of their fellows to whom co-operation was an unknown term ; to fix and fasten ideas of leadership and authority among those who had always looked to others for guidance and command. For these reasons the present efforts of Negroes in working together along various lines are peculiarly promising for the future of both races.

CHAPTER XIII.

THE NEGRO CRIMINAL.

37. History of Negro Crime in the City.[1]—From his earliest advent the Negro, as was natural, has figured largely in the criminal annals of Philadelphia. Only such superficial study of the American Negro as dates his beginning with 1863 can neglect this past record of crime in studying the present. Crime is a phenomenon of organized social life, and is the open rebellion of an individual against his social environment. Naturally then, if men are suddenly transported from one environment to another, the result is lack of harmony with the new conditions; lack of harmony with the new physical surroundings leading to disease and death or modification of physique; lack of harmony with social surroundings leading to crime. Thus very early in the history of the colony characteristic complaints of the disorder of the Negro slaves is heard. In 1693, July 11, the Governor and Council approved an ordinance, "Upon the Request of some of the members of Council, that an order be made by the Court of Quarter Sessions for the Countie of philadelphia, the 4th July instant (proceeding upon a presentment of the Grand Jurie for the bodie of the sd countie), agt the tumultuous gatherings of the Negroes of the towne of philadelphia, on the

---

[1] Throughout this chapter the basis of induction is the number of prisoners received at different institutions and *not* the prison population at particular times. This avoids the mistakes and distortions of the latter method. (Cf. Falkner: "Crime and the Census," Publications of the American Academy of Political and Social Science, No. 190)· Many writers on Crime among Negroes, as *e. g.*, F. L. Hoffman, and all who use the Eleventh Census uncritically, have fallen into numerous mistakes and exaggerations by carelessness on this point.

first dayes of the weeke, ordering the Constables of philadelphia, or anie other person whatsoever, to have power to
take up Negroes, male or female, whom they should find
gadding abroad on the said first dayes of the weeke, without a ticket from their Mr. or Mris., or not in their Compa,
or to carry them to gaole, there to remain that night, and
that without meat or drink, and to Cause them to be pub-
lickly whipt next morning with 39 Lashes, well Laid on,
on their bare backs, for which their sd. Mr. or Mris. should
pay 15d. to the whipper," etc. [2]

Penn himself introduced a law for the special trial and
punishment of Negroes very early in the history of the
colony, as has been noted before.[3]   The slave code finally
adopted was mild compared with the legislation of the
period, but it was severe enough to show the unruly character of many of the imported slaves.[4]

Especially in Philadelphia did the Negroes continue to
give general trouble, not so much by serious crime as by
disorder.   In 1732, under Mayor Hasel, the City Council
" taking under Consideration the frequent and tumultuous
meetings of the Negro Slaves, especially on Sunday, Gaming, Cursing, Swearing, and committing many other Disorders, to the great Terror and Disquiet of the Inhabitants
of this city," ordered an ordinance to be drawn up against
such disturbances.[5]   Again, six years later, we hear of the
draft of another city ordinance for " the more Effectual
suppressing Tumultuous meetings and other disorderly
doings of the Negroes, Mulattos and Indian servts. and
slaves." [6]   And in 1741, August 17, " frequent complaints
having been made to the Board that many disorderly persons meet every ev'g about the Court house of this city,

---

[2] "Pennsylvania Colonial Records," I, 380–81.
[3] See Chapter III, and Appendix B.
[4] Cf. "Pennsylvania Statutes at Large," Ch. 56.
[5] Watson's "Annals," I, 62.
[6] *Ibid.*

and great numbers of Negroes and others sit there with milk pails and other things late at night, and many disorders are there committed against the peace and good government of this city," Council ordered the place to be cleared "in half an hour after sunset." [7]

Of the graver crimes by Negroes we have only reports here and there which do not make it clear how frequently such crimes occurred. In 1706 a slave is arrested for setting fire to a dwelling; in 1738 three Negroes are hanged in neighboring parts of New Jersey for poisoning people, while at Rocky Hill a slave is burned alive for killing a child and burning a barn. Whipping of Negroes at the public whipping post was frequent, and so severe was the punishment that in 1743 a slave brought up to be whipped committed suicide. In 1762 two Philadelphia slaves were sentenced to death for felony and burglary; petitions were circulated in their behalf but Council was obdurate.[8]

Little special mention of Negro crime is again met with until the freedmen under the act of 1780 began to congregate in the city and other free immigrants joined them. In 1809 the leading colored churches united in a society to suppress crime and were cordially endorsed by the public for this action. After the war immigration to the city increased and the stress of hard times bore heavily on the lower classes. Complaints of petty thefts and murderous assaults on peaceable citizens now began to increase, and in numbers of cases they were traced to Negroes. The better class of colored citizens felt the accusation and held a meeting to denounce crime and take a firm stand against their own criminal class. A little later the Negro riots commenced, and they received their chief moral support from the increasing crime of Negroes; a Cuban slave

---

[7] *Ibid.*, pp. 62–63.

[8] "Pennsylvania Colonial Records," II, 275; IX, 6; "Watson's Annals," I, 309.

brained his master with a hatchet, two other murders by
Negroes followed, and gambling, drunkenness and debauch-
ery were widespread wherever Negroes settled. The
terribly vindictive insurrection of Nat Turner in a neighboring State frightened the citizens so thoroughly that
when some black fugitives actually arrived at Chester from
Southampton County, Virginia, the Legislature was
hastily appealed to, and the whole matter came to a climax
in the disfranchisement of the Negro in 1837, and the riots
in the years 1830 to 1840.[9]

Some actual figures will give us an idea of this, the
worst period of Negro crime ever experienced in the city.
The Eastern Penitentiary was opened in 1829 near the close
of the year. The total number of persons received here for
the most serious crimes is given in the next table. This
includes prisoners from the Eastern counties of the State,
but a large proportion were from Philadelphia :[10]

Years.	Total Commit- ments.	Negroes.	Per Cent of Negroes.	Per Cent of Negroes of Total Population.
1829–34	339	99	29.0	8.27 (1830)
1835–39	878	356	40.5	7.39 (1840)
1840–44	701	209	29.8	7.39 (1840)
1845–49	633	151	23.8	4.83 (1850)
1850–54	664	106	16.0	4.83 (1850)

Or to put it differently the problem of Negro crime in
Philadelphia from 1830 to 1850 arose from the fact that
less than one-fourteenth of the population was responsible
for nearly a third of the serious crimes committed.

These figures however are apt to relate more especially
to a criminal class. A better measure of the normal
criminal tendencies of the group would perhaps be found
in the statistics of Moyamensing, where ordinary cases of
crime and misdemeanor are confined and which contains

[9] Cf. Chapter IV.
[10] Reports Eastern Penitentiary.

only county prisoners.   The figures for Moyamensing prison are:

Years.	Total White Prisoners Received.	Total Negro Prisoners Received.	Per Cent of Negroes of Total Prisoners.	Per Cent of Negroes of Total Population.
1836–45	1164	1087	48.29	7.39 (1840)
1846–55	1478	696	32.01	4.83 (1850)
Total	2642	1783	. . .	. . . . .

Here we have even a worse showing than before; in 1896 the Negroes forming 4 per cent of the population furnish 9 per cent of the arrests, but in 1850 being 5 per cent of the population they furnished 32 per cent of the prisoners received at the county prison.   Of course there are some considerations which must not be overlooked in interpreting these figures for 1836–55.   It must be remembered that the discrimination against the Negro was much greater then than now: he was arrested for less cause and given longer sentences than whites.[11]   Great numbers of those arrested and committed for trial were never brought to trial so that their guilt could not be proven or disproven; of 737 Negroes committed for trial in six months of the year 1837, it is stated that only 123 were actually brought to trial; of the prisoners in the Eastern Penitentiary, 1829 to 1846, 14 per cent of the whites were pardoned and 2 per cent of the Negroes.   All these considerations increase the statistics to the disfavor of the Negro.[12]   Nevertheless making all reasonable allowances it is undoubtedly true that the crime of Negroes in this period reached its high tide for this city.

The character of the crimes committed by Negroes compared with whites is shown by the following table,

---

[11] Average length of sentences for whites in Eastern Penitentiary during nineteen years, 2 years 8 months 2 days; for Negroes, 3 years 3 months 14 days.   Cf. "Health of Convicts" (pam.), pp. 7, 8.

[12] *Ibid.*, "Condition of Negroes," 1838, pp. 15–18; "Condition," etc., 1848, pp. 26, 27.

which covers the offences of 1359 whites and 718 Negroes committed to the Eastern Penitentiary, 1829–1846. If we take simply petty larceny we find that 48.8 per cent of the whites and 55 per cent of the Negroes were committed for this offence.[13]

Kinds of Crime.	Whites.		Negroes.	
	Number.	Per Cent.	Number.	Per Cent.
Offences *vs.* the person	166	11.4	89	12.4
Offences *vs.* property with violence .	191	13.1	165	22.9
Offences *vs.* property without violence	873	59.8	432	60.2
Malicious offences *vs.* property . . .	22	1.5	14	2.0
Offences *vs.* Currency and forgery . .	167	11.5	7	1.0
Miscellaneous	40	27.0	11	1.5
All offences	1359	100	718	100

38. Negro Crime Since the War.—Throughout the land there has been since the war a large increase in crime, especially in cities. This phenomenon would seem to have sufficient cause in the increased complexity of life, in industrial competition, and the rush of great numbers to the large cities. It would therefore be natural to suppose that the Negro would also show this increase in criminality and, as in the case of all lower classes, that he would show it in greater degree. His evolution has, however, been marked by some peculiarities. For nearly two decades after emancipation he took little part in many of the great social movements about him for obvious reasons. His migration to city life, therefore, and his sharing in the competition of modern industrial life, came later than was the case with the mass of his fellow citizens. The Negro began to rush to the cities in large numbers after 1880, and consequently the phenomena attendant on that momentous change of life are tardier in his case. His rate of criminality has in the last two decades risen rapidly, and this is a parallel phenomenon to the rapid rise of the

---

[13] "Condition of Negroes," 1849, pp. 28, 29. "Condition," etc., 1838, pp. 15-18.

white criminal record two or three decades ago. Moreover, in the case of the Negro there were special causes for the prevalence of crime : he had lately been freed from serfdom, he was the object of stinging oppression and ridicule, and paths of advancement open to many were closed to him. Consequently the class of the shiftless, aimless, idle, discouraged and disappointed was proportionately larger.

In the city of Philadelphia the increasing number of bold and daring crimes committed by Negroes in the last ten years has focused the attention of the city on this subject. There is a widespread feeling that something is wrong with a race that is responsible for so much crime, and that strong remedies are called for. One has but to visit the corridors of the public buildings, when the courts are in session, to realize the part played in law-breaking by the Negro population. The various slum centres of the colored criminal population have lately been the objects of much philanthropic effort, and the work there has aroused discussion. Judges on the bench have discussed the matter. Indeed, to the minds of many, this is the real Negro problem.[14]

That it is a vast problem a glance at statistics will show ;[15] and since 1880 it has been steadily growing. At the same time crime is a difficult subject to study, more

---

[14] " The large proportion of colored men who, in April, had been before the criminal court, led Judge Gordon to make a suggestion when he yesterday discharged the jurors for the term. ' It would certainly seem,' said the Court, ' that the philanthropic colored people of the community, of whom there are a great many excellent and intelligent citizens sincerely interested in the welfare of their race, ought to see what is radically wrong that produces this state of affairs and correct it, if possible. There is nothing in history that indicates that the colored race has a propensity to acts of violent crime; on the contrary, their tendencies are most gentle, and they submit with grace to subordination.' " *Philadelphia Record*, April 29, 1893; Cf. *Record*, May 10 and 12; *Ledger*, May 10, and *Times*, May 22, 1893.

[15] Except as otherwise noted, the statistics of this section are from the official reports of the police department.

difficult to analyze into its sociological elements, and most difficult to cure or suppress. It is a phenomenon that stands not alone, but rather as a symptom of countless wrong social conditions.

The simplest, but crudest, measure of crime is found in the total arrests for a period of years. The value of such figures is lessened by the varying efficiency and diligence of the police, by discrimination in the administration of law, and by unwarranted arrests. And yet the figures roughly measure crime. The total arrests and the number of Negroes is given in the next table for thirty-two years, with a few omissions :

ARRESTS IN PHILADELPHIA, 1864–96.

Date.	Total Number Arrested.	Total Negroes Arrested.	Percentage of Negroes.
1864	34,221	3,114	9.1
1865	43,226	2,722	6.3
1869	38,749	2,907	7.5
1870	31,717	2,070	6.5
1873	30,400	1,380	4.5
1874	32,114	1,257	3.9
1875	34,553	1,539	4.5
1876	. . .	. . .	. . .
1877	44,220	2,524	5.7
1879	40,714	2,360	5.8
1880	44,097	2,204	4.98
1881	45,129	2,327	5.11
1882	46,130	2,183	4.73
1883	45,295	2,022	4.46
1884	49,468	2,134	4.31
1885	51,418	2,662	5.11
1886	. . .	. . .	. . .
1887	57,951	3,256	5.61
1888	46,899	2,910	6.20
1889	42,673	2,614	6.10
1890	49,148	3,167	6.44
1891	53,184	3,544	6.66
1892	52,944	3,431	6.48
1893	57,297	4,078	7.11
1894	61,478	4,805	7.81
1895	60,347	5,137	8.5
1896	58,072	5,302	9.1

We find that the total arrests in the city per annum have risen from 34,221 in 1864 to 61,478 in 1894, an increase of

80 per cent in crime, parallel to an increase of 85 per cent
in population. The Negroes arrested have increased from
3114 in 1864 to 4805 in 1894, an increase of 54 per cent in
crime, parallel to an increase of 77 per cent in the Negro
population of the city. So, too, the percentage of Negroes
in the total arrests is less in 1894 than in 1864. If, however, we follow the years between these two dates we see
an important development : 1864 was the date bounding
the ante-bellum period of crime; thereafter the proportion of
Negro arrests fell steadily until, in 1874, the Negroes came
as nearly as ever furnishing their normal quota of
arrests, 3.9 per cent from 3.28 per cent (1870) of the population. Then slowly there came a change. With the
Centennial Exposition in 1876 came a stream of immigrants, and once started the stream increased in speed by
its own momentum. With this immigration the proportion of Negro arrests arose rapidly at first as a result of the
exposition ; falling off a little in the early eighties, but with
1885 rising again steadily and quickly to over 6 per cent
in 1888, 6.4 per cent in 1890, 7 per cent in 1893, 8.5 per
cent in 1895, 9 per cent in 1896. This is, as has been said
before, but a rough indication of the amount of crime for
which the Negro is responsible ; it must not be relied on
too closely, for the number of arrests cannot in any city
accurately measure wrongdoing save in a very general way;
probably increased efficiency in the police force since 1864
has had large effect ; and yet we can draw the legitimate
conclusion here that Negro crime in the city is far less,
according to population, than before the war ; that after the
war it decreased until the middle of the seventies and then,
coincident with the beginning of the new Negro immigration to cities,[16] it has risen pretty steadily.

These same phenomena can be partially verified by statistics of Moyamensing prison. If we take the tried and

---

[16] Cf. Chapters IV and VII.

untried prisoners committed to this county prison from 1876 to 1895 we find the same gradual increase of crime :

MOYAMENSING PRISON.
Both Tried and Untried Prisoners.

Date.	Total Receptions.	Negroes.	Per Cent of Negroes.
1876	21,736	1,530	7.8
1877	22,666	1,460	6.44
1878	22,147	1,356	6.12
1879	20,736	1,136	5.48
1880	22,487	1,030	4.58
1881	22,478	1,168	5.19
1882	24,176	1,274	5.27
1883	23,245	1,175	5.05
1884	25,081	1,218	4.86
1885	24,725	1,427	5.77
1886	27,286	1,708	6.26
1887	28,964	1,724	5.97
1888	21,399	1,399	6.54
1889	18,476	1,338	7.24
1890	20,582	1,611	7.83
1891	22,745	1,723	7.57
1892	22,460	1,900	8.46
1893	25,209	2,234	8.86
1894	25,777	2,452	9.51
1895	22,584	2,317	10.26
Total	464,959	31,180	6.70
1876–1885	229,477	12,774	5.57
1886–1895	235,482	18,406	7.81

If we compare in this table the period 1876–85 with that of 1886–95 we find that the proportion of Negro criminals in the first period was 5.6 per cent, in the second 7.8 per cent.

The statistics of inmates of the House of Correction, where mild cases and juveniles are sent, for the last few years go to tell the same tale :

Year.	Total Receptions.	Negroes.	Percentage of Negroes.
1891	5907	274	4.6
1892	5297	254	4.8
1893	. .	. .	. .
1894	6579	1055	16.0
1895	7548	672	8.9

Gathering up the statistics presented let us make a rough diagram of some of the results. First let us scan the record of the Negro in serious crime, such as entails incarceration in the Eastern Penitentiary. In these figures the Philadelphia convicts are not separated from those in the eastern counties of the state prior to 1885. A large proportion of the prisoners however are from Philadelphia ; perhaps the net result of the error is somewhat to reduce the apparent proportion of Negroes in the earlier years. Taking then the proportion of Negro prisoners received to total receptions since the founding of the Penitentiary we have this diagram :

PROPORTION OF NEGROES TO TOTAL CONVICTS RECEIVED AT THE
EASTERN PENITENTIARY, 1829–1895.

The general rate of criminality may be graphically represented from the proportion of Negroes in the county prison,

although changes in the policy of the courts make the
validity of this somewhat uncertain :

PROPORTION OF NEGROES IN MOYAMENSING PRISON TO TOTAL PRISONERS
"   "   "   " TOTAL POPULATION OF CITY
PROPORTION ETC. ESTIMATED FROM ARRESTS.

It thus seems certain[17] that general criminality as
represented by commitments to the county prison has
decreased markedly since 1840, and that its rapid increase
since 1880 leaves it still far behind the decade 1830 to 1840.
Serious crime as represented by commitments to the penitentiary shows a similar decrease but one not so marked
indicating the presence of a pretty distinct criminal class.

---

[17] The chief element of uncertainty lies in the varying policy of the
courts, as for instance, in the proportion of prisoners sent to different
places of detention, the severity of sentence, etc. Only the general
conclusions are insisted on here.

CONVICTS COMMITTED TO THE EASTERN PENITENTIARY.

Years.	Total Commitments.	Negroes.	Percentage of Negroes.
1835–39	878	356	40.5
1855–59	941	126	13.4
1860–64	909	129	14.2
1865–69	1474	179	12.1
1870–74	1291	174	13.4
1875–79	2347	275	11.7
1880–84	2282	308	13.5
1885–89*	1583	223	14.09
1890–95*	1418	318	22.43

* Only convicts from Philadelphia; the statistics for the year 1891 are not available and are omitted.

The record of arrests per 1000 of Negro population 1864 to 1896 seems to confirm these conclusions for that period:

---- NEGRO ARRESTS TO EVERY 1000 OF NEGRO POPULATION.
——— WHITE   "   "   ·   1000   "   WHITE   "

The increase in crime between 1890 and 1895 is not without pretty adequate explanation in the large Negro immigration cityward and especially in "the terrible business depression of 1893" to which the police bureau attributes the increase of arrests. The effect of this would naturally be greater among the economic substrata.

This brings us to the question, Who are the Negro criminals and what crimes do they commit? To obtain an answer to this query let us make a special study of a typical group of criminals.

39. A Special Study in Crime.[18]—During ten years previous to and including 1895, there were committed to the Eastern Penitentiary, the following prisoners from the city of Philadelphia:

PHILADELPHIA WHITES AND NEGROES COMMITTED TO THE EASTERN PENITENTIARY.

Date.	Total Convictions.	Negroes.	Per Cent of Negroes.	
1885	313	40	12.78	⎫
1886	347	45	12.97	⎪
1887	363	53	14.60	⎬ 14.9
1888	269	39	14.49	⎪
1889	291	46	15.81	⎭
1890	271	63	23.25	⎫
1891*	. .	. .	. .	⎪
1892	213	42	19.71	⎬ 22.43
1893	320	74	23.13	⎪
1894	329	69	20.97	⎪
1895	285	70	24.56	⎭
Total	3,001	541	18.2 average.	

* Statistics for this year were not available. Throughout this section, therefore, this year is omitted.

Let us now take the 541 Negroes who have been the perpetrators of the serious crimes charged to their race during the last ten years and see what we may learn. These are all criminals convicted after trial for periods

---

[18] For the collection of the material here compiled, I am indebted to Mr. David N. Fell, Jr., a student of the Senior Class, Wharton School, University of Pennsylvania, in the year '96–'97. As before noted the figures in this Section refer to the number of prisoners received at the Eastern Penitentiary, and not to the total prison population at any particular time.

varying from six months to forty years. It seems plain in the first place that the 4 per cent of the population of Philadelphia having Negro blood furnished from 1885 to 1889, 14 per cent of the serious crimes, and from 1890 to 1895, 22½ per cent. This of course assumes that the convicts in the penitentiary represent with a fair degree of accuracy the crime committed. The assumption is not wholly true; in convictions by human courts the rich always are favored somewhat at the expense of the poor, the upper classes at the expense of the unfortunate classes, and whites at the expense of Negroes. We know for instance that certain crimes are not punished in Philadelphia because the public opinion is lenient, as for instance embezzlement, forgery, and certain sorts of stealing; on the other hand a commercial community is apt to punish with severity petty thieving, breaches of the peace, and personal assault or burglary. It happens, too, that the prevailing weakness of ex-slaves brought up in the communal life of the slave plantation, without acquaintanceship with the institution of private property, is to commit the very crimes which a great centre of commerce like Philadelphia especially abhors. We must add to this the influences of social position and connections in procuring whites pardons or lighter sentences. It has been charged by some Negroes that color prejudice plays some part, but there is no tangible proof of this, save perhaps that there is apt to be a certain presumption of guilt when a Negro is accused, on the part of police, public and judge.[19] All these considerations modify somewhat our judgment of the moral status of the mass of Negroes. And yet, with all allowances, there remains a vast problem of crime.

The chief crimes for which these prisoners were convicted were:

---

[19] Witness the case of Marion Stuyvesant accused of the murder of the librarian Wilson, in 1897.

Theft 243
Serious assaults on persons 139
Robbery and burglary 85
Rape 24
Other sexual crimes 23
Homicide 16
All other crimes 11

Total 541

Following these crimes from year to year we have :

Crime.	1885.	1886.	1887.	1888.	1889.	1890.	1892.	1893.	1894.	1895.	Total.
Theft, etc.	20	21	23	13	24	39	20	32	23	28	243
Robbery and burglary . . .	2	8	8	5	5	9	7	14	19	8	85
Serious assaults	10	9	11	15	9	12	9	19	18	27	139
Homicide	.	.	3	2	5	.	2	1	1	2	16
Sexual crimes	6	7	7	4	4	4	4	5	3	3	47
All others	2	.	1	1	.	.	.	2	3	2	11
Total	40	45	53	40	47	64	42	73	67	70	541

The course of the total serious crime for this period may
be illustrated by this diagram:

Drawing a similar diagram for the different sorts of
crime we have :

THEFT &C. ——— SEXUAL CRIMES ------- ASSAULTS ———
HOMICIDE ━━━━ BURGLARY & ROBBERY ———

In ten years convictions to the penitentiary for theft
have somewhat increased, robbery, burglary and assault
have considerably increased, homicide has remained about
the same, and sexual crimes have decreased. Detailed
statistics are given in the following table:

CRIMES OF 541 CONVICTS IN EASTERN PENITENTIARY, 1885-1895.

Crimes.	1885.	1886.	1887.	1888.	1889.	1890.	1892.	1893.	1894.	1895.
Assault and battery	3	.	1	2	.	1	.	.	.	
Aggravated assault and battery . .	3	3	3	7	3	6	3	6	6	9
Assault to kill	4	6	7	6	6	5	4	13	11	17
Manslaughter	.	.	.	1	3	.	1	1	.	1
Murder	.	.	3	1	2	.	1	.	1	1
Assault to murder	.	.	1	.	.	.	.	.	.	
Assault to steal	.	.	.	.	.	.	2	.	1	1
Larceny	20	21	23	13	24	39	17	27	22	28
Robbery	2	3	3	1	.	4	3	5	9	6
Burglary	.	5	5	4	5	5	4	9	10	2
Embezzlement	.	.	.	.	.	.	.	1	.	
Sodomy	2	1	1	3	2	3	2	.	.	1
Abortion	1	.	.	.	.	.	1	.	.	
Rape	1	.	.	.	.	.	.	2	1	.
Attempt to rape	1	6	1	1	1	1	1	3	2	1
Incest	1	.	.	.	.	.	.	.	.	
Keeping bawdy house	.	.	4	.	.	.	.	.	.	1
Enticing female child	.	.	1	.	1	.	.	.	.	
Carrying concealed weapons . . .	1	.	.	.	.	.	.	1	.	
Forgery	1	.	.	.	.	.	.	.	1	1
False pretence	.	.	.	.	1	.	1	.	1	.
Receiving stolen goods	.	.	.	.	.	.	2	4	1	.
Mayhem	.	.	.	.	.	.	.	1	.	
Indecent exposure	.	.	.	.	.	.	.	.	.	1
Conspiracy	.	.	.	.	.	.	.	.	1	.
Total	40	45	53	40	47	64	42	73	67	70

The total crime can be classified also in this way:

Crimes against property	. . . . . .	328	60.63 per cent.
" " persons	. . . .	157	29.02 "
" " persons and property	.	8	1.48 "
Sexual crimes	. . . .	48	8.87 "
		541	100. per cent.

Let us now turn from the crime to the criminals. 497 of them (91.87 per cent) were males and 44 (8.13 per cent) were females. 296 (54.71 per cent) were single, 208 (34.45 per cent) were married, and 37 (6.84 per cent) were widowed. In age they were divided as follows:

Age.	Number.	Percentage.	
15–19	58	10.73 }	
20–24	170	} 56.19	66.92
25–29	132		
30–39	132	24.03	
40–49	34	6.29	
50–59	10	1.85 }	34.08
60 and over	5	.91	
Total	541	100.	

The mass of criminals are, it is easy to see, young single men under thirty. Detailed statistics of sex and age and conjugal condition are given in the next tables.

AGE AND SEX OF CONVICTS IN EASTERN PENITENTIARY.
NEGROES, 1885–1895.

Ages.	Males.	Females.	Total.
15–19	53	5	58
20–24	153	17	170
25–29	119	13	132
30–34	80	5	85
35–39	45	2	47
40–44	21	1	22
45–49	11	1	12
50–59	3	.	3
60 and over	15	.	15
Total	497	44	541

CONJUGAL CONDITION OF CONVICTS IN EASTERN PENITENTIARY.

Age.	Males.			Females.		
	Single.	Married.	Widowed.	Single.	Married.	Widowed.
15–19	48	5	0	4	1	0
20–24	117	35	0	7	9	1
25–29	59	54	8	3	10	0
30–34	30	38	6	0	4	1
35–39	11	30	4	0	0	2
40–49	8	16	8	0	2	0
50–59	3	3	4	0	0	0
60 and over .	0	2	3	0	0	0

The convicts were born in the following States:

Philadelphia	114
Other parts of Pennsylvania	48
New Jersey	21
Maryland	99
Virginia	77
Delaware	37
District of Columbia	35
North Carolina	19
New York	11
South Carolina	9
Georgia	8
Other parts of the North	13
" " " South	22
The West	13
Foreign Countries	15
	541

Altogether 21 per cent were natives of Philadelphia; 217 were born in the North, and 309, or 57 per cent, were born in the South. Two-thirds of the Negroes of the city, judging from the Seventh Ward, were born outside the city, and this part furnishes 79 per cent of the serious crime. 54 per cent were born in the South, and this part furnishes 57 per cent of the crime, or more, since many giving their birthplace as in the North were really born in the South.

The total illiteracy of this group reaches 26 per cent or adding in those who can read and write imperfectly, 34 per cent compared with 18 per cent for the Negroes of the city in 1890. In other words the illiterate fifth of the Negro population furnished a third of the worst criminals.

ILLITERACY OF CONVICTS IN THE EASTERN STATE PENITENTIARY.

Year.	Read and Write.		Read and Write Imperfectly.		Totally Illiterate.	
	Number.	Per Cent.	Number.	Per Cent.	Number.	Per Cent.
1885	20	50.0	6	15.0	14	35.0
1886	25	55.55	4	8.88	16	35.55
1887	27	50.94	13	24.53	13	24.53
1888	25	64.10	6	15.38	8	20.51
1889	26	56.52	10	21.74	10	21.74
1890	43	68.25	3	4.76	17	26.98
1892	33	78.57	0	0	9	21.43
1893	55	74.32	0	0	19	25.68
1894	49	71.01	0	0	20	28.99
1895	55	78.57	0	0	15	21.43
Total	358	66.17	42	7.76	141	26.06

Naturally as the general intelligence of a community increases the general intelligence of its criminals increases, though seldom in the same proportion, showing that some crime may justly be attributed to pure ignorance. The number of criminals able to read and write has increased from 50 per cent in 1885 to 79 per cent in 1895. The number of colored men from fifteen to thirty who can read and write was about 90 per cent in the Seventh Ward in 1896. This shows how little increased intelligence alone avails to stop crime in the face of other powerful forces. It would of course be illogical to connect these phenomena directly as cause and effect and make Negro crime the result of Negro education—in that case we should find it difficult to defend the public schools in most modern lands. Crime comes either in spite of intelligence or as a result of misdirected intelligence under severe economic and moral strain. Thus we find here, as is apparently true in France, Italy and Germany, increasing crime and decreasing illiteracy as concurrent phenomena rather than as cause and effect. However the rapid increase of intelligence in Negro convicts does point to some grave social changes: first, a large number of young

Negroes are in such environment that they find it easier to be rogues than honest men ; secondly, there is evidence of the rise of more intelligent and therefore more dangerous crime from a trained criminal class, quite different from the thoughtless, ignorant crime of the mass of Negroes.

A separation of criminals according to sex and age and the kind of crime is of interest. (See p. 256 for males.)

CRIMINALS IN EASTERN STATE PENITENTIARY.—FEMALES, BY AGE AND CRIME.

Ages.	Crimes.							
	Larceny.	Assault and Battery.	Aggravated Assault.	Assault to Kill.	Murder.	Bawdy and Disorderly Houses.	Accessory to Murder.	Abduction.
15-19	5	. .	. .			. .	. .	. .
20-24	10	1	3	2	1	. .	. .	. .
25-29 . . .	11		1	. .	. .	1	. .	. .
30-34	3	. .	. .	. .	. .	. .	1	1
35-39	1	. .	. .	. .	. .	1	. .	. .
40-44	1	. .	. .	. .				
45-49 . .	1	. .	. .		. .	. .	. .	. .

The women are nearly all committed for stealing and fighting. They are generally prostitutes from the worst slums. The boys of fifteen to nineteen are sentenced largely for petty thieving :

Whole number of male convicts, 15-19 years of age . .　53
Convicted for larceny . . . .　27
　"　　"　assault and fighting . . . .　8
　"　　"　sexual crimes . . . .　5
　"　　"　burglary . . . .　5
　"　　"　other crimes . . . .　8
　　　　　　　　　　　　　　　　　　　　—　53

Making a similar table for two other age periods we have :

Men, 20-24 Years.		**Men, 25-29 Years.**	
Larceny	62	Larceny	45
Assault	41	Assault	33
Burglary and robbery	30	Burglary and robbery	22
Sexual crimes	6	Sexual crimes	13
Other crimes	14	Homicide	4
		Other crimes	3
	153		119

CRIMINALS IN EASTERN STATE PENITENTIARY.—MALES, BY AGE AND CRIME.

Ages	Larceny	Assault and Battery	Receiving Stolen Goods	Assault to Steal	Concealed Weapons	Aggravated Assault and Battery	Assault to Kill	Burglary	Robbery	Sodomy	Assault to Rape	Rape	Manslaughter	Forgery	Murder	Conspiracy	False Pretense	Embezzlement	Mayhem	Bawdy houses	Enticement to Rape	Indecent Exposure	Incest	Abortion
15-19	27	1	2	1	1	2	4	5		1	3	1	1	1	3									
20-24	62	4	2	1	1	16	24	14	16	4	1	1	1		1	1	2	1	1					
25-29	45	1	1	2		9	22	12	10	3	3	4	1		3					1	2			
30-34	23	1	1			6	17	12	9	3	2		1	1	2					1		1		
35-39	23		1			6	3	3			4		1	1			1			1			1	
40-44	9					4	2	1	1		2		1											1
45-49	3				1	2	2	1			1		1											
50-59	2						1	2	1	3														
60 and over	3						1																	1
Total	197	7	7	4	3	45	76	50	37	15	16	6	7	3	9	1	3	1	1	3	2	1	1	2

There is here revealed no especial peculiarity: stealing and fighting are ever the besetting sins of half-developed races.

It would be very instructive to know how many of the 541 criminals had been in the hands of the law before. This is however very difficult to ascertain correctly since in many, if not the majority of cases, the word of the prisoner must be taken. Even these methods however reveal the startling fact that only 315 or 58 per cent of these 541 convicts are reported as being incarcerated for the first time. 226 or 42 per cent can be classed as habitual criminals, who have been convicted as follows :

Twice	. . . .	105	46.5 per cent.
Three times	. . . .	60	26.5 "
Four "	. . . .	24	11.0 "
Five "	. . . .	19	8.0 "
Six "	. . . .	9	4.0 "
Seven "	. . . .	4	1.8 "
Nine "	. . . .	1	
Ten "	. . . .	1	2.2 "
Eleven "	. . . .	2	
Twelve "	. . . .	1	
		226	100 per cent.

When we realize that probably a large number of the other convicts are on their second or third term we begin to get an idea of the real Negro criminal class.[19]

---

[19] The following Negroes were measured by the Bertillon system in Philadelphia during the last three years:

1893	. . . . 64 (Whites 101).
1894	. . . . 66 (Whites 248).
1895	. . . . 56 (Whites 267).
1896	. . . . 75 (Whites 347).

The arrests by detectives for five years are given on the following page (258).

A few other facts are of interest: if we tabulate crime according to the illiteracy of its perpetrators, we have:

Larceny . . . .   31 per cent of illiteracy.
Assault, burglary and homicide . .   34   "   "   "
Sexual crimes   55   "   "   "

Or in other words, the more serious and revolting the crime the larger part does ignorance play as a cause. If we separate prisoners convicted for the above crimes according to length of sentence, we have:

Under five years   464   90.5 per cent.
Five and under ten years   40   8.0   "
Ten years and over   9   1.5   "
                                        ———
                                        513

Of the 49 sentenced for 5 years and over, 18 or 37 per

CRIMES OF NEGROES ARRESTED BY DETECTIVES, 1878-1892.

CRIMES.	1887.	1888.	1889.	1890.	1891.	1892.
Fugitives from justice	. . .	10	2	4	4	9
Larceny	10	19	17	19	18	29
Pickpocket	7	4	1	. . .	. . .	13
Burglary	1	. . .	2	. . .	2	4
Professional thief	1	4	2	1	2	3
Sodomy	. . .	. . .	. . .	. . .	. . .	1
Misdemeanor	. . .	1	. . .	1	. . .	1
Absconding	. . .	. . .	. . .	. . .	. . .	1
Assault to kill	5	6	1	1	4	4
Stabbing	. . .	. . .	. . .	. . .	. . .	1
False pretense	. . .	2	. . .	1	. . .	1
Forgery	. . .	. . .	. . .	. . .	. . .	1
Receiving stolen goods	1	4	8	. . .	3	. . .
Murder	3	2	1	3	2	. . .
Abortion	. . .	. . .	. . .	1	1	. . .
Breach of peace	. . .	. . .	. . .	2	. . .	. . .
Abandonment	. . .	. . .	1	1	. . .	. . .
Gambling house	. . .	4	. . .	5	. . .	. . .
Fornication and adultery . . .	. . .	. . .	1	. . .	. . .	. . .
Infanticide	. . .	1	. . .	. . .	. . .	. . .
House robbery	. . .	1	. . .	. . .	. . .	. . .
Lottery	1	8	. . .	. . .	. . .	. . .
Embezzlement	. . .	1	. . .	. . .	. . .	. . .
Perjury	. . .	1	. . .	. . .	. . .	. . .
Seduction	1	. . .	. . .	. . .	. . .	. . .
Bawdy house	1	. . .	. . .	. . .	. . .	. . .

cent were illiterate; of those sentenced for less than 5 years, 160 or 35 per cent were illiterate.

From this study we may conclude that young men are the perpetrators of the serious crime among Negroes; that this crime consists mainly of stealing and assault; that ignorance, and immigration to the temptations of city life, are responsible for much of this crime but not for all; that deep social causes underlie this prevalence of crime and they have so worked as to form among Negroes since 1864 a distinct class of habitual criminals; that to this criminal class and not to the great mass of Negroes the bulk of the serious crime perpetrated by this race should be charged.

40. Some Cases of Crime.—It is difficult while studying crime in the abstract to realize just what the actual crimes committed are, and under what circumstances they take place. A few typical cases of the crimes of Negroes may serve to give a more vivid idea than the abstract statistics give. Most of these cases are quoted from the daily newspapers.

First let us take a couple of cases of larceny:

Edward Ashbridge, a colored boy, pleaded guilty to the larceny of a quart of milk, the property of George Abbott. The boy's mother said he was incorrigible, and he was committed to the House of Refuge.

William Drumgoole, colored, aged thirty-one years, of Lawrenceville, Va., was shot in the back and probably fatally wounded late yesterday afternoon by William H. McCalley, a detective, employed in the store of John Wanamaker, Thirteenth and Chestnut streets. Drumgoole, it is alleged, stole a pair of shoes from the store, and was followed by McCalley to the corner of Thirteenth and Chestnut streets, where he placed him under arrest. Drumgoole broke away from the detective's grasp, and running down Thirteenth street turned into Drury street, a small thoroughfare above Sansom street. McCalley started in pursuit, calling upon him to stop, but the fugitive darted into an alleyway, and when his pursuer came up within a few yards of him, he threatened to "do him up" if he followed him any further. McCalley drew his revolver from his pocket, and as Drumgoole again broke into a run he pointed the weapon at his legs and fired. Drumgoole fell to the ground, and when McCalley came up to him he was unable to rise. McCalley saw at a glance that, instead of wounding him in the leg, as he had intended, the bullet had lodged in the man's back. He hurriedly sought assistance, and had the wounded man taken to the Jefferson Hospital. McCalley then surrendered himself to Reserve Policeman Powell, and was taken to the Central Station.

Fighting and quarreling among neighbors and associates is common in the slum districts :

Etta Jones, colored, aged twenty-one years, residing on Hirst street, above Fifth, was stabbed near her home last night, it is alleged, by Lottie Lee, also colored, of Second and Race streets. The other woman was taken to the Pennsylvania Hospital, where her injuries were found to consist of several cuts on the left shoulder and side, none of which are dangerous. Her assailant was arrested later by Policeman Dean and locked up in the Third and Union streets station house. The assault is said by the police to have been the outcome of an old grudge.

Joseph Cole, colored, aged twenty-four years, residing in Gillis' alley, was dangerously stabbed shortly before midnight on Saturday, as is alleged, by Abraham Wheeler, at the latter's house, on Hirst street. Cole was taken to the Pennsylvania Hospital, where it was found the knife had penetrated to within a short distance of the right lung. Wheeler fled from the house after the cutting and eluded arrest until yesterday afternoon, when he was captured by Policeman Mitchell, near Fifth and Lombard streets. When brought to the station house Wheeler denied having cut Cole, but acknowledged having struck him because he was insulting his wife. He was locked up, however, to await the result of Cole's injuries.

Sometimes servants are caught pilfering :

Theodore Grant, colored, residing on Burton street, attempted to pledge a woman's silk dress for $15 at McFillen's, Seventeenth and Market streets, several days ago. The pawnbroker refused, under his rule, to take women's raiment from a man, and told Grant to bring the owner. Grant went away and returned with Ella Jones, a young colored woman, who consented to take $7 for the dress. Since that time C. F. Robertson, residing at Sixtieth and Spruce streets, made complaint to the police of the loss of the dress, and as the result of an investigation made by Special Policemen Gallagher and Ewing, Grant and Ella Jones were arrested yesterday charged with the larceny of the silk dress, which was recovered. Grant admitted to the special policemen that Ella had given him the dress to pawn, but asserted that he had nothing to do with the matter except to offer to pledge the article. At a hearing before Magistrate Jermon, at the City Hall, yesterday, Mr. Robertson stated that the girl had made a statement to him, saying that Grant had induced her to take the dress. He said the girl had been perfectly trustworthy up to the time of her acquaintance with Grant, and had been left in full charge of the house, and that nothing was ever missed. He said he also expected to show that Grant had been concerned in two or three robberies. Ella Jones, a neatly dressed girl, who said she came from Maryland, stated to the magistrate that Grant had been coming to see her for about a year past. She said he had been importuning her to take something and let him pawn it, so that he could raise some money, until she finally consented. After she started to go to her mistress' room to get the dress her heart failed and she turned back, but he persuaded her, telling her that Mrs. Robertson would not miss it, and then she took the dress. Mr. Robertson informed the magistrate, and Ella assented to the statement, that Grant had taken every cent of her earnings from her for weeks past and had also pawned all of her clothing, so that at the present time she was penniless and had not a single garment except what she wore. The magistrate said it was undoubtedly a hard case, but he would have to hold Grant and Ella on the charge of larceny, and Grant under additional bail for a further hearing next Thursday on the charges referred to by Mr. Robertson. The police say that Grant, who is a smooth-faced, cross-eyed mulatto, is a "crap fiend," and that whatever money he has managed to obtain by threats and cajolery from his victim, Ella Jones, has gone into the pockets of the small-fry gamblers.

There is growing evidence of the appearance of a set of thieves of intelligence and cunning: sneak thieves, confidence-men, pickpockets, and "sharpers." Some typical cases follow:

Marion Shields and Alice Hoffman, both colored and residing on Fitzwater street, above Twelfth, had a further hearing yesterday before Magistrate South, at the City Hall, and were held for trial on the charge of pilfering wearing apparel, money, vases, umbrellas, surgical instruments, and other portable property from physicians' offices and houses, where they had made visits, under the pretence of desiring to hold consultations with the doctors. The Magistrate said there were ten cases against Marion Shields individually on which she would be placed under $2500 bail, and six cases against both women on which the bail would be $1500. For her frankness, Marion Shields was given the lighter sentence, one year in the Eastern Penitentiary, and Alice Hoffman was sentenced to eighteen months in the same institution.

Two daring thieves yesterday entered the jewelry store of Albert Baudschopfs , 468½ North Eighth street, and secured a number of articles of jewelry from under the very eyes of the proprietor. They had left the store and proceeded leisurely down the street before the jeweller discovered his loss, with the result that before an alarm could be given the thieves had traveled a considerable distance. One of the men was captured after a long chase, but the other's whereabouts is unknown. About half-past one o'clock two colored men entered the store and upon their request were shown trays of various articles. One of the men engaged the proprietor in conversation while the other continued to inspect the jewelry. They said they did not intend buying then and would call again and opening the door walked hurriedly down the street. Mr. Baudschopfs says the men got away with a gold-filled watch case, a silver watch, three gold lockets, each set with a small diamond ; two dozen ladies' gold rings, not jewelled; a gold scarf pin and a man's gold watch.

A crime for which Negroes of a certain class have become notorious is that of snatching pocketbooks on the streets :

While passing down Eleventh street, near Mount Vernon, shortly after nine o'clock, Mrs. K. Nichun, of 1947 Warnock street, was approached from behind by a Negro, who snatched a pocketbook containing $2 from her hand and ran down a small thoroughfare towards Tenth street. Very few pedestrians were upon the street at the time, but two men, who were attracted by the woman's scream, started in pursuit of the thief. The latter had too much of a start, however, and escaped.

William Williams, colored, of Dayton, O., was locked up in the Central Station yesterday, by Reserve Policeman A. Jones, on the charge of snatching a pocketbook from the hands of Mrs. Mary Tevis, of 141 Mifflin street. The theft occurred at Eighth and Market streets. After securing the pocketbook Williams ran until he reached the old office of the city solicitor, at Sixth and Locust streets. He was followed by Reserve Jones, who captured him in the cellar of the building. Williams was taken to Eighth and Sansom streets to await the arrival of the patrol wagon, and while getting into the vehicle the pocketbook dropped from out of his trousers.

Detectives Bond and O'Leary and Special Policeman Duffy, of the Eighth and Lombard streets station, arrested last night Sylvester Archer, of Fifth street, below Lombard, William Whittington, alias " Piggy," of Florida street, and William Carter, of South Fifteenth street, all colored and about twenty-one years of age, on the charge of assault upon and robbery of Mrs. Harrington Fitzgerald, wife of the editor of the *Evening Item.* The assault occurred on Monday at noon. As Mrs. Fitzgerald was passing Thirteenth and Spruce streets, a purse which she carried in her hand, and which contained $20, was snatched from her by one of three colored men. They took advantage of the crowd to strike her after the robbery had been perpetrated and escaped before her outcry was heard. When the men were brought to the Central Station last night and questioned by Captain of Detectives Miller, Whittington, it is said, confessed complicity in the crime. He told the captain that they had been following a band up Thirteenth street, and as they reached Spruce street Carter said, " There's a pocketbook; I'm going to get it." " All right; get it," came the response. Carter ran up to Mrs. Fitzgerald and and in a moment shouted, " I've got it ! " Then he and Archer ran up Thirteenth street. Each man has a criminal record, and the picture of each is in the Rogues' Gallery.   Carter has just completed a six months' sentence for purse-snatching, while Williams and Archer have each served time for larceny.

So frequent have these crimes become that sometimes Negroes are wrongfully suspected; whoever snatches a pocketbook on a dark night is supposed to be black.

A favorite method of stealing is to waylay and rob the frequenters of bawdy houses; very little of this sort of crime, naturally, is reported.   Here are some cases of such "badger thieves," as they are called :

William Lee, colored, and Kate Hughes, a white woman, were convicted of robbing Vincenzo Monacello of $10. Lee was sentenced to three years and three months in the Eastern Penitentiary and his accomplice to three years in the county prison. Mary Roach, jointly indicted with them, was acquitted. Monacello testified that, while walking along Christian street, between Eighth and Ninth streets, on Thursday night of last week, he was accosted by Mary Roach and accompanied her to her home on Essex street. Here he met Lee and Kate Hughes and they all drank considerable beer. Later in the night he started with Kate Hughes, at her suggestion, to a house further up the street. While on their way the prosecutor said he was struck in the face with a brick by Lee, after which the money was stolen from him. Mary Roach took the stand against the other two defendants and the case against her was abandoned.

Ella Jones, colored, claiming to be from Baltimore, was arrested yesterday by Policeman Dean on the charge of the larceny of a $10 bill from Joseph Gosch, a Pole, who came from Pittsburg on Sunday, and claims that while he was looking for lodging he was taken to the woman's house and robbed.

From pocketbook snatching to highway robbery is but a step :

Before Judge Yerkes, in Court No. 1, Samuel Buckner, a young colored man, was convicted of robbing George C. Goddard of a gold watch and chain and a pocketbook containing $3. He was sentenced to ten years in the Eastern Penitentiary. Mr. Goddard, with his head swathed in bandages, was called to the stand. He said that a few minutes past midnight of November 28 he was returning to his home, No. 1220 Spruce street, after a visit. He placed his hand in his pocket, drew out his key and was about to mount the steps when a dark form appeared from Dean street, a small, poorly-lighted thoroughfare, next door but one to his home, and at the same instant he was struck a violent blow full in the face with a brick. He sank to the pavement unconscious. When he recovered his senses he was in the Pennsylvania Hospital. There was a long, deep cut on his right cheek, another across the forehead, both eyes were blackened and swollen, and his nose was also bruised. At the same time he discovered the loss of his pocketbook and jewelry. Judge Yerkes reviewed the facts of the case, and in imposing sentence said: "When you committed this offence you were absolutely indifferent as to the consequences of your cowardly attack. You rifled this man's person of all his valuables and left him lying unconscious on the pavement, and for aught you knew he might have been dead. It is necessary not only that society be protected from the depredations of such fiends as you, but also that an example be made of such ruffians. The sentence of the Court is that you undergo an imprisonment of ten years at labor in the Eastern Penitentiary, and stand committed until this sentence shall be complied with." The official record shows that Buckner was arrested on December 11, 1893, by policeman Logan, of the Lombard street station, on the charge of the larceny of a purse from Mrs. Caroline Lodge, of 2416 North Fifteenth street, on the street, and was sentenced December 14, 1893, by Judge Biddle, to one year's imprisonment.

Cases of aggravated assaults, for various reasons, are frequent :

Rube Warren, colored, thirty years, of Foulkrod and Cedar streets, was held in $1000 bonds, by Magistrate Eisenbrown, for an alleged aggravated assault and battery on Policeman Haug, of the Frankford station, during a dog fight about a month ago. The policeman attempted to stop the fight when Warren, it is charged, assisted by several companions, assaulted him, broke his club and took away his revolver. During the free fight that followed, in which other policemen took part, Warren escaped and went to Baltimore. There, it is said, he was sent to prison for thirty days. As soon as he was released he went back to Frankford, where he was arrested on Saturday night.

William Braxton, colored, aged twenty-eight years, of Irving street, above Thirty-seventh, was yesterday held in $800 bail for a further hearing, charged with having committed an aggravated assault on William Keebler, of South Thirtieth street. The assault occurred about three o'clock yesterday morning on Irving street, near Thirty-seventh, where the colored folks of the neighborhood were having a party. Keebler and two friends, none of whom were colored, forced their company on the invited guests, it is said, and a fight ensued. Keebler was found a short time afterward lying in the snow with one eye almost gouged out. He was conveyed to the University Hospital and the police of the Woodland avenue station, under Acting Sergeant Ward, upon being notified of the affair, hurried to the Irving street house and arrested twenty of the guests just in the height of their merrymaking. All of them, however, were discharged at the hearing, upon Braxton's being recognized as the man who struck Keebler. The physician at the hospital says that the injured man will very likely lose the sight of one eye.

Gambling goes on almost openly in the slum sections and occasions, perhaps, more quarreling and crime than any other single cause. Reporters declared in 1897 that—

"Policy playing is rampant in Philadelphia. Under the very noses of the police officials and, it is safe to say, with the knowledge of some of them, policy shops are conducted openly and with amazing audacity. They are doing a 'land office' business. Hundreds of poor people every day place upon the infatuating lottery money that had better be spent for food and clothing. They actually deny themselves the necessaries of life to gamble away their meagre income with small chance of getting any return. Superintendent of Police Linden, discussing the general subject of policy playing with a *Ledger* reporter, said: 'There are not words enough in the dictionary to express my feelings upon this matter. I regard policy as the worst evil in a large city among the poor people. There are several reasons for this. One is that women and children may play. Another is that players may put a few cents on the lottery. Policy may do more harm than all the saloons and "speak easies" in the city. The price of a drink of liquor is five or ten cents and the cost of a "growler" is ten cents, but a man or a woman can buy two cents' worth of policy. The effect of this is obvious. Persons who have not the price of a drink may gamble away the few pennies they do possess in a policy shop. Then the drain is constant. Policy "fiends" play twice a day, risking from two cents to a dollar upon the chance. They become so infatuated with the play that they will spend their last cent upon it in the hope of making a "hit." Many children go hungry and with insufficient clothing as a result of policy playing. I have heard of young children engaging in this sort of gambling. Of course the effect of this is very bad. The policy evil is, to my mind, the very worst that exists in our large cities as affecting the poorer classes of people.' " [20]

---

[20] Although the police lieutenants have reported to the Superintendent that few policy shops exist, the *Ledger* has information which leads it to state that such is not the fact. Many complaints against the evil have been received at this office. A reporter found it easy to locate and gain admittance to a number of houses where policy is written. A policy writer who is thoroughly informed as to the inside working of the system is authority for the statement that at no time in recent years has policy playing been so prevalent or the business carried on as openly as it is now.

While the locations of the policy shops are well known and the writers familiar to many persons, the backers, who, after all, are the substantial part of the system, are hard to reach, for they exercise an unusual cunning in the direction of the business. There are several backers in

Once in a while gambling houses are raided:

Twenty-three colored men, who were arrested in a raid of the police on an alleged gambling house, on Rodman street, above Twelfth, had

---

Philadelphia of greater or less pretensions, but a young man who resides uptown and operates principally in the territory north of Girard avenue, is said to be the heaviest backer of the game in this city. He owns sixty or seventy " books," and his income from their combined receipts is sufficient to support himself and several relatives in magnificent style.

A *Ledger* reporter spent one day last week looking up the policy shops in one of the sections where this backer operates. He found, in addition to several places where policy is written, the rendezvous of the writers and the headquarters of the policy king himself.

The writers who hold " books " from the backer in question meet twice every day, Sundays excepted, in a mean, dirty little house overlooking the Reading tracks, just below Montgomery avenue. They enter by the rear through a narrow alley leading off Delhi street, several yards below Montgomery avenue. At noon and at 6 o'clock in the evening the writers hurry to this rendezvous.

The unusual number of men gathering at this point at regular intervals, and the business-like manner in which they go through the alley and back gate is enough to attract the attention of the Twelfth District policeman on this beat and arouse his suspicions. Whether he notices it or not, these proceedings have been going on for months.

Each writer, when he reaches this central point, turns in his " book " and receipts. There are two drawings daily, hence the two meetings. Two relatives of the backer receive the " books " and the money. A copy of each writer's " book " and all the money are carried by one of these men to the house of an ex-special policeman, a few squares away, and there turned over to the backer, who has received a telegram from Cincinnati stating the numbers that have come out at that drawing.

The " books " are carefully gone over, to see if there are any " hits." If there are they are computed, and the backer sends to each writer the amount necessary to pay his losses. The numbers that appear at each drawing are printed with rubber stamps in red ink, on slips of white paper and given to the writers to distribute among the players.

These drawings are usually carried to the rendezvous by the ex-policeman. The backer pockets the half day's receipts, mounts his bicycle and rides away.

To establish beyond a doubt the character of the building in which the writers meet, the reporter made his way into it on the afternoon in question. It is a well-known policy shop, conducted by a colored man, who has been writing policy for years. He is president of a colored political club, with headquarters near by. On the occasion of the visit the back gate was ajar. Pushing it open, the reporter walked in without challenge.—From the *Public Ledger*, December 3, 1897.

a hearing yesterday, before Magistrate South, at the City Hall. One man, residing on Griscom street, testified that the house was supposed to be a "club," and that it was customary to pay a dollar before admission could be secured, and that he had been gambling at "crap" and a card game known as "five-up," and had lost $18. He said there was a president, marshal and sergeant-at-arms. He pointed out Bolling, Jordan and Phillips as the principals. Special Policeman Duffy testified that the crowd was playing "crap" with dice on the floor when he headed the raid on Monday night. He said he had notified Bolling, as the head of the house, three months ago, when he had heard that gambling was going on there, to stop it. On cross-examination the witness said he did not know that it was a social club called the "Workingmen's Club." Patrolman William Harvey testified that he went to the house on last Saturday night and got in readily, and was not called on to pay a dollar initiation fee, as had been claimed was the rule. He said he played "sweat" and lost twenty-five cents, but did not win anything. He said Bolling was running the game. He said that when he entered the house somebody called out "Sam's got a new man," and that was all that was said.

More and more frequently in the last few years, have crime, excess, and disappointment led to attempted suicide :

Policeman Wynne, of the Fifth and Race streets station, last evening found an unknown colored woman lying unconscious in an alleyway at Delaware avenue and Race street. Beside the woman was an empty bottle labeled benzine. Wynne immediately summoned the patrol wagon and had the woman removed to the Pennsylvania Hospital, where her condition was said to be critical. The physicians said there was no doubt the woman had drunk the contents of the bottle, and narcotics were at once administered to counteract the effect of the poison. At midnight the woman showed signs of returning consciousness and it was thought that she would recover. The police have no clue to her identity, as she could not tell her name, and the alleyway where she was found is surrounded by business houses, and no one could be found who knew her.

It is but fair to add that many unsustained charges of crime are made against Negroes, and possibly more in proportion than against other classes. Some typical cases of this sort are of interest :

W. M. Boley, colored, thirty years old, who said he resided in Mayesville, South Carolina, was a defendant before Magistrate Jermon, at the City Hall, yesterday, on the charge of assault with intent to steal. Detective Gallagher and Special Policeman Thomas testified that their attention was attracted to the prisoner by his actions in a crowd at the

New York train gate at Broad street station on Saturday. He had with
him several parcels which he laid on the floor near the gate, and they
said they saw him make several attempts to pick women's pockets, and
arrested him. The man however proved by documentary evidence that
he was a clergyman, a graduate of Howard University, and financial
agent of a Southern school. He was released.

Under instructions from Judge Finletter, a jury rendered a verdict of
not guilty in the case of George Queen, a young colored man, charged
with the murder of Joseph A. Sweeney and John G. O'Brien. Dr.
Frederick G. Coxson, pastor of the Pitman Methodist Episcopal
Church, at Twenty-third and Lombard streets, testified that on the night
in question he was about to retire, when he heard a disturbance on
the street. Upon going out he saw three young men, two of whom were
leading the other and persuading him to come with them. At the
same time the prisoner, Queen, came along in the middle of the street,
walking leisurely. Immediately upon seeing him the three men attacked
him, and were shortly afterward joined by three others, and the entire
crowd, among whom were Sweeney and O'Brien, continued beating and
striking the colored man. Suddenly the crowd scattered and Queen was
placed under arrest ; he had fatally stabbed two of his assailants. This
testimony showed that the accused was not the aggressor, and without
hearing the defence Judge Finletter ordered the jury to render a verdict
of not guilty. The case, he said, was one of justifiable homicide, the
defendant having a right to resist the attack by force. The judge further
said he thought the case would have a tendency to repel the brutal attacks
made on inoffensive persons in the community, and to make the streets
safe for every man to walk on at any hour without fear.

Leaving for a moment the question of the deeper social
causes of crime among Negroes, let us consider two closely
allied subjects, pauperism and the use of alchoholic liquors.

CHAPTER XIV.

PAUPERISM AND ALCOHOLISM.

41. Pauperism.—Emancipation and pauperism must ever go hand in hand; when a group of persons have been for generations prohibited from self-support, and self-initiative in any line, there is bound to be a large number of them who, when thrown upon their own resources, will be found incapable of competing in the race of life. Pennsylvania from early times, when emancipation of slaves in considerable numbers first began, has seen and feared this problem of Negro poverty. The Act of 1726 declared: "Whereas free Negroes are an idle and slothful people and often prove burdensome to the neighborhood and afford ill examples to other Negroes, therefore be it enacted   *   *   *   *   that if any master or mistress shall discharge or set free any Negro, he or she shall enter into recognizance with sufficient securities in the sum of £30 to indemnify the county for any charge or incumbrance they may bring upon the same, in case such Negro through sickness or otherwise be rendered incapable of self-support."

The Acts of 1780 and 1788 took pains to provide for Negro paupers in the county where they had legal residence, and many decisions of the courts bear upon this point. About 1820 when the final results of the Act of 1780 were being felt, an act was passed "To prevent the increase of pauperism in the Commonwealth;" it provided that if a servant was brought into the state over twenty-eight years of age (the age of emancipation) his master was to be liable for his support in case he became a pauper.[1]

Thus we can infer that much pauperism was prevalent among the freedmen during these years although there are

---

[1] See Appendix B for these various laws.

no actual figures on the subject. In 1837, 235 of the 1673 inmates of the Philadelphia County Almshouse were Negroes or 14 per cent of paupers from 7.4 per cent of the population. These paupers were classed as follows:[2]

Males.		Females.	
Under 21 years	18	Under 18 years	33
21 to 50 "	57	18 to 40 "	59
50 to 75 "	18	40 to 60 "	17
Unknown	13	60 " and over . . .	10
		Unknown	10
	106		129

Lunatics and defective	16 males,	31 females,		
Defective from exposure	11 "	11 "		
Consumption, rheumatism, etc. . . .	9 "			
Pleurisy, typhus fever, etc.	12 "			
Destitute	13 "			
Paupers	32 "	35 "		
Unclassed	13 "	28 "		
Women lying-in, children and orphans,		24 "		

106 males, 129 females.

Ten years later there were 196 Negro paupers in the Almshouse, and those receiving outdoor relief were reported as follows:[3]

In the City:
 Of 2562 Negro families, 320 received assistance.
In Spring Garden:
 Of 202 Negro families, 3 received assistance.
In Northern Liberties:
 Of 272 Negro families, 6 received assistance.
In Southwark:
 Of 287 Negro families, 7 received assistance.
In West Philadelphia:
 Of 73 Negro families, 2 received assistance.
In Moyamensing:
 Of 866 Negro families, 104 received assistance.
Total, of 4262 Negro families, 442 received assistance, or 10 per cent.

---

[2] " Condition," etc., 1838.
[3] " Condition," etc., 1848.

This practically covers the available statistics of the past; it shows a large amount of pauperism and yet perhaps not more than could reasonably be expected.

To-day it is very difficult to get any definite idea of the extent of Negro poverty; there is a vast amount of alms-giving in Philadelphia, but much of it is unsystematic and there is much duplication of work; and, at the same time, so meagre are the records kept that the real extent of pauperism and its causes are very hard to study.[4]

The first available figures are those relating to lodgers at the station houses—*i. e.,* persons without shelter who have applied for and been given lodging :[5]

1891, total lodgers . . 13,600, of whom 365, or 2.7 per cent were Negroes.
1892,   "   "   . . 11,884,   "   345, or 2.9   "   "   "
1893,   "   "   . . 20,521,   "   622, or 3.0   "   "   "
1894,   "   "   . . 43,726,   "   1247, or 2.9   "   "   "
1895,   "   "   . . 45,788,   "   2247, or 4.9   "   "   "
1896,   "   "   . . 46,121,   "   2359, or 5.0   "   "   "

Somewhat similar statistics are furnished by the report of arrests by the vagrant detective for the last ten years :

1887 . . . total arrests, 581. Negroes . . . 55   9.5 per cent.
1888 . . .   "   "   574.   "   . . . 48   8.4   "
1889 . . .   "   "   588.   "   . . . 36   6.1   "
1890 . . .   "   "   523.   "   . . . 48   9.1   "
1891 . . .   "   "   554.   "   . . . 47   8.5   "
1892 . . .   "   "   505.   "   . . . 65   12.9   "
1893 . . .   "   "   586.   "   . . . 67   11.0   "
1894 . . .   "   "   688.   "   . . . 66   9.6   "
1895 . . .   "   "   557.   "   . . . 56   10.0   "
1896 . . .   "   "   629.   "   . . . 59   9.3   "

The Negro vagrants arrested during the last six years were thus disposed of :

---

[4] Cf. The "Civic Club Digest" for general information.

[5] From reports of police department. Many other official reports might be added to these, but they are easily accessible.

Disposal.	1891.	1892.	1893.	1894.	1895.	1896.
Given temporary shelter . . .	21	27	29	39	26	32
Transported from city	3	2	5	4	2	3
Arrested for vagrancy, beggary, etc.	5	10	4	4	2	5
Arrested for vicious conduct, etc	15	10	16	11	14	5
Sent to House of Refuge . . .	3	14	7	2	5	0
Sent to societies and institutions	0	2	6	6	7	13

These records give a vague idea of that class of persons just hovering between pauperism and crime—tramps, loafers, defective persons and unfortunates—a class difficult to deal with because made up of diverse elements.

Turning to the true paupers, we have the record of the paupers admitted to the Blockley Almshouse during six years:

ADULTS—SIXTEEN YEARS OF AGE AND OVER.

Year.	Total Receptions	Negroes.	Per Cent of Negroes.
1891	6764	569	8.4
1892	6231	537	8.8
1893	6451	567	8.8
1894	6108	569	9.3
1895	6318	606	9.3
1896	6414	593	9.2

CHILDREN UNDER SIXTEEN YEARS OF AGE.

Year.	Total Receptions	Negroes.	Per Cent of Negroes.
1891	380	38	12.3
1892	262	38	14.5
1893	295	38	12.9
1894	304	35	11.1
1895	401	42	10.5
1896	410	51	12.4

In 1891, 4.2 per cent of the whites admitted were insane and 2.3 per cent of the Negroes; in 1895, 8.3 per cent of the whites and 8.6 per cent of the Negroes:

THE INSANE.

Year.	Whites.		Negroes.	
	Total Receptions	Insane.	Total Receptions	Insane.
1891	6195	264	569	13
1892	5694	450	537	45
1893	5884	427	567	39
1894	5539	441	569	38
1895	5712	463	606	52

We have already seen that in the Seventh Ward about 9 per cent of the Negroes can be classed as the "very poor," needing public assistance in order to live. From this we may conclude that between three and four thousand Negro families in the city may be classed among the semi-pauper class. Thus it is plain that there is a large problem of poverty among the Negro problems; 4 per cent of the population furnish according to the foregoing statistics at least 8 per cent of the poverty. Considering the economic difficulties of the Negro, we ought perhaps to expect rather more than less than this. Beside these permanently pauperized families there is a considerable number of persons who from time to time must receive temporary aid, but can usually get on without it. In time of stress as during the year 1893 this class is very large.

There is especial suffering and neglect among the children of this class of people: in the last ten years the Children's Aid Society has received the following children: [6]

	From 1887 to 1897.	Negroes.	Total.
Received from judges and magistrates (so-called delinquents)		19	181
Deserted babies		7	55
Orphans		4	147
Half-orphans, including those with mothers in delicate health and worthless fathers; also both parents worthless		12	448
From Blockley Almshouse		7	

---

[6] From the Society records, by courtesy of the officers.

From Blockley Almshouse (foundlings)	12	362
From Society for Prevention of Cruelty to Children . .	3	45
From County Poor Boards	26	151
	110	1389

The total receptions during these ten years have been
1389, of which the Negroes formed 8 per cent. This but
emphasizes the fact of poor family life among the lower
classes which we have spoken of before.

A little better light can be thrown on the problem of
poverty by a study of concrete cases; for this purpose 237
families have been selected. They live in the Seventh
Ward and are composed of those families of Negroes
whom the Charity Organization Society, Seventh District,
has aided for at least two winters.[7] First, we must notice
that this number nearly corresponds with the previously
estimated per cent of the " very poor." [8] Arranging these
families according to size, we have:

Number in Family.	Families.	Persons.
1	48	48
2	61	122
3	54	162
4	31	124
5	19	95
6	10	60
7	1	7
11	1	11
Unknown	9	?
Total	234	638

The reported causes of poverty, which were in all cases
verified by visitors so far as possible, were as follows:

---

[7] From the C. O. S. records, Seventh District, by courtesy of Miss
Burke.

[8] This coincidence in figures was entirely unnoticed until both had
been worked out by independent methods.

Lack of work . . . . 115 families.
Sickness, accident, or physical disability . . . 39   "
Death of bread-winner and old age 24   "
Probable gambling, criminal shiftlessness, etc., 16   "
Desertion of bread-winner 15   "
Laziness and improvidence 10   "
Intemperate use of alcoholic liquors 8   "
Financial reverses 7   "
                                            ———
                                            234 families.

From as careful a consideration of these cases as the necessarily meagre information of records and visitors permit, it seems fair to say that Negro poverty in the Seventh Ward was, in these cases, caused as follows:

By sickness and misfortune . . . . 40 per cent.
By lack of steady employment 30   "
By laziness, improvidence and intemperate drink 20   "
By crime 10   "

Of course this is but a rough estimate; many of these causes indirectly influence each other: crime causes sickness and misfortune; lack of employment causes crime; laziness causes lack of work, etc.

Several typical families will illustrate the varying conditions encountered:

No. 1.—South Eighteenth street. Four in the family; husband intemperate drinker; wife decent, but out of work.

No. 2.—South Tenth street. Five in the family; widow and children out of work, and had sold the bed to pay for expense of a sick child.

No. 3.—Dean street. A woman paralyzed; partially supported by a colored church.

No. 4.—Carver street. Worthy woman deserted by her husband five years ago; helped with coal, but is paying the Charity Organization Society back again.

No. 5.—Hampton street. Three in family; living in three rooms with three other families. "No push, and improvident."

No. 6.—Stockton street. The woman has just had an operation performed in the hospital, and cannot work yet.

No. 7.—Addison street. Three in family; left their work in Virginia through the misrepresentations of an Arch street employment bureau; out of work.

No. 8.—Richard street. Laborer injured by falling of a derrick; five in the family. His fellow workmen have contributed to his support, but the employers have given nothing.

No. 9.—Lombard street. Five in family; wife white; living in one room; hard cases; rum and lies; pretended one child was dead in order to get aid.

No. 10.—Carver street. Woman and demented son; she was found very drunk on the street; plays policy.

No. 11.—Lombard street. Worthy woman sick with a tumor; given temporary aid.

No. 12.—Ohio street. Woman and two children deserted by her husband; helped to pay her rent.

No. 13.—Rodman street. A widow and child; out of work. "One very little room, clean and orderly."

No. 14.—Fothergill street. Two in the family; the man sick, half-crazy and lazy; "going to convert Africa and didn't want to cook;" given temporary help.

No. 15.—Lombard street. An improvident young couple out of work; living in one untidy room, with nothing to pay rent.

No. 16.—Lombard street. A poor widow of a wealthy caterer; cheated out of her property; has since died.

No. 17.—Ivy street. A family of four; husband was a stevedore, but is sick with asthma, and wife out of work; decent, but improvident.

No. 18.—Naudain street. Family of three; the man, who is decent, has broken his leg; the wife plays policy.

No. 19.—South Juniper street. Woman and two children; deserted by her husband, and in the last stages of consumption.

No. 20.—Radcliffe street. Family of three; borrowed of Charity Organization Society $1.00 to pay rent, and repaid it in three weeks.

No. 21.—Lombard street. "A genteel American white woman married to a colored man; he is at present in the South looking for employment; have one child;" both are respectable.

No. 22.—Fothergill street. Wife deserted him and two children, and ran off with a man; he is out of work; asked aid to send his children to friends.

No. 23.—Carver street. Man of twenty-three came from Virginia for work; was run over by cars at Forty-fifth street and Baltimore avenue, and lost both legs and right arm; is dependent on colored friends and wants something to do.

No. 24.—Helmuth street. Family of three; man out of work all winter, and wife with two and one-half days' work a week; respectable.

No. 25.—Richard street. Widow, niece and baby; the niece betrayed and deserted. They ask for work.

42. The Drink Habit.—The intemperate use of intoxicating liquors is not one of the Negro's special offences; nevertheless there is considerable drinking and the use of beer is on the increase. The Philadelphia liquor saloons are conducted under an unusually well-administered system, and are not to so great an extent centres of brawling and loafing as in other cities; no amusements, as pool and billiards, are allowed in rooms where liquor is sold. This is not an unmixed good for the result is that much of the drinking is thus driven into homes, clubs and "speakeasies." The increase of beer-drinking among all classes, black and white, is noticeable; the beer wagons deliver large numbers of bottles at private residences, and much is carried from the saloons in buckets.

An attempt was made in 1897 to count the frequenters of certain saloons in the Seventh Ward during the hours from 8 to 10 on a Saturday night. It was impracticable to make this count simultaneously or to cover the whole ward, but eight or ten were watched each night.[9] The results are a rough measurement of the drinking habits in this ward.

There are in the ward 52 saloons of which 26 were watched in districts mostly inhabited by Negroes. In these two hours the following record was made:

Persons entering the saloons :

Negroes—male, 1373; female, 213. Whites—male, 1445; female, 139.

Of those entering, the following are known to have carried liquor away :

Negroes—male, 238; female, 125. Whites—male, 275; female, 81.

3170 persons entered half the saloons of the Seventh Ward in the hours from 8 to 10 of one Saturday night in December, 1897; of these, 1586 were Negroes, and 1584 were whites; 2818 were males, and 352 were females.[10] Of those entering these saloons at this time a part carried away liquor—mostly beer in tin buckets; of those thus visibly carrying away liquor there were in all 719; of these 363 were Negroes, and 356 were whites; 513 were males, and 206 were females.

The observers stationed near these saloons saw, in the two hours they were there, 79 drunken persons.

The general character of the saloons and their frequenters can best be learned from a few typical reports. The numbers given are the official license numbers :

No. 516. Persons entering saloon :

Men—white, 40; Negro, 68. Women—white, 12; Negro, 12.

---

[9] I am indebted to Dr. S. M. Lindsay and the students of the Wharton School for the carrying out of this plan.

[10] No comparison of the number of Negroes and whites for the ward can be made, because many of the saloons omitted are frequented by whites principally.

Persons carrying liquor away :
Men—white, 8; Negro, 16. Women—white, 1; Negro, 3.
Drunken persons seen, 12.

General character of saloon and frequenters :—" A small corner saloon, kept by a white man. The saloon appears to be a respectable one and has three entrances : one on Thirteenth street and the two on a small court. The majority of the colored patrons are poor people and of the working class. The white patrons are, for the greater part, of the better class. Among the latter very few were intoxicated."

No. 488. Persons entering:
Men—white, 24; Negro, 102. Women—white, 2; Negro, 3.

Carrying liquor away, 12; drunken persons seen, 8.

General character :—" The saloon was none too orderly; policemen remained near all the time ; the Negro men entering were as a rule well dressed—perhaps one-third were laborers ; the white men were well dressed but suspicious looking characters."

No. 515. Persons entering :
Men—white, 81; Negro, 59. Women—white, 4; Negro, 10.

Persons carrying liquor away :
Men—white, 15 (one a boy of 12 or 14 years of age); Negro, 11. Women—white, 4; Negro, 8.

Drunken persons seen, 2 (to one nothing was sold).

General character of saloon and frequenters :—" There were two Negro men and seven white men in saloon when the count was started. The place has three doors but all are easily observed. Trade is largely in distilled liquors, and a great deal is sold in bottles—a ' barrel shop.' "

No. 527. Persons entering saloon :

	8 to 9 P. M.	9 to 10 P. M.	Total.
Men, White	49	54	104
" Negro	29	37	68
Women, White	3	3	6
" Negro	5	2	7
	88	97	185

Persons carrying liquor away:

Men, White	6	11	17
" Negro	4	9	13
Women, White	0	1	1
" Negro	4	0	4
Boys, "	1	0	1
	15	21	36

Drunken persons seen, none.

General character of saloon and frequenters :—" Quiet, orderly crowd—quick trade—no loafing. Three boys were among those entering."

No. 484. Persons entering saloon :
Men—white, 70; Negro, 32. Women—white, 10; Negro, 1.

Persons carrying liquor away :
Men—white, 10; Negro, 12. Women—white, 4; Negro, 0.

Drunken persons seen, 11, six of whom were white and five black. "I cannot say that the saloon was responsible for all of them, but they were all in or about it."

This saloon is in the worst slum section of the ward and is of bad character. Frequenters were a mixed lot, "fast, tough, criminal and besotted."

No. 487. Persons entering :
Men—white, 79; Negro, 129. Women—white, 13; Negro, 34.

Persons carrying liquor away :
Men—white, 15; Negro, 25. Women—white, 5; Negro, 8.

"No drunken men seen. Frequented by a sharp class of criminals and loafers. Near the notorious 'Middle Alley.'"

No. 525.

Total Negroes entering, 14; total whites entering, 13.

"No loafers about the front of the saloon. Streets well lighted and neighborhood quiet, according to the policeman. There was a barber shop next door and a saloon on the corner ten doors below. Very few drunken people were seen. Trade was most brisk between eight and nine o'clock. In two hours one more Negro than white entered. Two more Negroes, men, than whites carried away liquor. One white man, a German, returned three times for beer in a kettle. Two Negro women carried beer away in kettles; one white woman (Irish) made two trips. All women entered by side door. The saloon is under a residence, three stories, corner of Waverly and Eleventh streets. Waverly street has a Negro population which fairly swarms—good position for Negro trade. Proprietor and assistant were both Irish. The interior of the saloon was finished in white pine stained to imitate cherry. Extremely plain. Barkeeper said, 'A warm night, but we are doing very well.' One beggar came in, a colored 'Auntie;' she wanted bread, not gin. Negroes were well dressed, as a rule, many smoking. The majority of frequenters by their bustling air and directness with which they found the place, showed long acquaintance with the neighborhood; especially this corner."

No. 500.   Persons entering saloon:

Men—white, 40; Negro, 73.   Women—white 4; Negro, 6.

Persons carrying liquor away:

Men—white, 6; Negro, 23.   Women—white, 5; Negro, 4.

Drunken persons seen, 1.

General character of saloon and frequenters:—" Four
story building, plain and neat ; three entrances; iron
awning ; electric and Welsbach lights. Negroes generally
tidy and appear to be pretty well-to-do. Whites not so
tidy as Negroes and generally mechanics. Almost all
smoke cigars. Liquor carried away openly in pitchers and
kettles. Three of the white women, carrying away liquor,
looked like Irish servant girls. Some of the Negroes
carried bundles of laundry and groceries with them."

Few general conclusions can be drawn from this data.
The saloon is evidently not so much a moral as an economic
problem among Negroes ; if the 1586 Negroes who went
into the saloons within two hours Saturday night spent five
cents apiece, which is a low estimate, they spent $79.30.
If, as is probable, at least $100 was spent that Saturday
evening throughout the ward, then in a year we would not
be wrong in concluding their Saturday night's expenditure
was at least $5000, and their total expenditure could
scarcely be less than $10,000, and it may reach $20,000—a
large sum for a poor people to spend in liquor.

43. The Causes of Crime and Poverty.—A study of
statistics seems to show that the crime and pauperism of
the Negroes exceeds that of the whites ; that in the main,
nevertheless, it follows in its rise and fall the fluctuations
shown in the records of the whites, *i. e.*, if crime increases
among the whites it increases among Negroes, and *vice
versa*, with this peculiarity, that among the Negroes the
change is always exaggerated—the increase greater, the
decrease more marked in nearly all cases. This is what we
would naturally expect: we have here the record of a low
social class, and as the condition of a lower class is by its
very definition worse than that of a higher, so the situation
of the Negroes is worse as respects crime and poverty than
that of the mass of whites. Moreover, any change in social
conditions is bound to affect the poor and unfortunate more
than the rich and prosperous. We have in all probability

an example of this in the increase of crime since 1890 ;
we have had a period of financial stress and industrial
depression ; the ones who have felt this most are the poor,
the unskilled laborers, the inefficient and unfortunate, and
those with small social and economic advantages : the
Negroes are in this class, and the result has been an increase
in Negro crime and pauperism ; there has also been an
increase in the crime of the whites, though less rapid by
reason of their richer and more fortunate upper classes.

So far, then, we have no phenomena which are new or
exceptional, or which present more than the ordinary social
problems of crime and poverty—although these, to be sure,
are difficult enough.   Beyond these, however, there are
problems which can rightly be called Negro problems:
they arise from the peculiar history and condition of the
American Negro.   The first peculiarity is, of course, the
slavery and emancipation of the Negroes.   That their
emancipation has raised them economically and morally is
proven by the increase of wealth and co-operation, and the
decrease of poverty and crime between the period before
the war and the period since ; nevertheless, this was manifestly no simple process : the first effect of emancipation
was that of any sudden social revolution : a strain upon
the strength and resources of the Negro, moral, economic
and physical, which drove many to the wall.   For this reason
the rise of the Negro in this city is a series of rushes and
backslidings rather than a continuous growth.   The second
great peculiarity of the situation of the Negroes is the fact
of immigration ; the great numbers of raw recruits who
have from time to time precipitated themselves upon the
Negroes of the city and shared their small industrial opportunities, have made reputations which, whether good or bad,
all their race must share ; and finally whether they failed or
succeeded in the strong competition, they themselves must
soon prepare to face a new immigration.

Here then we have two great causes for the present

condition of the Negro : Slavery and emancipation with their attendant phenomena of ignorance, lack of discipline, and moral weakness ; immigration with its increased competition and moral influence. To this must be added a third as great—possibly greater in influence than the other two, namely the environment in which a Negro finds himself—the world of custom and thought in which he must live and work, the physical surrounding of house and home and ward, the moral encouragements and discouragements which he encounters. We dimly seek to define this social environment partially when we talk of color prejudice —but this is but a vague characterization ; what we want to study is not a vague thought or feeling but its concrete manifestations. We know pretty well what the surroundings are of a young white lad, or a foreign immigrant who comes to this great city to join in its organic life. We know what influences and limitations surround him, to what he may attain, what his companionships are, what his encouragements are, what his drawbacks.

This we must know in regard to the Negro if we would study his social condition. His strange social environment must have immense effect on his thought and life, his work and crime, his wealth and pauperism. That this environment differs and differs broadly from the environment of his fellows, we all know, but we do not know just how it differs. The real foundation of the difference is the widespread feeling all over the land, in Philadelphia as well as in Boston and New Orleans, that the Negro is something less than an American and ought not to be much more than what he is. Argue as we may for or against this idea, we must as students recognize its presence and its vast effects.

At the Eastern Penitentiary where they seek so far as possible to attribute to definite causes the criminal record of each prisoner, the vast influence of environment is shown. This estimate is naturally liable to error, but the

peculiar system of this institution and the long service and
wide experience of the warden and his subordinates gives
it a peculiar and unusual value.   Of the 541 Negro prisoners previously studied 191 were catalogued as criminals by
reason of " natural and inherent depravity." The others
were divided as follows :

Crimes due to

(*a*) Defects of the law :

Laxity in administration	33
Unsuitable laws for minor offences	48
Inefficient police	22
License given to the young	16
Inefficient laws in regard to saloons	11
Poor institutions and lack of institutions	12
	—— 142

(*b*) Immediate environment:

Association	53
Amusements	16
Home and family influences	25
	—— 94

(*c*) Lack of training, lack of opportunity, lack of desire to work	56
(*d*) General environment	6
(*e*) Disease	16
(*f*) Moral weakness and unknown	36
	—— 114

This rough judgment of men who have come into daily
contact with five hundred Negro criminals but emphasizes
the fact alluded to ; the immense influence of his peculiar
environment on the black Philadelphian ; the influence of
homes badly situated and badly managed, with parents
untrained for their responsibilities ; the influence of social
surroundings which by poor laws and inefficient administration leave the bad to be made worse; the influence of
economic exclusion which admits Negroes only to those
parts of the economic world where it is hardest to retain
ambition and self-respect ; and finally that indefinable but
real and mighty moral influence that causes men to have

a real sense of manhood or leads them to lose aspiration and self-respect.

For the last ten or fifteen years young Negroes have been pouring into this city at the rate of a thousand a year; the question is then what homes they find or make, what neighbors they have, how they amuse themselves, and what work they engage in? Again, into what sort of homes are the hundreds of Negro babies of each year born? Under what social influences do they come, what is the tendency of their training, and what places in life can they fill? To answer all these questions is to go far toward finding the real causes of crime and pauperism among this race; the next two chapters, therefore, take up the question of environment.

CHAPTER XV.

THE ENVIRONMENT OF THE NEGRO.

44. Houses and Rent.—The inquiry of 1848 returned quite full statistics of rents paid by the Negroes.[1] In the whole city at that date 4019 Negro families paid $199,665.46 in rent, or an average of $49.68 per family each year. Ten years earlier the average was $44 per family. Nothing better indicates the growth of the Negro population in numbers and power when we compare with this the figures for 1896 for one ward; in that year the Negroes of the Seventh Ward paid $25,699.50 each month in rent, or $308,034 a year, an average of $126.19 per annum for each family. This ward may have a somewhat higher proportion of renters than most other wards. At the lowest estimate, however, the Negroes of Philadelphia pay at least $1,250,000 in rent each year.[2]

The table of rents for 1848 is as follows (see page 288):

We see that in 1848 the average Negro family rented by the month or quarter, and paid between four and five dollars per month rent. The highest average rent for any section was less than fifteen dollars a month. For such rents the poorest accommodations were afforded, and we know from descriptions that the mass of Negroes had small and unhealthful homes, usually on the back streets and alleys. The rents paid to-day in the Seventh Ward, according to the number of rooms, are tabulated on page 289.

---

[1] "Condition," etc., 1848, p. 16.

[2] Not taking into account sub-rent repaid by sub-tenants; subtracting this and the sum would be, perhaps, $1,000,000—see *infra*, p. 291. That paid by single lodgers ought not, of course, to be subtracted as it has not been added in.

RENTS PAID BY NEGROES OF PHILADELPHIA, 1848.

	City.	Spring Garden.	Northern Liberties.	Southwark.	Moyamensing.	West Philadelphia.	Total.
Total rent paid annually	$124,979.37	$8,697.06	$11,128.00	$11,924.15	$40,809.51	$2,127.37	$199,665.46
Number tenements rented by the year	4	4	5	7	18	12	59
Annual average rent paid for same	$147.81	$125.00	$167.40	$148.43	$163.00	$66.60	
Number tenements rented by the quarter	1131	35	73	79	210	19	1547
Annual average rent paid for same	$58.80	$56.97	$58.41	$55.37	$67.23	$37.48	
Number tenements rented by the month	1078	98	143	139	373	16	1847
Annual average rent paid for same	$45.20	$40.68	$38.53	$38.78	$43.08	$32.78	
Number tenements rented by the week	248	38	34	34	205	4	563
Annual average rent paid for same	$36.47	$42.84	$30.00	$32.94	$35.47	$22.84	
Number tenements rented by the night					12		12
Annual average rent paid for same					$34.68		
Number persons whose rent is repaid by sub-tenants	6	1					7
Number who pay tax for rent			3				3
Rent free	2	1	1		1		5
Own their houses	88	23	38	28	44	20	241
Not reported	5	3			3		11
Average annual rent per family							$49.68
Same for 1837							$44.00

Negro Homes, According to Rents and Rooms.[3]
Seventh Ward, Philadelphia.

Amount of Rent per Month.	One and less.	Two.	Three.	Four.	Five.	Six.	Seven.	Eight.	Nine.	Ten.	Eleven and over.	Unknown.	Grand Total Rent.
Free	.	4	1	1	.	.	.	.	.	.	.	.	. . .
$1.00	.	.	.	.	.	.	.	.	.	.	.	.	. .
1.50	2	.	.	.	.	.	.	.	.	.	.	.	$3.00
2.00	5	.	.	.	.	.	.	.	.	.	.	1	12.00
2.50	6	.	.	.	.	.	.	.	.	.	.	.	15.00
3.00	36	.	.	.	.	.	.	.	.	.	.	.	108.00
3.50	17	.	.	.	.	.	.	.	.	.	.	.	59.50
4.00	161	4	.	.	.	.	.	.	.	.	.	.	660.00
4.50	237	11	3	1	.	.	.	.	.	.	.	.	1134.00
5.50	14	2	.	.	.	.	.	.	.	.	.	.	88.00
6.00	175	18	15	.	.	.	.	.	.	.	.	1	1254.00
6.50	6	4	.	.	.	.	.	.	.	.	.	.	65.00
7.00	39	11	47	.	.	.	.	.	.	.	.	.	679.00
7.50	2	1	5	1	.	.	.	.	.	.	.	.	67.50
8.00	88	28	76	9	4	.	.	.	.	.	.	1	1648.00
8.50	.	2	10	.	.	.	.	.	.	.	.	.	102.00
9.00	3	2	68	9	.	1	.	.	.	.	.	.	747.00
9.50	.	.	1	.	.	.	.	.	.	.	.	.	9.50
10.00	17	8	43	32	7	3	1	.	.	.	.	.	1110.00
10.50	.	2	.	.	.	.	.	.	.	.	.	.	21.00
11.00	.	1	19	10	3	.	.	.	.	.	.	.	363.00
11.50	.	2	.	.	.	.	.	.	.	.	.	.	23.00
12.00	.	8	48	46	25	11	1	.	.	.	.	.	139.00
13.00	.	.	11	18	10	3	1	.	.	.	.	.	569.00
14.00	.	.	8	17	13	9	3	.	.	.	.	.	700.00
15.00	.	.	10	15	18	31	2	1	1	.	.	.	1170.00
16.00	.	.	.	5	21	28	5	1	.	.	.	.	960.00
17.00	.	.	.	.	3	8	1	1	.	.	.	.	221.00
18.00	.	1	.	1	8	52	20	6	2	.	.	.	1620.00
19.00	.	.	.	.	.	6	2	2	1	.	.	.	209.00
20.00	.	.	.	2	4	50	35	16	7	1	.	.	2300.00
21.00	.	.	.	.	.	3	5	4	2	.	.	.	294.00
22.00	.	.	.	.	.	11	12	5	2	.	.	.	660.00
23.00	.	.	.	.	2	8	8	18	7	1	.	.	1012.00
24.00	.	.	.	.	.	.	3	1	1	.	.	.	120.00
25.00	.	.	.	1	2	21	27	38	21	12	9	.	3275.00
26.00–28.00 . .	.	.	.	.	2	1	4	9	15	3	2	.	972.00
30.00	.	.	.	.	1	2	6	8	15	7	10	.	1470.00
35.00	.	.	.	.	.	1	2	3	4	6	9	.	875.00
40.00	.	.	.	.	.	1	1	1	1	4	6	.	560.00
45.00	.	.	.	.	.	.	.	.	1	1	1	.	135.00
50.00	.	.	.	.	.	.	.	.	.	1	1	.	100.00
65.00	.	.	.	.	.	.	.	.	.	.	1	.	65.00
75.00	.	.	.	.	.	.	.	.	.	1	.	.	75.00
Owned and unknown . . .	21	.	3	2	4	12	12	29	16	12	14	51	. . .

Total rent per month $25,699.50	Aver. rent per year per family . $126.19
Total rent per year $308,034.00	Aver. rent per year per individual, $31.83
Aver. rent per month per family, $10.50+	

[3] The returns as to rents paid are among the most reliable of the statistics gathered. The amount of rent is always well known, and there are

Condensing this table somewhat we find that the Negroes pay rent as follows :

> Under $5 per month . . . . . . 490 families, or 21.9 per cent.
> $5 and under $10 . . . . . . 643 " " 28.7 "
> $10 " " $15 . . . . . . 380 " " 17.0 "
> $15 " " $20 . . . . . . 252 " " 11.3 "
> $20 " " $30 . . . . . . 375 " " 17.0 "
> $30 and over . . . . 95 " " 4.1 "

The lodging system so prevalent in the Seventh Ward makes some rents appear higher than the real facts warrant. This ward is in the centre of the city, near the places of employment for the mass of the people and near the centre of their social life ; consequently people crowd here in great numbers. Young couples just married engage lodging in one or two rooms ; families join together and hire one house ; and numbers of families take in single lodgers ; thus the population of the ward is made up of

Families owning or renting their homes and living
alone . . . . 738, or 31 per cent.
Families owning or renting their homes, who take
lodgers or sub-renters . . . . 937, " 38 "
Families sub-renting under other families . . . . . 766, " 31 "

Total individuals 7751   100 "
Total families 2441
Individuals lodging with families 1924

Total individuals 9675

The practice of sub-renting is found of course in all degrees : from the business of boarding-house keeper to the

---

few motives for deception. Moreover in Philadelphia there is a tendency to build rows and streets of houses with the same general design. These rent for the same sum, and thus particular instances of false report are easily detected. One feature of the returns must be noted, *i. e.*, the large number of cases where high rents are paid for one- and two-room tenements. In nearly all of these cases this rent is paid for large front bedrooms in good localities, and often includes furniture. Sometimes a limited use of the family kitchen is also included. In such cases it is misleading to call these one-room tenements. No other arrangement, however, seemed practical in these tables.

case of a family which rents out its spare bed-chamber. In the first case the rent is practically all repaid, and must in some cases be regarded as income ; in the other cases a small fraction of the rent is repaid and the real rent and the size of the home reduced. Let us endeavor to determine what proportion of the rents of the Seventh Ward are repaid in sub-rents, omitting some boarding and lodging-houses where the sub-rent is really the income of the house-wife. In most cases the room-rent of lodgers covers some return for the care of the room. The next table gives detailed statistics :

PROPORTION OF RENT REPAID IN SUB-RENT.
Negroes of Seventh Ward, Philadelphia.

Proportion Repaid in Sub-rent.	Monthly Rent Paid: Dollars											Total Families.	Approximate Total Sub-rent: Dollars.
	5 and under.	Over 5 and under 8.	8 and under 10.	10 and under 12.	12 and under 15.	15 and under 18.	18 and under 20.	20 and under 25.	25 and under 30.	30 and over.	Unknown.		
One-eighth rep'd	.	.	1	1	.	.	.	4	7	6	.	19	61.08
One-sixth "	.	.	.	.	.	.	.	.	1	1	.	2	9.16
One-fourth "	1	.	1	1	8	23	16	31	9	8	1	99	460.51
One-third "	2	3	18	16	45	26	8	17	23	11	.	170	871.33
One-half "	2	17	37	20	17	26	23	55	31	14	1	243	1748.75
Two-thirds "	.	2	11	6	24	11	10	7	21	6	1	109	1246.33
Three-fourths "	.	2	4	2	6	11	7	23	19	6	.	80	1201.08
Four-fifths "	.	.	.	.	.	.	.	1	.	1	.	2	48.00
Whole rent "	.	2	11	3	12	8	13	19	14	10	1	94	} 3167.00
More than the whole rent repaid	1	.	4	3	5	2	2	14	13	13	.	57	
Unknown . . .	.	.	.	.	.	.	.	.	.	.	62	62	. . .
Total families .	.	.	.	.	.	.	.	.	.	.	.	937	. . .
Approximate total of sub-rent repaid monthly . . .	.	.	.	.	.	.	.	.	.	.	.		8813.24

It appears from this table that nearly $9000 is paid by the sub-renting families and lodgers to the renting families. A part of this ought to be subtracted from the total rent paid if we would get at the net rent; just how much, however, should be called wages for care of room, or other conveniences furnished sub-renters, it is difficult to say. Possibly the net rent of the ward is $20,000, and of the city about $1,000,000.[4]

The accommodations furnished for the rent paid must now be considered. The number of rooms occupied is the simplest measurement, but is not very satisfactory in this case owing to the lodging system which makes it difficult to say how many rooms a family really occupies. A very large number of families of two and three rent a single bedroom and these must be regarded as one-room tenants, and yet this renting of a room often includes a limited use of a common kitchen; on the other hand this sub-renting family cannot in justice be counted as belonging to the renting family. The figures are:

829 families live in 1 room, including families lodging, or 35.2 per cent.
104   "   "   " 2 rooms . . . . or 4.4   "
371   "   "   " 3   "   . . . . or 15.7   "
170   "   "   " 4   " ⎫
127   "   "   " 5   " ⎬ . . . . or 12.7   "
754   "   "   " 6   "   or more . . . . or 32.0   "

The number of families occupying one room is here exaggerated as before shown by the lodging system; on the other hand the number occupying six rooms and more is also somewhat exaggerated by the fact that not all sub-rented rooms have been subtracted, although this has been done as far as possible.

Of the 2441 families only 334 had access to bathrooms and water-closets, or 13.7 per cent. Even these 334 families have poor accommodations in most instances. Many share the use of one bathroom with one or more other families. The bath-tubs usually are not supplied with hot water and very often have no water-connection at all. This condition is largely owing to the fact that the Seventh

---

[4] Here, again, the proportion paid by single lodgers must not be subtracted as it has not been added in before.

Ward belongs to the older part of Philadelphia, built
when vaults in the yards were used exclusively and bathrooms could not be given space in the small houses. This
was not so unhealthful before the houses were thick
and when there were large back yards. To-day, however,
the back yards have been filled by tenement houses and the
bad sanitary results are shown in the death rate of the ward.

Even the remaining yards are disappearing. Of the
1751 families making returns, 932 had a private yard
12 x 12 feet, or larger; 312 had a private yard smaller than
12 x 12 feet; 507 had either no yard at all or a yard and
outhouse in common with the other denizens of the tenement or alley.

Of the latter only sixteen families had water-closets. So
that over 20 per cent and possibly 30 per cent of the Negro
families of this ward lack some of the very elementary
accommodations necessary to health and decency. And
this too in spite of the fact that they are paying comparatively high rents. Here too there comes another consideration, and that is the lack of public urinals and water-closets
in this ward and, in fact, throughout Philadelphia. The
result is that the closets of tenements are used by the
public. A couple of diagrams will illustrate this; the
houses of older Philadelphia were built like this:

A HOME
B OUTHOUSE
C YARD
D PASSAGE TO STREET

When, however, certain districts like the Seventh Ward
became crowded and given over to tenants, the thirst for

money-getting led landlords in large numbers of cases to
build up their back yards like this :

A FRONT TENEMENT FACING ST.
C BACK TENEMENT FACING ALLEY
D ALLEY
B COMMON OUTHOUSÉ
  FOR 3 TENANTS

This is the origin of numbers of the blind alleys and
dark holes which make some parts of the Fifth, Seventh
and Eighth Wards notorious.   The closets in such cases are
sometimes divided into compartments for different tenants,
but in many cases not even this is done; and in all cases
the alley closet becomes a public resort for pedestrians and
loafers.   The back tenements thus formed rent usually for
from $7 to $9 a month, and sometimes for more.   They
consist of three rooms one above the other, small, poorly
lighted and poorly ventilated.   The inhabitants of the
alley are at the mercy of its worst tenants; here policy
shops abound, prostitutes ply their trade, and criminals
hide.   Most of these houses have to get their water at a
hydrant in the alley, and must store their fuel in the
house.   These tenement abominations of Philadelphia are
perhaps better than the vast tenement houses of New York,
but they are bad enough, and cry for reform in housing.

The fairly comfortable working class live in houses of
3–6 rooms, with water in the house, but seldom with a
bath.   A three room house on a small street rents from
$10 up ; on Lombard street a 5–8 room house can be
rented for from $18 to $30 according to location.   The
great mass of comfortably situated working people live in
houses of 6–10 rooms, and sub-rent a part or take lodgers.
A 5–7 room house on South Eighteenth street can be had
for $20 ; on Florida street for $18 ; such houses have

usually a parlor, dining room and kitchen on the first floor
and two to four bedrooms, of which one or two are apt to
be rented to a waiter or coachman for $4 a month, or to a
married couple at $6–10 a month. The more elaborate
houses are on Lombard street and its cross streets.

The rents paid by the Negroes are without doubt far
above their means and often from one-fourth to three-fourths
of the total income of a family goes in rent. This leads to
much non-payment of rent both intentional and uninten-
tional, to frequent shifting of homes, and above all to
stinting the families in many necessities of life in order to
live in respectable dwellings. Many a Negro family eats
less than it ought for the sake of living in a decent
house.

Some of this waste of money in rent is sheer ignorance
and carelessness. The Negroes have an inherited distrust
of banks and companies, and have long neglected to take
part in Building and Loan Associations. Others are simply
careless in the spending of their money and lack the
shrewdness and business sense of differently trained peoples.
Ignorance and carelessness however will not explain all
or even the greater part of the problem of rent among
Negroes. There are three causes of even greater importance : these are the limited localities where Negroes may
rent, the peculiar connection of dwelling and occupation
among Negroes and the social organization of the Negro.
The undeniable fact that most Philadelphia white people
prefer not to live near Negroes [5] limits the Negro very
seriously in his choice of a home and especially in the
choice of a cheap home. Moreover, real estate agents
knowing the limited supply usually raise the rent a dollar
or two for Negro tenants, if they do not refuse them
altogether. Again, the occupations which the Negro
follows, and which at present he is compelled to follow, are

---

[5] The sentiment has greatly lessened in intensity during the last two
decades, but it is still strong ; cf. section 47.

of a sort that makes it necessary for him to live near the best portions of the city; the mass of Negroes are in the economic world purveyors to the rich—working in private houses, in hotels, large stores, etc.[6] In order to keep this work they must live near by; the laundress cannot bring her Spruce street family's clothes from the Thirtieth Ward, nor can the waiter at the Continental Hotel lodge in Germantown. With the mass of white workmen this same necessity of living near work, does not hinder them from getting cheap dwellings; the factory is surrounded by cheap cottages, the foundry by long rows of houses, and even the white clerk and shop girl can, on account of their hours of labor, afford to live further out in the suburbs than the black porter who opens the store. Thus it is clear that the nature of the Negro's work compels him to crowd into the centre of the city much more than is the case with the mass of white working people. At the same time this necessity is apt in some cases to be overestimated, and a few hours of sleep or convenience serve to persuade a good many families to endure poverty in the Seventh Ward when they might be comfortable in the Twenty-fourth Ward. Nevertheless much of the Negro problem in this city finds adequate explanation when we reflect that here is a people receiving a little lower wages than usual for less desirable work, and compelled, in order to do that work, to live in a little less pleasant quarters than most people, and pay for them somewhat higher rents.

The final reason of the concentration of Negroes in certain localities is a social one and one peculiarly strong: the life of the Negroes of the city has for years centred in the Seventh Ward; here are the old churches, St. Thomas', Bethel, Central, Shiloh and Wesley; here are the halls of the secret societies; here are the homesteads of old families. To a race socially ostracised it means far more to move to

---

[6] At the same time, from long custom and from competition, their wages for this work are not high.

remote parts of a city, than to those who will in any part
of the city easily form congenial acquaintances and new ties.
The Negro who ventures away from the mass of his people
and their organized life, finds himself alone, shunned and
taunted, stared at and made uncomfortable; he can make
few new friends, for his neighbors however well-disposed
would shrink to add a Negro to their list of acquaintances. Thus he remains far from friends and the con-
centred social life of the church, and feels in all its
bitterness what it means to be a social outcast. Consequently emigration from the ward has gone in groups and
centred itself about some church, and individual initiative
is thus checked. At the same time color prejudice makes
it difficult for groups to find suitable places to move to—
one Negro family would be tolerated where six would be
objected to; thus we have here a very decisive hindrance
to emigration to the suburbs.

It is not surprising that this situation leads to considerable crowding in the homes, *i. e.*, to the endeavor to get as
many people into the space hired as possible. It is this
crowding that gives the casual observer many false notions
as to the size of Negro families, since he often forgets that
every other house has its sub-renters and lodgers. It is
however difficult to measure this crowding on account of
this very lodging system which makes it very often uncertain as to just the number of rooms a given group of
people occupy. In the following table therefore it is likely
that the number of rooms given is somewhat greater than is
really the case and that consequently there is more crowding than is indicated. This error however could not be
wholly eliminated under the circumstances; a study of the
table (page 298) shows that in the Seventh Ward there are
9302 rooms occupied by 2401 families, an average of 3.8
rooms to a family, and 1.04 individuals to a room. A
division by rooms will better show where the crowding
comes in.

HOMES ACCORDING TO ROOMS AND PERSONS LIVING IN THEM.

Rooms	Persons																		Homes, Total	Total Rooms
	One	Two	Three	Four	Five	Six	Seven	Eight	Nine	Ten	Eleven	Twelve	Thirteen	Fourteen	Fifteen	Sixteen	Seventeen and over	Unknown		
One	47	572	154	58	25	6	5	.	1	2	.	.	.	.	.	.	.	.	870	870
Two	5	38	33	19	6	1	2	.	1	.	.	1	.	.	.	.	.	.	105	210
Three	13	54	69	87	60	36	25	17	8	2	1	3	1	.	.	1	.	.	375	1125
Four	6	24	35	42	19	19	7	7	5	4	.	.	.	.	.	.	.	.	171	684
Five	.	11	20	21	21	17	14	8	7	5	3	5	.	.	.	.	.	.	127	635
Six	1	5	14	46	38	47	40	24	20	9	10	5	2	1	1	1	.	.	263	1578
Seven	.	2	10	26	19	23	13	12	14	7	7	9	3	3	2	.	4	.	148	1036
Eight	4	9	7	17	17	19	12	15	11	8	6	2	2	2	.	1	3	.	143	1144
Nine	.	2	10	13	8	14	10	8	12	7	5	3	1	1	1	1	.	.	95	855
Ten	.	1	5	6	2	4	5	4	.	5	2	.	3	.	1	1	4	.	48	480
Eleven	.	1	.	1	5	3	4	2	3	2	.	1	1	1	2	4	.	.	28	308
Twelve and over	.	.	1	1	1	.	2	1	4	4	2	.	2	.	.	.	7	.	28	377
Unknown	.	.	2	4	1	1	.	.	.	.	.	.	.	.	.	.	.	32	40	.
Total	76	720	360	341	222	190	139	98	86	55	36	29	15	8	7	9	18	32	2141	9302

Families occupying five rooms and less: 1648, total rooms per family, 2.17 ; total individuals per room, 1.53.

Families occupying three rooms and less: 1350, total rooms per family, 1.63 ; total individuals per room, 1.85.

The worst cases of crowding are as follows :

> Two cases of 10 persons in 1 room.
> One case of   9   "   1   "
> Five cases of   7   "   1   "
> Six cases of   6   "   1   "
> Twenty-five cases of 5 persons in 1 room.
> One case of   9 persons in 2 rooms.
> One case of 16   "   3   "
> One case of 13   "   3   "
> One case of 11   "   3   "

As said before, this is probably something under the real truth, although perhaps not greatly so. The figures show considerable overcrowding, but not nearly as much as is often the case in other cities. This is largely due to the character of Philadelphia houses, which are small and low, and will not admit many inmates. Five persons in one room of an ordinary tenement would be almost suffocating. The large number of one-room tenements with two persons should be noted. These 572 families are for the most part young or childless couples, sub-renting a bedroom and working in the city.[7]

45. Sections and Wards.—The spread of Negro population in the city during the nineteenth century is worth studying. In 1793,[8] one-fourth of the black inhabitants —or 538 persons—lived north of Market street and south of Vine, and were either in the homes of white families as

---

[7] One room under such circumstances may not by any means denote excessive poverty or indecency ; the room is usually rented in a good locality and is well furnished. Cf. note 3.

[8] During the plague of that year a census of the inhabitants remaining in the city was taken. Five-sixths of the Negroes remained, so the census gives a good idea of the distribution of the Negro population. The results are published in the report printed afterward by order of Councils.

servants, or in the alleys, as Shively's, Pewter Platter,
Croomb's, Sugar, Cresson's, etc. Between Market and South
lived one-half of the blacks, crowded in a region that centred at Sixth and Lombard: in Strawberry alley and lane,
Elbow lane, Grey's alley, Shippen's alley, etc., besides in
the families of the whites on Walnut, Spruce, Pine, etc.
The remaining fourth of the population was in Southwark,
south of South street, and in the Northern Liberties, north
of Vine. Details are given in the next table:

NUMBER AND DISTRIBUTION OF THE NEGRO INHABITANTS OF PHILA- DELPHIA IN 1793—OCTOBER TO DECEMBER.

(Taken from the Census of the Plague Committee.)

BETWEEN MARKET AND VINE STREETS.

Streets, etc.	Negroes.	Streets, etc.	Negroes.
Market	63	Quarry	4
Water	31	Cherry alley	25
Front	40	South alley	1
Second	29	North alley	4
Third	37	Sugar alley	14
Fourth	42	Appletree alley	7
Fifth	24	Cresson's alley	10
Sixth	32	Shively's alley	11
Seventh	8	Pewter Platter alley	3
Eighth	13	Croomb's alley	5
Ninth	3	Baker's alley	7
Arch	56	Brooks' court	1
Race	38	Priest's alley	6
Vine (south side)	9	Says alley	6
New	3		
Church alley	2	Total	538

BETWEEN MARKET AND SOUTH STREETS.

Streets, etc.	Negroes.	Streets, etc.	Negroes.
Water	12	Penn	11
Front	129	Chestnut	50
Second	116	Walnut	83
Third	66	Spruce	66
Fourth	81	Pine	31
Fifth	63	South (north side)	32
Sixth	37	Strawberry lane	4
Seventh	0	Strawberry alley	2
Eighth	16	Elbow lane	10
Ninth	0	Beetles' alley	5

Streets, etc.	Negroes.	Streets, etc.	Negroes.
Grey's alley	13	Willing's alley . . .	1
Norris alley	4	Blackberry alley . . .	2
Dock	5	Carpenter	7
Union	32	Gaskill	7
Cypress alley	1	Georges to South . . .	5
Pear	5	Little Water	5
Lombard	57	Stamper's alley . . .	8
Emslie's alley	6	Taylor's alley	1
Laurel court	1	York court	7
Shippen's alley . . .	26		
		Total . . .	1007

NORTHERN LIBERTIES.

Streets, etc.	Negroes.	Streets, etc.	Negroes.
Water	1	Green	6
Front	59	Coates	32
Second	41	Brown	15
Third	1	Cable lane	1
Fourth	3	St. John	6
Fifth	1	St. Tammany	2
Vine (north side) . . .	18	Willow	1
Callowhill	10	Wood's alley	1
Noble, or Bloody lane .	4	Crown	3
Artillery lane (or Duke)	26		
		Total . . .	233

DISTRICT OF SOUTHWARK.

Streets, etc.	Negroes.	Streets, etc.	Negroes.
Swanson	22	Christian	6
South Penn	3	Queen	5
Front	15	Meade's alley	10
Second	22	German	3
Third	34	Plumb	5
Fifth	5	Moll Tuller's alley . .	4
Cedar court (south side)	19	George	8
Shippen	50	Ball alley	3
Almond	9	Crabtree alley	2
Catharine	33		
		Total . . .	258

SUMMARY.

Between Market and Vine streets	538
Between Market and South streets	1007
North of Vine street	233
South of South street	258
Total	2036
Total inhabitants of county by census of 1790	2489

The changes from 1793 to 1838, nearly a half century, may thus be shown:

Place.	1793.	1838.
City	1545—75.0%	8462—60%
Northern Liberties		878 ⎫
Kensington	233—11.5%	359 ⎬ 1744—15%
Spring Garden		507 ⎭
Southwark	258—13.5%	931 ⎫ 3385—25%
Moyamensing		2454 ⎭
Total	2036	13,591+5000 servants.

Thus we see in 1838 that the centre of Negro population had gone southward toward Moyamensing. The Cedar, Locust, Newmarket, Pine and South Wards, as they were then called, had the bulk of the population, and they corresponded approximately to the Fourth, Fifth, Seventh and Eighth Wards of to-day.

Ten years later than this, in 1848,[9] we have a more detailed account of the distribution of the Negroes in the various sections of the city. They were mostly crowded into narrow courts and alleys. The colored population north of Vine and east of Sixth streets consisted of 272 families with 1285 persons. One hundred and one families of these (415 persons) lived on Apple street and its courts, and in Paschall's alley (now Lynd street). Apple street itself, including Hick's court, had 37 families, with 138 persons, living in 16 houses ; Shotwell's row, on the same street, had 16 families with 65 persons in 7 houses ; the rooms were about 8 feet square. Paschall's alley contained 48 families with 212 persons, in 28 houses ; one house had 7 families, 33 persons, living in 13 rooms, 8 feet square. The rent of the whole house was $266 per year ; "yet all of them [*i. e.*, these families] have comfortable beds and bedding."

About a third of the total Negro population of Moya-

---

[9] The figures for 1838 and 1848 are from the inquiries of those dates ; cf. census of 1840.

mensing (the district "south of Cedar street and west of Passyunk road") was crowded into the space between Fifth and Eighth streets, and South and Fitzwater; for instance:

	Families.		Families.
Shippen street	55	Black Horse alley	5
Bedford street	63	Hutton's court	9
Small street	73	Yeager's court	9
Baker street	21	Dickerson's court	5
Seventh and South streets	14	Britton's court	5
Spafford street	16	Cryder's court	4
Freytag's alley	9	Sherman's court	13
Prosperous alley	11		
		Total	302

"It is in this district and in the adjoining portion of the city, especially Mary street and its vicinity, that the great destitution and wretchedness exist." The personal property of 176 of the above 302 families is returned as $603.50, or $3.43 per family; 15 families (42 persons) on Small street (Alaska street) above Sixth, have their whole property valued at $7. Most of these Negroes were rag-pickers, and 29 out of 42 families were not natives of the State. Mary street and its courts had 80 families, with 281 persons living in 35 houses. Some were industrious and temperate, but there was "much surrounding misery." In Gile's alley (from Cedar to Lombard street) were 42 families, 147 persons, in 20 houses. Eighty-three of these persons were not natives of the State, and 13 of the families received public charity. A description of this district in 1847 is interesting:

"The vicinity of the place we sought was pointed out by a large number of colored people congregated on the neighboring pavements. We first inspected the rooms, yards and cellars of the four or five houses next above Baker street on Seventh. The cellars were wretchedly dark, damp and dirty, and were generally rented for twelve and a half cents per night. These are occupied by one or more families at the present time, but in the winter season when the frost drives those who in summer sleep abroad in fields, in boardyards and in sheds, to seek more effectual shelter, they often contain from twelve to twenty lodgers per night. Commencing at the back of each house are small wooden buildings roughly put together, about six feet square, without windows or fireplaces, a hole about a foot square being left in front along side of the door to let in fresh air and light, and to let out foul air and smoke. These desolate pens, the roofs of which are generally leaky, and their floors so low that more or less water comes in on them from the yard in rainy weather, would not give comfortable winter accommodations to a cow. Although as dismal as dirt, damp and insufficient ventilation can make them, they are nearly all inhabited. In one of the first we entered, we found the dead body of a large Negro man who had died suddenly there. This pen was about eight feet deep by six wide. There was no bedding in it, but a box or two around the sides furnished places where two colored persons, one said to be the wife of the deceased, were lying either drunk or fast asleep. The body of the dead man was on the wet floor beneath an old torn coverlet." [10]

In 1853 a similar description of the crime, filth and poverty of this district shows us that the present slums do not compare with those in misfortune and depravity. [11] Much of this poverty and degradation could in 1847 be laid at the door of the new immigrants, and although some of the immigrants were in good circumstances, yet in general most of the poverty was found where most of the immigrants were. The immigrants formed the following percentages of the total population in 1847:

City	47.7	per cent.
Moyamensing	46.3	"
Southwark	35.9	"
West Philadelphia	34.3	"
Spring Garden	31.4	"
Northern Liberties	14.2	"

[10] "Condition of Negroes," 1848, pp. 34-41.
[11] "Mysteries and Miseries of Philadelphia." (Pamphlet.)

The historic centre of Negro settlement in the city can thus be seen to be at Sixth and Lombard. From this point it moved north, as is indicated for instance by the establishment of Zoar Church in 1794. Immigration of foreigners and the rise of industries, however, early began to turn it back and it found outlet in the alleys of Southwark and Moyamensing. For a while about 1840 it was bottled up here, but finally it began to move west. A few early left the mass and settled in West Philadelphia; the rest began a slow steady movement along Lombard street. The influx of 1876 and thereafter sent the wave across Broad street to a new centre at Seventeenth and Lombard. There it divided into two streams; one went north and joined remnants of the old settlers in the Northern Liberties and Spring Garden. The other went south to the Twenty-sixth, Thirtieth and Thirty-sixth Wards. Meantime the new immigrants poured in at Seventh and Lombard, while Sixth and Lombard down to the Delaware was deserted to the Jews, and Moyamensing partially to the Italians. The Irish were pushed on beyond Eighteenth to the Schuylkill, or emigrated to the mills of Kensington and elsewhere. The course may be thus graphically represented (see page 306):

This migration explains much that is paradoxical about Negro slums, especially their present remnant at Seventh and Lombard. Many people wonder that the mission and reformatory agencies at work there for so many years have so little to show by way of results. One answer is that this work has new material continually to work upon, while the best classes move to the west and leave the dregs behind. The parents and grandparents of some of the best families of Philadelphia Negroes were born in the neighborhood of Sixth and Lombard at a time when all Negroes, good, bad and indifferent, were confined to that and a few other localities. With the greater freedom of domicile which has since come, these slum districts have

sent a stream of emigrants westward. There has, too, been
a general movement from the alleys to the streets and
from the back to the front streets. Moreover it is untrue

MIGRATION OF THE NEGRO POPULATION, 1790–1890.

that the slums of Seventh and Lombard have not greatly
changed in character ; compared with 1840, 1850 or even
1870 these slums are much improved in every way. More

and more every year the unfortunate and poor are being sifted out from the vicious and criminal and sent to better quarters.

And yet with all the obvious improvement, there are still slums and dangerous slums left. Of the Fifth Ward and adjoining parts of the Seventh, a city health inspector says :

" Few of the houses are underdrained, and if the closets have sewer connections the people are too careless to keep them in order. The streets and alleys are strewn with garbage, excepting immediately after the visit of the street cleaner. Penetrate into one of these houses and beyond into the back yard, if there is one (frequently there is not), and there will be found a pile of ashes, garbage and filth, the accumulation of the winter, perhaps of the whole year. In such heaps of refuse what disease germ may be breeding ? " [12]

To take a typical case :

"Gillis' Alley, famed in the Police Court, is a narrow alley, extending from Lombard street through to South street, above Fifth street, cobbled and without sewer connections. Houses and stables are mixed promiscuously. Buildings are of frame and of brick. No. — looks both outside and in like a Southern Negro's cabin. In this miserable place four colored families have their homes. The aggregate rent demanded is $22 a month, though the owner seldom receives the full rent. For three small dark rooms in the rear of another house in this alley, the tenants pay, and have paid for thirteen years, $11 a month. The entrance is by a court not over two feet wide. Except at midday the sun does not shine in the small open space in the rear that answers for a yard. It is safe to say that not one house in this alley could pass an inspection without being condemned as prejudicial to health. But if they are so condemned and cleaned, with such inhabitants how long will they remain clean ? " [13]

---

[12] Dr. Frances Van Gasken in a tract published by the Civic Club.
[13] *Ibid.*

Some of the present characteristics of the chief alleys where Negroes live are given in the following table:

SOME ALLEYS WHERE NEGROES LIVE.

	Cross Alley.	McCann's Court.	Alley off Carver Street.	Turner's Court.	Lombard Row.	Horstman's Court.	Allen's Court.	Hines' Court.	Govett's Court.
General Character	Bad.	Poor.	Fair.	Wretched.	Fair.	Squalid.	Very Poor.	Poor.	Poor.
Width, in feet	12	12	6	3-12	9	12	6	3-6.	3
Paved with	Asphalt.	Bricks.	Bricks.	Bricks.	Bricks.	Bricks.	Bricks.	Bricks.	Bricks.
Character of Dwelling	Wood and Brick.	Old Brick Tenements	Old Brick Tenements	Old Wooden Houses.	Fair.	Back Yard Tenements	Back Yard Tenements	Back Yard Tenements	Poor.
Number of Stories in Houses	2 to 3.	2 to 3.	3	1 to 3.	3	2 and 3.	3	3	3
Inhabitants	Jews and Negroes.	All Negroes.	Jews and Negroes.	All Negroes.	Negroes and Jews.	All Negroes.	All Negroes.	All Negroes.	All Negroes.
Cleanliness, etc.	Dirty.	Fair.	Fair.	Fair.	Fair.	Dirty.	Dirty.	Fair.	Fair.
Width of Sidewalk . . feet.	None.	None.	None.	None.	None.	None.	6	5	4
Lighted by	No Lights.	1 Gas Lamp.	1 Gas Lamp.	1 Gas Lamp.	1 Gas Lamp.	1 Gas Lamp.	No Lights.	No Lights.	No Lights.
Privies in Common or Private	Common.	Common.	Common.	Common.	Private.	5 in open Court.	½ for each House.	2 for whole Alley.	Common.
Remarks.	Some Bad Characters.	Poor People and some Question-able.	"Blind" Alley; Fairly Respect-able.	Many Empty Houses; Poor and Doubtful People.	Respectable Homes mingled with Gamblers and Prostitutes.	Very Poor People.	Poor and Doubt-ful Characters.	Emigrants from 5th Ward slums.	

The general characteristics and distribution of the Negro population at present in the different wards can only be indicated in general terms. The wards with the best Negro population are parts of the Seventh, Twenty-sixth, Thirtieth and Thirty-sixth, Fourteenth, Fifteenth, Twenty-fourth, Twenty-seventh and Twenty-ninth. The worst Negro population is found in parts of the Seventh, and in the Fourth, Fifth and Eighth. In the other wards either the classes are mixed or there are very few colored people. The tendency of the best migration to-day is toward the Twenty-sixth, Thirtieth and Thirty-sixth Wards, and West Philadelphia.

46. Social Classes and Amusements.—Notwithstanding the large influence of the physical environment of home and ward, nevertheless there is a far mightier influence to mold and make the citizen, and that is the social atmosphere which surrounds him: first his daily companionship, the thoughts and whims of his class; then his recreations and amusements; finally the surrounding world of American civilization, which the Negro meets especially in his economic life. Let us take up here the subject of social classes and amusements among Negroes, reserving for the next chapter a study of the contact of the Whites and Blacks.

There is always a strong tendency on the part of the community to consider the Negroes as composing one practically homogeneous mass. This view has of course a certain justification: the people of Negro descent in this land have had a common history, suffer to-day common disabilities, and contribute to one general set of social problems. And yet if the foregoing statistics have emphasized any one fact it is that wide variations in antecedents, wealth, intelligence and general efficiency have already been differentiated within this group. These differences are not, to be sure, so great or so patent as those among the whites of to-day, and yet they un-

doubtedly equal the difference among the masses of the
people in certain sections of the land fifty or one hundred
years ago; and there is no surer way of misunderstanding the
Negro or being misunderstood by him than by ignoring
manifest differences of condition and power in the 40,000
black people of Philadelphia.

And yet well-meaning people continually do this. They
regale the thugs and whoremongers and gamblers of
Seventh and Lombard streets with congratulations on what
the Negroes have done in a quarter century, and pity for
their disabilities ; and they scold the caterers of Addison
street for the pickpockets and paupers of the race. A
judge of the city courts, who for years has daily met a
throng of lazy and debased Negro criminals, comes from
the bench to talk to the Negroes about their criminals : he
warns them first of all to leave the slums and either forgets
or does not know that the fathers of the audience he is
speaking to, left the slums when he was a boy and that the
people before him are as distinctly differentiated from the
criminals he has met, as honest laborers anywhere differ
from thieves.

Nothing more exasperates the better class of Negroes
than this tendency to ignore utterly their existence. The
law-abiding, hard-working inhabitants of the Thirtieth
Ward are aroused to righteous indignation when they see
that the word Negro carries most Philadelphians' minds to
the alleys of the Fifth Ward or the police courts. Since
so much misunderstanding or rather forgetfulness and carelessness on this point is common, let us endeavor to try and
fix with some definiteness the different social classes which
are clearly enough defined among Negroes to deserve
attention. When the statistics of the families of the
Seventh Ward were gathered, each family was put in one
of four grades as follows :

Grade 1. Families of undoubted respectability earning
sufficient income to live well; not engaged in menial

service of any kind ; the wife engaged in no occupation
save that of house-wife, except in a few cases where she
had special employment at home. The children not compelled to be bread-winners, but found in school ; the family
living in a well-kept home.

Grade 2. The respectable working-class ; in comfortable
circumstances, with a good home, and having steady
remunerative work. The younger children in school.

Grade 3. The poor; persons not earning enough to
keep them at all times above want; honest, although not
always energetic or thrifty, and with no touch of gross
immorality or crime. Including the very poor, and the
poor.

Grade 4. The lowest class of criminals, prostitutes and
loafers ; the " submerged tenth."

Thus we have in these four grades the criminals, the
poor, the laborers, and the well-to-do. [14] The last class
represents the ordinary middle-class folk of most modern
countries, and contains the germs of other social classes
which the Negro has not yet clearly differentiated. Let
us begin first with the fourth class.

The criminals and gamblers are to be found at such
centres as Seventh and Lombard streets, Seventeenth and
Lombard, Twelfth and Kater, Eighteenth and Naudain,
etc. Many people have failed to notice the significant
change which has come over these slums in recent years ;
the squalor and misery and dumb suffering of 1840 has
passed, and in its place have come more baffling and sinister
phenomena: shrewd laziness, shameless lewdness, cunning

---

[14] It will be noted that this classification differs materially from the
economic division in Chapter XI. In that case grade four and a part of
three appear as the "poor ;" grade two and the rest of grade three, as
the "fair to comfortable ;" and a few of grade two and grade one as the
well-to-do. The basis of division there was almost entirely according to
income ; this division brings in moral considerations and questions of
expenditure, and consequently reflects more largely the personal judgment of the investigator.

crime. The loafers who line the curbs in these places are no fools, but sharp, wily men who often outwit both the Police Department and the Department of Charities. Their nucleus consists of a class of professional criminals, who do not work, figure in the rogues' galleries of a half-dozen cities, and migrate here and there. About these are a set of gamblers and sharpers who seldom are caught in serious crime, but who nevertheless live from its proceeds and aid and abet it. The headquarters of all these are usually the political clubs and pool-rooms; they stand ready to entrap the unwary and tempt the weak. Their organization, tacit or recognized, is very effective, and no one can long watch their actions without seeing that they keep in close touch with the authorities in some way. Affairs will be gliding on lazily some summer afternoon at the corner of Seventh and Lombard streets ; a few loafers on the corners, a prostitute here and there, and the Jew and Italian plying their trades. Suddenly there is an oath, a sharp altercation, a blow; then a hurried rush of feet, the silent door of a neighboring club closes, and when the policeman arrives only the victim lies bleeding on the sidewalk ; or at midnight the drowsy quiet will be suddenly broken by the cries and quarreling of a half-drunken gambling table ; then comes the sharp, quick crack of pistol shots—a scurrying in the darkness, and only the wounded man lies awaiting the patrol-wagon. If the matter turns out seriously, the police know where in Minster street and Middle alley to look for the aggressor; often they find him, but sometimes not.[15]

The size of the more desperate class of criminals and their shrewd abettors is of course comparatively small, but it is large enough to characterize the slum districts. Around this central body lies a large crowd of satellites

---

[15] The investigator resided at the College Settlement, Seventh and Lombard streets, some months, and thus had an opportunity to observe this slum carefully.

and feeders: young idlers attracted by excitement, shift-less and lazy ne'er-do-wells, who have sunk from better things, and a rough crowd of pleasure seekers and liber-tines. These are the fellows who figure in the police courts for larceny and fighting, and drift thus into graver crime or shrewder dissoluteness. They are usually far more ignorant than their leaders, and rapidly die out from disease and excess. Proper measures for rescue and reform might save many of this class. Usually they are not natives of the city, but immigrants who have wandered from the small towns of the South to Richmond and Washington and thence to Philadelphia. Their environ-ment in this city makes it easier for them to live by crime or the results of crime than by work, and being without ambition—or perhaps having lost ambition and grown bitter with the world—they drift with the stream.

One large element of these slums, a class we have barely mentioned, are the prostitutes. It is difficult to get at any satisfactory data concerning such a class, but an attempt has been made. There were in 1896 fifty-three Negro women in the Seventh Ward known on pretty satisfactory evidence to be supported wholly or largely by the proceeds of prostitution; and it is probable that this is not half the real number;[16] these fifty-three were of the following ages:

14 to 19	2
20 to 24	11
25 to 29	9
30 to 39	17
40 to 49	3
50 and over	2
Unknown	9
Total	53

Seven of these women had small children with them and had probably been betrayed, and had then turned to this

---

[16] These figures were taken during the inquiry by the visitor to the houses.

sort of life. There were fourteen recognized bawdy houses in the ward; ten of them were private dwellings where prostitutes lived and were not especially fitted up, although male visitors frequented them. Four of the houses were regularly fitted up, with elaborate furniture, and in one or two cases had young and beautiful girls on exhibition. All of these latter were seven- or eight-room houses for which $26 to $30 a month was paid. They are pretty well-known resorts, but are not disturbed. In the slums the lowest class of street walkers abound and ply their trade among Negroes, Italians and Americans. One can see men following them into alleys in broad daylight. They usually have male associates whom they support and who join them in " badger " thieving. Most of them are grown women though a few cases of girls under sixteen have been seen on the street.

This fairly characterizes the lowest class of Negroes. According to the inquiry in the Seventh Ward at least 138 families were estimated as belonging to this class out of 2395 reported, or 5.8 per cent. This would include between five and six hundred individuals. Perhaps this number reaches 1000 if the facts were known, but the evidence at hand furnishes only the number stated. In the whole city the number may reach 3000, although there is little data for an estimate.[17]

The next class are the poor and unfortunate and the casual laborers; most of these are of the class of Negroes who in the contact with the life of a great city have failed to find an assured place. They include immigrants who cannot get steady work; good-natured, but unreliable and shiftless persons who cannot keep work or spend their earnings thoughtfully; those who have suffered accident and misfortune; the maimed and defective classes,

---

[17] This includes not simply the actual criminal class, but its aiders and abettors, and the class intimately associated with it. It would, for instance, include much more than Charles Booth's class A in London.

and the sick ; many widows and orphans and deserted wives ; all these form a large class and are here considered. It is of course very difficult to separate the lowest of this class from the one below, and probably many are included here who, if the truth were known, ought to be classed lower. In most cases, however, they have been given the benefit of the doubt. The lowest ones of this class usually live in the slums and back streets, and next door. or in the same house often, with criminals and lewd women. Ignorant and easily influenced, they readily go with the tide and now rise to industry and decency, now fall to crime. Others of this class get on fairly well in good times, but never get far ahead. They are the ones who earliest feel the weight of hard times and their latest blight. Some correspond to the " worthy poor " of most charitable organizations, and some fall a little below that class. The children of this class are the feeders of the criminal classes. Often in the same family one can find respectable and striving parents weighed down by idle, impudent sons and wayward daughters. This is partly because of poverty, more because of the poor home life. In the Seventh Ward 30½ per cent of the families or 728 may be put into this class, including the very poor, the poor and those who manage just to make ends meet in good times. In the whole city perhaps ten to twelve thousand Negroes fall in this third social grade.

Above these come the representative Negroes; the mass of the servant class, the porters and waiters, and the best of the laborers. They are hard-working people, proverbially good-natured ; lacking a little in foresight and forehandedness, and in " push." They are honest and faithful, of fair and improving morals, and beginning to accumulate property. The great drawback to this class is lack of congenial occupation especially among the young men and women, and the consequent wide-spread dissatisfaction and complaint. As a class these persons are ambitious ; the majority can read and write, many have a common school training, and all are anxious to rise in the world. Their wages are low compared with corresponding classes of white workmen, their rents are high, and the field of advancement opened to them is very limited. The best expression of the life of this group is the Negro church, where their social life centres, and where they discuss their situation and prospects.

A note of disappointment and discouragement is often heard at these discussions and their work suffers from a growing lack of interest in it. Most of them are probably best fitted for the work they are doing, but a large percentage deserve better ways to display their talent, and better remuneration. The whole class deserves credit for its bold advance in the midst of discouragements, and for the distinct moral improvement in their family life during the last quarter century. These persons form 56 per cent or 1,252 of the families of the Seventh Ward, and include perhaps 25,000 of the Negroes of the city. They live in 5–10-room houses, and usually have lodgers. The houses are always well furnished with neat parlors and some musical instrument. Sunday dinners and small parties, together with church activities, make up their social intercourse. Their chief trouble is in finding suitable careers for their growing children.

Finally we come to the 277 families, 11.5 per cent of those of the Seventh Ward, and including perhaps 3,000 Negroes in the city, who form the aristocracy of the Negro population in education, wealth and general social efficiency. In many respects it is right and proper to judge a people by its best classes rather than by its worst classes or middle ranks. The highest class of any group represents its possibilities rather than its exceptions, as is so often assumed in regard to the Negro. The colored people are seldom judged by their best classes, and often the very existence of classes among them is ignored. This is

partly due in the North to the anomalous position of those
who compose this class : they are not the leaders or the
ideal-makers of their own group in thought, work, or
morals. They teach the masses to a very small extent,
mingle with them but little, do not largely hire their
labor. Instead then of social classes held together by
strong ties of mutual interest we have in the case of the
Negroes, classes who have much to keep them apart, and
only community of blood and color prejudice to bind them
together. If the Negroes were by themselves either a
strong aristocratic system or a dictatorship would for the
present prevail. With, however, democracy thus prema-
turely thrust upon them, the first impulse of the best, the
wisest and richest is to segregate themselves from the mass.
This action, however, causes more of dislike and jealousy
on the part of the masses than usual, because those masses
look to the whites for ideals and largely for leadership. It
is natural therefore that even to-day the mass of Negroes
should look upon the worshipers at St. Thomas' and
Central as feeling themselves above them, and should dislike them for it. On the other hand it is just as natural
for the well-educated and well-to-do Negroes to feel themselves far above the criminals and prostitutes of Seventh
and Lombard streets, and even above the servant girls and
porters of the middle class of workers. So far they are
justified ; but they make their mistake in failing to recognize that, however laudable an ambition to rise may be, the
first duty of an upper class is to serve the lowest classes.
The aristocracies of all peoples have been slow in learning
this and perhaps the Negro is no slower than the rest, but
his peculiar situation demands that in his case this lesson be
learned sooner. Naturally the uncertain economic status
even of this picked class makes it difficult for them to
spare much time and energy in social reform ; compared
with their fellows they are rich, but compared with white

Americans they are poor, and they can hardly fulfill their duty as the leaders of the Negroes until they are captains of industry over their people as well as richer and wiser. To-day the professional class among them is, compared with other callings, rather over-represented, and all have a struggle to maintain the position they have won.

This class is itself an answer to the question of the ability of the Negro to assimilate American culture. It is a class small in numbers and not sharply differentiated from other classes, although sufficiently so to be easily recognized. Its members are not to be met with in the ordinary assemblages of the Negroes, nor in their usual promenading places. They are largely Philadelphia born, and being descended from the house-servant class, contain many mulattoes. In their assemblies there are evidences of good breeding and taste, so that a foreigner would hardly think of ex-slaves. They are not to be sure people of wide culture and their mental horizon is as limited as that of the first families in a country town. Here and there may be noted, too, some faint trace of careless moral training. On the whole they strike one as sensible, good folks. Their conversation turns on the gossip of similar circles among the Negroes of Washington, Boston and New York; on questions of the day, and, less willingly, on the situation of the Negro. Strangers secure entrance to this circle with difficulty and only by introduction. For an ordinary white person it would be almost impossible to secure introduction even by a friend. Once in a while some well-known citizen meets a company of this class, but it is hard for the average white American to lay aside his patronizing way toward a Negro, and to talk of aught to him but the Negro question; the lack, therefore, of common ground even for conversation makes such meetings rather stiff and not often repeated. Fifty-two of these families keep servants regularly; they

live in well-appointed homes, which give evidence of taste
and even luxury.[18]

Something must be said, before leaving this subject, of
the amusements of the Negroes.   Among the fourth grade
and the third, gambling, excursions, balls and cake-walks
are the chief amusements.   The gambling instinct is widespread, as in all low classes, and, together with sexual
looseness, is their greatest vice ; it is carried on in clubs,
in private houses, in pool-rooms and on the street.   Public
gambling can be found at a dozen different places every
night at full tilt in the Seventh Ward, and almost any
stranger can gain easy access.   Games of pure chance are
preferred to those of skill, and in the larger clubs a sort of
three-card monte is the favorite game, played with a dealer
who gambles against all comers.   In private houses in the
slums, cards, beer and prostitutes can always be found.   In
the public pool-rooms there is some quiet gambling and
playing for prizes.   For the new comer to the city the
only open places of amusement are these pool-rooms and
gambling clubs ; here are crowds of young fellows, and

---

[18] A comparison of the size of families in the highest and lowest class
may be of interest:

Number in Family.	First Grade.	Fourth Grade.
One	22 — 8%	17 — 12%
Two	66 — 24%	58 — 42%
Three	54 — 19%	27 — 20%
Four	48 ⎫	21 ⎫
Five	25 ⎬ —33%	6 ⎬ —24%
Six	18 ⎭	6 ⎭
Seven	20 ⎫	2 ⎫
Eight	7 ⎬ —12%	0 ⎬ — 2%
Nine	5 ⎭	1 ⎭
Ten	7 ⎫	0 ⎫
Eleven	0 ⎬ 4%%	0 ⎬ — 0%
Twelve or more	5 ⎭	0 ⎭
Total.	277	138

Average size of family, first grade, 4.07% ; fourth grade, 2.08%.

This certainly looks like the survival of the fittest, and is hardly an
argument for the extinction of the civilized Negro.

once started in this company no one can say where they may not end.

The most innocent amusements of this class are the balls and cake-walks, although they are accompanied by much drinking, and are attended by white and black prostitutes. The cake-walk is a rhythmic promenade or slow dance, and when well done is pretty and quite innocent. Excursions are frequent in summer, and are accompanied often by much fighting and drinking.

The mass of the laboring Negroes get their amusement in connection with the churches. There are suppers, fairs, concerts, socials and the like. Dancing is forbidden by most of the churches, and many of the stricter sort would not think of going to balls or theatres. The younger set, however, dance, although the parents seldom accompany them, and the hours kept are late, making it often a dissipation. Secret societies and social clubs add to these amusements by balls and suppers, and there are numbers of parties at private houses. This class also patronizes frequent excursions given by churches and Sunday schools and secret societies; they are usually well conducted, but cost a great deal more than is necessary. The money wasted in excursions above what would be necessary for a day's outing and plenty of recreation, would foot up many thousand dollars in a season.

In the upper class alone has the home begun to be the centre of recreation and amusement. There are always to be found parties and small receptions, and gatherings at the invitations of musical or social clubs. One large ball each year is usually given, which is strictly private. Guests from out of town are given much social attention.

Among nearly all classes of Negroes there is a large unsatisfied demand for amusement. Large numbers of servant girls and young men have flocked to the city, have no homes, and want places to frequent. The churches supply this need partially, but the institution which will supply this want

better and add instruction and diversion, will save many
girls from ruin and boys from crime. There is to-day little
done in places of public amusement to protect colored
girls from designing men. Many of the idlers and rascals
of the slums play on the affections of silly servant girls,
and either ruin them or lead them into crime, or more
often live on a part of their wages. There are many cases
of this latter system to be met in the Seventh Ward.

It is difficult to measure amusements in any enlightening
way. A count of the amusements reported by the *Tribune*,
the chief colored paper, which reports for a select part of
the laboring class, and the upper class, resulted as follows
for nine weeks:[19]

Parties at homes in honor of visitors	16
" " homes	11
" " " with dancing	10
Balls in halls	10
Concerts in churches	7
Church suppers, etc.	7
Weddings	7
Birthday parties	7
Lectures and literary entertainments at churches	6
Card parties	4
Fairs at churches	3
Lawn parties and picnics	3
	91

These, of course, are the larger parties in the whole city,
and do not include the numerous small church socials and
gatherings. The proportions here are largely accidental,
but the list is instructive.

---

[19] These weeks were not consecutive but taken at random.

CHAPTER XVI.

THE CONTACT OF THE RACES.

47. Color Prejudice.—Incidentally throughout this study the prejudice against the Negro has been again and again mentioned. It is time now to reduce this somewhat indefinite term to something tangible. Everybody speaks of the matter, everybody knows that it exists, but in just what form it shows itself or how influential it is few agree. In the Negro's mind, color prejudice in Philadelphia is that widespread feeling of dislike for his blood, which keeps him and his children out of decent employment, from certain public conveniences and amusements, from hiring houses in many sections, and in general, from being recognized as a man. Negroes regard this prejudice as the chief cause of their present unfortunate condition. On the other hand most white people are quite unconscious of any such powerful and vindictive feeling; they regard color prejudice as the easily explicable feeling that intimate social intercourse with a lower race is not only undesirable but impracticable if our present standards of culture are to be maintained; and although they are aware that some people feel the aversion more intensely than others, they cannot see how such a feeling has much influence on the real situation or alters the social condition of the mass of Negroes.

As a matter of fact, color prejudice in this city is something between these two extreme views: it is not to-day responsible for all, or perhaps the greater part of the Negro problems, or of the disabilities under which the race labors; on the other hand it is a far more powerful social force than most Philadelphians realize. The practical results of the attitude of most of the inhabitants of Philadelphia toward persons of Negro descent are as follows :

1. As to getting work :

No matter how well trained a Negro may be, or how fitted for work of any kind, he cannot in the ordinary course of competition hope to be much more than a menial servant.

He cannot get clerical or supervisory work to do save in exceptional cases.

He cannot teach save in a few of the remaining Negro schools.

He cannot become a mechanic except for small transient jobs, and cannot join a trades union.

A Negro woman has but three careers open to her in this city : domestic service, sewing, or married life.

2. As to keeping work :

The Negro suffers in competition more severely than white men.

Change in fashion is causing him to be replaced by whites in the better paid positions of domestic service.

Whim and accident will cause him to lose a hard-earned place more quickly than the same things would affect a white man.

Being few in number compared with the whites the crime or carelessness of a few of his race is easily imputed to all, and the reputation of the good, industrious and reliable suffer thereby.

Because Negro workmen may not often work side by side with white workmen, the individual black workman is rated not by his own efficiency, but by the efficiency of a whole group of black fellow workmen which may often be low.

Because of these difficulties which virtually increase competition in his case, he is forced to take lower wages for the same work than white workmen.

3. As to entering new lines of work :

Men are used to seeing Negroes in inferior positions ; when, therefore, by any chance a Negro gets in a better position, most men immediately conclude that he is not fitted for it, even before he has a chance to show his fitness.

If, therefore, he set up a store, men will not patronize him.

If he is put into public position men will complain.

If he gain a position in the commercial world, men will quietly secure his dismissal or see that a white man succeeds him.

4. As to his expenditure :

The comparative smallness of the patronage of the Negro, and the dislike of other customers makes it usual to increase the charges or difficulties in certain directions in which a Negro must spend money.

He must pay more house-rent for worse houses than most white people pay.

He is sometimes liable to insult or reluctant service in some restaurants, hotels and stores, at public resorts, theatres and places of recreation ; and at nearly all barber shops.

5. As to his children :

The Negro finds it extremely difficult to rear children in such an atmosphere and not have them either cringing or impudent : if he impresses upon them patience with their lot, they may grow up satisfied with their condition ; if he inspires them with ambition to rise, they may grow to despise their own people, hate the whites and become embittered with the world.

His children are discriminated against, often in public schools.

They are advised when seeking employment to become waiters and maids.

They are liable to species of insult and temptation peculiarly trying to children.

6. As to social intercourse :

In all walks of life the Negro is liable to meet some objection to his presence or some discourteous treatment ; and the ties of friendship or memory seldom are strong enough to hold across the color line.

If an invitation is issued to the public for any occasion, the Negro can never know whether he would be welcomed or not ; if he goes he is liable to have his feelings hurt and get into unpleasant altercation ; if he stays away, he is blamed for indifference.

If he meet a lifelong white friend on the street, he is in a dilemma ; if he does not greet the friend he is put down as boorish and impolite ; if he does greet the friend he is liable to be flatly snubbed.

If by chance he is introduced to a white woman or man, he expects to be ignored on the next meeting, and usually is.

White friends may call on him, but he is scarcely expected to call on them, save for strictly business matters.

If he gain the affections of a white woman and marry her he may invariably expect that slurs will be thrown on her reputation and on his, and that both his and her race will shun their company.[1]

When he dies he cannot be buried beside white corpses.

7. The result :

Any one of these things happening now and then would not be remarkable or call for especial comment ; but when one group of people suffer all these little differences of treatment and discriminations and insults continually, the result is either discouragement, or bitterness, or over-sensitiveness, or recklessness. And a people feeling thus cannot do their best.

Presumably the first impulse of the average Philadelphian would be emphatically to deny any such marked and blighting discrimination as the above against a group of citizens in this metropolis. Every one knows that in the

---

[1] Cf. Section 49.

past color prejudice in the city was deep and passionate; living men can remember when a Negro could not sit in a street car or walk many streets in peace. These times have passed, however, and many imagine that active discrimination against the Negro has passed with them. Careful inquiry will convince any such one of his error. To be sure a colored man to-day can walk the streets of Philadelphia without personal insult; he can go to theatres, parks and some places of amusement without meeting more than stares and discourtesy; he can be accommodated at most hotels and restaurants, although his treatment in some would not be pleasant. All this is a vast advance and augurs much for the future. And yet all that has been said of the remaining discrimination is but too true.

During the investigation of 1896 there was collected a number of actual cases, which may illustrate the discriminations spoken of. So far as possible these have been sifted and only those which seem undoubtedly true have been selected.[2]

1. As to getting work.

It is hardly necessary to dwell upon the situation of the Negro in regard to work in the higher walks of life: the white boy may start in the lawyer's office and work himself into a lucrative practice; he may serve a physician as office boy or enter a hospital in a minor position, and have his talent alone between him and

---

[2] One of the questions on the schedule was: "Have you had any difficulty in getting work?" another: "Have you had any difficulty in renting houses?" Most of the answers were vague or general. Those that were definite and apparently reliable were, so far as possible, inquired into further, compared with other testimony and then used as material for working out a list of discriminations; single and isolated cases without corroboration were never taken. I believe those here presented are reliable, although naturally I may have been deceived in some stories. Of the general truth of the statement I am thoroughly convinced.

affluence and fame ; if he is bright in school, he may
make his mark in a university, become a tutor with some
time and much inspiration for study, and eventually fill
a professor's chair.   All these careers are at the very
outset closed to the Negro on account of his color ; what
lawyer would give even a minor case to a Negro assistant?
or what university would appoint a promising young
Negro as tutor ?   Thus the young white man starts in life
knowing that within some limits and barring accidents,
talent and application will tell.   The young Negro starts
knowing that on all sides his advance is made doubly
difficult if not wholly shut off by his color.   Let us come,
however, to ordinary occupations which concern more
nearly the mass of Negroes.   Philadelphia is a great industrial and business centre, with thousands of foremen,
managers and clerks—the lieutenants of industry who
direct its progress.   They are paid for thinking and for
skill to direct, and naturally such positions are coveted
because they are well paid, well thought-of and carry some
authority.   To such positions Negro boys and girls may
not aspire no matter what their qualifications.   Even as
teachers and ordinary clerks and stenographers they find
almost no openings.   Let us note some actual instances :

A young woman who graduated with credit from the
Girls' Normal School in 1892, has taught in the kindergarten, acted as substitute, and waited in vain for a permanent position.   Once she was allowed to substitute in a
school with white teachers ; the principal commended her
work, but when the permanent appointment was made a
white woman got it.

A girl who graduated from a Pennsylvania high school
and from a business college sought work in the city as a
stenographer and typewriter.   A prominent lawyer undertook to find her a position ; he went to friends and said,
"Here is a girl that does excellent work and is of good
character ; can you not give her work ? "   Several imme-

diately answered yes. "But," said the lawyer, "I will be
perfectly frank with you and tell you she is colored ;" and
not in the whole city could he find a man willing to
employ her. It happened, however, that the girl was so
light in complexion that few not knowing would have
suspected her descent. The lawyer therefore gave her
temporary work in his own office until she found a position
outside the city. "But," said he, "to this day I have not
dared to tell my clerks that they worked beside a Negress."
Another woman graduated from the high school and the
Palmer College of Shorthand, but all over the city has met
with nothing but refusal of work.

Several graduates in pharmacy have sought to get their
three years required apprenticeship in the city and in only
one case did one succeed, although they offered to work for
nothing. One young pharmacist came from Massachusetts
and for weeks sought in vain for work here at any price;
"I wouldn't have a darky to clean out my store, much
less to stand behind the counter," answered one druggist.
A colored man answered an advertisement for a clerk in
the suburbs. "What do you suppose we'd want of a
nigger ?" was the plain answer. A graduate of the
University of Pennsylvania in mechanical engineering,
well recommended, obtained work in the city, through an
advertisement, on account of his excellent record. He
worked a few hours and then was discharged because he
was found to be colored. He is now a waiter at the
University Club, where his white fellow graduates dine.[3]
Another young man attended Spring Garden Institute and
studied drawing for lithography. He had good references
from the institute and elsewhere, but application at the
five largest establishments in the city could secure him no
work. A telegraph operator has hunted in vain for an
opening, and two graduates of the Central High School

---

[3] And is, of course, pointed out by some as typifying the educated
Negro's success in life.

have sunk to menial labor. "What's the use of an education?" asked one. Mr. A—— has elsewhere been employed as a traveling salesman. He applied for a position here by letter and was told he could have one. When they saw him they had no work for him.

Such cases could be multiplied indefinitely. But that is not necessary ; one has but to note that, notwithstanding the acknowledged ability of many colored men, the Negro is conspicuously absent from all places of honor, trust or emolument, as well as from those of respectable grade in commerce and industry.

Even in the world of skilled labor the Negro is largely excluded. Many would explain the absence of Negroes from higher vocations by saying that while a few may now and then be found competent, the great mass are not fitted for that sort of work and are destined for some time to form a laboring class. In the matter of the trades, however, there can be raised no serious question of ability ; for years the Negroes filled satisfactorily the trades of the city, and to-day in many parts of the South they are still prominent. And yet in Philadelphia a determined prejudice, aided by public opinion, has succeeded nearly in driving them from the field:

A——, who works at a bookbinding establishment on Front street, has learned to bind books and often does so for his friends. He is not allowed to work at the trade in the shop, however, but must remain a porter at a porter's wages.

B—— is a brushmaker ; he has applied at several establishments, but they would not even examine his testimonials. They simply said : "We do not employ colored people."

C—— is a shoemaker ; he tried to get work in some of the large department stores. They "had no place" for him.

D—— was a bricklayer, but experienced so much trouble in getting work that he is now a messenger.

E—— is a painter, but has found it impossible to get work because he is colored.

F—— is a telegraph line man, who formerly worked in Richmond, Va. When he applied here he was told that Negroes were not employed.

G—— is an iron puddler, who belonged to a Pittsburg union. Here he was not recognized as a union man and could not get work except as a stevedore.

H—— was a cooper, but could get no work after repeated trials, and is now a common laborer.

I—— is a candy-maker, but has never been able to find employment in the city; he is always told that the white help will not work with him.

J—— is a carpenter; he can only secure odd jobs or work where only Negroes are employed.

K—— was an upholsterer, but could get no work save in the few colored shops, which had workmen; he is now a waiter on a dining car.

L—— was a first-class baker; he applied for work some time ago near Green street and was told shortly, "We don't work no niggers here."

M—— is a good typesetter; he has not been allowed to join the union and has been refused work at eight different places in the city.

N—— is a printer by trade, but can only find work as a porter.

O—— is a sign-painter, but can get but little work.

P—— is a painter and gets considerable work, but never with white workmen.

Q—— is a good stationary engineer, but can find no employment; is at present a waiter in a private family.

R—— was born in Jamaica; he went to England and worked fifteen years in the Sir Edward Green Economizing Works in Wakefield, Yorkshire. During dull times he emigrated to America, bringing excellent references. He applied for a place as mechanic in nearly all the large iron working establishments in the city. A locomotive works assured him that his letters were all right, but that their men would not work with Negroes. At a manufactory of railway switches they told him they had no vacancy and he could call again ; he called and finally was frankly told that they could not employ Negroes. He applied twice to a foundry company : they told him : "We have use for only one Negro—a porter," and refusing either further conversation or even to look at his letters showed him out. He then applied for work on a new building; the man told him he could leave an application, then added : "To tell the truth, it's no use, for we don't employ Negroes." Thus the man has searched for work two years and has not yet found a permanent position. He can only support his family by odd jobs as a common laborer.

S—— is a stone-cutter ; he was refused work repeatedly on account of color. At last he got a job during a strike and was found to be so good a workman that his employer refused to dismiss him.

T—— was a boy, who, together with a white boy came to the city to hunt work. The colored boy was very light in complexion, and consequently both were taken in as apprentices at a large locomotive works; they worked there some months, but it was finally disclosed that the boy was colored; he was dismissed and the white boy retained.

These all seem typical and reliable cases. There are, of course, some exceptions to the general rule, but even these seem to confirm the fact that exclusion is a matter of prejudice and thoughtlessness which sometimes yields to determination and good sense. The most notable case in point is that of the Midvale Steel Works, where a large number of Negro workmen are regularly employed as mechanics and work alongside whites.[4] If another foreman should take charge there, or if friction should arise, it would be easy for all

---

[4] Cf. Section 23.

this to receive a serious set-back, for ultimate success in such matters demands many experiments and a widespread public sympathy.

There are several cases where strong personal influence has secured colored boys positions; in one cabinet-making factory, a porter who had served the firm thirty years, asked to have his son learn the trade and work in the shop. The workmen objected strenuously at first, but the employer was firm and the young man has been at work there now seven years. The S. S. White Dental Company has a colored chemist who has worked up to his place and gives satisfaction. A jeweler allowed his colored fellow-soldier in the late war to learn the gold beaters' trade and work in his shop. A few other cases follow:

A—— was intimately acquainted with a merchant and secured his son a position as a typewriter in the merchant's office.

B——, a stationary engineer, came with his employer from Washington and still works with him.

C——, a plasterer, learned his trade with a firm in Virginia who especially recommended him to the firm where he now works.

D—— is a boy whose mother's friend got him work as cutter in a bag and rope factory; the hands objected but the friend's influence was strong enough to keep him there.

All these exceptions prove the rule, viz., that without strong effort and special influence it is next to impossible for a Negro in Philadelphia to get regular employment in most of the trades, except he work as an independent workman and take small transient jobs.

The chief agency that brings about this state of affairs is public opinion; if they were not intrenched, and strongly intrenched, back of an active prejudice or at least passive acquiescence in this effort to deprive Negroes of a decent livelihood, both trades unions and arbitrary bosses would be powerless to do the harm they now do; where, however, a large section of the public more or less openly applaud the stamina of a man who refuses to work with a "Nigger," the results are inevitable. The object of the trades union is purely business-like; it aims to restrict the labor market, just as the manufacturer aims to raise the price of his goods. Here is a chance to keep out of the market a vast number of workmen, and the unions seize the chance save in cases where they dare not as in the case of the cigar-makers and coal-miners. If they could keep out the foreign workmen in the same way they would; but here public opinion within and without their ranks forbids hostile action. Of course, most unions do not flatly declare their discriminations; a few plainly put the word "white" into their constitutions; most of them do not and will say that they consider each case on its merits. Then they quietly blackball the Negro applicant. Others delay and temporize and put off action until the Negro withdraws; still others discriminate against the Negro in initiation fees and dues, making a Negro pay $100, where the whites pay $25. On the other hand in times of strikes or other disturbances cordial invitations to join are often sent to Negro workmen.[5]

At a time when women are engaged in bread-winning to a larger degree than ever before, the field open to Negro women is unusually narrow. This is, of course, due largely to the more intense prejudices of females on all subjects,

---

[5] Two newspaper clippings will illustrate the attitude of the workmen; the first relates to the Chinese apprentices taken into the Baldwin Locomotive Works:

The announcement that the Baldwins had taken five Chinese apprentices made quite a stir among labor leaders. Some of them worked themselves into quite a fever of indignation. Charles P. Patrick, grand organizer of the Boilermakers' Union, was quite outspoken on the subject.

He said: "All this plan of putting Chinamen in to learn trades sounds nice and charitable to the Christian League, but how does it sound to the ears of American mechanics who are walking the streets in search of

and especially to the fact that women who work dislike to
be in any way mistaken for menials, and they regard Negro
women as menials *par excellence.*

A——, a dressmaker and seamstress of proven ability,

employment? I have traveled all over this country and Mexico, and I
have never before seen Chinamen given places over the heads of Americans. In the West and in Mexico, Chinese labor is plentiful, but the
Chinamen are given only menial positions. They are servants, helpers
in the mines and laborers. I never before heard of a Chinaman being
given a place as an apprentice in a shop.

" Our government excludes Chinese labor from this country, yet here
is the Christian League seeking to put forbidden immigrants in a position
where they, with their peculiarly cheap, even beggarly style of living,
can compete with American labor. I have only been in this city for a
few days, but I venture to say I have seen more beggars and men out of
work around Eighth and Market streets than I have seen in the whole
City of Mexico."

Missionary Frederic Poole disposed of this argument in a few words.
He said: " It is not my idea, nor the idea of Mr. Converse, that these
men should at any time compete with American workingmen. It is not
the wish of the men themselves. Mr. Converse would not have given
them employment had any such thing been intended.

" To-day China is building a vast railroad to Pekin that will open up
all the wealthy and fertile region of Central China. The enterprise is
under the direction of the government. It will be in operation in about
four years. Men of intelligence will be needed for engineers, and there
my five protégés will find their life work. It is not unlikely that the
Chinese Government will send for them before their apprenticeship is
over."

John H. Converse was rather interested when he learned of objections
to his Chinese apprentices. " We might have expected such objections
from professional agitators," he said, "but I do not think you will learn
of any among our employes."

Continuing, he said: "The Baldwin Locomotive Works is now con-
structing eight locomotives for the Chinese Government, which will be
the first to run over the great new railroad being built from Pekin to
Tien-Tsin. American workingmen would be very narrow indeed if they
cannot see that it is to their own immediate advantage that Chinese
mechanics fit to look after American locomotives shall be trained at once,
for the time is coming when thousands of American workingmen may be
kept busy from the extension of railroad building in China.

"These five boys are Philadelphians. They were not brought here,
and every broad-minded mechanic will believe that their apprenticeship
in our shops, should they, as they probably will, return to China, must
mean something for the American locomotive. They are the first to be

sought work in the large department stores. They all commended her work, but could not employ her on account of her color.

B—— is a typewriter, but has applied at stores and

---

admitted to a locomotive works in this country, and the news will in all likelihood create a more friendly feeling in the railroad department of the Chinese Government for American products."

Mr. Converse said that his firm had no thought of extending the privilege beyond the present number of Chinese apprentices.—Philadelphia *Public Ledger*, January 5, 1897.

No Negro apprentices have ever been admitted.

The other clipping is a report of the discussion in the annual meeting of the Federation of Labor:

The Negro question occupied the major portion of the session, and a heated discussion was brought on by a resolution by Henry Lloyd, reaffirming the declarations of the Federation that all labor, without regard to color, is welcome to its ranks—denouncing as untrue in fact the reported statements of Booker T. Washington that the trades unions were placing obstacles in the way of the material advancement of the Negro, and appealing to the records of the Federation Conventions as complete answers to such false assertions.

This resolution caused much spirited discussion. Delegate Jones, of Augusta, Ga., spoke, claiming that the white laborer could not compete with the Negro laborer, though organization would improve conditions materially. President Gompers took part in the discussion, explaining that the movement was not against the Negro laborer, but against the cheap laborer, and that the textile workers of the East had been compelled to contribute most of their means to teach laborers in the South the benefits of organization.

He also made the point that the capitalist would profit by the failure of the Negro laborers to organize, thus making the Negro an impediment to labor movements.

C. P. Frahey, a Nashville delegate, insisted that the Negro was not the equal of the white man socially or industrially. He grew warm in speaking of President Gompers' remarks regarding the Negro in the labor movement, and stated that the President had not revoked the commission of a National Organizer who had patronized a non-union white barber shop in preference to a union Negro barber shop.

The organizer had simply been allowed to resign and no publicity had been given the matter. In answer to a question desiring the name of the party, Frahey stated it was Jesse Johnson, president of the pressmen.

James O'Connell and P. J. McGuire spoke for the resolution. The latter insisted that Booker T. Washington was attempting to put the Negro before the public as the victim of gross injustice, and himself as the offices in vain for work; "very sorry" they all say, but they can give her no work. She has answered many advertisements without result.

C—— has attended the Girls, High School for two years, and has been unable to find any work; she is washing and sewing for a living now.

D—— is a dressmaker and milliner, and does bead work. "Your work is very good," they say to her, "but if we hired you all of our ladies would leave."

E——, a seamstress, was given work from a store once, to do at home. It was commended as satisfactory, but they gave her no more.

F—— had two daughters who tried to get work as stenographers, but got only one small job.

G—— is a graduate of the Girls, High School, with excellent record; both teachers and influential friends have been seeking work for her but have not been able to find any.

H—— a girl, applied at seven stores for some work not menial; they had none.

I—— started at the Schuylkill, on Market street, and applied at almost every store nearly to the Delaware for work; she was only offered scrubbing.[6]

Moses of the race. M. D. Rathford insisted that drawing the color line would be a blow to the miners' organization.

W. D. Mahon charged that Jones was not a representative of Southern trades unionism, having just joined the ranks. Jones then, in his own defence, declared he did not oppose the Negro, but did contend that the Negro laborer was lower than the white, citing an Atlanta case, where whites and blacks had been jointly employed and the whites struck.

He wanted to know if there had been any efforts made in the East to organize Chinese who came in conflict with the union labor. President Gompers then ruled that the discussion must cease.

The resolution which had caused the heated debate was adopted, and the delegates went into executive session.—*Public Ledger*, December 17, 1897.

[6] From the facts tabulated, it appears that one-twentieth of the colored domestic servants of Philadelphia have trades, while in addition to this one-tenth have had some higher school training and are presumably

2. So much for the difficulty of getting work. In addition to this the Negro is meeting difficulties in keeping the work he has, or at least the better part of it. Outside of all dissatisfaction with Negro work there are whims

---

fitted to be something more than ordinary domestics. Why then do they not enter these fields instead of drifting into or deliberately choosing domestic service as a means of livelihood? The answer is simple. In a majority of cases the reason why they do not enter other fields is because they are colored not because they are incompetent. Many instances might be cited in proof of this, were proof needed. The following cases are only some of those that were personally encountered by the investigator in one ward of one city.

One very fair young girl, apparently a white girl, was employed as a clerk in one of the large department stores for over two years, so that there was no question of her competency as a clerk. At the end of this time it was discovered that she had colored blood and she was promptly discharged. One young woman who had been a teacher and is now a school janitress, teaching occasionally when extra help is needed, states that she had received an appointment as typewriter in a certain Philadelphia office, on the strength of her letter of application and when she appeared and was seen to be a colored girl, the position was refused her. She said that her brother—whom people usually take to be a white man —after serving in the barbershop of a certain hotel for more than ten years, was summarily discharged when it was learned that he was of Negro birth. One woman, who was a seamstress and dressmaker, stated that she had on several occasions gotten work from a certain church home when she wore a heavy veil, on making her application at the office, but that on the first occasion when she wore no veil her application was refused and had been every time since. Of course many of the men in domestic service have had similar experiences. Ten men out of one hundred and fifty-six had trades, but none of them were members of the trades unions.

Mr. McGuire, vice-president of the Federation of Labor, stated to the present investigator that the Federation claims that colored men may be members of any trade union represented in the Federation. But what this profession amounts to may be judged from Mr. McGuire's further statement, quoted verbatim: "A majority are willing to have them admitted, but a strong minority will oppose it. Not a word will be said against it in discussion, but quietly at the ballot they will rule them out."

How this profession of admission, which amounts to practical exclusion, looks from the workingman's point of view is shown in the experience of a first-rate colored carpenter and builder in the Seventh Ward who was induced to apply for admission to the Carpenters' Union. He asked an officer of the Amalgamated Association of Carpenters and

and fashions that affect his economic position; to-day
general European travel has made the trained English
servant popular and consequently well-shaven white men-
servants, whether English or not, find it easy to replace

Joiners, one of the allied societies of the American Federation of Labor,
if it would be of any use for him to apply to the Union for membership.
"If you know your trade and are a carpenter in good and regular
standing, I see no reason why you should not become a member," said
the officer. "So he sent me to the present secretary of the association,
and when I put the question to him, he said, 'Well, he didn't know
whether I could join or not, because they had never *had* a colored man
in the Union, but he would report it to the association here [Philadelphia]
and would write to headquarters in New York to see if it would be admis-
sible to enter a colored man.' He put it on the ground of my color, you
see." This application was made in December, 1896. The applicant was
told that the matter would be acted on in the Union on a certain night in
January, 1897, and every attempt was made to send a man to report that
particular meeting, but without success. What occurred is not hard to
guess, however, since the colored carpenter whose case was then considered has received no word from the Union from that day to this. He has
called at the secretary's office three or four times and left word that he
would like to hear what action was taken regarding his application for
admission to the Union, but December 1, 1897, he had received no answer
to his application made in December, 1896.

The effect of this is well illustrated by the case of a young colored
"waiter man" on Pine street, whose case may be taken as typical. He
had studied three years at Hampton, where he had learned in that time
the stone-cutter's trade. He could practice this in Georgia, he said, but
in the South stone-cutters get only $2.00 a day as compared with $3.50,
sometimes $4.00 a day, in the North. So he came North with the promise
of a job of stone-cutting for a new block of buildings to be erected by a
Philadelphian he had met in Georgia. He received $3.50 a day, but when
the block was done he could get no other job at stone-cutting and so
went into domestic service, where he is receiving $6.25 a week instead of
the $21.00 a week he should be receiving as a stone-cutter.

The effect on domestic service is to swell its already over-full ranks with
discontented young men and women whom one would naturally expect
to find rendering half-hearted service because they consider their domestic
work only a temporary makeshift employment. One sometimes hears it
said that "our waiter has graduated from such and such a school, but we
notice that he is not even a very good waiter." Such comments give rise
to the speculation as to the success in ditch digging which would be likely
to attend upon the labors of college professors, or indeed, how many of
the young white men who have graduated from college and from law

Negro butlers and coachmen at higher wages. Again, though a man ordinarily does not dismiss all his white mill-hands because some turn out badly, yet it repeatedly happens that men dismiss all their colored servants and condemn their race because one or two in their employ have proven untrustworthy. Finally, the antipathies of lower classes are so great that it is often impracticable to mix races among the servants. A young colored girl went to work temporarily in Germantown; " I should like so much to keep you permanently," said the mistress, " but all my other servants are white." She was discharged. Usually now advertisements for help state whether white or Negro servants are wanted, and the Negro who applies at the wrong place must not be surprised to have the door slammed in his face.

The difficulties encountered by the Negro on account of sweeping conclusions made about him are manifold; a large building, for instance, has several poorly paid Negro janitors, without facilities for their work or guidance in its prosecution. Finally the building is thoroughly overhauled or rebuilt, elevators and electricity installed and a well paid set of white uniformed janitors put to work under a responsible salaried chief. Immediately the public concludes that the improvement in the service is due to the change of color. In some cases, of course, the change is due to a widening of the field of choice in selecting servants; for assuredly one cannot expect that one twenty-fifth of the population can furnish as many good workmen or as uniformly good ones as the other twenty-four twenty-fifths. One actual case illustrates this tendency to exclude the

---

schools would show themselves excellent waiters, particularly if they took up the work simply as a temporary expedient. A "match" between Yale and Hampton, where mental activities must be confined to the walls of the butler's pantry, and where there were to be no "fumbles" with soup plates, might bring out interesting and suggestive points.

ISABEL EATON.

Negro without proper consideration from even menial employment:

A great church which has a number of members among the most respectable Negro families in the city has recently erected a large new building for its offices, etc., in the city. As the building was nearing completion a colored clergyman of that sect was surprised to hear that no Negroes were to be employed in the building; he thought that a peculiar stand for a Christian church to take and so he went to the manager of the building; the manager blandly assured him that the rumor was true; and that there was not the shadow of a chance for a Negro to get employment under him, except one woman to clean the water-closet. The reason for this, he said, was that the janitors and help were all to be uniformed and the whites would not wear uniforms with Negroes. The clergyman thereupon went to a prominent member of the church who was serving on the building committee; he denied that the committee had made any such decision, but sent him to another member of the committee; this member said the same thing and referred to the third, a blunt business man. The business man said: "That building is called the ———— Church House, but it is more than that, it is a business enterprise, to be run on business principles. We hired a man to run it so as to get the most out of it. We found such a man in the present manager, and put all power in his hands." He acknowledged then, that while the committee had made no decision, the question of hiring Negroes had come up and it was left solely to the manager's decision. The manager thought most Negroes were dishonest and untrustworthy, etc. And thus the Christian church joins hands with trades unions and a large public opinion to force Negroes into idleness and crime.

Sometimes Negroes, by special influence, as has been pointed out before, secure good positions; then there are other cases where colored men have by sheer merit and pluck secured positions.   In all these cases, however, they are liable to lose their places through no fault of their own and primarily on account of their Negro blood.   It may be that at first their Negro descent is not known, or other causes may operate ; in all cases the Negro's tenure of office is insecure :

A—— worked in a large tailor's establishment on Third street for three weeks.   His work was acceptable. Then it became known he was colored and he was discharged as the other tailors refused to work with him.

B——, a pressman, was employed on Twelfth street, but a week later was discharged when they knew he was colored ; he then worked as a door-boy for five years, and finally got another job in a Jewish shop as pressman.

C—— was nine years a painter in Stewart's Furniture Factory, until Stewart failed four years ago.   Has applied repeatedly, but could get no work on account of color. He now works as a night watchman on the streets for the city.

D—— was a stationary engineer ; his employer died, and he has never been able to find another.

E—— was light in complexion and got a job as driver ; he " kept his cap on," but when they found he was colored they discharged him.

F—— was one of many colored laborers at an ink factory. The heads of the firm died, and now whenever a Negro leaves a white man is put in his place.

G—— worked for a long time as a typesetter on Taggart's *Times ;* when the paper changed hands he was discharged and has never been able to get another job ; he is now a janitor.

H—— was a brickmason, but his employers finally refused to let him lay brick longer as his fellow workmen were all white ; he is now a waiter.

L—— learned the trade of range-setting from his employer ; the employer then refused him work and he went into business for himself ; he has taught four apprentices.

M—— is a woman whose husband was janitor for a firm twenty years ; when they moved to the new Betz Building they discharged him as all the janitors there were white ; after his death they could find no work for his boy.

N—— was a porter in a book store and rose to be head postmaster of a sub-station in Philadelphia which handles $250,000, it is said, a year ; he was also at the head of a very efficient Bureau of Information in a large department store. Recently attempts have been made to displace him, for no specified fault but because " we want his place for another [white] man."

O—— is a well-known instance ; an observer in 1898 wrote : " If any Philadelphian who is anxious to study the matter with his own eyes, will walk along South Eleventh street, from Chestnut down, and will note the most tasteful and enterprising stationery and periodical store along the way, it will pay him to enter it. On entering he will, according to his way of thinking, be pleased or grieved to see that it is conducted by Negroes. If the proprietor happens to be in he may know that this keen-looking pleasant young man was once assistant business manager of a large white religious newspaper in the city. A change of management led to his dismissal. No fault was found, his work was commended, but a white man was put into his place, and profuse apologies made.

"The clerk behind the counter is his sister; a neat lady-like woman, educated, and trained in stenography and typewriting. She could not find in the city of Philadelphia, any one who had the slightest use for such a colored woman.

" The result of this situation is this little store, which is remarkably successful. The proprietor owns the stock, the store and the building. This is one tale of its sort with a pleasant ending. Other tales are far less pleasing."

Much discouragement results from the persistent refusal to promote colored employes. The humblest white employe knows that the better he does his work the more chance there is for him to rise in the business. The black employe knows that the better he does his work the longer he may do it ; he cannot often hope for promotion. This makes much of the criticism aimed against Negroes, because some of them want to refuse menial labor, lose something of its point. If the better class of Negro boys could look on such labor as a stepping-stone to something higher it would be different; if they must view it as a lifework we cannot wonder at their hesitation :

A—— has been a porter at a great locomotive works for ten years. He is a carpenter by trade and has picked up considerable knowledge of machinery ; he was formerly allowed to work a little as a machinist ; now that is stopped and he has never been promoted and probably never will be.

B—— has worked in a shop eight years and never been promoted from his porter's position, although he is a capable man.

C—— is a porter ; he has been in a hardware store six years ; he is bright and has repeatedly been promised advancement but has never got it.

D—— was for seven years in a gang of porters in a department store, and part of the time acted as foreman. He had a white boy under him who disliked him ; eventually the boy was promoted but he remained a porter. Finally the boy became his boss and discharged him.

E——, a woman, worked long in a family of lawyers ; a white lad went into their office as office-boy and came to be a member of the firm ; she had a smart, ambitious son and asked for any sort of office work for him—anything in which he could hope for promotion. "Why don't you make him a waiter?" they asked.

F—— has for twenty-one years driven for a lumber

firm; speaks German and is very useful to them, but they have never promoted him.

G—— was a porter; he begged for a chance to work up; offering to do clerical work for nothing, but was refused. White companions were repeatedly promoted over his head. He has been a porter seventeen years.

H—— was a servant in the family of one of the members of a large dry goods firm; he was so capable that the employer sent him down to the store for a place which the manager very reluctantly gave him. He rose to be registering clerk in the delivering department where he worked fourteen years and his work was commended. Recently without notice or complaint he was changed to run an elevator at the same wages. He thinks that pressure from other members of the firm made him lose his work.

Once in a while there are exceptions to this rule. The Pennsylvania Railroad has promoted one bright and persistent porter to a clerkship, which he has held for years. He had, however, spent his life hunting chances for promotion and had been told "You have ability enough, George, if you were not colored ——— ."

There is much discrimination against Negroes in wages.[7]

---

[7] In the case of the Colored people, the number of mother wage-earners more than doubles the number of widows. This is due to the small average wage of the Colored husband—the smallest among the twenty-seven nationalities. The laundress is the economic supplement of the porter. . . . It is not because the Colored husband of this district neglects his responsibility as a wage-winner that so many Colored women are forced into supplemental toil, for 98.7 per cent of the Colored husbands are wage-earners, and only 92.2 per cent of the American, 90.3 per cent of the Irish, 96 per cent of the German, 93.7 per cent of the Italian, 93.1 per cent of the French. The Danes, 80 per cent; Canadians, 81.8 per cent; Russians, 85.7 per cent, and Hungarians, 88.8 per cent, have the smallest percentages. Of the more largely represented nationalities, the French most nearly approach the Colored people in the percentage of their wives who are wage-earners; but while the French percentage is 21.6 per cent, the Colored people's percentage is 53.6 per cent." Dr. W. Laidlaw in the "Report of a Sociological Canvass of the Nineteenth Assembly District," a slum section of New York City, in 1897.

The Negroes have fewer chances for work, have been used to low wages, and consequently the first thought that occurs to the average employer is to give a Negro less than he would offer a white man for the same work. This is not universal, but it is widespread. In domestic service of the ordinary sort there is no difference, because the wages are a matter of custom. When it comes to waiters, butlers and coachmen, however, there is considerable difference made; while white coachmen receive from $50–$75, the Negroes do not get usually more than $30–$60. Negro hotel waiters get from $18–$20, while whites receive $20–$30. Naturally when a hotel manager replaces $20 men with $30 men he may expect, outside any question of color, better service.

In ordinary work the competition forces down the wages outside mere race reasons, though the Negro is the greatest sufferer; this is especially the case in laundry work. "I've counted as high as seven dozen pieces in that washing," said a weary black woman, "and she pays me only $1.25 a week for it." Persons who throw away $5 a week on gew-gaws will often haggle over twenty-five cents with a washerwoman. There are, however, notable exceptions to these cases, where good wages are paid to persons who have long worked for the same family.

Very often if a Negro is given a chance to work at a trade his wages are cut down for the privilege. This gives the workingman's prejudice additional intensity:

A—— got a job formerly held by a white porter; the wages were reduced from $12 to $8.

B—— worked for a firm as china packer, and they said he was the best packer they had. He, however, received but $6 a week while the white packers received $12.

C—— has been porter and assistant shipping clerk in an Arch street store for five years. He receives $6 a week and whites get $8 for the same work.

D—— is a stationary engineer; he learned his trade

with this firm and has been with them ten years. Formerly he received $9 a week, now $10.50; whites get $12 for the same work.

E—— is a stationary engineer and has been in his place three years. He receives but $9 a week.

F—— works with several other Negroes with a firm of electrical engineers. The white laborers receive $2 a day : "We've got to be glad to get $1.75."

G—— was a carpenter, but could get neither sufficient work nor satisfactory wages. For a job on which he received $15 a week, his white successor got $18.

H——, a cementer, receives $1.75 a day; white workmen get $2-$3. He has been promised more next fall.

I——, a plasterer, has worked for one boss twenty-seven years. Regular plasterers get $4 or more a day; he does the same work, but cannot join the union and is paid as a laborer—$2.50 a day.

J—— works as a porter in a department store; is married, and receives $8 a week. "They pay the same to white unmarried shop girls, who stand a chance to be promoted."

3. If a Negro enters some line of employment in which people are not used to seeing him, he suffers from an assumption that he is unfit for the work. It is reported that a Chestnut street firm once took a Negro shop girl, but the protests of their customers were such that they had to dismiss her. A great many merchants hesitate to advance Negroes lest they should lose custom. Negro merchants who have attempted to start business in the city at first encounter much difficulty from this prejudice:

A—— has a bakery; white people sometimes enter and finding Negroes in charge abruptly leave.

B—— is a baker and had a shop some years on Vine street, but prejudice against him barred him from gaining much custom.

C—— is a successful expressman with a large business;

he is sometimes told by persons that they prefer to patronize white expressmen.

D—— is a woman and keeps a hair store on South street. Customers sometimes enter, look at her, and leave.

E—— is a music teacher on Lombard street. Several white people have entered and seeing him, said : " Oh ! I thought you were white—excuse me ! " or " I'll call again ! "

Even among the colored people themselves some prejudice of this sort is met. Once a Negro physician could not get the patronage of Negroes because they were not used to the innovation. Now they have a large part of the Negro patronage. The Negro merchant, however, still lacks the full confidence of his own people though this is slowly growing. It is one of the paradoxes of this question to see a people so discriminated against sometimes add to their misfortunes by discriminating against themselves. They themselves, however, are beginning to recognize this.

4. The chief discrimination against Negroes in expenditure is in the matter of rents. There can be no reasonable doubt but that Negroes pay excessive rents :

A—— paid $13 a month where the preceding white family had paid $10.

B—— paid $16 ; " heard that former white family paid $12."

C—— paid $25 ; " heard that former white family paid $20."

D—— paid $12 ; neighbors say that former white family paid $9.

E—— paid $25, instead of $18.

F—— paid $12, instead of $10.

G——,the Negro inhabitants of the whole street pay $12 to $14 and the whites $9 and $10. The houses are all alike.

H——, whites on this street pay $15–$18 ; Negroes pay $18–$21.

Not only is there this pretty general discrimination in

rent, but agents and owners will not usually repair the
houses of the blacks willingly or improve them. In
addition to this agents and owners in many sections utterly
refuse to rent to Negroes on any terms. Both these sorts
of discrimination are easily defended from a merely business
point of view; public opinion in the city is such that the
presence of even a respectable colored family in a block
will affect its value for renting or sale; increased rent to
Negroes is therefore a sort of insurance, and refusal to
rent a device for money-getting. The indefensible cruelty
lies with those classes who refuse to recognize the right of
respectable Negro citizens to respectable houses. Real
estate agents also increase prejudice by refusing to discriminate between different classes of Negroes. A quiet
Negro family moves into a street. The agent finds no
great objection, and allows the next empty house to go to
any Negro who applies. This family may disgrace and
scandalize the neighborhood and make it harder for decent
families to find homes.[8]

In the last fifteen years, however, public opinion has so
greatly changed in this matter that we may expect much
in the future. To-day the Negro population is more widely
scattered over the city than ever before. At the same time
it remains true that as a rule they must occupy the worst
houses of the districts where they live. The advance
made has been a battle for the better class of Negroes. An
ex-Minister to Hayti moved to the northwestern part of
the city and his white neighbors insulted him, barricaded
their steps against him, and tried in every way to make
him move; to-day he is honored and respected in the
whole neighborhood. Many such cases have occurred; in

---

[8] Undoubtedly certain classes of Negroes bring much deserved criticism on themselves by irregular payment or default of rent, and by the
poor care they take of property. They must not, however, be con-
founded with the better classes who make good customers; this is again
a place for careful discrimination.

others the result was different. An estimable young Negro, just married, moved with his bride into a little street. The neighborhood rose in arms and besieged the tenant and the landlord so relentlessly that the landlord leased the house and compelled the young couple to move within a month. One of the bishops of the A. M. E. Church recently moved into the newly purchased Episcopal residence on Belmont avenue, and his neighbors have barricaded their porches against his view.

5. The chief discrimination against Negro children is in the matter of educational facilities. Prejudice here works to compel colored children to attend certain schools where most Negro children go, or to keep them out of private and higher schools.

A—— tried to get her little girl into the kindergarten nearest to her, at Fifteenth and Locust. The teachers wanted her to send it down across Broad to the kindergarten chiefly attended by colored children and much further away from its home. This journey was dangerous for the child, but the teachers refused to receive it for six months, until the authorities were appealed to.

In transfers from schools Negroes have difficulty in getting convenient accommodations; only within comparatively few years have Negroes been allowed to complete the course at the High and Normal Schools without difficulty. Earlier than that the University of Pennsylvania refused to let Negroes sit in the Auditorium and listen to lectures, much less to be students. Within two or three years a Negro student had to fight his way through a city dental school with his fists, and was treated with every indignity. Several times Negroes have been asked to leave schools of stenography, etc., on account of their fellow students. In 1893 a colored woman applied at Temple College, a church institution, for admission and was refused and advised to go elsewhere. The college then offered scholarships to churches, but would not admit applicants from colored

churches.   Two years later the same woman applied again.
The faculty declared that they did not object, but that the
students would ; she persisted and was finally admitted
with evident reluctance.

It goes without saying that most private schools, music
schools, etc., will not admit Negroes and in some cases
have insulted applicants.

Such is the tangible form of Negro prejudice in Philadelphia.   Possibly some of the particulur cases cited can
be proven to have had extenuating circumstances unknown
to the investigator ; at the same time many not cited would
be just as much in point.   At any rate no one who has with
any diligence studied the situation of the Negro in the city
can long doubt but that his opportunities are limited and
his ambition circumscribed about as has been shown.   There
are of course numerous exceptions, but the mass of the
Negroes have been so often refused openings and discouraged in efforts to better their condition that many of them
say, as one said, " I never apply—I know it is useless."
Beside these tangible and measurable forms there are
deeper and less easily described results of the attitude of
the white population toward the Negroes : a certain
manifestation of a real or assumed aversion, a spirit of
ridicule or patronage, a vindictive hatred in some, absolute
indifference in others ; all this of course does not make
much difference to the mass of the race, but it deeply
wounds the better classes, the very classes who are attaining to that to which we wish the mass to attain.   Notwithstanding all this, most Negroes would patiently await the
effect of time and commonsense on such prejudice did it
not to-day touch them in matters of life and death ;
threaten their homes, their food, their children, their hopes.
And the result of this is bound to be increased crime,
inefficiency and bitterness.

It would, of course, be idle to assert that most of the
Negro crime was caused by prejudice ; the violent economic

and social changes which the last fifty years have brought
to the American Negro, the sad social history that preceded
these changes, have all contributed to unsettle morals and
pervert talents. Nevertheless it is certain that Negro
prejudice in cities like Philadelphia has been a vast factor
in aiding and abetting all other causes which impel a
half-developed race to recklessness and excess. Certainly
a great amount of crime can be without doubt traced to the
discrimination against Negro boys and girls in the matter
of employment. Or to put it differently, Negro prejudice
costs the city something.

The connection of crime and prejudice is, on the other
hand, neither simple nor direct. The boy who is refused
promotion in his job as porter does not go out and snatch
somebody's pocketbook. Conversely the loafers at Twelfth
and Kater streets, and the thugs in the county prison are
not usually graduates of high schools who have been
refused work. The connections are much more subtle and
dangerous ; it is the atmosphere of rebellion and discontent
that unrewarded merit and reasonable but unsatisfied
ambition make. The social environment of excuse, listless
despair, careless indulgence and lack of inspiration to
work is the growing force that turns black boys and girls
into gamblers, prostitutes and rascals. And this social
environment has been built up slowly out of the dis-
appointments of deserving men and the sloth of the un-
awakened. How long can a city say to a part of its citizens,
" It is useless to work ; it is fruitless to deserve well of
men ; education will gain you nothing but disappointment
and humiliation ? " How long can a city teach its black
children that the road to success is to have a white face ?
How long can a city do this and escape the inevitable
penalty ?

For thirty years and more Philadelphia has said to its
black children : " Honesty, efficiency and talent have little
to do with your success ; if you work hard, spend little and

are good you may earn your bread and butter at those sorts
of work which we frankly confess we despise; if you are
dishonest and lazy, the State will furnish your bread free."
Thus the class of Negroes which the prejudices of the city
have distinctly encouraged is that of the criminal, the lazy
and the shiftless; for them the city teems with institutions
and charities; for them there is succor and sympathy; for
them Philadelphians are thinking and planning; but for
the educated and industrious young colored man who
wants work and not platitudes, wages and not alms, just
rewards and not sermons—for such colored men Philadelphia apparently has no use.

What then do such men do? What becomes of the
graduates of the many schools of the city? The answer
is simple: most of those who amount to anything leave
the city, the others take what they can get for a livelihood.
Let us for a moment glance at the statistics of three colored
schools: [9]

1. The O. V. Catto Primary School.
2. The Robert Vaux Grammar School.
3. The Institute for Colored Youth.

There attended the Catto school, 1867–97, 5915 pupils.
Of these there were promoted from the full course, 653.
129 of the latter are known to be in positions of higher
grade; or taking out 93 who are still in school, there
remain 36 as follows: 18 teachers, 10 clerks, 2 physicians,
2 engravers, 2 printers, 1 lawyer and 1 mechanic.

The other 524 are for the most part in service, laborers
and housewives. Of the 36 more successful ones fully half
are at work outside of the city.

Of the Vaux school there were, 1877–89, 76 graduates.
Of these there are 16 unaccounted for; the rest are:

Teachers	27	Barbers	4
Musicians	5	Clerks	3
Merchants	3	Physician	1

---

[9] Kindly furnished by the principals of these schools.

Mechanic	1	Deceased	8
Clergymen	3	Housewives	5

47

From one-half to two-thirds of these have been compelled to leave the city in order to find work ; one, the artist, Tanner, whom France recently honored, could not in his native land much less in his native city find room for his talents. He taught school in Georgia in order to earn money enough to go abroad.

The Institute of Colored Youth has had 340 graduates, 1856–97 ; 57 of these are dead. Of the 283 remaining 91 are unaccounted for. The rest are :

Teachers	117	Electrical Engineer	1
Lawyers	4	Professor	1
Physicians	4	Government clerks	5
Musicians	4	Merchants	7
Dentists	2	Mechanics	5
Clergymen	2	Clerks	23
Nurses	2	Teacher of cooking	1
Editor	1	Dressmakers	4
Civil Engineer	1	Students	7

192

Here, again, nearly three-fourths of the graduates who have amounted to anything have had to leave the city for work. The civil engineer, for instance, tried in vain to get work here and finally had to go to New Jersey to teach.

There have been 9, possibly 11, colored graduates of the Central High School. These are engaged as follows :

Grocer	1	Porter	1
Clerks in service of city	2	Butler	1
Caterer	1	Unknown	3 or 5

It is high time that the best conscience of Philadelphia awakened to her duty ; her Negro citizens are here to remain ; they can be made good citizens or burdens to the community ; if we want them to be sources of wealth and power and not of poverty and weakness then they must be given employment according to their ability and encouraged to train that ability and increase their talents by the hope of reasonable reward. To educate boys and girls and then refuse them work is to train loafers and rogues.[10]

From another point of view it could be argued with much cogency that the cause of economic stress, and consequently of crime, was the recent inconsiderate rush of Negroes into cities ; and that the unpleasant results of this migration, while deplorable, will nevertheless serve to check the movement of Negroes to cities and keep them in the country where their chance for economic development is widest. This argument loses much of its point from the fact that it is the better class of educated Philadelphia-born Negroes who have the most difficulty in obtaining employment. The new immigrant fresh from the South is much more apt to obtain work suitable for him than the black boy born here and trained in efficiency. Nevertheless it is undoubtedly true that the recent migration has both directly and indirectly increased crime and competition. How is this movement to be checked ? Much can be done by correcting misrepresentations as to the opportunities of city life made by designing employment bureaus and thoughtless persons ; a more strict surveillance of criminals might prevent the influx of undesirable elements. Such efforts, however, would not touch the main stream of immigration. Back of that stream is the world-wide desire to rise in the world, to escape the choking narrowness of the plantation, and the lawless repression of the village, in the South. It is a search for better opportunities of living, and as such it must be discouraged and repressed with great care and delicacy, if at all. The real movement of reform is the raising of economic standards and increase of economic opportunity in the South. Mere land and climate without law and

---

[10] Cf. on this point the interesting article of John Stevens Durham in the *Atlantic Monthly*, 1898.

order, capital and skill, will not develop a country. When Negroes in the South have a larger opportunity to work, accumulate property, be protected in life and limb, and encourage pride and self-respect in their children, there will be a diminution in the stream of immigrants to Northern cities. At the same time if those cities practice industrial exclusion against these immigrants to such an extent that they are forced to become paupers, loafers and criminals, they can scarcely complain of conditions in the South. Northern cities should not, of course, seek to encourage and invite a poor quality of labor, with low standards of life and morals. The standards of wages and respectability should be kept up ; but when a man reaches those standards in skill, efficiency and decency no question of color should, in a civilized community, debar him from an equal chance with his peers in earning a living.

48. Benevolence.[11]—In the attitude of Philadelphia toward the Negro may be traced the same contradictions so often apparent in social phenomena ; prejudice and apparent dislike conjoined with widespread and deep sympathy ; there can, for instance, be no doubt of the sincerity of the efforts put forth by Philadelphians to help the Negroes. Much of it is unsystematic and ill-directed and yet it has behind it a broad charity and a desire to relieve suffering and distress. The same Philadelphian who would not let a Negro work in his store or mill will contribute handsomely to relieve Negroes in poverty and distress. There are in the city the following charities exclusively designed for Negroes :

Home for Aged and Infirm Colored Persons, Belmont and Girard avenues.[12]

---

[11] No attempt has been made here to make any intensive study of the efforts to help Negroes, which are widespread and commendable; they need, however, a study which would extend the scope of this inquiry too far.

[12] Founded, and supported in part, by Negroes. Cf. Chap. XII.

Home for Destitute Colored Children, Berks street and Old Lancaster road.

St. Mary Day Nursery, 1627 Lombard street.

The Association for the Care of Colored Orphans, Forty-fourth and Wallace streets.

Frederick Douglass Memorial Hospital and Training School, 1512 Lombard street.[13]

Magdalen Convent House of the Good Shepherd (Roman Catholic), Penn and Chew streets, Germantown.

St. Mary's Mission for Colored People, 1623–29 Lombard street.

Raspberry Street School, 229 Raspberry street.

The Star Kitchen, and allied enterprises, Seventh and Lombard streets.

Colored Industrial School, Twentieth street, below Walnut.

Sisters of the Blessed Sacrament, for Indians and Colored People, Cornwell's Station, Pa.

Men's Guild House, 1628 Lombard street.

House of St. Michael and All Angels, 613 North Forty-third street.

The Industrial Exchange Training School and Dormitory, 756 South Twelfth street.[13]

Fifty-nine of the charities mentioned in the Civic Club Digest discriminate against colored persons. Fifty-one societies profess to make no discrimination ; in the case of the larger and better known societies this is true, as, for instance, the Home Missionary Society, the Union Benevolent Association, the Protestant Episcopal City Mission, the Charity Organization Society, the Children's Aid Society, the Society to Prevent Cruelty to Children, etc. Others, however, exercise a silent policy against Negroes. The Country Week Association, for instance, would rather Negroes should not apply, although it sends a few away

---

[13] Founded, and supported in part, by Negroes. Cf. Chap. XII.

each summer.   Colored applicants at the building of the
Young Woman's Christian Association are not very
welcome.   So with many other societies and institutions.
This veiled discrimination is very unjust, for it makes it
seem as though the Negro had more help than he does.
On the other hand between donors, prejudiced persons,
friends of the Negro, and the beneficiaries, the managers of
many of these enterprises find it by far the easiest method
silently to draw the color line.

Fifty-seven other charities make no explicit statement as
to whether they discriminate or not.   To sum up then :

```
Charitable agencies exclusively for Negroes . . . . . .  14
      "          "          "          " Whites . . . . . . .  59
      "          "        which  profess not  to discriminate,
                           but in some cases do . . . . . .  51
      "          "        which make no statements, but usu-
                           ally discriminate . . . . . . . .  57
                                                            ———
                                                            181
```

On the whole it is fair to say that about one half of
the charities of Philadelphia, so far as mere numbers
are concerned, are open to Negroes.   In the different
kinds of charity, however, some disproportion is noticeable.   Of direct almsgiving, the most questionable and
least organized sort of charity, the Negroes receive
probably far more than their just proportion, as a study
of the work of the great distributing societies clearly
shows.   On the other hand, protective, rescue and reformatory work is not applied to any great extent among them.
Consequently, while actual poverty and distress among
Negroes is quickly relieved, there are only a few agencies
to prevent the better classes from sinking or to reclaim
the fallen or to protect the helpless and the children.
Even the agencies of this sort open to the Negroes are not
always taken advantage of, partly through ignorance and
carelessness, partly because they fear discrimination or because they are apt to be treated the same whether they be
from Addison street or Middle alley.

Much of the benevolence of the whites has been checked because the classes on whom it has been showered have not appreciated it, and because there has been no careful attempt to discriminate between different sorts of Negroes. After all, the need of the Negro, as of so many unfortunate classes, is " not alms but a friend."

There are a few homes, asylums, nurseries, hospitals and the like for work among Negroes, which are doing excellent work and deserve commendation. It is to be hoped that this sort of work will receive needed encouragement.

49. The Intermarriage of the Races.—For years much has been said on the destiny of the Negro with regard to intermarriage with the whites. To many this seems the difficulty that differentiates the Negro question from all other social questions which we face, and makes it seemingly insoluble ; the questions of ignorance, crime and immorality, these argue, may safely be left to the influence of time and education ; but will time and training ever change the obvious fact that the white people of the country do not wish to mingle socially with the Negroes or to join blood in legal wedlock with them ? This problem is, it must be acknowledged, difficult. Its difficulty arises, however, rather from an ignorance of surrounding facts than from the theoretic argument. Theory in such case is of little value ; the white people as members of the races now dominant in the world naturally boast of their blood and accomplishments, and recoil from an alliance with a people which is to-day represented by a host of untrained and uncouth ex-slaves. On the other hand, whatever his practice be, the Negro as a free American citizen must just as strenuously maintain that marriage is a private contract, and that given two persons of proper age and economic ability who agree to enter into that relation, it does not concern any one but themselves as to whether one of them be white, black or red. It is thus that theoretical argument comes to an unpleasant standstill, and its further pursuit really settles nothing, nay, rather unsettles much, by bringing men's thoughts to a question that is, at present at least, of little practical importance. For in practice the matter works itself out: the average white person does not marry a Negro; and the average Negro, despite his theory, himself marries one of his race, and frowns darkly on his fellows unless they do likewise. In those very circles of Negroes who have a large infusion of white blood, where the freedom of marriage is most strenuously advocated, white wives have always been treated with a disdain bordering on insult, and white husbands never received on any terms of social recognition.

Notwithstanding theory and the practice of whites and Negroes in general, it is nevertheless manifest that the white and black races have mingled their blood in this country to a vast extent. Such facts puzzle the foreigner and are destined to puzzle the future historian. A serious student of the subject gravely declares in one chapter that the races are separate and distinct and becoming more so, and in another that by reason of the intermingling of white blood the " original type of the African has almost completely disappeared ; " [14] here we have reflected the prevailing confusion in the popular mind. Race amalgamation is a fact, not a theory; it took place, however, largely under the institution of slavery and for the most part, though not wholly, outside the bonds of legal marriage. With the abolition of slavery now, and the establishment of a self-protecting Negro home the question is, what have been the tendencies and the actual facts with regard to the intermarriage of races? This is the only question with which students have to do, and this singularly enough has been the one which they, with curious unanimity, have neglected. We do not know the facts

[14] Hoffman's "Race Traits and Tendencies," etc., pp. 1 and 177.

with regard to the mingling of white and black blood in
the past save in a most general and unsatisfactory way ;
we do not know the facts for to-day at all. And yet, of
course, without this knowledge all philosophy of the
situation is vain ; only long observation of the course of
intermarriage can furnish us that broad knowledge of facts
which can serve as a basis for race theories and final conclusions.[15]

The first legal obstacle to the intermarriage of whites
and blacks in Pennsylvania was the Act of 1726, which
forbade such unions in terms that would seem to indicate
that a few such marriages had taken place. Mulattoes early
appeared in the State, and especially in Philadelphia, some
being from the South and some from up the State. Sailors
from this port in some cases brought back English, Scotch
and Irish wives, and mixed families immigrated here at the
time of the Haytian revolt. Between 1820 and 1860 many
natural children were sent from the South and in a few
cases their parents followed and were legally married here.
Descendants of such children in many cases forsook the
mother's race ; one became principal of a city school, one
a prominent sister in a Catholic church, one a bishop, and
one or two officers in the Confederate army.[16] Some marriages with Quakers took place, one especially in 1825,
when a Quakeress married a Negro, created much comment. Descendants of this couple still survive. Since
the War the number of local marriages has considerably
increased.

In this work there was originally no intention of treating
the subject of intermarriage, for it was thought that the data
would be too insignificant to be enlightening. When,

---

[15] Hoffman has the results of some intermarriages recorded, but they
are chiefly reports of criminals in the newspapers, and thus manifestly
unfair for generalization.

[16] From a personal letter of a life long Philadelphian, whose name I am
not at liberty to quote.

however, in one ward of the city thirty-three cases of mixed marriages were found, and it was known that there were others in that ward, and probably a similar proportion in many other wards, it was thought that a study of these thirty-three families might be of interest and be a small contribution of fact to a subject where facts are not easily accessible.

The size of these families varies, of course, with the question as to what one considers a family ; if we take the " census family," or all those living together under circumstances of family life in one home, the average size of the thirty-three families of the Seventh Ward in which there were intermarried whites was 3.5. If we take simply the father, mother and children, the average size was 2.9. There were ninety-seven parents and children in these families, and twenty other relatives living with them, making 117 individuals in the families. Tabulated they are as follows :

Number of Persons in the Real Family.	Number of Persons in the Census Family.						Total Real Families.	Total Individuals in Real Family.
	2	3	4	5	6	13		
Two	11	4	1	1	. . .	. . .	17	34
Three . . .	.	5	. .	. . .	. . .	1	6	18
Four . . .	. . .	. .	6	. .	. . .	. . .	6	24
Five. . . .	. .	. .	. . .	2	1	. . .	3	15
Six . .	. .	. .	. . .	. . .	1	. . .	1	6
Total Census Families.	11	9	7	3	2	1	33	97
Total Individuals in Census Family.	22	27	28	15	12	13	117 Individuals in Census Family.	

Of the intermarried whites there are four husbands and twenty-nine wives. Let us first consider the families having the four white husbands :

FOUR WHITE HUSBANDS.

	No. 1.	No. 2.	No. 3.	No. 4.
Age	48	52	31	32
Birthplace . .	Philadelphia.	Georgia.	Cuba?	?
No. of years resident in Philadelphia . .	48	7	?	12
Reads and Writes?	Reads.	Yes.	Yes.	Yes.
Occupation . .	Street car driver, laborer.	Motorman on electric cars.	Tobacconist.	Painter.
No. of Children by this Marriage	4	0	0	0
Social grade . .	Third.	Second.	Fourth.	?

THEIR FOUR NEGRO WIVES.

	No. 1.	No. 2.	No. 3.	No. 4.
Age	38	29	30	28
Birthplace . .	Maryland.	Georgia.	?	Virginia.
Years resident in Philadelphia	25	7	?	11
Reads and Writes . . .	No.	Reads.	Yes.	Yes.
Occupation . .	Housewife and day's work.	Housewife.	Housewife.	Cook.
Children by this Marriage . .	4	0	0	0
Social grade .	Third.	Second.	Fourth.	?

The third family may be simply a case of cohabitation, and not enough is known of the fourth to make any judgment. The second family lives in a comfortable home and appears contented. The first family is poor and the man lazy and good-natured.

The twenty-nine white wives were of the following ages:

15 to 19	1	40 to 49	3
20 to 24	7	50 and over	1
25 to 29	8	Unknown	1
30 to 39	8		—
		Total	29

They were born as follows :

Philadelphia	6	Hungary	1
Ireland	6	Virginia	1
England	3	Maryland	1
Scotland	2	Delaware	1
New York	2	Unknown	3
Germany	2		—
Canada	1	Total	29

By rearranging this table we have for the known cases :

Born in Philadelphia	6
" " the United States	11
" " " North	8
" " " South	3
" " foreign lands	15

Those not born in Philadelphia have resided there as follows :

Less than 1 year	1
One to three years	1
Five to ten years	3
Over ten years	8
Unknown	10
	23
Born in Philadelphia	6
	29

These wives are occupied as follows :

Housewives	18
" and day's work	3
Waitresses	2
No occupation or unknown	3
Cook	1
Merchant	1
Service	1
	29

Only one of these women was reported as illiterate, and in the case of three no return was made as to illiteracy.

Fourteen of these wives had no children by this marriage ; 6 had 1 child, 6 had 2 children, 3 had 3 children ;

making 27 children in all.   Of the 14 having no children 5 were women under twenty-five recently married ; 2 were women over forty and probably past child-bearing.   Several of the remaining 7 were, in all probability, lewd.

Of the colored husbands of these white wives we have the following statistics :

Age—20 to 24	2	50 and over	1
25 to 29	5	Unknown	2
30 to 39	12		
40 to 49	7	Total	29

Birthplace—Philadelphia	5	North Carolina	1
Maryland	5	Massachusetts	1
Virginia	5	Alabama	1
District of Columbia	3	New York	1
Delaware	2	Unknown	2
Kentucky	1		
New Jersey	1	Total	29
Texas	1		

Born in Philadelphia	5
" " North	8
" " South	19

Illiteracy—Can read and write	23
Illiterate	4
Unknown	2
Total	29

Occupations—			
Waiter	9	Baker and Merchant	1
Porter	3	Stationary Engineer	1
Barber	2	Laborer	1
Steward	2	Stevedore	1
Cook	2	Caterer	1
Restaurant Keeper	2	Messenger	1
Helper and Engineer	1	Bootblack	1
		Unknown	1
		Total	29

The social grade of thirty-two of these families is thought to be as follows :

First grade, four families.   These all live well and are

comfortable ; the wife stays at home and the children at school. Everything indicates comfort and contentment.

Second grade, fifteen families. These are ordinary working-class families ; the wife in some cases helps as a breadwinner ; none of them are in poverty, many are young couples just starting in married life. All are decent and respectable.

Third grade, six families. These are poor families of low grade, but not immoral; some are lazy, some unfortunate.

Fourth grade, seven families. Many of these are cases of permanent cohabitation and the women for the most part are or were prostitutes. They live in the slums mostly, and in some cases have lived together many years. None of them have children, or at least have none living with them at present.

Let us now glance a moment at the 31 children of these mixed marriages : 27 born of white mothers by Negro husbands, and 4 of Negro mothers by white husbands:

Age.	Male.	Female.	Total.
Under 1 year	0	3	3
1–2	2	3	5
3–5	4	3	7
6–10	3	5	8
11–15	3	1	4
16–19	2	—	2
20–29	2	—	2
Total	16	15	31

Of school age, 5–20 14
Number in school 12
Number over 10 who are illiterate 0
At work, 1, as porter.

The homes occupied by these families and the rents paid monthly are :

Number of Rooms.	$5 and under.	$6–10.	$11–15.	$16–20.	Over $20.	Total Families.
1 (tenant)	2	2	—	—	—	4
1 (lodging)	3	—	—	—	—	3
2	—	—	—	—	—	—
3	—	5	4	—	—	9
4	—	—	4	—	—	4
5	—	—	2	—	—	2
6	—	—	3	1	2	6
7	—	—	—	—	2	2
8 or more	—	—	—	—	3	3
Total	5	7	13	1	7	33

One family owns real estate (building lots).
One family belongs to a building and loan association.

The data here presented constitute too narrow a basis for many general conclusions even for a single city. Of the 2441 families in the ward these families represent 1.35 per cent. There are two or more other cases in the Seventh Ward not catalogued. If this percentage holds good in the remaining parts of the city there would be about one hundred and fifty such marriages in the city; there are no data on this point.

It is often said that only the worst Negroes and lowest whites intermarry. This is certainly untrue in Philadelphia; to be sure among the lowest classes there is a large number of temporary unions and much cohabitation. In the case of the Seventh Ward several of such cases were not noticed at all in the above record as they savor more of prostitution than of marriage. On the other hand it is an error certainly in this ward to regard marriages of this sort as confined principally to the lower classes; on the contrary they take place most frequently in the laboring classes, and especially among servants, where there is the most contact between the races. Among the best class of Negroes and whites such marriages seldom occur although one notable case occurred in 1897 in Philadelphia, where there could be no question of the good social standing of the parties.

As to the tendencies of the present, and the general result of such marriages there are no reliable data. That more separations occur in such marriages than in others is very probable. It is certainly a strain on affections to have to endure not simply the social ostracism of the whites but of the blacks also. Undoubtedly this latter acts as a more practical deterrent than the first. For, while a Negro expects to be ostracized by the whites, and his white wife agrees to it by her marriage vow, neither of them are quite prepared for the cold reception they invariably meet with among the Negroes. This is the consideration that makes the sacrifice in such marriages great, and makes it perfectly proper to give the aphoristic marriage advice of Punch to those contemplating such alliances. Nevertheless one must candidly acknowledge that there are respectable people who are thus married and are apparently contented and as happy as the average of mankind. It is difficult to see whose concern their choice is but their own, or why the world should see fit to insult or slander them.

CHAPTER XVII.

NEGRO SUFFRAGE.

50. The Significance of the Experiment.—The indiscriminate granting of universal suffrage to freedmen and foreigners was one of the most daring experiments of a too venturesome nation. In the case of the Negro its only justification was that the ballot might serve as a weapon of defence for helpless ex-slaves, and would at one stroke enfranchise those Negroes whose education and standing entitled them to a voice in the government. There can be no doubt but that the wisest provision would have been an educational and property qualification impartially enforced against ex-slaves and immigrants. In the absence of such a provision it was certainly more just to admit the untrained and ignorant than to bar out all Negroes in spite of their qualifications; more just, but also more dangerous.

Those who from time to time have discussed the results of this experiment have usually looked for their facts in the wrong place, *i. e.*, in the South. Under the peculiar conditions still prevailing in the South no fair trial of the Negro voter could have been made. The "carpet-bag" governments of reconstruction time were in no true sense the creatures of Negro voters, nor is there to-day a Southern State where free untrammeled Negro suffrage prevails. It is then to Northern communities that one must turn to study the Negro as a voter, and the result of the experiment in Pennsylvania while not decisive is certainly instructive.

51. The History of Negro Suffrage in Pennsylvania.—The laws for Pennsylvania agreed upon in England in 1682 declared as qualified electors "every inhabitant in the said province, that is or shall be a purchaser of one hundred acres of land or upwards, ... and every person that hath been a servant or bondsman, and is free by his service, that shall have taken up his fifty acres of land, and cultivated twenty thereof;" and also some other taxpayers.[1]

These provisions were in keeping with the design of partially freeing Negroes after fourteen years service and contemplated without doubt black electors, at least in theory. It is doubtful if many Negroes voted under this provision although that is possible. In the call for the Convention of 1776 no restriction as to color was mentioned,[2] and the constitution of that year gave the right of suffrage to "every freeman of the full age of twenty-one years, having resided in this State for the space of one whole year."[3] Probably some Negro electors in Pennsylvania helped choose the framers of the Constitution.

In the Convention of 1790 no restriction as to color was adopted and the suffrage article as finally decided upon read as follows :

"Article III, Section 1. In elections by the citizens, every freeman of the age of twenty-one years, having resided in the State two years next before the election, and within that time paid a State or county tax, which shall have been assessed at least six months before the election, shall enjoy the rights of an elector."[4]

Nothing in the printed minutes of the convention indicates any attempt in the convention to prohibit Negro suffrage, but Mr. Albert Gallatin declared in 1837 : "I have a lively recollection that in some stages of the discussion the proposition pending before the convention limited

---

[1] " Minutes of the Conventions of 1776 and 1790," (Ed. 1825) pp. 32–33; Cf. p. 26.

[2] *Ibid.*, pp. 38–39.

[3] *Ibid.*, p. 57.

[4] *Ibid.*, p. 300. Cf. " Purdon's Digest," sixth edition.

the right of suffrage to 'free white citizens,' etc., and that the word white was struck out on my motion." [5]

It was alleged afterward that in 1795 the question came before the High Court of Errors and Appeals and that its decision denied the right to Negroes. No written decision of this sort was ever found, however, and it is certain that for nearly a half century free Negroes voted in parts of Pennsylvania. [6]

As the Negro population increased, however, and ignorant and dangerous elements entered, and as the slavery controversy grew warmer, the feeling against Negroes increased and with it opposition to their right to vote. In July, 1837, the Supreme Court sitting at Sunbury took up the celebrated case of Hobbs *et al.* against Fogg. Fogg was a free Negro and taxpayer, and had been denied the right to vote by Hobbs and others, the judges and inspectors of election in Luzerne County. He brought action and was sustained in the Court of Common Pleas, but the Supreme Court under Judge Gibson reversed this judgment. The decision rendered was an evident straining of law and sense. The judge sought to refer to the decision of 1795, but could cite no written record ; he explained the striking out of the word " white " in the constitutional convention as done to prevent insult to " dark colored white men," and held that a Negro, though free, could never be a freeman. [7]

All doubt was finally removed by the reform constitutional convention of 1837–38. The article on suffrage as reported to the convention May 17, 1837, was practically the same as in the Constitution of 1790. [8] This

---

[5] "Proceedings and Debates of the Convention of 1837," X, 45. Cf. Purvis in "Appeal of 40,000 Citizens." The printed minutes give only the main results with few details.

[6] 6 Watts, 553–560, " Pennsylvania Reports." " Proceedings, etc., Convention 1837-8, II, 476.

[7] 6 Watts, 553–60, " Pennsylvania Reports."

[8] "Proceedings and Debates," I, 233.

article was taken up June 19, 1837. There was an
attempt to amend the report and to restrict the suffrage
to "free white male" citizens. The attempt was defended as being in consonance with the regulations of
other States, and with the real facts in Pennsylvania,
since "In the county of Philadelphia the colored man
could not with safety appear at the polls." [9] The amendment, however, met opposition and was withdrawn. The
matter arose again a few days later but was voted down by
a vote of 61 to 49. [10]

The friends of exclusion now began systematic efforts to
stir up public opinion. No less than forty-five petitions
against Negro suffrage were handed in, especially from
Bucks County, where a Negro had once nearly succeeded
in being elected to the legislature. Many petitions too
in favor of retaining the old provisions came in, but it was
charged that the convention would not print petitions in
favor of Negro suffrage, and some members did not wish
even to receive petitions from Negroes. [11]

The discussion of the Third Article recurred January 17,
1838, and a long argument ensued. Finally the word
"white" was inserted in the qualifications of voters by a
vote of 77 to 45. A protracted struggle took place to
soften this regulation in various ways, but all efforts failed
and the final draft, which was eventually adopted by
popular vote, had the following provisions: [12]

"Article III, Section 1. In elections by the citizens,
every white freeman of the age of twenty-one years, having
resided in this State one year, and in the electoral district
where he offers to vote ten days immediately preceding
such election, and within two years paid a State or county
tax, which shall have been assessed at least ten days

[9] "Proceedings and Debates," II, 478.
[10] *Ibid.*, III, 82–92.
[11] *Ibid.*, Volumes IV–IX.
[12] *Ibid.*, IX, 320–397, X, 1–134.

before the election, shall enjoy the rights of an elector." [13]
This disfranchisement lasted thirty-two years, until the
passage of the Fifteenth Amendment. The Constitution
of 1874 formally adopted this change. [14] Since 1870 the
experiment of untrammeled Negro suffrage has been made
throughout the State.

52. **City Politics.**—About 5500 Negroes were eligible
to vote in the city of Philadelphia, in 1870. The question
first arises, Into what sort of a political atmosphere were
they introduced, and what training did they receive for
their new responsibilities?

Few large cities have such a disreputable record for mis-
government as Philadelphia. In the period before the
war the city was ruled by the Democratic party, which
retained its power by the manipulation of a mass of
ignorant and turbulent foreign voters, chiefly Irish. Riots,
disorder, and crime were the rule in the city proper and
especially in the surrounding districts. About the time of
the breaking out of the war, the city was consolidated and
made coterminous with the county. The social up-
heaval after the Civil War gave the political power to the
Republicans and a new era of misrule commenced. Open
disorder and crime were repressed, but in its place came
the rule of the boss, with its quiet manipulation and cal-
culating embezzlement of public funds. To-day the government of both city and State is unparalleled in the
history of republican government for brazen dishonesty
and bare-faced defiance of public opinion. The supporters
of this government have been, by a vast majority, white
men and native Americans; the Negro vote has never
exceeded 4 per cent of the total registration.

---

[13] " Purdon," sixth edition.

[14] The Constitution of 1874 gave the right of suffrage to "Every male
citizen of the United States of the age of twenty-one years. . . . ."
—"Debates," etc., I, 503, etc. See Index "Constitution of Pennsylvania,"
Article VIII; and also the Act of 6 April, 1870.

Manifestly such a political atmosphere was the worst possible for the new untutored voter. Starting himself without political ideals, he was put under the tutelage of unscrupulous and dishonest men whose ideal of government was to prostitute it to their own private ends. As the Irishman had been the tool of the Democrats, so the Negro became the tool of the Republicans. It was natural that the freedman should vote for the party that emancipated him, and perhaps, too, it was natural that a party with so sure a following, should use it unscrupulously. The result to be expected from such a situation was that the Negro should learn from his surroundings a low ideal of political morality and no conception of the real end of party loyalty. At the same time we ought to expect individual exceptions to this general level, and some evidences of growth.

53. Some Bad Results of Negro Suffrage.—The experiment of Negro suffrage in Philadelphia has developed three classes of Negro voters: a large majority of voters who vote blindly at the dictates of the party and, while not open to direct bribery, accept the indirect emoluments of office or influence in return for party loyalty; a considerable group, centering in the slum districts, which casts a corrupt purchasable vote for the highest bidder; lastly, a very small group of independent voters who seek to use their vote to better present conditions of municipal life.

The political morality of the first group of voters, that is to say, of the great mass of Negro voters, corresponds roughly to that of the mass of white voters, but with this difference: the ignorance of the Negro in matters of government is greater and his devotion to party blinder and more unreasoning. Add to this the mass of recent immigrants from the South, with the political training of reconstruction and post-bellum days, and one can easily see how poorly trained this body of electors has been.

Under such circumstances it is but natural that political

morality and knowledge should be even slower in spreading among Negroes than wealth and general intelligence.
One consequently finds among those of considerable intelligence and of upright lives such curious misapprehension
of political duties as is illustrated by the address of the
Afro-American League to the mayor of the city, February
8, 1897 :

" MR. MAYOR:—We desire first and foremost, to tender you our pro-
found thanks for the honor of this cordial reception. We regard it, sir,
as proof of the recognition on your part of that just and most admirable
custom of our country's government, which permits the subjects, however
humble may be their condition in life, to see their ruler as well as feel
the workings of his power.

" We are here to state to your excellency that the colored citizens of
Philadelphia are penetrated with feelings of inexpressible grief at the
manner in which they have thus far been overlooked and ignored by the
Republican party in this city, in giving out work and otherwise distributing the enormous patronage in the gift of the party. We are therefore
here, sir, to earnestly beseech of you as a faithful Republican and our
worthy chief executive, to use your potent influence as well as the good
offices of your municipal government, if not inconsistent with the public
weal, to procure for the colored people of this city a share at least, of the
public work and the recognition which they now ask for and feel to be
justly due to them, no less as citizens and taxpayers, than on a basis of
their voting strength of something over 14,000 in the Republican party
here in Philadelphia.

" As the chosen organ of this body of men I am actuated by a due sense
of their earnestness of purpose in this matter and I regret to be inade-
quate to the task of convincing you, Mr. Mayor, of the deep interest
which is being universally manifested by the colored element in Philadelphia in this somewhat important question. The colored people neither
ask for nor expect extremes; we only claim that our loyal fidelity to the
Republican party should count, at some time, for some benefits to at least
a reasonable number of the colored race when our friends are installed
into place and power; and, cherishing as we do, sir, the most implicit
confidence in your justice as the chief executive of this great city, we
firmly believe that this most unfair treatment of which our people now
complain, would not fail, when brought thus to your attention, in moving
you in our humble behalf. We, therefore, have here to present for your
candid consideration a paper containing the names of some worthy and
reliable men of our race and they are respectfully urged for appointment
as indicated on the face of that paper, and out of a desire, Mr. Mayor, to
facilitate your efforts should you take favorable action upon this matter,
these men, as we will state, have been selected as near as possible from

every section of the city, as well as upon the proof of their fitness for the places named."

The organization which here speaks is not large or nearly as representative as it claims to be ; it is simply a small faction of " outs " who are striving to get " in." The significant thing about the address is the fact that a considerable number of fairly respectable and ordinarily intelligent citizens should think this a perfectly legitimate and laudable demand. This represents the political morality of the great mass of ordinary Negro voters. And what more does it argue than that they have learned their lesson well and recited it bluntly but honestly ? What more do the majority of American politicians and voters to-day say in action if not in word than : " Here is my vote, now where is my pay in office or favor or influence ?" What thousands are acting, this delegation had the charming simplicity to say plainly and then to print.

Moreover one circumstance makes this attitude of mind more dangerous among Negroes than among whites ; Negroes as a class are poor and as laborers are restricted to few and unremunerative occupations ; consequently the bribe of office is to them a far larger and alluring temptation than to the mass of whites. In other words here are a people more ignorant than their fellows, with stronger tendencies to dishonesty and crime, who are offered a far larger bribe than ordinary men to enter politics for personal gain. The result is obvious : " Of course I'm in politics," said a Negro city watchman, " it's the only way a colored man can get a position where he can earn a decent living." He was a fireman by trade, but Philadelphia engineers object to working with " Niggers."

If this is the result in the case of an honest man, how great is the temptation to the vicious and lazy. This brings us to the second class of voters—the corrupt class, which sells its votes more or less openly.

The able-bodied, well-dressed loafers and criminals who

infest the sidewalks of parts of the Fifth, Seventh and other wards are supported partly by crime and gambling, partly by the prostitution of their female paramours, but mainly from the vast corruption fund gathered from office-holders and others, and distributed according to the will of the party Boss. The *Public Ledger* said in 1896:

> "It is estimated that the Republican City Committee realized nearly if not all of $100,000 from the 1½ per cent assessment levied upon municipal officeholders for this campaign. Of this sum $40,000 has been paid for the eighty thousand tax receipts to qualify Republican voters. This leaves $60,000 at the disposal of David Martin, the Combine leader." [15]

How is this corruption fund used? Without doubt a large part of it is spent in the purchase of votes. It is of course difficult to estimate the directly purchasable vote among the whites or among the Negroes. Once in a while when "thieves fall out" some idea of the bribery may be obtained; for instance in a hearing relative to a Third Ward election:

> William Reed, of Catharine street, below Thirteenth, was first on the stand. He was watcher in the Fifteenth Division on election day.
>
> "Did you make up any election papers for voters?" asked Mr. Ingham.
>
> "I marked up about seventy or eighty ballots; I got $20 off of Roberts' brother, and used $100 altogether, paying the rest out of my own pocket."
>
> "How did you spend the money?"
>
> "Oh, well, there were some few objectionable characters there to make trouble. We'd give 'em a few dollars to go away and attend to their business." Then he addressed Mr. Ingham directly, "You know how it works."
>
> "I'd give 'em a dollar to buy a cigar. And if they didn't want to pay $1 for a cigar, why, they could put it in the contribution box at church."
>
> "Was this election conducted in the usual way?" inquired Mr. Sterr.
>
> "Oh, yes, the way they're conducted in the Third Ward—with vote buying, and all the rest of it."
>
> "Did the other side have any money to spend?"
>
> "Saunders had $16 to the division."
>
> "What did your side have?"
>
> "Oh, we had about $60; there was money to burn. But our money went to three people. The other fellows saved theirs. I spent mine—like a sucker."

---

[15] October 5, 1896.

James Brown, a McKinley-Citizen worker, began his testimony indignantly.

"Election? Why Reed and Morrow, the judges of the election, run the whole shootin' match," he declared. " It was all a farce. I brought voters up; and Reed would take 'em away from me. When we challenged anybody, Reed and the others would have vouchers ready."

"Did they use money?"

"There was a good deal of money through the division. We wasn't even allowed to mark ballots for our own people who asked for help. The judge would ask 'em if they could read and write. When they said 'yes,' he'd tell 'em they were able to mark their own ballot. There were even some people who wanted to mark their own ballots. Reed would simply grab 'em and mark their ballots, whether they liked it or not."

Lavinia Brown, colored, of the rear of 1306 Kater street, said that Mr. Bradford was judge on election day, of the Sixteenth Division, and that on the morning of the election she cooked his breakfast. She said that I. Newton Roberts came to the house, and in her presence gave Bradford a roll of notes, at the same time throwing her $2, but she did not know for what purpose he gave it.

George W. Green, colored, of 1224 Catharine street, said he was a watcher at the polls of the Sixteenth Division. He told of fraud and how the voters were treated.

"Were you offered any money?"

"Yes, sir. Lincoln Roberts came over to me and shoved $50 at me, but I turned him down and would not take it, because I didn't belong to that crowd." Continuing, he said: " Seven or eight men were challenged, but it did not amount to anything, because Lincoln Roberts would tell the police to eject them. He also vouched for men who did not live in the ward. This condition of affairs continued all day."

Several other witnesses followed, whose testimony was similar to Green's, and who declared that money was distributed freely by the Roberts faction to buy over voters. They said that challenges were disregarded, and that the election was a farce. Voters were kept out, and when it was known that any of Saunders' adherents were coming a rush would be made, making it impossible for that side to enter the booth.

Philip Brown, a McKinley-Citizen watcher, said that the election was a fraud. He saw Mr. Roberts with a pile of money, going around shouting, " That's the stuff that wins !" When asked what the judge was doing all this time he said:

"Why, the judge belonged to Mr. Roberts, who had full control of the polling place all day."

William Hare, of 1346 Kater street, proved an interesting witness. His story is as follows :

" Mr. Lincoln Roberts brought my tax receipt and told me to come around to the club. I went and was given a bundle of tax receipts, marked for other men, and told to deliver them. The next day being election day I made it a point to watch, and saw that every man to whom I gave a receipt came to the polls and voted for Mr. Roberts. I saw Mr. Newton Roberts mark the ballots over six times myself."

Many of the men mentioned here are white, and this happened in a ward where there are more white than Negro voters, but the same open bribery goes on at every election in the slum districts of the Fourth, Fifth, Seventh and Eighth Wards, where a large Negro vote is cast. In a meeting of Negroes held in 1896 one politician calmly announced that " through money from my white friends I control the colored vote in my precinct." Another man arose and denounced the speaker pretty plainly as a trickster although his allegation was not denied. This brought on general discussion in which there were uncontradicted statements that in certain sections votes were bought for " fifty cents and a drink of whisky " and men " driven in droves to the polls." There was some exaggeration here and yet without doubt many Negroes sell their votes directly for a money consideration. This sort of thing is confined to the lowest classes, but there it is widespread. Such bribery, however, is the least harmful kind because it is so direct and shameless that only men of no character would accept it.

Next to this direct purchase of votes, one of the chief and most pernicious forms of bribery among the lowest classes is through the establishment of political clubs, which abound in the Fourth, Fifth, Seventh and Eighth Wards, and are not uncommon elsewhere. A political club is a band of eight or twelve men who rent a club house with money furnished them by the boss, and support themselves partially in the same way. The club is often named after some politician—one of the most notorious gambling hells of the Seventh Ward is named after a United States Senator—and the business of the club is to see that its precinct is carried for the proper candidate, to get "jobs" for some of its "boys," to keep others from arrest and to

secure bail and discharge for those arrested. Such clubs
become the centre of gambling, drunkenness, prostitution
and crime. Every night there are no less than fifteen of
these clubs in the Seventh Ward where open gambling goes
on, to which almost any one can gain admittance if properly
introduced; nearly every day some redhanded criminal
finds refuge here from the law. Prostitutes are in easy
reach of these places and sometimes enter them. Liquor
is furnished to "members" at all times and the restrictions
on membership are slight. The leader of each club is boss
of his district; he knows the people, knows the ward boss,
knows the police; so long as the loafers and gamblers
under him do not arouse the public too much he sees that
they are not molested. If they are arrested it does not
mean much save in grave cases. Men openly boast on the
streets that they can get bail for any amount. And certainly they appear to have powerful friends at the Public
Buildings. There is of course a difference in the various
clubs; some are of higher class than others and receive
offices as bribes; others are openly devoted to gambling
and receive protection as a bribe; one of the most notorious
gambling houses of the Seventh Ward was recently raided,
and although every school boy knows the character of the
proprietor he was released for "lack of evidence." Still
other clubs are simply winter quarters for thieves, loafers
and criminals well known to the police. There are of
course one or two clubs, mainly social and only partially
political, to which the foregoing statements do not apply
—as for instance the Citizens' Club on Broad street, which
has the best Negroes of the city in its membership, allows
no gambling and pays its own expenses. This club,
however, stands almost alone and the other twelve or
fifteen political clubs of the Seventh Ward represent a
form of political corruption which is a disgrace to a
civilized city. In the Fourth, Fifth and Eighth Wards
there are ten or twelve more clubs, and probably in the

whole city the Negroes have forty such places with a possible membership of five or six hundred. The influence of these clubs on the young immigrants, on growing boys, on the surrounding working people is most deplorable. At the polls they carry the day with high-handed and often riotous proceedings, voting "repeaters" and "colonists" often with impunity.

Among the great mass of Negro voters, whose votes cannot be directly purchased, a less direct but, in the long run, more demoralizing bribery is common. It is the same sort of bribery as that which is to-day corrupting the white voters of the land, viz:

(*a*) Contributions to various objects in which voters are interested.

(*b*) Appointment to public office or to work of any kind for the city.

Men accept from political organizations, contributions to charitable and other objects which they would not think of accepting for themselves. Others less scrupulous get contributions or favors for enterprises in which they are directly interested. Fairs, societies, clubs and even churches have profited by this sort of political corruption, and the custom is by no means confined to Negroes.

A better known method of political bribery among the mass of Negroes is through apportionment of the public work or appointment to public office. The work open to Negroes throughout the city is greatly restricted as has been pointed out. One class of well-paid positions, the city civil service, was once closed to them, and only one road was open to them to secure these positions and that was unquestioning obedience to the "machine." The emoluments of office are a temptation to most men, but how much greater they are for Negroes can only be realized on reflection: Here is a well-educated young man, who despite all efforts can get no work above that of porter at $6 or $8 a week. If he goes into "politics," blindly votes for the candidate of the party boss, and by hard, steady and astute work persuades most of the colored voters in his precinct to do the same, he has the chance of being rewarded by a city clerkship, the social prestige of being in a position above menial labor, and an income of $60 or $75 a month. Such is the character of the grasp which the "machine" has on even intelligent Negro voters.

How far this sort of bribery goes is illustrated by the fact that 170 city employes are from the Fifth Ward and probably forty of these are Negroes. The three Negro members of the machine in this ward are all office-holders. About one-fourth of the fifty-two members of the Seventh Ward machine are Negroes, and one-half of these are office-holders. The Negro's record as an office-seeker is, it is needless to say, far surpassed by his white brother and it is only in the last two decades that Negroes have appeared as members of councils and clerks.[16]

In spite of the methods employed to secure these offices it cannot as yet justly be charged that many of the Negro office-holders are unfitted for their duty. There is always the possibility however that incompetent Negro officers may increase in number; and there can be no doubt but that corrupt and dishonest white politicians have been kept in power by the influence thus obtained to sway the Negro vote of the Seventh and Eighth and other wards. The problem of the Negro voter then is one of the many problems that baffle all efforts at political reform in Philadelphia: the small corrupt vote of the slums which disgraces republican government; the large vote of the masses which mistaken political ideals, blind party loyalty and economic stress now holds imprisoned and shackled to the service of dishonest political leaders.

---

[16] Cf. "A Woman's Municipal Campaign." Publications of Amer. Acad. of Pol. and Soc. Science.

54. Some Good Results of Negro Suffrage.—It is wrong to suppose that all the results of this hazardous experiment in widening the franchise have been evil. First the ballot has without doubt been a means of protection in the hands of a people peculiarly liable to oppression. Its first bestowal gained Negroes admittance to street-cars after a struggle of a quarter century; and frequently since private and public oppression has been lightened by the knowledge of the power of the black vote. This fact has greatly increased the civic patriotism of the Negro, made him strive more eagerly to adapt himself to the spirit of the city life, and has kept him from becoming a socially dangerous class.

At the same time the Negro has never sought to use his ballot to menace civilization or even the established principles of this government. This fact has been noticed by many students but it deserves emphasis. Instead of being radical light-headed followers of every new political panacea, the freedmen of Philadelphia and of the nation have always formed the most conservative element in our political life and have steadfastly opposed the schemes of inflationists, socialists and dreamers. Part of this conservatism may to be sure be the inertia of ignorance, but even such inertia must anchor to some well-defined notions as to what the present situation is; and no element of our political life seems better to comprehend the main lines of our social organization than the Negro. In Philadelphia he has usually been allied with the better elements although too often that "better" was far from the best. And never has the Negro been to any extent the ally of the worst elements.

In spite of the fact that unworthy officials could easily get into office by the political methods pursued by the Negroes, the average of those who have obtained office has been good. Of the three colored councilmen one has received the endorsement of the Municipal League, while the others seem to be up to the average of the councilmen. One Negro has been clerk in the tax office for twenty years or more and has an enviable record. The colored policemen as a class are declared by their superiors to be capable, neat and efficient. There are some cases of inefficiency— one clerk who used to be drunk most of his time, another who devotes his time to work outside his office, and many cases of inefficient watchmen and laborers. The average of efficiency among colored officeholders however is good and much higher than one might naturally expect.

Finally, the training in citizenship which the exercise of the right of suffrage entails has not been lost on the Philadelphia Negro. Any worthy cause of municipal reform can secure a respectable Negro vote in the city, showing that there is the germ of an intelligent independent vote which rises above even the blandishments of decent remunerative employment. This class is small but seems to be growing.

55. The Paradox of Reform.—The growth of a higher political morality among Negroes is to-day hindered by their paradoxical position. Suppose the Municipal League or the Woman's School-board movement, or some other reform is brought before the better class of Negroes to-day; they will nearly all agree that city politics are notoriously corrupt, that honest women should replace ward heelers on school-boards, and the like. But can they vote for such movements? Most of them will say No; for to do so will throw many worthy Negroes out of employment: these very reformers who want votes for specific reforms, will not themselves work beside Negroes, or admit them to positions in their stores or offices, or lend them friendly aid in trouble. Moreover Negroes are proud of their councilmen and policemen. What if some of these positions of honor and respectability have been gained by shady "politics"— shall they be nicer in these matters than the mass of the whites? Shall they surrender these tangible evidences of the rise of their race to forward the good-hearted but hardly imperative demands of a crowd of women? Especially, too, of women who did not apparently know there were any Negroes on earth until they wanted their votes? Such logic may be faulty, but it is convincing to the mass of Negro voters. And cause after cause may gain their respectful attention and even applause, but when election-day comes, the "machine" gets their votes.

Thus the growth of broader political sentiment is hindered and will be until some change comes. When industrial exclusion is so broken down that no class will be unduly tempted by the bribe of office; when the apostles of civil reform compete within the ward Boss in friendliness and kindly consideration for the unfortunate; when the league between gambling and crime and the city authorities is less close, then we can expect the more rapid development of civic virtue in the Negro and indeed in the whole city. As it is to-day the experiment of Negro suffrage with all its glaring shortcomings cannot justly be called a failure, but rather in view of all circumstances a partial success. Whatever it lacks can justly be charged to those Philadelphians who for thirty years have surrendered their right of political leadership to thieves and tricksters, and allowed such teachers to instruct this untutored race in whose hand lay an unfamiliar instrument of civilization.

CHAPTER XVIII.

A FINAL WORD.

56. The Meaning of All This.—Two sorts of answers are usually returned to the bewildered American who asks seriously: What is the Negro problem? The one is straightforward and clear: it is simply this, or simply that, and one simple remedy long enough applied will in time cause it to disappear. The other answer is apt to be hopelessly involved and complex—to indicate no simple panacea, and to end in a somewhat hopeless—There it is; what can we do? Both of these sorts of answers have something of truth in them: the Negro problem looked at in one way is but the old world questions of ignorance, poverty, crime, and the dislike of the stranger. On the other hand it is a mistake to think that attacking each of these questions single-handed without reference to the others will settle the matter: a combination of social problems is far more than a matter of mere addition,—the combination itself is a problem. Nevertheless the Negro problems are not more hopelessly complex than many others have been. Their elements despite their bewildering complication can be kept clearly in view: they are after all the same difficulties over which the world has grown gray: the question as to how far human intelligence can be trusted and trained; as to whether we must always have the poor with us; as to whether it is possible for the mass of men to attain righteousness on earth; and then to this is added that question of questions: after all who are Men? Is every featherless biped to be counted a man and brother? Are all races and types to be joint heirs of the

(385)

new earth that men have striven to raise in thirty centuries
and more? Shall we not swamp civilization in barbarism and drown genius in indulgence if we seek a mythical
Humanity which shall shadow all men? The answer of
the early centuries to this puzzle was clear: those of any
nation who can be called Men and endowed with rights are
few: they are the privileged classes—the well-born and the
accidents of low birth called up by the King. The rest,
the mass of the nation, the *pöbel*, the mob, are fit to follow,
to obey, to dig and delve, but not to think or rule or play
the gentleman. We who were born to another philosophy
hardly realize how deep-seated and plausible this view of
human capabilities and powers once was; how utterly in-
comprehensible this republic would have been to Charle-
magne or Charles V or Charles I. We rather hasten to
forget that once the courtiers of English kings looked upon
the ancestors of most Americans with far greater contempt
than these Americans look upon Negroes—and perhaps,
indeed, had more cause. We forget that once French
peasants were the " Niggers " of France, and that German
princelings once discussed with doubt the brains and
humanity of the *bauer*.

Much of this—or at least some of it—has passed and the
world has glided by blood and iron into a wider humanity,
a wider respect for simple manhood unadorned by ancestors
or privilege. Not that we have discovered, as some hoped
and some feared, that all men were created free and equal,
but rather that the differences in men are not so vast as we
had assumed. We still yield the well-born the advantages
of birth, we still see that each nation has its dangerous
flock of fools and rascals ; but we also find most men have
brains to be cultivated and souls to be saved.

And still this widening of the idea of common Humanity is of slow growth and to-day but dimly realized. We
grant full citizenship in the World Commonwealth to the
" Anglo-Saxon " (whatever that may mean), the Teuton

and the Latin; then with just a shade of reluctance we extend it to the Celt and Slav. We half deny it to the yellow races of Asia, admit the brown Indians to an ante-room only on the strength of an undeniable past; but with the Negroes of Africa we come to a full stop, and in its heart the civilized world with one accord denies that these come within the pale of nineteenth-century Humanity. This feeling, widespread and deep-seated, is, in America, the vastest of the Negro problems; we have, to be sure, a threatening problem of ignorance but the ancestors of most Americans were far more ignorant than the freedmen's sons; these ex-slaves are poor but not as poor as the Irish peasants used to be; crime is rampant but not more so, if as much, as in Italy; but the difference is that the ancestors of the English and the Irish and the Italians were felt to be worth educating, helping and guiding because they were men and brothers, while in America a census which gives a slight indication of the utter disappearance of the American Negro from the earth is greeted with ill-concealed delight.

Other centuries looking back upon the culture of the nineteenth would have a right to suppose that if, in a land of freemen, eight millions of human beings were found to be dying of disease, the nation would cry with one voice, "Heal them!" If they were staggering on in ignorance, it would cry, "Train them!" If they were harming themselves and others by crime, it would cry, "Guide them!" And such cries are heard and have been heard in the land; but it was not one voice and its volume has been ever broken by counter-cries and echoes, "Let them die!" "Train them like slaves!" "Let them stagger downward!"

This is the spirit that enters in and complicates all Negro social problems and this is a problem which only civilization and humanity can successfully solve. Meantime we have the other problems before us—we have the problems arising from the uniting of so many social questions about one centre. In such a situation we need only to avoid underestimating the difficulties on the one hand and overestimating them on the other. The problems are difficult, extremely difficult, but they are such as the world has conquered before and can conquer again. Moreover the battle involves more than a mere altruistic interest in an alien people. It is a battle for humanity and human culture. If in the hey-day of the greatest of the world's civilizations, it is possible for one people ruthlessly to steal another, drag them helpless across the water, enslave them, debauch them, and then slowly murder them by economic and social exclusion until they disappear from the face of the earth—if the consummation of such a crime be possible in the twentieth century, then our civilization is vain and the republic is a mockery and a farce.

But this will not be; first, even with the terribly adverse circumstances under which Negroes live, there is not the slightest likelihood of their dying out; a nation that has endured the slave-trade, slavery, reconstruction, and present prejudice three hundred years, and under it increased in numbers and efficiency, is not in any immediate danger of extinction. Nor is the thought of voluntary or involuntary emigration more than a dream of men who forget that there are half as many Negroes in the United States as Spaniards in Spain. If this be so then a few plain propositions may be laid down as axiomatic:

1. The Negro is here to stay.

2. It is to the advantage of all, both black and white, that every Negro should make the best of himself.

3. It is the duty of the Negro to raise himself by every effort to the standards of modern civilization and not to lower those standards in any degree.

4. It is the duty of the white people to guard their civilization against debauchment by themselves or others; but in order to do this it is not necessary to hinder and

retard the efforts of an earnest people to rise, simply because they lack faith in the ability of that people.

5. With these duties in mind and with a spirit of self-help, mutual aid and co-operation, the two races should strive side by side to realize the ideals of the republic and make this truly a land of equal opportunity for all men.

57. The Duty of the Negroes.—That the Negro race has an appalling work of social reform before it need hardly be said.   Simply because the ancestors of the present white inhabitants of America went out of their way barbarously to mistreat and enslave the ancestors of the present black inhabitants gives those blacks no right to ask that the civilization and morality of the land be seriously menaced for their benefit.   Men have a right to demand that the members of a civilized community be civilized ; that the fabric of human culture, so laboriously woven, be not wantonly or ignorantly destroyed.   Consequently a nation may rightly demand, even of a people it has consciously and intentionally wronged, not indeed complete civilization in thirty or one hundred years, but at least every effort and sacrifice possible on their part toward making themselves fit members of the community within a reasonable length of time; that thus they may early become a source of strength and help instead of a national burden.   Modern society has too many problems of its own, too much proper anxiety as to its own ability to survive under its present organization, for it lightly to shoulder all the burdens of a less advanced people, and it can rightly demand that as far as possible and as rapidly as possible the Negro bend his energy to the solving of his own social problems—contributing to his poor, paying his share of the taxes and supporting the schools and public administration.   For the accomplishment of this the Negro has a right to demand freedom for self-development, and no more aid from without than is really helpful for furthering that development.   Such aid must of necessity be considerable : it must furnish schools and reformatories, and relief and preventive agencies ; but the bulk of the work of raising the Negro must be done by the Negro himself, and the greatest help for him will be not to hinder and curtail and discourage his efforts. Against prejudice, injustice and wrong the Negro ought to protest energetically and continuously, but he must never forget that he protests because those things hinder his own efforts, and that those efforts are the key to his future.

And those efforts must be mighty and comprehensive, persistent, well-aimed and tireless; satisfied with no partial success, lulled to sleep by no colorless victories ; and, above all, guided by no low selfish ideals ; at the same time they must be tempered by common sense and rational expectation. In Philadelphia those efforts should first be directed toward a lessening of Negro crime ; no doubt the amount of crime imputed to the race is exaggerated, no doubt features of the Negro's environment over which he has no control, excuse much that is committed ; but beyond all this the amount of crime that can without doubt rightly be laid at the door of the Philadelphia Negro is large and is a menacé to a civilized people. Efforts to stop this crime must commence in the Negro homes ; they must cease to be, as they often are, breeders of idleness and extravagance and complaint. Work, continuous and intensive; work, although it be menial and poorly rewarded ; work, though done in travail of soul and sweat of brow, must be so impressed upon Negro children as the road to salvation, that a child would feel it a greater disgrace to be idle than to do the humblest labor. The homely virtues of honesty, truth and chastity must be instilled in the cradle, and although it is hard to teach self-respect to a people whose million fellow-citizens half-despise them, yet it must be taught as the surest road to gain the respect of others.

It is right and proper that Negro boys and girls should desire to rise as high in the world as their ability and just desert entitle them. They should be ever encouraged and urged to do so, although they should be taught also that idleness and crime are beneath and not above the lowest work. It should be the continual object of Negroes to open up better industrial chances for their sons and daughters. Their success here must of course rest largely with the white people, but not entirely. Proper co-operation among forty or fifty thousand colored people ought to open many chances of employment for their sons and daughters in trades, stores and shops, associations and industrial enterprises.

Further, some rational means of amusement should be furnished young folks. Prayer meetings and church socials have their place, but they cannot compete in attractiveness with the dance halls and gambling dens of the city. There is a legitimate demand for amusement on the part of the young which may be made a means of education, improvement and recreation. A harmless and beautiful amusement like dancing might with proper effort be rescued from its low and unhealthful associations and made a means of health and recreation. The billiard table is no more wedded to the saloon than to the church if good people did not drive it there. If the Negro homes and churches cannot amuse their young people, and if no other efforts are made to satisfy this want, then we cannot complain if the saloons and clubs and bawdy houses send these children to crime, disease and death.

There is a vast amount of preventive and rescue work which the Negroes themselves might do : keeping little girls off the street at night, stopping the escorting of unchaperoned young ladies to church and elsewhere, showing the dangers of the lodging system, urging the buying of homes and removal from crowded and tainted neighborhoods, giving lectures and tracts on health and habits, exposing the dangers of gambling and policy-playing, and inculcating respect for women. Day-nurseries and sewing-schools, mothers' meetings, the parks and

airing places, all these things are little known or appreciated among the masses of Negroes, and their attention
should be directed to them.

The spending of money is a matter to which Negroes
need to give especial attention. Money is wasted to-day
in dress, furniture, elaborate entertainments, costly church
edifices, and " insurance " schemes, which ought to go
toward buying homes, educating children, giving simple
healthful amusement to the young, and accumulating
something in the savings bank against a " rainy day." A
crusade for the savings bank as against the " insurance "
society ought to be started in the Seventh Ward without
delay.

Although directly after the war there was great and
remarkable enthusiasm for education, there is no doubt but
that this enthusiasm has fallen off, and there is to-day
much neglect of children among the Negroes, and failure
to send them regularly to school. This should be looked
into by the Negroes themselves and every effort made to
induce full regular attendance.

Above all, the better classes of the Negroes should
recognize their duty toward the masses. They should not
forget that the spirit of the twentieth century is to be the
turning of the high toward the lowly, the bending of
Humanity to all that is human ; the recognition that in
the slums of modern society lie the answers to most of our
puzzling problems of organization and life, and that only as
we solve those problems is our culture assured and our
progress certain. This the Negro is far from recognizing
for himself; his social evolution in cities like Philadelphia is approaching a mediæval stage when the centrifugal forces of repulsion between social classes are becoming more powerful than those of attraction. So hard
has been the rise of the better class of Negroes that
they fear to fall if now they stoop to lend a hand to
their fellows. This feeling is intensified by the blindness

of those outsiders who persist even now in confounding the good and bad, the risen and fallen in one mass. Nevertheless the Negro must learn the lesson that other nations learned so laboriously and imperfectly, that his better classes have their chief excuse for being in the work they may do toward lifting the rabble. This is especially true in a city like Philadelphia which has so distinct and creditable a Negro aristocracy; that they do something already to grapple with these social problems of their race is true, but they do not yet do nearly as much as they must, nor do they clearly recognize their responsibility.

Finally, the Negroes must cultivate a spirit of calm, patient persistence in their attitude toward their fellow citizens rather than of loud and intemperate complaint. A man may be wrong, and know he is wrong, and yet some finesse must be used in telling him of it. The white people of Philadelphia are perfectly conscious that their Negro citizens are not treated fairly in all respects, but it will not improve matters to call names or impute unworthy motives to all men. Social reforms move slowly and yet when Right is reinforced by calm but persistent Progress we somehow all feel that in the end it must triumph.

58. **The Duty of the Whites.**—There is a tendency on the part of many white people to approach the Negro question from the side which just now is of least pressing importance, namely, that of the social intermingling of races. The old query : Would you want your sister to marry a Nigger? still stands as a grim sentinel to stop much rational discussion. And yet few white women have been pained by the addresses of black suitors, and those who have easily got rid of them. The whole discussion is little less than foolish; perhaps a century from to-day we may find ourselves seriously discussing such questions of social policy, but it is certain that just as long as one group deems it a serious *mésalliance* to marry with another just

so long few marriages will take place, and it will need neither law nor argument to guide human choice in such a matter. Certainly the masses of whites would hardly acknowledge that an active propaganda of repression was necessary to ward off intermarriage. Natural pride of race, strong on one side and growing on the other, may be trusted to ward off such mingling as might in this stage of development prove disastrous to both races. All this therefore is a question of the far-off future.

To-day, however, we must face the fact that a natural repugnance to close intermingling with unfortunate ex-slaves has descended to a discrimination that very seriously hinders them from being anything better. It is right and proper to object to ignorance and consequently to ignorant men; but if by our actions we have been responsible for their ignorance and are still actively engaged in keeping them ignorant, the argument loses its moral force. So with the Negroes: men have a right to object to a race so poor and ignorant and inefficient as the mass of the Negroes; but if their policy in the past is parent of much of this condition, and if to-day by shutting black boys and girls out of most avenues of decent employment they are increasing pauperism and vice, then they must hold themselves largely responsible for the deplorable results.

There is no doubt that in Philadelphia the centre and kernel of the Negro problem so far as the white people are concerned is the narrow opportunities afforded Negroes for earning a decent living. Such discrimination is morally wrong, politically dangerous, industrially wasteful, and socially silly. It is the duty of the whites to stop it, and to do so primarily for their own sakes. Industrial freedom of opportunity has by long experience been proven to be generally best for all. Moreover the cost of crime and pauperism, the growth of slums, and the pernicious influences of idleness and lewdness, cost the public far more than would the hurt to the feelings of a carpenter to work beside a black man, or a shop girl to stand beside a darker mate. This does not contemplate the wholesale replacing of white workmen for Negroes out of sympathy or philanthropy; it does mean that talent should be rewarded, and aptness used in commerce and industry whether its owner be black or white; that the same incentive to good, honest, effective work be placed before a black office boy as before a white one—before a black porter as before a white one; and that unless this is done the city has no right to complain that black boys lose interest in work and drift into idleness and crime. Probably a change in public opinion on this point to-morrow would not make very much difference in the positions occupied by Negroes in the city: some few would be promoted, some few would get new places—the mass would remain as they are; but it would make one vast difference: it would inspire the young to try harder, it would stimulate the idle and discouraged and it would take away from this race the omnipresent excuse for failure: prejudice. Such a moral change would work a revolution in the criminal rate during the next ten years. Even a Negro bootblack could black boots better if he knew he was a menial not because he was a Negro but because he was best fitted for that work.

We need then a radical change in public opinion on this point; it will not and ought not to come suddenly, but instead of thoughtless acquiescence in the continual and steadily encroaching exclusion of Negroes from work in the city, the leaders of industry and opinion ought to be trying here and there to open up new opportunities and give new chances to bright colored boys. The policy of the city to-day simply drives out the best class of young people whom its schools have educated and social opportunities trained, and fills their places with idle and vicious immigrants. It is a paradox of the times that young men and women from some of the best Negro families of the city—families born and reared here and schooled in the

best traditions of this municipility have actually had to go
to the South to get work, if they wished to be aught but
chambermaids and bootblacks.　Not that such work may
not be honorable and useful, but that it is as wrong to
make scullions of engineers as it is to make engineers of
scullions.　Such a situation is a disgrace to the city—a
disgrace to its Christianity, to its spirit of justice, to its
common sense ; what can be the end of such a policy but
increased crime and increased excuse for crime ?　Increased
poverty and more reason to be poor ?　Increased political
serfdom of the mass of black voters to the bosses and
rascals who divide the spoils ?　Surely here lies the first
duty of a civilized city.

Secondly, in their efforts for the uplifting of the Negro
the people of Philadelphia must recognize the existence of
the better class of Negroes and must gain their active aid
and co-operation by generous and polite conduct.　Social
sympathy must exist between what is best in both races and
there must no longer be the feeling that the Negro who
makes the best of himself is of least account to the city
of Philadelphia, while the vagabond is to be helped and
pitied.　This better class of Negro does not want help or
pity, but it does want a generous recognition of its difficulties, and a broad sympathy with the problem of life as
it presents itself to them.　It is composed of men and
women educated and in many cases cultured ; with proper
co-operation they could be a vast power in the city, and the
only power that could successfully cope with many phases
of the Negro problems.　But their active aid cannot be
gained for purely selfish motives, or kept by churlish
and ungentle manners ; and above all they object to being
patronized.

Again, the white people of the city must remember that
much of the sorrow and bitterness that surrounds the life
of the American Negro comes from the unconscious prejudice and half-conscious actions of men and women who do

not intend to wound or annoy.   One is not compelled to
discuss the Negro question with every Negro one meets or
to tell him of a father who was connected with the Underground Railroad; one is not compelled to stare at the
solitary black face in the audience as though it were not
human; it is not necessary to sneer, or be unkind or boorish, if the Negroes in the room or on the street are not all
the best behaved or have not the most elegant manners; it
is hardly necessary to strike from the dwindling list of
one's boyhood and girlhood acquaintances or school-day
friends all those who happen to have Negro blood, simply
because one has not the courage now to greet them on the
street.   The little decencies of daily intercourse can go
on, the courtesies of life be exchanged even across the
color line without any danger to the supremacy of the
Anglo-Saxon or the social ambition of the Negro.   Without doubt social differences are facts not fancies and cannot lightly be swept aside; but they hardly need to be
looked upon as excuses for downright meanness and
incivility.

A polite and sympathetic attitude toward these striving
thousands; a delicate avoidance of that which wounds and
embitters them; a generous granting of opportunity to
them; a seconding of their efforts, and a desire to reward
honest success—all this, added to proper striving on their
part, will go far even in our day toward making all men,
white and black, realize what the great founder of the
city meant when he named it the City of Brotherly Love.

APPENDICES.

APPENDIX A.—SCHEDULES USED IN THE HOUSE-TO-HOUSE INQUIRY.

UNIVERSITY OF PENNSYLVANIA.

CONDITION OF THE NEGROES OF PHILADELPHIA, WARD SEVEN.—*Family Schedule,* 1.

DECEMBER 1, 1896.   No. ———   Investigator.

1. NUMBER OF PERSONS IN THIS FAMILY ———

INQUIRIES.	1	2	3	4	5
2 Relationship to head of family?					
3 Sex?					
4 Age at nearest birthday?					
5 Conjugal condition?					
6 Place of birth?					
7 Length of residence in Philadelphia?					
8 Length of residence in this house?					
9 Able to read?					
10 Able to write?					
11 Months in school during last school year?					
12 Graduate or attendant at any time of any higher school?					
13 Attendant of any industrial school?					
14 Occupations since December 1, 1891?					
15 Present occupation?					
16 Place of work?					
17 Average income from present occupation { weekly? monthly? yearly? }					
18 Weeks unemployed at above occupation during last twelve months?					
19 Weeks employed at any other occupation during last twelve months?					
20 Name of such other occupation?					
21 Average weekly earnings at such other occupation?					
22 Number of days sick during last twelve months?					
23 Nature of illness?					
24 Sound and healthy in mind, sight, hearing, speech, limbs and body?					
25 When and where have attempts been made to find other employment?					
26 Why was application refused?					

27	Amount of real estate owned?		
28	Situation of such real estate?		
29	Amount of other property?		
30	Member of what building, secret, beneficial or insurance societies, or labor union?		
31	Average monthly dues to such societies?		

32 Budget:
Total income of family from all sources for one year?
Expenditure for one year?

Expenditure for	Weekly.	Monthly.	Yearly.
Rent			
Food			
Fuel			
Clothing			

Expenditure for	Weekly.	Monthly.	Yearly.
Amusements			
Tobacco			
Alcoholic drinks			
Sickness and Death			
All other Purposes			

Total expenditure for one year?
Total savings for one year?

33	Chief form of amusement?	
34	Member or attendant of what church?	
35	Non-resident members of family?	
36	Occupation and address of same?	
37	Remarks	

UNIVERSITY OF PENNSYLVANIA.

INVESTIGATION INTO THE CONDITION OF THE NEGROES OF PHILADELPHIA.

Instructions for Family Schedule.

A family schedule must be made out for every group of two or more related persons living under conditions of family life. Boarders, lodgers and servants, are to be entered on separate individual schedules. Hotels, etc., should be entered on an institution schedule, and the inmates on family and individual schedules.

Question 1. Enter here the number of persons in the family, exclusive of lodgers, boarders, visitors or servants.

Question 2. Facts for the head of the family should be entered in the first column, and he or she should be designated as *Head*, whether man, woman, married or single. Give the other members the term which will indicate their relation to the head; as wife, son, daughter, sister, etc, or mother (*i. e.* mother of head of family), etc.

Question 3. Abbreviate to M. (male), or F. (female).

Question 4. Give exact years, as, 17, 29, 31, 43, etc., and do not say "about" 25, 30, 35, 40. Enter children less than one year old on the 1st of December, in twelfths of a month, as 6-12, 3-12, etc.; or if not one month old, as 0-12.

Question 5. Enter as married (mar.), single (sing.), widowed (wid.), and separated (sep.).

Question 6. Give State and town.

Questions 7 and 8. Give approximate number of years.

Question 11. This refers to the children of the family.

Questions 12 and 13. Write "Graduate—Girls' High, '96"; or "Attendant Institute for Colored Youth, 3 yrs.," etc. Schools higher than common schools are here referred to. Answer this for all members of the family.

Questions 14 and 15. This is an important inquiry. Simple as it appears, it is always difficult in census work to get satisfactory replies to this question. Inaccuracy and insufficiency of statement are the most prominent evils to be avoided:

For instance, *remember:* we want to know not what a man "works in," but just what he does.

We want to *distinguish between:* the owner or director of a business and one who works at it; between waiters and head-waiters; between cooks in private families and in hotels; between coachmen, hackmen, and draymen; between merchants and pedlars, and those who keep stands.

Do not say:
"Printer," but "compositor," or "pressman;" not "mechanic," but "carpenter" or "plumber;" not "agent," but "real-estate agent;" not "merchant" or "pedlar," but "dry-goods merchant" or "pedlar—tinware"; not "clerk" but "salesman in hardware-store," "stenographer," "bookkeeper," etc.

Describe women who keep house at home as "housewives;" those who keep house for others as "housekeepers." If the woman does her own housework, and in addition pursues a gainful occupation, as dressmaking, enter: "housewife—dressmaker," or "housewife—day's-work-out."

Daughters, etc., who help with housework, should be entered: "housework—no pay." Those who do nothing should be entered as "no occupation." Children, too young to have an occupation, should be entered "at home," or "at school."

Question 17. Answer only one of these—preferably one of the first two. Seek to approximate the truth as nearly as possible.

Question 22. This refers to sickness that was severe enough to interfere seriously with daily work.

Question 23. Give the name of the disease or ailment.

Question 25. Give dates as nearly as possible, and addresses.

Question 26. Enter either the reason given or the reason surmised, or both.

Question 28. Give street and number.

Question 30. Give names of societies.

Question 32. This question is optional, and is only for those who are able to give their expenditure in some detail. Fill only *one* of the three columns for each particular item (*e. g.* rent *yearly*, food *weekly*, etc.) and seek by reference to written accounts to make this report accurate. Remember that *income, expenditure* and *savings* must *balance*.

Question 33. Enter this under one of the following heads: A. Athletics (bicycling, baseball, etc.). B. Music. C. Church entertainments. D. Indoor games (cards, billiards, etc.). E. Balls. F. House-parties. G. Picnics and excursions. H. Theatres.

Remember to enter here the actual chief amusement, not merely the one the person likes best, but does not often enjoy.

Question 35. Give relationship to head of family.

Where the question only applies to certain members of the family, put a cross in the spaces where there are no answers expected. Where no information is given, put "unknown," or "unanswered."

Finally, remember that the information given is confidential; the University of Pennsylvania will strictly guard it as such, and allow no one to have access to the schedules for other than scientific purposes. We ask, under these conditions, careful, accurate, and truthful answers.

UNIVERSITY OF PENNSYLVANIA.

CONDITION OF THE NEGROES OF PHILADELPHIA, WARD SEVEN.

Individual Schedule, 2.

DECEMBER 1, 1896. No.———— Investigator.

1 | Relationship to head of family? . . . .
2 | Sex? . . . .
3 | Age at nearest birthday? . . . .
4 | Conjugal condition? . . . .
5 | Place of birth? . . . .
6 | Length of residence in Philadelphia? . . . .
7 | Length of residence in this house? . . . . .
8 | Able to read? . . . .
9 | Able to write? . . . .
10 | Months in school during last school year? . . .
11 | Graduate or attendant at any time of any higher school? . . . .
12 | Attendant of any industrial school? . . . .
13 | Occupations since November 1, 1891? . . . .
14 | Present occupation? . . . .
15 | Place of work? . . . .
16 | Average income from present occupation { weekly? monthly? yearly?
17 | Weeks unemployed at above occupation during last twelve months? . . . . . .
18 | Weeks employed at any other occupation during last twelve months? . . . .
19 | Name of such other occupation? . . . .
20 | Average weekly earnings at such other occupation? .
21 | Number of days sick during last twelve months?
22 | Nature of illness? . . . .
23 | Sound and healthy in mind, sight, hearing, speech, limbs and body? . . . .
24 | When and where have attempts been made to find other employment? . . . .
25 | Why was application refused? . . . .
26 | Amount of real estate owned? . . . .
27 | Situation of such real estate? . . . .
28 | Amount of other property? . . . .
29 | Member of what building, secret, beneficial or insurance societies, or labor union? . . . .
30 | Average monthly dues to such societies? . . . . .

31 | Budget:
Total income for one year?
Expenditure for one year?

Expenditure for	W'kly.	Monthly.	Yearly.	Expenditure for	W'kly.	Monthly.	Yearly.
Rent				Amusements .			
Food				Tobacco			
Fuel				Alcoholic drinks			
Clothing				Sick's and dt'h.			
				All other purposes			

Total expenditure for one year?
Total savings for one year?

32 | Chief form of amusement?
33 | Member or attendant of what church?
34 | Remarks.

See Instructions for Family Schedule, 1.

UNIVERSITY OF PENNSYLVANIA.

CONDITION OF THE NEGROES OF PHILADELPHIA, WARD SEVEN.

Home Schedule, 3.

DECEMBER 1, 1896.   No.————   Investigator.

1	Material of house?. . . . .
2	Stories in house above basement? . . . .
3	Number of homes in house? . . . .
4	In which story is this home? . . . .
5	Number of rooms in this home? . . . .
6	Is this home rented directly of the landlord? . . . .
7	Number of boarders in this home? . . . . . .
8	Number of lodgers in this home? . . . .
9	Number of servants kept? . . . .
10	Total number of persons in this home? . . . .
11	House owned by . . . .
12	Rent paid monthly? . . . .
13	Rent received from sub-letting? . . . .
14	Bath-room? . . . .
15	Water-closet? . . . .
16	Privy? . . . .
17	Yard, and size? . . . .
18	Where is washing hung to dry? . . . .
19	Light? . . . .
20	Ventilation and air? . . . .
21	Cleanliness? . . . .
22	Outside sanitary conditions? . . . .

THE HOME.

	Room No. 1.	Room No. 2.	Room No. 3.	Room No. 4.	Room No. 5.	Room No. 6.
23 Use?						
24 Dimensions?						
25 Outside windows?						
26 Furniture?						
27 Occupants at night?						
28 Additional rooms?						

29 | When and where have you had difficulty in renting houses?

INSTRUCTIONS FOR HOME SCHEDULE.

Every structure in which persons live is a dwelling for the purposes of this investigation, whether wholly so occupied or not. In each dwelling there will be one or more homes; for each such home a Home Schedule must be made out, and at its top the schedule number of the corresponding family or individual inserted.

Question 4. If it occupies the house, put "whole house."

Questions 14, 15, 16, 17. Answer *Yes* or *No*. Note whether these facilities are used by one or more homes?

Questions 19, 20, 21, 22. Answer *excellent, good, fair* or *bad*.

Question 26. This refers primarily to the living room. Note the presence of the following articles: piano, organ, parlor-suit, sewing-machine, bookshelves, couch, centre-table, rocking-chair, etc.

UNIVERSITY OF PENNSYLVANIA.

CONDITION OF THE NEGROES OF PHILADELPHIA, WARD SEVEN.

House Servant Schedule, 4.

DECEMBER 1, 1896.   No.————————   Investigator.

1 Street and number? . . . .
2 Occupation of employer? . . . .
3 Sex? . . . .
4 Age at nearest birthday? . . . . ?
5 Conjugal condition? . . . .
6 Any home in the city? . . . .
7 Address of same? . . . .
8 Place of birth? . . . .
9 Number of days sick in last twelve months? . . . .
10 Nature of illness? . . . .
11 Able to read? . . . .
12 Able to write? . . . .
13 Graduate or attendant at any time of any higher
       school? . . . .
14 Occupations since November 1, 1891? . . . .
15 Present occupation? . . . .
16 Length of service here? . . . .
17 Weekly earnings? . . . .
18 Is board given in addition to this? . . . .
19 Is lodging given in addition to this? . . . .
20 Number of hours free each month? . . . .
21 Who besides yourself is supported by your wages? .
22 How much is given for this purpose weekly? . . . .
23 Member or attendant of what church? . . . .
24 When and where have you attempted to get other
       employment? . . . .
25 Why was application refused? . . . .
26 What is your chief amusement? . . . .

27 Budget:
Total income for one year:

Expenditure for	W'kly.	Monthly.	Yearly.	Expenditure for	W'kly.	Monthly.	Yearly.
Clothing . . .				Sickness			
Amusement . .				Dues to Societies			
Lodging				All other purposes			

Total expense for one year?
Total savings?
28 Amount of property owned?

For Instructions, see Family Schedule, 1.

UNIVERSITY OF PENNSYLVANIA.

CONDITION OF THE NEGROES OF PHILADELPHIA, WARD SEVEN.

Street Schedule, 5. —————*Street, between*—————*Streets.*

DECEMBER 1, 1896.   NO.————   Investigator.

1	General Character?	
2	Width?	
3	Paved with?	
4	Street-car line?	
5	Character of houses?	
6	Stories in houses?	
7	Material of houses?	
8	Proportion occupied as dwellings?	
9	Proportion of Whites to Blacks?	
10	Nationality of Whites?	
11	Cleanliness of street?	
12	Width of sidewalks?	
13	Lighted by?	
14	Hydrants?	
15	Schools?	
16	Churches?	
17	Saloons?	
18	Pool-rooms?	
19	Public institutions?	
20	Public conveniences?	
21	Shops?	
22	Remarks?	

INSTRUCTIONS FOR STREET SCHEDULE.

A "street" in this Schedule is meant to designate not necessarily the whole street which bears one name—as Lombard from river to river—but rather such parts of streets as have a common character; thus four or five Schedules would be necessary for the distinctive parts of Lombard Street, two for Juniper, several for Pine, one for Wetherill.

1. Characterize the street concisely; as, "respectable residence street," or "blind alley with tumble-down brick houses."
4. Answer by *Yes* or *No.*
5. Note whether the houses are dwellings, stables, etc., respectable, suspicious, etc.
8. Estimate carefully; as one-third dwellings, or one-half back yards, etc.
9 and 10. Ask a policeman, or one or two of the persons dwelling there. Do not depend on your own observation, unless it extends over some time.
11. Answer by *excellent, good, fair,* or *bad.*
14. Give number.
15. Give names.
16. Give number, names and denomination.
17 and 18. Give number.
19. This includes hospitals, clubs, missions, manufactories. Note clubs of all sorts carefully, and ascertain their character if possible. Enter all these institutions by name.
20. This refers to public water-closets, baths, urinals, and lavatories.
21. Give approximate distribution and character of shops.
22. Make here any concise statement that will throw light on the street and its inhabitants.

UNIVERSITY OF PENNSYLVANIA.

CONDITION OF THE NEGROES OF PHILADELPHIA, WARD SEVEN.

Institution Schedule, 6.

DECEMBER 1, 1896.   NO.————————   Investigator.

1 | Name? . . . .
2 | Street and number? . . . .
3 | Character? . . . .
4 | Proprietors? . . . .
5 | Number of members or partners? . . . .
6 | Amount of capital invested? . . . .
7 | Real estate owned? . . . .
8 | Value of same? . . . .
9 | Taxes paid last year on same? . . . .
10 | Value of other property? . . . .
11 | Income last twelve months? . . . .
12 | Source of said income? . . . .
13 | Expenditures last twelve months? . . . .
14 | Objects of expenditures? . . . .
15 | History? . . . .
16 | Description and remarks: . . . .

INSTRUCTIONS FOR INSTITUTION SCHEDULE.

This includes all institutions conducted by Negroes wholly or partially, or wholly or partially in the interest of the Negroes; as, *e. g.*, churches, missions, clubs, shops, stands, stores, agencies, societies, associations, halls, newspapers, etc.

Find out the object of the enterprise (philanthropic, social, business, etc.), the capital invested, the property owned, taxes paid, income for past twelve months, character and amount of expenditure, sort of quarters occupied, and persons connected, etc., aiming, in all cases, to collect essential facts.

Especially try and find out whether the enterprise is that of one person, of a partnership, or is a co-operative enterprise among a large number. If in any degree co-operative, bring out the extent, character and objects of the co-operation.

APPENDIX B.

1682. *Negro Serfdom Recognized.* The charter of the Free
Society of Traders of Pennsylvania recognizes the slavery of
Blacks. Slaves were to be freed after fourteen years of service,
upon condition that they cultivate land allotted to them, and
surrender two-thirds of the produce annually.—Hazard's "Annals" (Ed. 1850), 553.

1693, July 11. *Tumults of Slaves.* Action of City Council
of Philadelphia against tumults by slaves.—Penna. Col. Rec.,
I, 380–81.

1700. *Slave Marriages.* Penn proposes a bill regulating
slave marriages; bill is lost in Council.—Bettle, 368; Thomas,
266.

1700, November 27. *Trial of Slaves.* "An Act for the
Trial of Negroes." Introduced by Penn. This act provided
that Negroes accused of high crime should be tried by two
justices of the peace and six freeholders; rape of white women
to be punished by death, and attempts by castration; Negroes
were not to carry arms without special license; over four Negroes meeting together on Sundays or other days "upon no
lawful business of their masters or owners" were to be whipped.
—Statutes-at-Large, ch. 56. (Disallowed January 7, 1706.)

1700, November 27. *Traffic with Slaves.* "An Act for the
Better Regulation of Servants in this Province and Territories."
Traffic with slaves forbidden, among other things.—Statutes-
at-Large, ch. 49.

1700, November 27. *Duty on Slaves.* "An Act for Granting an Impost upon Wines, Rum, Beer, Ale, Cider, etc., Imported, Retorted and Sold in this Province and Territories."
§ 2. . . . "for every Negro, male or female, imported, if
above sixteen years of age, twenty shillings; for every Negro
under the age of sixteen, six shillings.—Statutes-at-Large,
ch. 85.

1706, January 12. *Duty on Slaves.* "An Act for Raising a Supply. . . . ." Imported Negroes, except those who lived at least two years in Jersey, 40s. (or 10s. ?) per head.—Statutes-at-Large, ch. 164.

1706, January 12. *Trial of Negroes.* "An Act for the Trial of Negroes." Practically the same as the Act of 1700; attempt to rape and robbery of £5 or more, punished by branding and exportation.—Statutes-at-Large, ch. 143. (Repealed by Act of 1780, q. v.)

1708. *Protest to Legislature.* Protest of Mechanics against hiring out of Negroes.—Scharf-Wescott: "History of Philadelphia," I, 200.

1710, December 28. *Duty Act.* "An Impost Act, laying a Duty on Negroes. . . ."—40s. on Negroes imported.—Carey and Bioren, I, 82.

1711, February 28. *Duty Act.* "An Impost Act, laying a Duty on Negroes. . . ." 40s. on Negroes not imported for importers own use.—Statutes-at-Large, ch. 181. (Disallowed 20 February, 1714.)

1712. *Petition for Emancipation.* Petition of Southeby for Abolition of Slavery.—DuBois'"Slave Trade," p. 22.

1712. *Negro Plot.* Negro plot in New York.—*Ibid.*

1712, June 11. *Duty Act.* "A Supplementary Act to. . ." the Act of 1810.—Carey and Bioren, I, 87-88. (Disallowed in 1713.)

1712, June 7. *Prohibitory Duty Act.* "An Act to Prevent the Importation of Negroes and Indians into this Province." £20 prohibitory duty laid on slaves imported, because of their plots and insurrections.—Statutes-at-Large, ch. 192. Cf. DuBois'"Slave Trade," p. 22. (Disallowed 1713.)

1713. *Assiento Treaty.* Contract for importing slaves into Spanish West Indies signed by Great Britain.—DuBois'"Slave Trade," pp. 207-9.

1715, May 28. *Duty Act.* "An Act for Laying a Duty on Negroes Imported into this Province." £5 duty ; slaves of immigrants not to be sold for a year.—Statutes-at-Large, III, 121. (Disallowed 21 July, 1719.)

1718, February 22. *Duty Act.* "An Act for Continuing a Duty on Negroes. . . ." £5 duty; slaves of immigrants not to be sold for 16 months.—Statutes-at-Large, III, 164.

1721, February 24. *Duty Act.* "An Act for Continuing several Acts. . . ." Act of 1718 continued.—Statutes-at-Large, III, 238.

1721, August 21. *Traffic with Negroes.* "A Supplementary Act to a Law. . . ." On Public Houses. No liquors to be sold Negroes or Indians without leave.—Statutes-at-Large, III, 250.

1721, August 26. *Police Regulation.* "An Act for Preventing Accidents that May Happen by Fire." Slaves shooting squibs or guns in Philadelphia without license to be whipped.—Statutes-at-Large, III, 254.

1722, May 12. *Duty Act.* "An Act for Laying a Duty on Negroes. . . ." £5 duty, as in 1718.—Statutes-at-Large, III, 275.

1722. *Petition of White Laborers.* Laborers petition General Assembly against employment of Blacks. Assembly resolves: That the principle is dangerous and injurious to the republic and not to be sanctioned.—"Watson's Annals," I, 98.

1726, March 5. *Duty Act.* "An Act for Laying a Duty on Negroes. . . ." Act of 1722 continued from 1726 to 1729.—Statutes-at-Large, IV, 52.

1726, March 26. *Status of Negroes Defined.* "An Act for the Better Regulation of Negroes in this Province."

"Whereas, it often happens that Negroes commit felonies and other heinous crimes, which by the laws of this Province are punishable by death, but the loss of such cases falling wholly on the owner, is so great a hardship that sometimes may induce him to conceal such crimes, or convey his Negro to some other place and so suffer him to escape justice to the ill example of others to commit like offences.

" Be it resolved, etc., That Negroes convicted of capital crime be valued and paid for out of money collected as duty on their importation." . . .

§ III. " Whereas, free Negroes are an idle and slothful people and often prove burdensome to the neighborhood and afford ill examples to other Negroes. Therefore, Be it enacted that if any master or mistress shall discharge or set free any Negro, he or she shall enter into recognizance with sufficient securities in the sum of £30 to indemnify the county for any charge or incumbrance they may bring upon the same in case such Negro, through sickness or otherwise, be rendered incapable of self-support.''

In case of freedom by will, the executor or administrator was required to give the bond, or such slaves should not be regarded as free.

Any Negro becoming free under age 21 might be bound to service until of age.

The Act further provided penalties for the harboring of Negroes by each other; for trading or dealing with each other without license—all on pain of being sold into slavery if unable to pay fine; also provided penalty of £100 for anybody who should marry a Negro and white person; £30 for Negro caught living in marriage relation with white person, in such cases Negro to be sold into slavery for life.

§ XI of Act prohibited masters, etc., from allowing Negro slaves to hire their own time.

One section also imposed a duty of £10 on imported slaves.—Statutes-at-Large, IV, 59.

1729, May 10. *Duty Act.* '' An Act for Laying a Duty on Negroes Imported into this Province.'' £2 duty.—Statutes-at-Large, IV, 128.

1732, April 17. *Slave Tumults.* Philadelphia Council order Ordinance drawn to prevent tumults of slaves on Sundays.— ''Watson's Annals,'' I, 62.

1738, July 3. *Slave Tumults.* Draft of Ordinance to suppress tumults of slaves considered in Philadelphia City Council.—*Ibid.*, I, 62.

1741, August 17. *Tumults of Negroes.* Order made by Philadelphia City Councils to suppress disorders of Negroes and others on court house square at night.—''Watson's Annals,'' I, 62–63.

1761, March 14. *Duty Act.* ''An Act for Laying a Duty on Negro and Mulatto Slaves imported into this province.'' £10 duty? Continued in 1768; repealed in 1780.—Carey and Bioren, I, 371, 451.

1761, April 22. *Duty Act.* ''A Supplement to. . . . '' the Act of 1761.—*Ibid.*, 371, 451.

1768, February 20. *Duty Act.* Acts of 1761 re-enacted.— Dallas, I, 490.

1773, February 26. *Duty Act.* ''An Act for Making

Perpetual the Act. . . . " of 1761. Additional £10 duty provided for.—Dallas, I, 671.

1775. *Bill on Importation.* Bill to prohibit importation oɪ slaves vetoed by Governor.—Bettle.

1778, September 7. *Recovery of Duties.* "An Act for the Recovery of the Duties on Negro and Mulatto Slaves. . . ." —Dallas, I, 782.

1779, February 5. *Plan of Emancipation.* Supreme Executive Council recommends a plan of gradual emancipation to Assembly.

1780, March 1. *Slavery Abolished.* "An Act for the Gradual Abolition of Slavery."

§ 1, 2. General condemnation of slavery.

§ 3. No child born hereafter in Pennsylvania to be a slave.

§ 4. Children of slaves born hereafter to be bound to service until twenty-eight years of age.

§ 5. All slaves to be registered.

§ 7. Negroes to be tried for crime like other inhabitants.

§ 10. None to be slaves except those registered.

§ 14. Acts of 1725, 1761 and 1773 repealed.—Carey and Bioren, ch. 881.

1786. *Petition for Potter's Field.* Petition of Philadelphia Negroes to Council for leave to enclose Potter's Field as a Negro burial ground.—Penna. Col. Rec., XIV, 637.

1788, March 29. *Act of 1780 Amended.* "An Act to Explain and Amend an Act Entitled 'An Act for the Gradual Abolition of Slavery.'"

§ 2. Slaves of immigrants to be free.

§ 3. Slaves not to be removed from without their consent given before two justices.

§ 4. Persons possessed of children liable to serve till twenty-eight years old must register them.

§ 5. Slave trading forbidden under penalty and forfeiture.

§ 6. Slaves serving for a term of years not to be separated from parents.—Carey and Bioren, ch. 394.

1790, September 2. *Negro Suffrage.* Constitution of Pennsylvania. Art. III, Sec. 1. In elections by the citizens, every freeman of the age of twenty-one years, having resided in the State two years next before the election, and within that time paid a State or county tax, which shall have been assessed at least six months before the election, shall enjoy the rights of an elector.—Purdon's "Digest," 6th ed.

1793, April 11. *Duty on Slaves.* "An Act to Establish a Board of Wardens for the Port of Philadelphia. . . ."

§ 22. Of passengers entering port only slaves to pay head money.—Carey and Bioren, ch. 178.

1800. *Petition to Congress.* Petition of Negroes to Legislature and Congress against slave-trade.—DuBois' "Slave Trade," p. 31–83.

1821, April. *Act vs. Pauperism.* "An Act to Prevent the Increase of Pauperism in the Commonwealth."

§ 1. If any black indentured servant over twenty-eight years of age is brought into the State, his master is liable for his charge if he becomes a pauper.—Laws of Penna., 1821.

1826, March 25. *Act vs. Kidnapping.* "An Act to Give Effect to the Provisions of the Constitution of the United States, Relative to Fugitives from Labor, for the Protection of the Free People of Color, and to prevent Kidnapping."

§ 1. Fine of $500–$2000 and imprisonment seven to twenty-one years for kidnapping.

§ 2. Aiding and abetting punished.

§§ 3–6. Claimed fugitives to be arrested on warrant and taken before a judge. Oath of alleged owner or of interested persons not received as evidence.—Laws of Penna., 1826. Cf. Prigg *vs.* Penna., 16 Peters, 500, U. S. Reports.

1827, April 17. *Sales of Fugitives.* "An Act to Prevent Certain Abuses of the Laws Relative to Fugitives from Labor." No sales of fugitive slaves to be made in the State of Pennsylvania.—Laws of Penna., 1827.

1832. *Restriction on Immigration.* Bill in Legislature to make free Negroes carry passes. Cf., p. 27.

1837, July. *Negro Suffrage.* Pennsylvania Supreme Court at Sunbury; case of Hobbs *et al. vs.* Fogg. Judgment of Common Pleas Court reversed and Negro declared not a "freeman" in the meaning of Constitution.—Penna. Reports, 6 Watts, 553–60.

1838. *Negro Suffrage.* Revised Constitution of Pennsylvania, Art. III, Sec. 1. "In elections by the citizens, every white freeman of the age of twenty-one years, having resided in this State one year, and in the election district where he offers to vote ten days immediately preceding such election, and within two years paid a State or county tax, which shall have been assessed at least ten days before the election, shall enjoy the right of an elector."—Purdon's"Digest,"Sixth Ed.

1854, May 8. "An Act for the Regulation and Continuance of a System of Education by Common Schools."

The Controllers and Directors of the several school districts of the State are hereby authorized and required to establish within their respective districts separate schools for Negro and Mulatto children wherever such schools can be located so as to accommodate twenty or more pupils; and wherever such schools shall be established and kept open four months in every year the Directors and Controllers shall not be compelled to admit such pupils into any other schools of the district.—Laws of Penna., 1854.

1863, March 6. *Immigration.* Petition against immigration of freedmen to Pennsylvania denied by Senate committee of Legislature.—Pamphlet, Phila. Library.

1867. *Separate Seats in Cars.* Pennsylvania Supreme Court; case of West Chester and Philadelphia Co. *vs.* Miles. Held that separation of Negroes to assigned seats for good order is not illegal on railways, etc.—Penna. Reports, 5 Smith, 209.

1867, March 22. *Civil Rights.* Negroes to have same rights on railway cars as white citizens.—Brightley's Purdon, Eleventh Ed., 1436.

1870, April 6. *Negro Suffrage.* § 10 of Act says: "That so much of every Act of Assembly as provides that only white freemen shall be entitled to vote or to register as voters, or as claiming to vote, at any general or special election in this Commonwealth, be and the same is hereby repealed; and that hereafter all freemen, without distinction of color, shall be enrolled and registered according to the provisions of the act approved April 17, 1869."—Laws of Penna., 1870.

1874. *Negro Suffrage.* New Constitution removes restrictions as to color.

1874, April 10. *Civil Rights.* Pennsylvania Supreme Court; case of Drew *vs.* Peer. Damages given Negroes for ejectment from a theatre.—12 Norris, 234.

1878, March 15. *Civil Rights.* Pennsylvania Supreme

Court; case of Central Railroad of New Jersey *vs.* Green and wife. Damages granted for compelling Negroes to go from one car to another on railway.—Penna. Reports, 5 Norris, 421, 427.

1881, June 8. *Mixed Schools.* § 1. It shall be unlawful for any school director, superintendent, or teacher to make any distinction whatever on account of, or by reason of, the race or color of any pupil or scholar who may be in attendance upon or seeking admission to any public or common school maintained wholly or in part under the school laws of the commonwealth.—Brightley's Purdon, Eleventh ed., p. 292.

1887, May 19. *Civil Rights.* "An Act to Provide Civil Rights for all People, Regardless of Race or Color." "§ 1. *Be it enacted, etc.*, that any person, company, corporation, being owner, lessee or manager of any restaurant, hotel, railroad, street railway, omnibus line, theatre, concert hall or place of entertainment or amusement, who shall refuse to accommodate, convey or admit any person or persons on account of race or color over their lines or into their hotel or restaurant, theatre, concert hall or place of amusement, shall upon conviction thereof be guilty of a misdemeanor and be punished by a fine of not less than fifty or more than one hundred dollars."—Laws of Penna., 1887, pp. 130–31.

1895, July 2. *Life Insurance.* Life insurance companies are not allowed to make any discriminations as to premiums, dividends, or otherwise, between insured of the same class and expectation of life.—Penna. Laws, 1895, p. 432.

APPENDIX C.

BIBLIOGRAPHY.

I. General Works.

Publications of Atlanta University :
  No. 1. Mortality Among Negroes in Cities.
  No. 2. Social and Physical Condition of Negroes.
  No. 3. Efforts of Negroes for Social Betterment.
                          —Atlanta, Ga., 1896-98.

Edward Bettle. Notices of Negro Slavery as Connected with Pennsylvania. In Mem. Hist. Soc. of Pennsylvania, I.

Charles Booth. Life and Labour of the People. London, 1892.

M. Carey and J. Bioren. Laws of Pennsylvania, 1700-1802. Philadelphia, 1803.

A. J. Dallas. Laws of Pennsylvania, 1700-1781. Philadelphia, 1797.

W. E. Burghardt DuBois. Suppression of the Slave Trade. New York, 1896.

————— The Study of the Negro Problems. Annals of the Amer. Acad. of Pol. and Soc. Science. Philadelphia, 1898.

————— The Negroes of Farmville, Va. (U. S. Bureau of Labor *Bulletin*, January, 1898.)

[Benjamin Franklin.] An Essay on the African Slave Trade. Philadelphia, 1790.

[Friends.] Germantown Friends' Protest Against Slavery, 1688. (Facsimile copy) Philadelphia, 1880.

[Friends.] The Appeal of the Religious Society of Friends in Pennsylvania, New Jersey, etc. . . . on behalf of the Colored Races. Philadelphia, 1858.

[Friends.] A Brief Statement of the Rise and Progress of the Testimony of the Religious Society of Friends against Slavery and the Slave Trade. Philadelphia, 1843.

Samuel Hazard. The Register of Pennsylvania. Philadelphia, 1828-36.

Hull House Maps and Papers. New York, 1895.

Samuel M. Janney. History of the Religious Society of Friends. Philadelphia, 1859-67.

Walter Laidlaw, Editor. The Federation of Churches and Christian Workers in New York City. First and Second Sociological Canvasses. New York, 1896–1897.

Marion J. McDougal. Fugitive Slaves. Boston, 1891.

Edward Needles. An Historical Memoir of the Pennsylvania Society for Promoting the Abolition of Slavery. Philadelphia, 1848.

William C. Nell. Services of Colored Americans in the Wars of 1776 and 1812. Reprinted, Philadelphia, 1894.

Statutes-at-Large of the State of Pennsylvania. Philadelphia.

Pennsylvania Colonial Records. Philadelphia.

Robert Proud. History of Pennsylvania. Philadelphia, 1797-98.

R. Mayo-Smith. Statistics and Sociology. New York, 1896.

Allen Clapp Thomas. The Attitude of the Society of Friends toward Slavery, etc. (Reprinted from Vol. VIII, American Society of Church History.) New York, 1897.

Census of the United States, First to the Eleventh. Washington, 1790-1898.

George W. Williams. History of the Negro Race in America from 1619 to 1880. New York, 1883.

Joseph T. Willson. The Black Phalanx. Hartford, 1889.

Carroll D. Wright. Slums of Great Cities. Seventh Special Report of the United States Department of Labor. Washington, 1894.

II. *Books and Pamphlets Relating to Philadelphia Negroes.*

Benjamin C. Bacon. Statistics of the Colored People of Philadelphia. Philadelphia, 1856.

———— *Ibid.*, Second Edition, with Statistics of Crime. Philadelphia, 1859.

A Brief History of the Movement to Abolish the Slums of Philadelphia. Philadelphia. (Pam.)

Collection of Reports of Charitable Institutions for Colored Persons. Philadelphia. (Ridgeway Library.)

Colored Enlistments. Philadelphia. (Pam. Philadelphia Library Co.)

Colored People in Philadelphia. Philadelphia. (Pam. Philadelphia Library Co.)

Colored Regiments. Philadelphia. (Pam. Philadelphia Library Co.)

Education and Employment Statistics of the Colored People of Philadelphia. (MS. in Library of Historical Association.)

Dr. E. O. Emerson. Vital Statistics of Philadelphia (in American Journal of Medical Sciences, July, 1848.)

[Friends.] A Brief Sketch of the Schools for Black People and Their Descendants Established by the Religious Society of Friends, in 1770. Philadelphia, 1867.

A. Mott. Biography of Colored People. Philadelphia. (Pam. Philadelphia Library Co.)

Edward Needles. Ten Years' Progress, or a Comparison of the State and Condition of the Colored People in the City and County of Philadelphia from 1837 to 1847. Philadelphia, 1849.

Daniel A. Payne. History of the A. M. E. Church. Nashville, 1891.

Report of the Committee Appointed for the Purpose of Securing to Colored People in Philadelphia the Right to the use of the Street Cars. Philadelphia, 1865. (Pam.)

Report of the Committee on the Comparative Health, Mortality, Length of Sentences, etc., of White and Colored Convicts. Philadelphia, 1849.

Frederick W. Spiers. The Street Railway System of Philadelphia, etc. Johns Hopkins University Studies. Ser. 15, Nos. 3–5. Baltimore, 1897.

The Present State and Condition of the Free People of Colour of the City of Philadelphia and Adjoining Districts, etc. Philadelphia, 1838.

A Statistical Inquiry into the Condition of the People of Color of the City and Districts of Philadelphia. Philadelphia, 1849.

Trades of the Colored People. Philadelphia, 1838.

John F. Watson. Annals of Philadelphia. Philadelphia, 1830.

A. W. Wayman. My Recollections of A. M. E. Ministers. Philadelphia, 1882.

Why Colored People in Philadelphia Are Excluded from the Street Cars. Philadelphia, 1866. (Pam., Two Editions.)

[John Woolman.] Considerations on Keeping Negroes. Philadelphia, 1784.

III. Books and Pamphlets Written by Philadelphia Negroes.

Act of Incorporation, Causes and Motives of the African Episcopal Church of Philadelphia. Philadelphia, 1810.

Richard Allen. (First Bishop of A. M. E. Church.) The Life, Experience and Gospel Labours of the Rt. Rev. Richard Allen, etc. Written by himself. Philadelphia, 1833.

Richard Allen and Jacob Tapsico. The Doctrine and Discipline of the A. M. E. Church. Philadelphia, 1819.

Matthew Anderson. Presbyterianism and Its Relation to the Negro. Philadelphia, 1897.

Appeal of Forty Thousand Colored Citizens, Threatened with Disfranchisement, to the People of Pennsylvania. Philadelphia, 1838. (Pam.)

Jeremiah Asher. Autobiography. Philadelphia, 1862.

E. D. Bassett. Handbook on Hayti. Philadelphia.

J. J. G. Bias. Synopsis of Phrenology. Philadelphia, 1859.

Lorenzo Blackson. Autobiography. Philadelphia, 1861.

C. H. Brooks. Manual and History of the Grand United Order of Odd Fellows. 360 pp. Philadelphia, 1864.

Robert Campbell. A Pilgrimage to My Motherland; an Account of a Journey among the Egbas and Yorubas of Central Africa. Philadelphia, 1861.

W. Y. Catto. History of the Presbyterian Movement. Philadelphia, 1858.

Levi J. Coffin. The Relation of Baptized Children to the Church. Philadelphia, 1890. 106 pp.

Martin Robinson Delaney. Condition, Elevation, Emigration and Destiny of the Colored People of the United States, etc. Philadelphia, 1852.

William Douglass. Sermons Preached in the African Protestant Episcopal Church of St. Thomas', Philadelphia. Philadelphia, 1854.

William Douglass. Annals of St. Thomas' Church. Philadelphia, 1862.

John S. Durham. To Teach the Negro History. Philadelphia, 1898.

Frances E. W. Harper. Miscellaneous Poems. Boston, 1854.

—— ——. Forest Leaves. Baltimore, 1855.

—— ——. Iola Leroy: A Novel. Third Edition. Philadelphia, 1892. 280 pp.

Absalom Jones. A Thanksgiving Sermon. . . . On Account of the Abolition of the African Slave Trade, etc. Philadelphia, 1808. (Pam.)

Robert Jones. Fifty Years in the Lombard Street Central Presbyterian Church. Philadelphia, 1894. 170 pp.

H. T. Johnson. The Divine Logos. Philadelphia, 1890.

Jarena Lee. Journal. Philadelphia, 1849.

—— ——. The Color of Solomon. Philadelphia, 1895. 93 pp.

Minutes of the First Annual Convention of the People of Colour. Philadelphia, 1831. (Pam.)

Minutes of Third Annual Convention of Free Negroes. Philadelphia, 1833. (Pam.)

Mrs. N. T. Mossell. The Work of Afro-American Women. Philadelphia, 1894. 178 pp.

Proceedings of Convention of Colored Freemen of Pennsylvania. Philadelphia. (Pam.)

Robert Purvis. Remarks on the Life and Character of James Forten. (Pam.)

William Still. The Underground Railroad. Philadelphia, 1872. 780 pp.

Benjamin T. Tanner. An Apology for African Methodism. Baltimore, 1867. 468 pp.

—— ——. Theological Lectures. Nashville, 1894. 185 pp.

—— ——. An Outline of History and Government for A. M. E. Churchmen. Philadelphia, 1884. 206 pp.

[Joseph Willson.] Sketches of the Higher Classes of Colored Society in Philadelphia. Philadelphia, 1841.

SPECIAL REPORT

ON

NEGRO DOMESTIC SERVICE

IN THE SEVENTH WARD

PHILADELPHIA

BY

ISABEL EATON, M. A.

Fellow of the College Settlements Association

I.

INTRODUCTION.

This paper is an attempt to give the most accurate facts obtainable bearing upon the question of colored domestic service in Philadelphia. It endeavors to show the relation of the colored domestic to the general domestic service problem on the one hand, and to the great mass of the Negro people on the other. The purpose, scope and methods of the work are the same as those already explained at length by Dr. W. E. B. Du Bois in the introduction to this volume, constituting the general report of the investigation conducted by the University of Pennsylvania.

The section treating Domestic Service is no unimportant division of the general subject. On the contrary, it is probably of more consequence than any other single aspect of the problem, since the number of domestic servants among colored wage-earners is shown by the last census to be greater in thirty-two out of forty-eight States than the number engaged in any other occupation; while in many cases it is greater than the number engaged in all other employments taken together. Indeed this predominance of domestic service over all other occupations followed by the Negroes, is recorded of every State in the Union, excepting the Southern States, where agriculture stands first and domestic service second. It will doubtless be surprising to many to hear that the census record shows that each of the Northern and Western States, with the single exception of Delaware, has more colored people in domestic service than in any other occupation, while in nearly seven in every ten of these States colored domestic service more than outnumbers the aggregate of all other occupations of colored people. The record for the State of Pennsylvania as given by the last census shows the following ·facts concerning occupations of Negroes throughout the State:

State.	All Occupations.		Domestic Service.	
	Males.	Females.	Males.	Females.
Pennsylvania.	37,534	15,704	22,505	14,297

It appears from this that very nearly 60 per cent of the colored workingmen of Pennsylvania are engaged in domestic service ; while over 91 per cent of the colored workingwomen of the State are in service. A graphic presentation of these facts makes clear the large proportion of the Negro population of Pennsylvania employed in domestic service:

PROPORTION OF COLORED DOMESTIC SERVANTS IN PENNSYLVANIA
AS COMPARED WITH WHOLE WORKING COLORED POPU-
LATION—ELEVENTH CENSUS.

In the city of Philadelphia nearly the same preponderance of domestic service in relation to other occupations of the colored people is found.

In this investigation a separate schedule for domestic service was used.[1] Like the other schedules, it was prepared under the direction of Dr. S. M. Lindsay, Assistant Professor of Sociology at the University of Pennsylvania, and was carefully revised by the national Department of Labor at Washington, as well as by prominent statisticians in New York and elsewhere. The facts here given were collected during a nine months, residence at the Philadelphia College Settlement, which is located in the heart of one of the most densely populated Negro quarters of the city.

This schedule was used throughout the residence streets of the Seventh Ward, and elsewhere in the ward limits wherever

[1] See Appendix A.

colored domestics were employed. [2] This ward includes among its inhabitants all grades of wealth and comfort, from the houses with a coachman and coachman's assistant, a butler and butler's assistant, and a retinue of female domestics as well, to those houses where only one woman is employed, who does "general housework," sometimes including not only cooking and laundry work, but also the furnace work, removal of ashes, "cleaning the front," and other outside work usually delegated to a man. And thus, since nearly all degrees of wealth are represented in the district investigated—that is to say, from the present point of view, all grades of service-employing families—it is probable that all grades of colored domestic service have been encountered in this survey.

In this house-to-house canvass, every domestic scheduled, with a very few exceptions, was personally interviewed. Occasionally the butler or waiter would answer for the cook, if both chanced to have served long in the same family, or sometimes the lady of the house would herself supply the answers, but in every case the information given was such as to warrant belief in its reliability. To the domestic servants personally interviewed in this way have been added the far greater number scheduled by Dr. DuBois in his canvass of the homes of the colored people within the ward limits. Altogether 677 men have been recorded and 1612 women, making a total of 2289 domestics, male and female, either working or living in the Seventh Ward.

---

[2] For map showing the ward boundaries see page 59.

ENUMERATION OF NEGRO DOMESTIC SERVANTS.

Recent Reform in Domestic Service.—Reform in the administration of the household has been called a "belated reform," one that has been so long a time in gaining the ear of intelligent people that it must somehow make up for lost time and gain a little on other reforms before it can hope to come abreast of the progress of the age. In view of the fact that college-bred women in greater numbers are assuming responsibility for the administration of the household, at the same time that reform of domestic service is being agitated, it is natural to think that the one thing partly accounts for the other. It is certainly true that the question is now for the first time being treated scientifically by some of the most intelligent women in the country. The Civic Club of Philadelphia has done honorable pioneer work in attempting to establish a standard of work and wages for domestic servants, and other similar clubs are following in their footsteps. Also, there is beginning to be a literature on the subject, best represented by Charles Booth's Study of Household Service in the eighth volume of his "Life and Labour of the People," and by the admirable work entitled "Domestic Service" by Miss Lucy M. Salmon, Professor of History at Vassar College. In the latter work, which is easily the best authority on this much discussed but little understood subject, the doctrine of survival through adaptation is for the first time applied to the economics of the household. One result has been the conviction that much of the friction in the modern household arises from its lack of adaptation to the civilization of to-day, and will disappear when domestic service gets in line with the march of progress and ceases to try to meet modern needs by the employment of mediæval methods. The higher is dependent on the lower, and as our social reforms deal with the houses and food of the poor for the sake of higher things than mere physical well being, so all our reforms must begin at the bottom and work up. We may take courage that reforms in domestic service and in household economics will spread, since they have now ceased to be regarded as impossibilities, and the problems involved are being fairly faced. With the widening of woman's mental horizon has come a realizing sense of the truth regarding household work, that "in no other occupation is there so much waste of labor and capital, and in no other would a fraction of this waste be overlooked."

This report endeavors to contribute to the problem the results of a study of facts concerning the domestic work of Negroes in Philadelphia.

Enumeration.—In presenting these facts, we shall begin with an enumeration of Negro domestics.

The first table shows the number of colored domestic servants[3] in the Seventh Ward of Philadelphia by sex and age periods:

TABLE I.

(*Domestic Service.*)

NUMBER OF COLORED DOMESTIC SERVANTS IN WARD SEVEN BY SEX AND AGE PERIODS.

Age.	Male.	Female.
Ten to twenty	48	274
Twenty-one to thirty	305	698
Thirty-one to forty	165	364
Forty-one and over	150	262
Age unknown	9	14
Total	677	1612

From this statement it will be seen that of the colored service in the ward about 30 per cent is furnished by men and 70 per cent by women. In the Seventh Ward of Philadelphia there were found to be 9675 colored persons, of whom 2289 are here seen to be domestic employes, or 23.7 per cent of the

---

[3] In this study of the condition of the colored people of Philadelphia, all persons scheduled as "domestic servants" are connected with private establishments, waiters in hotels, etc., being classified with public service.

total colored population of the ward. It is a little over 30 per cent of all the colored wage-earners of the ward.[4]

This per cent in domestic service agrees very nearly with the following table taken from the eleventh census, showing the proportion of Negro wage-earners engaged in domestic service the country over to be 31.4 to the hundred.[5]

TABLE FROM ELEVENTH CENSUS OF THE UNITED STATES SHOWING PERCENTAGES OF DIFFERENT ELEMENTS OF THE POPULATION ENGAGED IN DIFFERENT OCCUPATIONS.

	Native Whites. Per cent.	Foreign Born. Per cent.	Negro. Per cent.
Professions	5.5	2.2	1.1
Agriculture	41.0	25.5	57.2
Trade and transportation	17.0	14.0	4.7
Manufactures	22.9	31.3	5.6
Personal service	13.6	27.0	31.4
Total	100.0	100.0	100.0

When public waiters and waitresses in hotels and restaurants, as well as janitors and caretakers, are included in the count of domestic servants, it brings the ratio up nearly to 41 per cent of the whole number of colored wage-earners in the ward.

After considering what per cent of the colored people are domestics, it is interesting to notice what part of domestic service is colored. So we turn from the ratios just given to consider what proportion of the total of domestic service in the United States is performed by colored people. When we think of American domestic service as a whole, we have a more or

---

[4] The 2289 domestics which constitute 34 per cent of the 6661 Negroes in the Seventh Ward engaged in gainful occupations are those actually investigated in the special inquiry into domestic service. The number may not include all the domestics in the ward and does not include many classes of persons enumerated under "domestic and personal service" in the table on page 108 of this volume.

[5] Domestic service is classified in the census under "personal service," and includes persons classified elsewhere in this investigation, such as hotel proprietors, but the number of Negroes thus included is small, and the error of comparison, therefore, small.

less clear conception of a great army of the colored race in the south, of the Irish and Germans in the north, of the Swedes in the middle west, and of the Chinese on the Pacific Coast. The census of 1890 gives the relative numbers of native white, foreign white and colored (including Chinese) domestic employes in the United States as follows:

ELEMENTS OF THE POPULATION ENGAGED IN DOMESTIC SERVICE.

(From the Eleventh Census of the United States.)

Geographical Section.	Number.			Per cent.		
	Native White.	Foreign White.	Colored.	Native White.	For'gn White.	Col'd.
Pacific Coast	. . . .	. . . .	. . . .	37.58	35.83	†26.59
Eastern	. . . .	. . . .	. . . .	39.11	55.22	5.67
Middle*	176,194	175,819	42,049	44.71	44.62	10.67
Western	. . . .	. . . .	. . . .	59.98	33.11	6.91
Border (near the Mason-Dixon line) . .	. . . .	. . . .	. . . .	31.65	6.62	61.73
Southern	. . . .	. . . .	. . . .	16.77	3.10	80.13
United States	. . . .	. . . .	. . . .	41.65	29.55	28.80

* Includes New York, Pennsylvania, and New Jersey.
† This term includes also Chinese who are reckoned in the census as "colored."

These figures attribute nearly 29 per cent of the domestic service of the country to the colored, who comprise only 12½ per cent of the population.

The colored perform about three times as much domestic service in proportion to their numbers as the whites do. From this it will be seen that, while the study of domestic service in any consideration of the condition of the colored people is important, the study of the Negro domestic is equally important in any careful consideration of the domestic service problem. It will be noticed that the per cents for the middle section of States show only 10.67 per cent of the domestic service performed by colored people. The large urban populations of the New York cities doubtless reduce this below what it would be if only Pennsylvania and New Jersey were considered, as city servants are mostly drawn from our foreign white population, but if the rate be accepted as true for the city of

Philadelphia (though it is doubtless much too low for a city which has the largest colored population of any city in the United States, except New Orleans and Washington), if it be accepted for Philadelphia, where 4 per cent of the population is colored, we shall find that the Negro domestics "run ahead of their ticket" here also in this matter of household service.

The probable reason for this disproportion is not far to seek when we remember the unpopularity of domestic service which keeps whites out, and reflect that the colored prejudice, which is known to operate against the Negro in nearly all departments of labor excepting drudgery, actually works in his favor in the matter of domestic service, where the competence of Negro waiters and the superior skill of Negro cooks is generally admitted. Hence, Negro labor, following the line of least resistance, flows in enlarged streams into the channel of domestic service.

III.

SOURCES OF THE SUPPLY AND METHODS OF HIRING.

The question next arises as to the chief sources of Philadelphia's large supply of colored service. Are these people Southern Negroes, or Philadelphia born? The quality of service rendered and the standard of excellence may depend in some degree upon circumstances of birth and training. Hence the facts in regard to nativity as shown in Table II, which follows, are worth considering:

TABLE II.
NATIVITY OF COLORED DOMESTIC SERVANTS IN PHILADELPHIA.
Number and Per Cent by Sex and Birthplace.

Birthplace.	Number of Males.	Number of Females.	Total Number.	Total Per cent.
Philadelphia	78	215	293	12.08 } 18.52
Pennsylvania	37	94	131	5.72 }
New Jersey	18	50	68	3.
Delaware	34	99	133	5.08
Maryland	102	359	461	20.14 } 48.04
Virginia	199	439	638	27.90 }
West Virginia	5	14	19	
District of Columbia . . .	50	85	135	5.90
North Carolina	36	68	104	4.50
South Carolina	7	5	12	
Georgia	4	11	15	
South Georgia	28	51	79	3.90
West Georgia	2	3	5	
Ohio	0	5	5	
Missouri	0	2	2	
Kentucky	0	1	1	
Tennessee	2	4	6	
Louisiana	1	2	3	
Mississippi	0	2	2	
Alabama	2	2	4	
West Indies	15	4	19	
New York	8	10	18	
Maine	1	1	2	
Massachusetts	5	2	7	
Connecticut	1	4	5	
Rhode Island	2	0	2	
North Rhode Island	0	1	1	
Canada	1	2	3	
Florida	2	0	2	
Texas	0	2	2	
Hungary	0	1	1	
Scotland	0	1	1	
South America	0	1	1	
Unknown	37	72	109	
Total	677	1612	2289	

These facts show clearly that the greater part of Philadelphia's colored domestic service is supplied from Maryland and Virginia, particularly from the latter State. It will be noticed that less than one-fifth of it (18.5 per cent) is supplied from Philadelphia and the State of Pennsylvania, while very nearly one-half (48.4 per cent) comes from the two States of Maryland and Virginia. Some interesting indications in regard to nativity and quality of service as measured by length of service with the same employer, are brought out later in Table XXV.

Methods of Hiring.—Philadelphia is as much at the mercy of employment bureaus, and the frequently untrustworthy recommendations of previous employers, as are other large cities. Yet these and the method of advertising are the only ways open to the employer for accomplishing what has been called the "inevitable annual change of employes." The colored people in domestic service seldom seek employment through the Philadelphia intelligence offices or by applying in answer to advertisement unless it is particularly stated that colored help is acceptable or preferred. They generally offer the recommendations of former employers, though many of them, seldom the best ones, offer their services from door to door and are employed upon the recommendation of personal appearance and general bearing. The colored man's avoidance of the employment bureau is largely due to the fact that extortionate fees are usually charged him. He patronizes a few bureaus kept by colored people whom he trusts ; and his unwillingness to answer advertisements needs no explanation but the remark already offered.

Personnel of Colored Domestic Service.—In regard to the personnel of domestic service, the facts in Philadelphia correspond with those for all employes the world over ; Negro domestic servants are for the most part women rather than men, and young rather than middle-aged or old people. An examination of Table I will show that only about 30 in 100 of Philadelphia's colored domestics are men, while a study of the census figures of 1890 shows only 16 men in 100 in domestic service the country over; and the disproportion in English household service is even greater, there being only 7 men in 100 London servants. The sexes thus engaged in domestic work in

Philadelphia, in the United States and in London are here compared in tabular form:

TABLE III.

SEX IN DOMESTIC SERVICE OF DIFFERENT LOCALITIES COMPARED.

Locality.	Male. Per cent.	Female. Per cent.
Colored Domestic Service in Philadelphia	29.6	70.4
Domestic Service in United States (eleventh census)	15.8	84.2
Domestic Service in London (Charles Booth, Vol. 8, p. 211)	6.7	93.3

A comparison of the two columns shows very clearly that domestic work which has long been considered as "women's work" is still being done largely by women. A comparison of the items of the first column of Table II with each other shows that, taking the country over, where the domestic service is represented largely by Irish, German, English, Swedish and Norwegian elements as well as Negroes, the proportion of men servants falls to only about one-half that of colored men servants in Philadelphia. This again is probably to be accounted for by the fact that so many avenues of employment which are closed to colored men are open to men among the white foreign element which makes up the greater part of American service. In our shops and markets and in our building trades, on our trolley cars and our delivery wagons we see Irish and German and Swedish men, but no Negroes. The result upon domestic service of this closing of so many doors to the colored man is twofold. Many of them, being unable to better themselves financially by leaving service for other employments, remain in household work much longer than they otherwise would do, and when they marry many of them "turn waiter" because household service is one of the best paid employments open to the blacks. Thus colored men servants tend to remain in service longer than whites do, and the frequent addition to their ranks of married colored men also tends to increase the ratio of men servants among Negro domestics as well as to raise the average age.

Next to the small number of men in domestic service and the fact that a greater proportion of colored than of white men are domestics, a study of the personnel of domestic service reveals peculiarities concerning the age of servants. Nearly all household servants are comparatively young. This has been found to be true everywhere, where records have been made, and more especially among whites than among blacks. The colored people in service are older on the average than the whites (as would be expected from facts just given). Nearly one-half of all the colored domestics in the Seventh Ward of Philadelphia, both men and women, are included in the age period between twenty-one and thirty years as may be seen by reference to Table I. The average age among them is 31.9 years for the men, and 29.6 for the women, the combined average for both sexes being 30.3 years. This shows that Philadelphia's colored domestics are comparatively young people, but an examination of the age of London servants shows also 30.5 years as the average age of the men and 28.2 years as the average age of the women in service there. While the United States Census of 1890 shows men servants the country over to average 29.1 years, the women average only 26.8 years. These average ages are given in tabular form for convenience of comparison.

TABLE IV.

AVERAGE AGE IN DOMESTIC SERVICE OF DIFFERENT LOCALITIES COMPARED.

Locality.	Male. Aver. Age.	Female. Aver. Age.
Colored Domestic Service in Philadelphia	31.9	29.6
General Domestic Service in London (computed from Charles Booth's Diagram)	30.5	28.2
General Domestic Service in United States (computed from eleventh census)	29.1	26.8

DIAGRAM A.
ENGLISH DOMESTIC SERVICE.
DIAGRAM SHOWING AGES OF PERSONS
ENGAGED IN HOUSEHOLD SERVICE & OF THE
WHOLE OF OCCUPIED LONDON (MALES)
– – – – DOM. SERVICE
———— WHOLE OF OCCUPIED LONDON.

Taken from Booth's "Life and Labour of the People," Vol. 8, p. 211.

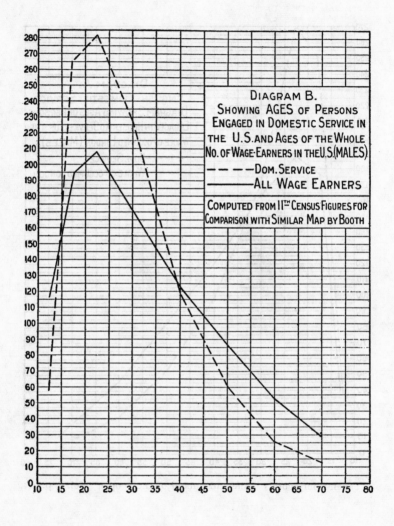

DIAGRAM B.
SHOWING AGES OF PERSONS ENGAGED IN DOMESTIC SERVICE IN THE U.S. AND AGES OF THE WHOLE NO. OF WAGE-EARNERS IN THE U.S. (MALES)
— — — DOM. SERVICE
———— ALL WAGE EARNERS
COMPUTED FROM 11TH CENSUS FIGURES FOR COMPARISON WITH SIMILAR MAP BY BOOTH

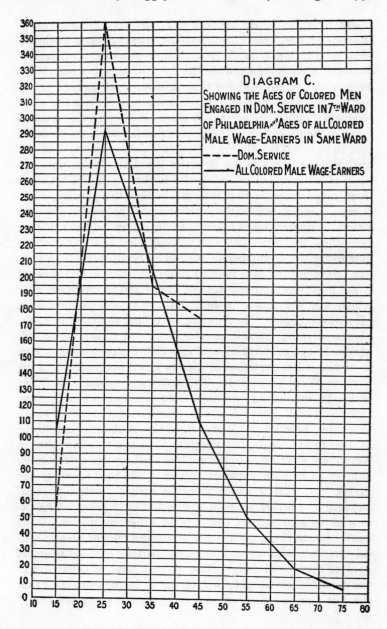

DIAGRAM C.

SHOWING THE AGES OF COLORED MEN ENGAGED IN DOM. SERVICE IN 7ᵀᴴ WARD OF PHILADELPHIA ᴬᴺᴰ AGES OF ALL COLORED MALE WAGE-EARNERS IN SAME WARD

– – – DOM. SERVICE
——— ALL COLORED MALE WAGE-EARNERS

But while these are average ages, the very great excess of the younger age periods over the older ones may be more clearly seen by the diagrams A, B and C, contrasting the ages of domestic men servants with the ages of all other male wage earners. Diagram A shows these differences of age, as exhibited in London, between men in household service and all of occupied London. Diagram B shows the contrast as it exists between men servants in the United States and all the occupied men in the total population. Diagram C contrasts ages of colored male servants in the Seventh Ward of Philadelphia and those of all occupied colored males in that ward. What these three maps mean is that the ratio which the young men in domestic service bear to the whole number of men in domestic service is greater (by as much as the diagram indicates in each case) than the ratio which the young men in all occupations bear to the whole number of men in all occupations. In London, according to Mr. Booth's diagram, there is an excess of youth in service between ages of fifteen and thirty-three, after which age the males in household work fall behind those otherwise occupied. In America, according to diagram B,[6] the excess of young men in service begins at fifteen, lasting till nearly the age of thirty-nine, after which the proportion of men in service is less than that of men otherwise occupied. In the Seventh Ward of Philadelphia, according to diagram C, we notice an interesting variation from the comparatively close agreement of diagrams A and B. The greatest excess of youth in service, here, as in A and B, is also at about twenty-three to twenty-five years, but diagram C seems to show that in Negro wage-earning in cities, the disproportionately large number of men in domestic service holds good for every age except that period which marks a man's greatest physical strength, the period between thirty and forty years. The excess of colored men of that age in other occupations is no doubt due to the large number of colored men of great physical strength who act as stevedores, porters, etc., between the ages of thirty and forty. The sudden bend at thirty-five in the domestic service line, in diagram C, is due to the fact that the last age period recorded was " forty-one years and over,"

---

[6] Computed on census figures and after Mr. Booth's method.

and, therefore, includes a few old servants about sixty. If each decade had been recorded, the curve would be more gradual, perhaps crossing the other between forty and forty-five. The excess of sixty-seven points on the forty-five-year line is almost equal to the excess at twenty-five years, and is, therefore, probably in need of modification, though there is little doubt of its indicating a real condition of Negro labor in cities.

The fact that the highest point of excess of youth in these three diagrams is reached at twenty-three to twenty-five years is significant, and suggests the query why it is that domestic service so clearly attracts the young of both sexes and of all races. It is safe to say that one of the most prominent determining causes is necessity for immediate income. Many young men and women are obliged by circumstances to undertake some form of work which, while requiring no capital and no particular course of training, still yields an immediate return, which is certain to provide them at least their board and lodging, with a small amount for living expenses. This is the chief reason why the first employment of young men and women just beginning to support themselves is so often "going out to service."

IV.

In his study of household service in the eighth volume of "Life and Labour of the People," Mr. Charles Booth distinguishes three grades or divisions among women in domestic service. The lowest group is made up of those employed in the "roughest single-handed places." The next group is made up of those in single-handed places, but of a better class; while the third group "includes those employed in many middle class homes and in the large establishments of the wealthy, it being scarcely possible to make any practical division between these two classes of servants." Each group merges imperceptibly into the next above it, so that it is practically impossible to separate them in statistical enumeration. If another grade be supplied between the second and third given here—a grade found in well-to-do Philadelphia families, where two women servants are employed—this grading of London service applies very fairly to the condition of colored service in Philadelphia. A considerable number of families in Philadelphia employ but one woman servant, and hire no extra help to do laundry work, house cleaning or outside work. The one woman does the "cooking, washing, ironing, and drags up all the ashes, tends furnace, cleans the front, and does every single thing"—as one woman put her own case. A second sort of household has only one domestic, but also hires extra service for laundry work, etc. Then follows the large number of houses where two women servants are kept, cook and "second girl," sometimes with and sometimes without the weekly extra service; and finally, the establishments with many domestics, each having his or her own special duties. The only classification of houshould servants which is at all practicable in this inquiry is that into sub-occupations or specialized kinds of work resulting from division of labor within domestic service. Such a classification of colored domestic service in Philadelphia shows seven sub-divisions of the work engaging the labor of men servants, while there are no fewer than twelve in which women are employed. These are here given in tabulated form:

TABLE V.

SUB-OCCUPATIONS IN PHILADELPHIA DOMESTIC SERVICE (SEVENTH WARD) BY NUMBER AND SEX.

MALE.		FEMALE.	
Bell and errand boys, etc. . .	23	Bell and errand girls, etc. . .	34
Butler	109	Child's nurse	21
Coachman	76	Chambermaid	114
Waiter	387	Waitress	44
Cook	47	Waitress and chambermaid .	22
Valet	4	Lady's maid	4
General work	31	Laundress	25
		Cook	365
		Cook and laundress	8
		Chambermaid and laundress .	6
		"Janitress"	4
		General housework	965

Work Required of Various Sub-occupations.—The work usually assigned to each of these sub-classes is known in a general way by everyone. In one of the appendices to her book on "Domestic Service," Miss Salmon publishes a circular letter from one of the committees of the Philadelphia Civic Club to the members of the club, submitting standards of work and wages for the various classes of sub-occupations among domestic servants. A single paragraph may be quoted, which gives the duties of one sub-occupation minutely and accurately, though all sorts of cross-classifications occur in practice, the waitress often being also chambermaid or laundress:

"Waitresses at $3.00 or $3.50 per week; must understand care of dining-room, of silver, glass and china; care and attention in waiting on table, care of parlor and halls and answering the doorbell properly."

The requirements for cooks, laundresses, chambermaids, nurses, etc., are given with equal accuracy of detail, but this is so generally understood that it is not necessary to dwell on the point here. The term "janitress" may need a word of explanation; this was what the hall servant and generally useful domestic at a large private boarding school called herself, and there were several others who seemed best classed with her. The duties of the butler in many cases extend to those of steward, and he is often to a large degree responsible for the selection and purchase of the food materials used in his particular establishment. The colored butler thus honorably commissioned generally styles himself "butler and steward," though he has not, in any case thus far personally encountered, the responsibility of engaging and paying the other servants, as is the case with the English steward. The Philadelphia use of the word is evidently a modification of the English term and bears a quite different significance.

The wages paid for these services vary in accordance with many modifying influences, as will be shown. Domestic service, however, is generally acknowledged to be well paid, as compared with other occupations which are open to women. A cook receiving $4.50 a week, the average pay in Boston, can save as much in a year as the average teacher in American public schools, as is shown by a comparison of the average teacher's salary, based on 6512 records,[7] and the statement is made on the authority of cashiers of banks in factory towns that domestics as a class save more than do factory hands. The question of the savings of colored domestics is treated in the latter part of this report.

Table VI, which follows, shows the range of wages paid to men in the various sub-divisions of colored domestic service and also the average wage in each class of service. This table and Table VII represent the statements of the workers themselves in regard to their earnings.

TABLE VI.

RANGE OF WAGES AND AVERAGE WAGES OF COLORED MEN SERVANTS IN PHILADELPHIA.

Sub-occupation.	Range of Wages.	Average Weekly Wage.*
Bell-boy, etc.	†$1.00— $4.50	$2.61
Butler	6.25— 13.50	8.24
Coachman	5.00— 14.00	8.58
Waiter	2.00— 8.00	6.14
Cook	1.00— 15.00	6.17
Valet	7.00— 10.00	8.00
General work	1.00— 10.00	5.38

* Computed on basis of reports from all individuals interviewed belonging to each sub-occupation.

† The figures given indicate the lowest and highest wages reported in each class, as reported by those interviewed in a canvass of 616 individuals in the Seventh Ward, Philadelphia.

[7] L. M. Salmon, "Domestic Service," p. 99.

The figures here given of course represent the *weekly* pay for the services classified; but such sums as $1.00 as the weekly pay for the service of a cook, or $2.00 as that of a waiter should be recognized as unusual and as recording facts which are far from typical, which represent the extreme of underpay offered only under extraordinary circumstances, probably to a young and inexperienced boy or to an aged or otherwise inefficient cook.

Table VII gives the same set of facts in regard to the earnings of women servants:

TABLE VII.

RANGE OF WAGES AND AVERAGE WAGES OF COLORED WOMEN SERVANTS IN PHILADELPHIA

Sub-occupation.	Range of Wages.	Average Weekly.†
Errand girls, etc.	*$0.00— $2.50	$2.00
Child's nurse	1.50— 10.00	3.35
Chambermaid	1.50— 4.00	3.17
Waitress	1.50— 4.00	3.31
Waitress and chambermaid	2.00— 3.50	3.17
Lady's maid	3.50— 4.00	3.63
Laundress	2.50— 7.00	4.04
Cook	2.50— 10.00	4.02
Cook and laundress	3.50— 5.00	4.00
Chambermaid and laundress	3.25— 4.00	3.58
Janitress	2.00— 7.00	4.06
General work	1.00— 5.00	3.24

* That is to say, "living and tips."
† The average is the actual average for all cases recorded.

These two tables show that in domestic service, as in every other department of the economic world, it is the office of skill or of trust which is the best paid. The offices of skill and trust among the men are those of butler and valet, or trusted personal attendant. Frequently the coachman is also butler. Comparison of the average pay of butlers with that of waiters or general work of " utility men," as they are called, shows very clearly the higher pay for skilled work. Men cooks' wages are here seen to be low in comparison with the butlers' or coachmen's, —this for several reasons: first, because in so small a number as were encountered one man receiving only $1.00 brings down the average appreciably; further, because in the wealthiest establishments almost no men-cooks were encountered. The majority of men-cooks reporting were employed in boarding houses, where presumably the pay was not allowed for on a lavish scale; but, finally and chiefly, wages of men-cooks are lower because a man servant who is a cook practically competes with the woman-cook. The services of an excellent woman can be gotten for $4.50 or $5.00, while no woman can take the place of a butler or coachman; hence butlers' wages are not affected by woman's competition. Doubtless the same tendency operates to lower the wages of waiters, now that such capable waitresses can be obtained. The same tendency is noticeable in England, where Mr. Booth says the butler is "giving place to the neat parlor-maid." In Table VII, showing women's wages, the skilled specialists are cooks and laundresses, while the office of trust is held by the janitress, and these are seen to head the list in the matter of pay, being the only women domestics who receive on the average more than $4.00. The Boston Employment Bureau publishes a list[8] showing the same thing. The average wages of cooks in Boston is given as $4.45, while chambermaids receive $3.86, waitresses $3.76, second girls $3.34 and general servants $3.16. The factotum, who does everything from cooking to furnace work and house cleaning, is evidently not considered a skilled hand, nor paid as such.

Secondly, these two tables also show clearly a very large difference between the pay of men and of women in domestic service; the men receiving on the average close upon 100 per cent more than the women. Miss Salmon's averages,[9] showing the wages of men and of women domestics throughout the country, are $167.96 yearly for women and $373.36 yearly for men. The difference here is more than 100 per cent. These figures, therefore, emphasize this difference between men's pay and women's pay, showing that men servants are generally paid more than double the wages which women accept.

Are wages in domestic service affected by race or color? How do theory and practice agree in this matter of wages?

---

[8] L. M. Salmon, "Domestic Service," p. 90.

[9] L. M. Salmon, "Domestic Service," p. 88, or see Table X, following.

How nearly does the wage which ought to be paid agree with the actual average pay of domestics? A comparison of the figures given in Table VII, with the standard of wages suggested by the ladies of the Philadelphia Civic Club in the letter already quoted, is interesting as showing the close agreement between pay which the best intelligence of the city believes to be just and the actual average wages of Philadelphia domestics. The following table compares these average wages with the Civic Club estimates:

TABLE VIII.

COMPARISON OF "THEORETICAL WAGES" WITH ACTUAL WAGES OF DOMESTICS IN PHILADELPHIA.

	Civic Club Estimate.	Actual Average Wage of Colored Domestics.
Cooks	At $3.50 or $4.00 per week.	$4.02
Waitresses	" 3.00 " 3.50 " "	3.31
Chambermaids . . .	" 3.00 " 3.50 " "	3.17
Child's nurse . . .	" 3.00 " 3.50 " "	3.35
Laundress	" 3.50 " 4.00 " "	4.04
Seamstress . . . . or Lady's maid . .	" 3.50 " 4.00 " "	3.63

This agreement points to the probability that among women in domestic service at least, there is no difference between "white pay and black pay," however much of it there may be in other departments of work in Philadelphia; for the Civic Club estimate is given for the whole field of service, white as well as black. Among men servants, however, there probably is a variation in wages determined largely by color. This first became evident on Rittenhouse Square,[10] where the colored butlers encountered were receiving on the average $36.90 monthly—(a slightly better wage than that of the Seventh Ward employes doing the same work), while the white butlers, according to the statement of one of their number, "generally get $40.00 to $45.00 a month in the houses that keep one man. Where there are two men—two white men—the first

[10] Rittenhouse Square is not in the Seventh Ward, but being probably the most fashionable quarter of the city, was investigated for purposes of comparison.

may get $50.00 and the second $45.00 ; but there are not many houses that pay $50.00." [11]

The variation in pay of colored and white butlers is probably partly due then to the fact already stated that there are relatively fewer white than colored men in service ; thus giving different ratios of supply and demand for white and colored men servants. But the matter of fashion counts much. It doubtless has more influence in determining the pay of an employee who is as much in evidence as is the butler or coachman than it has in fixing the pay of an "invisible employee" like the cook. The question of personal appearance and fashion holds also as between different grades of white employees, as will be seen from Mr. Booth's statements that in London "a second footman of five feet six inches would command £20 to £22, while one of five feet ten inches or six feet would not take under £28 or £30. Again, a short first footman could not expect more than £30, while a tall man would command £32 to £40." The same principle operating in Philadelphia often obliges colored men, like short footmen in London, to take what they can get. There is a relatively smaller demand for them for these two reasons, and so their pay varies from white men's pay, while among the women those cooks and maids who are the most skillful are in greatest demand ; so that color makes less difference in the women's wages.

Does "imported service" affect wages of colored domestic servants in Philadelphia ? There can be little doubt that in household service, where hardly anything else could have affected their secure hold on at least this one branch of employment, fashion has militated against the colored people of Philadelphia. A Spruce street colored butler said, "What are you

---

[11] The remainder of this conversation gives a side light on the reason for this difference in men's wages. The investigator, seeing this butler was communicative, said, "The colored butlers get less than that, I suppose you know, only $30 or $35, and a few get $40. Don't you think they make as good or better butlers and waiters than you white men do?" He laughed and said, "Yes, they're better at that than we are, and "— in a half-confidential, half-amused tone—"they aren't so lazy as we are. We're lazy, but they are always anxious to please, and they work harder 'an we do." "Well, why don't they get the same pay, then?" "Well," he said, stiffening, "but even if they do, you don't expect a white man is going to work for what a *nigger* will take. You can't expect *that*."

going to do when you're shut out of your work? I don't know no other country. I was born here. The colored are shut out more than when I come to Philadelphia in '65. The foreigners shut us out of even our ordinary work we've always done in service. I don't know why; because the colored people are just as good help as they ever was. And the worst is it throws them into the slums when they can't get their work. I've been praying the Lord to help our people," etc. A white butler on Rittenhouse Square sums up the situation from what might be called the impersonal point of view: "You see they (the employers) go to Europe and bring home Englishmen, and that knocks out the Negro." Many colored women— natives—say that it is harder now than formerly to get good places, because there are so many more white girls—foreigners— seeking household work.

It is difficult to reduce to figures information on this point, but the following enumeration which shows the distribution of colored service with reference to the fashionable quarter seems to confirm the opinions of the butlers quoted, or at least to indicate that the people who employ the greatest number of servants employ fewer colored people than are to be found in plainer establishments.

TABLE IX.

DISTRIBUTION OF COLORED SERVICE WITH REFERENCE TO THE FASHIONABLE QUARTER.

	Seven Blocks East of Broad Street.	Seven Blocks West of Broad Street.
On Spruce Street.	106 domestics, or 65 per cent of all colored domestic servants on Spruce Street.	58 domestics, or 35 per cent of all colored domestic servants on Spruce Street.
On Pine Street.	99 domestics, or 58 per cent of all colored domestic servants on Pine Street.	71 domestics, or 42 per cent of all colored domestic servants on Pine Street.

The smaller number of colored domestics employed in the fashionable section is noticeable both on Pine and Spruce streets, the number to the east of Broad on Spruce being very nearly double that in the more fashionable region to the west. The greater divergence of the ratios east and west is where we should expect it in accordance with the butler's theory—that is on Spruce, the more fashionable street.[12] On the whole, it seems probable that the fashion of importing English and French service has an appreciable effect in the direction of complicating Philadelphia's Negro problem.

"Importation" from the butler's point of view is easily explained. The willingness of English butlers to come to America is doubtless largely, indeed almost wholly, due to the fact that their absolute money wages are so much higher here than in England. Few of them are political economists enough to realize that $600 in America may be worth only half that sum in England. So glittering an offer as that of "double his present salary," is eagerly accepted by the majority of Englishmen of a certain grade of intelligence and this has quite definite results upon the domestic service of our large cities in America.

In the table which follows, the annual money wages of domestic servants in London are contrasted with the general yearly average wages for men's and women's work in thirty-seven of our States and also with the wages of colored domestic servants in Philadelphia.

TABLE X.

TABLE COMPARING ENGLISH AND AMERICAN "MONEY WAGES."

(*Annual Amounts Over and Above Board and Lodging.*)

Sub-occupation.		London.*	Colored Domestics in Philadelphia.	United States.†	Philadelphia.
Women.	Gen'l Servant	$77.50	$168.48	Average women's wages, $167.96.	Average woman's wages, $179.92.
	Housemaid .	82.50	164.84		
	Cook	109.50	209.04		
Men.	Errand boy . . .	55.00	135.72	Average men's wages, $373.36	Average colored men's wages, $335.40
	Footm'n, Coach'n	175.00	446.16		
	Butler	300.00	{ 428.48 (Colored) 540.00 (White)		

* Charles Booth, Vol. viii, pp. 217 and 223.

† Salmon, " Domestic Service," p. 28.

[12] In corroboration of this belief that colored men are displaced by imported English and foreign men servants comes the statement made to the investigator by the business manager of the Continental Hotel. He says that the Continental, which at the change of seasons often adds at one time as many as thirty colored waiters and bellmen to its force, "can always get as many colored waiters as are wanted at a few hours' notice," which certainly indicates that there are many unemployed colored men in Philadelphia who are anxious to work but are crowded out in the supply and demand adjustments.

The comparison here offered shows that in the most of the sub-occupations of domestic service the actual sums paid are twice as large in America as in London.

The range of wages in England as given by Mr. Booth also strengthens the belief that American wages must sound very large to English ears. " The actual wages earned," says Mr. Booth, on page 217 of his eighth volume, " begin as low as one shilling a week, this amount being received in three cases (out of a total of 1692 servants), while forty-two more were paid less than £5 per annum—at the other end of the scale we find three servants all over thirty years old, receiving from £26 to £36 a year, three more receiving £20 and £39, others receiving from £15 to £20." To an American this sounds far from lavish although it is of course impossible to know how much this money is worth until we know the cost of staple articles in London. Still,to a servant who has been receiving even £36 a year ($180), our highest women's wage ($520 yearly) would doubtless present remarkable attractions.

Do board and lodging enter into, or affect, wages? A comparison of the items of Table X shows a very large difference between the pay of American men servants and American women servants. This seems hardly to be accounted for by the fact that a much larger per cent of women in domestic service than of men receive board and lodging in addition to wages. Miss Salmon's investigation estimates that only 60 per cent of the men servants receive board and lodging while 98 per cent of the women do.

In the Philadelphia investigation the facts upon this point seem to indicate that the amount of wages is only slightly affected, if at all, by the question of board and lodging. When these are given in addition to wages they apparently do not stand, in the mind of either employer or domestic, as part payment for service. A comparison of the pay of women cooks who lodge at their place of work with that of women cooks who lodge at home will illustrate this. The average pay of those who lodge at their place of work,and therefore receive board and lodging in addition to wages, is $4.13 as contrasted with $3.95 received by those who go home at night. Here the difference will be seen to be in the opposite direction from what we should expect if board and lodging are reckoned as part of

the wages of cooks. The same facts hold good for the other
sub-occupations among colored domestic servants in the ward,
which would seem to indicate that in Philadelphia, at least, board
and lodging are customarily given or not according as it suits
the convenience or the preference of mistress or maid, but are
not, except rarely, considered a part of the wages paid for
service. Many employers doubtless believe that the service
rendered by girls who lodge in their place of work is better,
and they may perhaps consider the board and lodging given
as added pay for better quality of service. Be this as it may,
the actual money wages do not appear to be affected by it in
Philadelphia, where, as will be seen by the following table,
only 50 per cent of the colored women in service and only 24
per cent of the colored men lodge at their employers' establishments.

TABLE XI.

NUMBER AND PER CENT OF COLORED DOMESTIC SERVANTS, BY SEX,
IN SEVENTH WARD, WHO LODGE AT PLACE OF WORK.

Lodging Place.	MALE.		FEMALE.	
	No.	Per Cent.	No.	Per Cent.
At employers' house	38	24.4	207	50.7
At home or lodgings	118	75.6	201	49.3
Total	156	100.0	408	100.0

To the thoughtful and thrifty colored domestic this ought to
suggest an easy way of saving a good bit for the "old folks at
home" if they can only see it that way, for they reduce the
home expenses both for meals and for rent in many cases by
lodging at place of work, while they themselves receive the
same money wages and very likely higher ones, whether their
board and lodging comes out of their employer or is drawn
from their own home circle.

The majority of the single colored girls in service board and
lodge in their employers' establishments, only 38.7 per cent
of them going home at night; while most of the married
women in service, as is natural, do go home from work, only
27.5 per cent of them lodging in the employers' house. Of

the men reporting in regard to lodging place 29 per cent of the single men sleep at their places of work, while 71 per cent have lodgings elsewhere. Of the married men only 17.6 per cent lodge at the place of work while 82.4 per cent lodge at home.

V.

SAVINGS AND EXPENDITURE.

The question of the savings of Seventh Ward domestics
would naturally be discussed here. Table XII shows the
facts upon this point. It is based upon the records of those
who have been personally interviewed. In this table the
"societies" referred to are either sick benefit, death benefit, or
insurance societies, which are all very popular with the colored
people. Their tendency to use this method of saving rather
than to deposit in the bank is shown in many ways. They
frequently express their distrust of banks and banking. One
girl sums up her philosophy by saying, "I save in my pocket.
I'm a very poor spender, but I bank a little too, only the banks
are so shaky I'm afraid of them. A friend of mine lost $600
in the Keystone and I lost $100 and came near putting in
$50.00 just the day before the bank broke. Yes, I'm afraid of
banks." A waiter working on Spruce near Broad says, "I've
quit banking. I lost $300 in the Keystone." This distrust
of banks is traced by excellently qualified judges as far back
as the Freedman's Bank trouble, and it seems probable that
that first wave of distrust has been followed by a second one,
and that to the Philadelphia colored people the failure of the
Keystone stands for the same thing nearer home.

Table XII shows proportion of colored domestics who are
saving and who, therefore, not only are not a burden to the
community, but are adding something to the sum total of its
power. It shows also the methods of saving employed.

It will be noticed that the men do more banking in proportion than the women do, and less saving "at home" or by
means of the benefit societies. Three men use the bank where
one woman does, while three women save at home to one man
who does. It is also noticeable that the percentages of those
who do not save at all are about equal in both columns
of Table XII.

TABLE XII.

SAVINGS OF COLORED DOMESTICS IN PHILADELPHIA.

(*By Sex and by Method of Saving.*)

Method of Saving.	Per Cent of Men Who Save.	Per Cent of Women Who Save.
Saving in bank only	28.3	9.7
" in society only	20.7	30.2
" in bank and in society . .	18.6	15.9
" in society and owns property	3.5	1.2
" at home	6.2	15.9
" at home and society . . .	1.4	4.2
" in building association . .	2.1	.7
" in bank and owns property	. .	1.0
" in bank and society and owns property or has built a home	4.2	1.2
Not saving this year	. .	4.4
" " at all	15.0	15.6

In contrast with this 15 per cent which saves nothing, may be mentioned a few cases which seem particularly noteworthy as examples of unusual thrift :

1. The case of a young chore-man twenty years old, who said, " No, he wasn't saving any thing to speak of." And it would have passed at that, had not his employer said, " Why, Henry, you know you bring me $2.00 every month to save for you." And it came out that from the $14.00 he earned monthly he was regularly sending $5.00 each month to his aged mother and saving $2.00. The month before his report was taken he had sent $10.00 to his mother because she had had a destructive fire at home and needed new articles.

2. The case of a man cook thirty-one years old, who has been in his present situation over seven years, and earns $8.00 weekly. From this amount he has supported his family and built a home which he now owns. He also has a good bank account which, he says, his wife doesn't know about. He's " going to surprise her with it when he gets a good bit; or, if he dies she will have something to keep her." This man also has membership in two benefit societies.

3. The case of a young woman twenty-nine years of age, who receives $4.00 a week for cooking. She sends $10.00 a month to her mother who is a consumptive invalid and also "puts by" $2.00 every month.

4. A chambermaid, a widow fifty-three years old, who says, "I've got a little home in Virginia I bought and paid for myself." She earns $3.00 a week. She also has a bank account and belongs to a sick benefit society.

5. The case of a young woman of twenty-two years who "banks half she earns every week." She earns $3.50 weekly and saves $91.00 a year from her total yearly earnings, $182.00.

6. The case of a butler earning $35.00 a month, who owns five lots in Richmond, two more in New Jersey and one in Essington.

7. Another butler forty years old, who has been twenty-three years in the same family. He is paid $40.00 a month. He owns a Maryland stock farm which his uncle manages for him, several lots of land in south Philadelphia, has a term policy on which he pays $93.00 yearly and has membership in a sick benefit which insures him $10.00 a week in case of illness.

Perhaps the most popular way of saving among the colored servants of Philadelphia is now by means of the "society." Of all those reporting on savings 48.4 per cent of the men and 52.7 per cent of the women are saving in these societies. Whether this per cent of patronage of societies by domestic servants is greater or less than that for the whole community, very nearly two-thirds of all the women who save at all do so through one or more societies while the greater part of the other one-third do their saving at home, "in their pockets."

These societies, when they are *bona fide* insurance companies, often furnish fair investments to their contributors. A policy drawing a fee of $1.30 monthly when paid up entitles its holder to $10.00 a week in case of sickness. A policy drawing eighty cents a month entitles its holder to $5.00 a week sick benefit. These represent the sick benefit rates paid by two of the best and most reliable societies. The great value of such companies to such individuals as are subject to frequent illness and have no home for a refuge is clear at a glance. But it often happens that colored people who have iron constitutions will go into these societies and contribute year after year, reaping no benefit because they are never ill, and loath to stop paying their fees and begin to deposit in the bank for fear they should be ill. The fact that this sort of membership in sick benefits is a very *bad* investment was pointed out to a certain waiter on Pine street who had paid $30.00 a year for ten years into his two societies, but had never drawn a cent from either because he had never been sick. The fact that, had he banked his money he would have had now in hand the sum of $300, could not be denied, but this certainty was not sufficient to stifle the feeling that if he dropped the societies he " would lose all he had put in " and the question arising, " suppose I *should* be sick ?" which was not to be satisfactorily answered by statements of probabilities. The same thing, grown to greater proportions, is seen in the case of one quite aged butler, who for sixteen years has held policies in seven societies and has never drawn, except when his wife died. Many instances might be cited of domestics who have belonged to two or more societies for six years or more and have never drawn though their policies were paid up. Several instances were encountered of domestics who were saving in societies and also in the bank, and who when they were sick drew all their money out of the bank and " never thought of the society " and so did not draw at all, but exhausted their bank accounts and were then, presumably, helped by friends. One woman, who had been insured in one society for seventeen years and also held a sick benefit, exhausted her whole bank account and only drew on the society for two weeks (although she was ill some months) because she "didn't think of it" till she had spent all the money she had in the bank. All which goes to show how difficult it is for a people long unused to any financial responsibility to adjust their minds to it and how easy a matter it is for unscrupulous persons or societies to take advantage of their simplicity.

Assistance Given by Domestic Servants.—In connection with wages and savings may be considered the matter of assistance to dependents. Many colored domestics in Philadelphia either wholly support or very materially help toward the support of parents or other members of the family. Even, in many cases, taking entire care of more distant relatives, outside the immediate home circle.

The answers to Question 21 of the schedule (" Who besides yourself is supported by your wages?") were separated into four grades : (1) those wholly supporting one or both parents; (2), those helping parents ; (3), those wholly supporting others than parents ; (4), those helping, but not wholly supporting, others than parents.

In this matter, the men generally do less proportionately than the women. Of 187 men reporting on this point, 13, that is 7 per cent, are of the first class, who furnish from their earnings the whole support of one or both parents ; 40 (or 21.4 per cent) are of the second class, and are helping one or both parents; 25 (or 13.4 per cent), are of the third class, and are supporting some other member of the family, generally some younger brother or sister ; while 16 (or 8.6 per cent) are of the fourth class, and are helping, though not wholly supporting, some other member of the family; 8 (or 4.3 per cent) are doing more than one of these things; e. g., one young fellow of twenty years who earns only $3.00 a week, is responsible for the support of his father's entire family, seven in number, as the father drinks and can not be depended upon. One waiter, twenty-eight years old, receives $20.00 a month and is helping his own father and mother and both his wife's parents also. His wife too is earning, so what it practically amounts to is that the two young people are between them taking care of the four old people. The facts gathered in the Seventh Ward show 50.3 per cent of the men in domestic service are contributing toward the support of parents or others while 49.7 per cent have no one but themselves to look out for. These facts and similar ones for colored women domestics are here tabulated, 187 men in all reported on this subject and 420 women.

Table XIII presents approximately the actual condition in regard to responsibilities assumed for the help or support of parents and others. Whether the following table, which will show the proportion of wages thus given, is equally reliable, is an open question. It is difficult to estimate at a moment's notice what one spends or gives for any one object. To determine with any degree of accuracy the amount one

TABLE XIII.

NUMBER AND PERCENTAGE OF COLORED DOMESTIC SERVANTS IN PHIL-
ADELPHIA HAVING PARENTS OR OTHERS DEPENDENT ON THEM.

(607 Cases.)

		Support Parents.	Help Parents.	Support Others.	Help Others.	Total Having Dependents.	Total Independent Persons.
Men.	Number	13	40	25	16	94	93
	Per cent	7	21.4	13.4	8.6	50.3	49.7
Women.	Number	26	121	46	48	241	179
	Per cent	6.2	28.8	11	11.4	57.4	42.6

spends in a year for clothing is not always an easy thing to do.
So the answers given must involve a large amount of involuntary misstatement. The following table, therefore, may be
taken with allowances. It gives the result of many averages
thus hastily struck by the domestics interviewed, and shows
the number and percentage of colored servants who regularly
give one-half, more than one-half or less than one-half their
wages toward the support of those dependent on them.

TABLE XIV.

NUMBER AND PERCENTAGE OF COLORED DOMESTIC SERVANTS OF
PHILADELPHIA SUPPORTING OTHERS, BY SEX AND
PROPORTION OF WAGES GIVEN.

		Giving One-half Total Earnings.	Giving Less than One-half.	Giving More than One-half.
Men.	Number . . .	7	22	7
	Per cent . . .	3.7 (of 187)	11.8	3.7
Women.	Number . .	30	71	29
	Per cent . .	7.1 (of 420)	16.9	6.9

Many who do help their parents and others report that
they "can not estimate how much it takes." Fifteen, however, who give no estimate as to proportion of wages given,
say very plainly that it "takes all I make," or, it "takes everything but eno' to clothe me." One married man of forty

is supporting his " sister's little girl," who, he says, is "like an adopted child to us. Her father and mother are living but they have three or four besides her to support." This man earns thirty dollars a month, on which he supports his own family and his sister's little girl, and is also saving in the bank and has a one-dollar fee in a sick benefit society.

One young "waiter-man," earning twenty-five dollars a month, is "making a home for his mother" and helping three sisters besides. But none of these cases appear in Table XIV, since none of them could give any kind of an estimate of the proportion of earnings given. That considerable was given in each of these cases, however, is obvious, and many similar instances might be cited. It is almost invariably true of bell boys and errand boys and girls that they take their entire earnings home to their parents to swell the general store. One young bell boy said that he "took all he earned home to his mother except twenty-five cents he kept himself and she saved that for him."

Summary.—A large part of the earnings of the colored domestics of the ward are thus seen to go towards the support of parents and dependents. This generosity towards their own will be attested, it is believed, by everyone who has had any considerable knowledge of the colored people. When one remembers that the same thing is noticeably true of the Jews, the thought naturally occurs that it is perhaps an instinct of self-preservation, which reveals itself among oppressed races.

Again, that with a majority of Negroes, some part of their earnings are steadily " put by for a nest egg "—to use one of their own quaint expressions—will doubtless be similarly attested. There is of course much extravagance among Negroes. Much is doubtless spent for amusement, much certainly goes for finery. These outlays are comparatively large with some among the colored domestics of Philadelphia, although the facts which came to the knowledge of the investigator during these nine months in Philadelphia seemed to indicate that, speaking broadly, the colored domestics of that city are a thrifty class of people.

VI.

AMUSEMENTS AND RECREATIONS.

There can be little doubt that the monotony of the life of a domestic employee is one of the chief obstacles in the way of many competent workers who, but for this, might enter service as a permanent employment. Although household work is less arduous than many other forms of manual labor, yet it is true of it more than of almost any other occupation that it demands practically the whole of the worker's time. Nearly all of the restaurant waiters interviewed have "only two hours at a time," and it will readily be understood that with their leisure so broken they find it difficult to employ it to any very great advantage, either in the direction of study or of recreation. The liberty of the "private waiter" (except on his day out) is even less than that of the hotel waiter. Household work is a ceaseless round which, like woman's work, is "never done." And the private domestic, even when given considerable liberty and free time while within the household, must always hold himself in readiness to answer any call at a moment's notice. All this is a very serious objection in the minds of most young people, who, as has been seen, constitute the greater part of domestic service everywhere. Without doubt it deters many whites as well as blacks, and many rural as well as urban people, from entering household service. Indeed, it is probable that it determines in a very considerable degree the personnel of domestic service in England as well as throughout the United States, and somewhat modifies its character in the matter of permanence, as many English girls prefer factory work, and many girls in our cotton-growing and grape-raising regions, as well as in our factory towns, prefer field and factory work when it is to be had, and only fall back into the ranks of domestic service when the season is passed or factory work slack. Of the restlessness of household servants in England, Mr. Booth says: [13] "Many of this class (the middle grade)

[13] Charles Booth, vol. 8, chapter on Household Service.

only go to service when factory work is slack. They almost universally stipulate for one whole day's holiday in every month—indeed, with most of them, this seems to be the one thing which makes the servant's life worth living. . . The dullness and monotony of a domestic servant's life seems to be the most generally pressing question. The demand is for more Sundays and evenings out and a monthly holiday. . . Careful mistresses assert that they find that even quite young girls fresh from the country chafe under any restriction as to the manner in which they shall spend their leisure, or as to being out late alone.''

The same tendencies are noticeable throughout American domestic service, both with native whites, foreign whites, and colored domestics. This dissatisfaction is shown by the restless attempts of domestics to enter other occupations. Among American domestic employes the country over, 28 per cent are found to have been engaged in other occupations, such as hoppicking, grape- and cotton-picking and factory work.[14] That these people are now employed in domestic work, Miss Salmon believes, means not so much a preference for service as that it is a sort of *dernière ressort* to be taken up only when no better paid or more popular work offers. For the other kinds of work named the employes get wages so high as to enable them to live for a considerable time in idleness —hence its popularity among young people in many places.

Among the colored people in the city of Philadelphia, 524 domestics report in regard to other occupations. Of this number 91, or 17.4 per cent, have done, or attempted to get the opportunity to do, other work than domestic service, and it is noticeable that the employment which has occupied this 17.4 per cent of colored domestics has been very different in character from the field and factory work attracting young domestics in general. Among colored city domestics, the work done by the women before entering service has very generally been dressmaking, typewriting or teaching, while the men have worked as porters, or drug clerks, or have practiced trades or even professions. One man was encountered who had graduated from Hampton and from a law school as well, while several stone-

---

[14] L. M. Salmon, ''Domestic Service,'' p. 110.

cutters, brick masons and carpenters were found who had drifted or been forced into the ranks of domestic service.

The chief difference between the case of these Negro domestics in the city and the case of the grape-pickers and factory hands both in England and America who have tried to leave service for other work is indicated by the widely different character of the work sought in each case. The grape- and cotton-pickers and the factory hands leave service only temporarily, lured by the high wages and the "liveliness" of the work, fully expecting all the time to return to service when the harvesting is over and their wages spent; while the colored city employes who attempt to get other work wish to leave domestic service permanently. They wish to do this partly because they consider that service savors of slavery and that they are degraded by it, and, being ambitious of achieving respectability, they attempt to better their social standing by becoming teachers or dressmakers; partly also because they hope for higher wages from teaching and other work than they receive as domestics. The difference between the proportion of servants the country over who have done other work and the proportion of colored domestics in Philadelphia who have done or attempted to do other work is a large one. Twenty-eight per cent of general domestic service as contrasted with 17.4 per cent of colored domestic service shows a difference which is almost in the ratio of five to three. And also it must be remembered—and this accentuates the difference still further—that the colored servants who have tried to get other work and failed have also been counted, since the attempt showed their restlessness in service and their desire to leave it. There must be some reason for this apparent willingness to remain in service on the part of the colored people. In answer to the schedule question, "Have you ever tried to do other work?" a large number of domestics replied, "I never go any place I'm not sure of —I won't give them a chance to refuse me." One girl who had taught for four years and who thinks she lost her place at the end of that time from prejudice on the part of the school committee says, without the slightest apparent touch of resentment, "The reason I don't try to teach is because I know I'd have trouble, and I can save as much this way." Another ex-teacher has now been a chambermaid for several years for the same reason.

One Philadelphia carpenter and builder says, " We have five granddaughters—my son's children—from twenty-three years old to fourteen; and what can we do with them? They can't get teachers' places, though they are good students. Dressmaking is about played out. Service? They don't want to do *that.* Typewriting is about the only hope, and the oldest one was refused that the other day."

One man, now a waiter, was formerly a stock clerk for the Eureka Silk Company, of Cincinnati, Ohio, and held his place there for seven years. At the end of that time he applied by letter for a similar position in Philadelphia, and was told to " come along ; everything was satisfactory ; his record was good and they would try him." When he appeared in person they inquired, " Are *you* Mr. ——— ? " . . . " Well, we have another applicant on file who is coming around to-day. If we don't decide on him we'll let you know." He left his address and has not heard from the firm since. He says, " Waiting is all we can get to do, and lots will refuse us that. No man as dark as I am could get work at one of the large apartment houses. They want a ' bright skin.' It is the same in many hotels, and families, too." Another man states that when he applied for office work the clerk to whom he addressed his remarks looked at him and did not answer him at all ; while yet another, a fine looking young man of the type called a " brown skin," said he had been refused clerk's work with insults, which " it would be impossible for him to repeat before a lady—words he would not soil his lips with." Fortunately, however, this is becoming less common. When colored domestics are refused it appears to be generally with the simple statement that white help is preferred. It should be said here that among those who said that they had never attempted anything except domestic employment, fifty-two, or about 10 per cent, have even been refused domestic work when applying for it. Some of these were inclined to charge the refusal to race prejudice; some attribute it to the fact that unintelligent employers class all colored people together; or, to put it in their own words, " If the mistresses has bad luck with one colored girl they won't never have another. They think all colored is alike." Still others think it is not a race question at all, but merely one of supply and demand. As one man put it, " There isn't work enough or places enough to go round ; that's it." There are many well-authenticated cases also of "light" colored people who have retained their places from two to fifteen years, under the impression, on the part of the employer, that they were white people ; but on the discovery of the slight tincture of African blood, although it could not be detected, and although the work had been entirely satisfactory, their situations were immediately forfeited. Such instances might be multiplied indefinitely, as they were encountered upon every hand.

In consideration of all this, it appears highly probable that the Negroes are deterred in many cases from attempting to obtain other work, from unwillingness to run the risk of insult or failure. The moral certainty of "having trouble" is probably sufficient to account for the comparatively low percentage of colored domestics who have attempted to leave service, while the well-known fact that so many industries are closed against the race would account in large measure for the scarcity of those who have actually been engaged in other employments. These facts are sufficient to explain the 10.6 per cent difference in the two percentages compared.

Judging by the character of the work sought by the domestics who have left or attempted to leave service, it seems fair to conclude that,while the monotony of service and the low pay, as compared with harvest wages, are the chief things that rural American servants have against it, probably the chief objection of colored city domestics against service is the social stigma which rightly or wrongly attaches to it. It savors to them of the degradation of their slavery days, while they believe that to be a teacher is to achieve immediate social position and become a respected member of the community. Colored city domestics seek other work, therefore, from the desire to escape social degradation first, from the desire for greater personal freedom next, and finally from the hope of higher remuneration.

But while the social stigma is the city Negro's chief objection to domestic service there can be no doubt that from his point of view this dullness of the life is one of its most serious drawbacks—the most serious probably with the exception of the one already named. That the monotony of service is as keenly felt by the colored people as by any other domestics may easily be inferred both from the well-known fact of the natural

joyousness and gaiety of the Negro's disposition, and also from
the fact,shown in Table XI, that so large a proportion of them,
as compared with other domestics, stipulate for the freedom of
their evenings.   It was found from schedules relating to 564
cases that 75.6 per cent of all the Negro men servants interviewed and 49.3 per cent of all the women servants go home
from work.   When this is contrasted with the per cent of
domestic servants the country over who go home from work,
we find a remarkable divergence.   In general service [15] 40 per
cent of the men and only 2 per cent of the women lodge at
home, that is to say, outside the establishment of the employer.
This seems to show clearly the greater tendency of the colored
domestic to escape from the solitary confinement to which our
present system of household management condemns all the
servants in " single-handed " places.   It should be marked,
however, that the per cents relating to Philadelphia colored
people here are based on less than 600 schedules, while those
relating to general service are based upon over 2500.   Also, it
is much oftener the case among colored domestics that they
work in the same city in which their families and friends live,
while many white women domestics have no home nearer than
Ireland or Sweden, and so they naturally lodge at their working places, while the colored women as naturally lodge at home
when it is possible to do so.

Questions will arise as to the amount of leisure time usually
granted to colored domestics and how this leisure is employed.

It would be impossible to tabulate the statements returned in
answer to the question, "Number of hours free each month,"
but it may be said in general that a very great number of different arrangements obtain even in this one ward of one city.
The most of them include one afternoon each week and the
evening or the afternoon and evening of alternate Sundays.   For
the greater number of both men and women domestics report
this amount of leisure while some are allowed only one
afternoon and every third Sunday or one afternoon and every
fourth Sunday.   Still a considerable number are given the
usual afternoon of a week day and *every* Sunday afternoon
as well.   Some have their afternoon and alternate Sundays

---

[15] L. M. Salmon, "Domestic Service," p. 92.   Based on 2545 cases.

and one or more evenings, and a considerable number have this arrangement with the freedom of *all* their evenings. While still others have two afternoons weekly and alternate Sundays. The whole holiday every month which is so dear to the English household servant is not found in American domestic service. No Negro employe in the Philadelphia ward investigated reported such a whole holiday, however liberal might be the leisure granted in the shape of parts of different days; and Miss Salmon's treatment of the subject mentions no whole day of leisure for domestics, but states that "in the case of more than 1000 employees at least one afternoon each week is given, while more than 400 employers give a part of Sunday."

The question how their leisure is employed was answered by only 257 colored domestics, of whom 206 were women and only 51 were men. It will be seen from the tabulation of these returns that the Negro church is very closely bound up with the problem of the recreations of the Negro people, and in this connection a word of explanation is necessary to acquaint the general reader with the status of the Negro church. To quote from a well-known American scholar and writer who is an authority upon race questions : " Among most people the primitive sociological group was the family or at least the clan. Not so among American Negroes ; such vestiges of primitive organization among the Negro slaves were destroyed by the slaveship. In this country the first distinct voluntary organization of Negroes was the Negro church. The Negro church came before the Negro home ; it ante-dates their social life, and in every respect it stands to-day as the fullest, broadest expression of organized Negro life. . . . We are so familiar with churches, and church work is so near to us, that we have scarce time to view it in perspective and to realize that in origin and functions the Negro church is a broader, deeper and more comprehensive social organism than the churches of white Americans. The Negro church is not simply an organism for the propagation of religion ; it is the centre of social, intellectual and religious life of an organized group of individuals. It provides social intercourse, it provides amusements of various kinds, it serves as a newspaper and intelligence bureau, it supplants the theatre, it directs the picnic and excursion, it furnishes the music, it introduces the stranger to the community, it serves as a lyceum, library and lecture bureau ; it is, in fine, the central organ of the organized life of the American Negro, for amusement, relaxation, instruction and religion.   To maintain its pre-eminence the Negro church has been forced to compete with the dance-hall, the theatre and the home as an amusement-giving agency.   Aided by color proscription in public amusements, aided by the fact mentioned before—that the church among us is older than the home—the church has been peculiarly successful, so that of the 10,000 Philadelphia Negroes whom I asked, ' Where do you get your amusements? ' fully three-quarters could only answer, ' From the churches.' '' [17]

This centralization of amusements about the church shows itself very conspicuously in the following tabulation based on 257 records :

TABLE XV.

LEISURE TIME OF COLORED DOMESTICS—HOW EMPLOYED.

Usual Recreation.	MALE.		FEMALE.	
	No.	Per Cent.	No.	Per Cent.
Church and church entertaiments and at home	4	7.8	69	33.5
Church and visits to friends	11	21.6	22	10.7
Church and home (occasional concert or theatre)	4	7.8	15	7.3
Church and study	10	19.6	29	14.1
Theatre, concerts, balls, bicycling, etc.	5	9.8	10	4.8
Home resting (women " home resting and sewing ")	17	33.4	61	29.6
	51		206	

If these figures may be taken as typical nearly 57 per cent of the Negro men and nearly 66 per cent of the Negro women in domestic service look to the churches and the church entertainments for all their recreations except those engaged within the precincts of their own homes, such as home studies, music and social visits.   Indeed the number who depend upon the

[17] Dr. W. E. B. DuBois, in the ''College Settlement News,'' Philadelphia, July, 1897.   See also page 197 *et seq.*, in this volume.

church in this matter should be even greater than these figures
indicate, since it is true that many of those reporting that they
spend their leisure "at home, resting," or "at home, sewing
and clearing up," also in most cases report in answer to question twenty-three of the schedule, the church of which they
are members and whose regular services they regularly attend.
Of the seventeen men reporting that their leisure is spent in
"resting up" only two report that they attend no church and
of the sixty-one women thus classified only four attend no church.
If we count these "at home" domestics then where they really
belong, with the church-goers, we shall have 93.2 per cent of
the women and 86.3 per cent of the men among domestics who
depend on the church for their lectures, libraries, musicales,
festivals, etc., as well as for their religious instruction and
uplift. This gives a combined average of 91.8 per cent of all
colored domestics whose usual entertainment and instruction is
of this kind.

A comparison of the per cents of those whose leisure is
chiefly devoted to study shows that 19.6 per cent of the men
are so classified to 14.1 per cent of the women. Nearly a
third of the women so classed are music students; and if these
are counted out we shall have only 9.7 per cent of the women
domestics devoting their leisure chiefly to study and reading.
One young waiter, a West Indian, was devoting his spare time
to the study of English and meantime was taking his directions
from his employer in French. Another waiter reported that
he read "the classics" in his spare hours, and still another
confessed to a fondness for "the poets" while at the same time
he offered a pleasing contrast to many of the poets he admired,
in having his collar and white tie and complete costume quite
faultlessly neat and well ordered. The mistress of one household says, "Our waiter has the education of a gentleman,"
but on the other hand one employer whose judgments were
evidently free from bias says, "Our man may be a good lawyer
but he certainly is not a good waiter." This was however
the only adverse criticism offered in regard to any of the
domestics who were students and readers. It appears that
educated domestics are generally no worse workers than others,
if they are no better. In at least two cases it appeared that
the educated domestic did better household work than others.

These were a cook and maid whose employer said both her girls read a great deal and apparently spent their time upon good literature; her cook was then reading "Hyperion," she said. The question naturally followed, "Is she a good cook?" "Yes, I have never had a more efficient girl" was the ready reply, "and I have employed both white and colored. These are two of the cleanest girls I have ever had in the house."

Several of the women servants reported their leisure devoted chiefly to "literaries," all of which, so far as the investigator was able to learn, were connected with the churches. These students and readers among domestic servants doubtless are the more ambitious ones who are anxious to improve every opportunity with the hope of finally working their way out of service. This high per cent of readers among colored domestics, 20 per cent of the men and 10 per cent of the women, ought not to be surprising, however, when we remember that 10 per cent of these people have had some training higher than the common school and might therefore be expected to have literary taste.

In regard to the home-keeping domestics, if the first and last classes in Table XV be combined, we find 41.2 per cent of home-keeping women domestics who are either at home or at their churches during their leisure time. At the Pennsylvania Hospital the investigator was informed by one of the officials in charge that more late passes were given to the white than to the colored servants, and there are about equal numbers of each race employed.

The church affiliation of colored domestic servants in Philadelphia may be given in this connection. Reports from 548 persons were received on this point, 400 women and 148 men. The following table shows the various denominations by number and per cent :

TABLE XVI.

CHURCH AFFILIATION OF COLORED DOMESTICS IN THE SEVENTH
WARD OF PHILADELPHIA.

Church.	MEN.		WOMEN.	
	No.	Per Cent.	No.	Per Cent.
Methodist	63	42.6	184	46.0
Baptist	52	35.1	160	40.0
Episcopal	14	9.4	24	6.0
Presbyterian	5	3.4	7	1.7
Catholic	10	6.8	18	4.5
Attending all churches	2	1.4	6	1.5
Attending no church	2	1.3	1	0.3
Total	148	100.	400	100.

These per cents are united into combined averages and represented in graphic form in the following diagram :

DIAGRAM SHOWING CHURCH AFFILIATION OF THE COLORED DOMESTIC
SERVANTS OF THE SEVENTH WARD OF PHILADELPHIA.

VII.

LENGTH AND QUALITY OF NEGRO DOMESTIC SERVICE.

In regard to length of service, we have 284 reports from men employed in domestic service, and 591 from women, 875 altogether.

Of these 213 are from men personally interviewed, and since this question was uniformly asked, these 213 reports will represent the service of the rank and file of men servants.

The remaining 71 were recorded upon the family schedules, and were obtained, therefore, from the statements of their parents or sisters, and since no question regarding length of service appears in the family schedule, this information was evidently volunteered. From this fact it seems probable that the length of service in these 71 cases was put forward as being something unusual, as indeed it is, including as it does, 7 records of 10 to 15 years service with one family, 12 records of 16 to 20 years, and 10 records of over 20 years of service, one coachman having served 41 years in the same family. In view of the nature of this information it has been kept separate from the other records and dealt with by itself in order to avoid misrepresentation of facts.

The service periods shown in these 71 records range from 2 to 41 years, the average service period being 11 years and 5 months.

TABLE XVII.

(Domestic Service.)

SERVICE PERIODS OF SEVENTY-ONE "LONG-SERVICE MEN" IN THE SEVENTH WARD OF PHILADELPHIA.

Service Periods (in years)	1-5	6-9	10-15	16-20	Over 20.
Number of men servants	20	22	7	12	10

The following table (No. XVIII) gives the nativity of these 71 "long-service men."

TABLE XVIII.

(*Domestic Service.*)

NATIVITY OF SEVENTY-ONE "LONG-SERVICE MEN" IN THE SEVENTH
WARD OF PHILADELPHIA.

Birthplace.	Number.	Per Cent.
Philadelphia	6	8.5 } 18.4
Pennsylvania	7	9.9
District of Columbia	7	9.9
Maryland	15	21.1
Virginia	20	28.2
Delaware	5	7.0
New Jersey	3	4.2
North Carolina	4	5.6
The South	3	4.2
New York	1	1.4
Total	71	100.

Here the 18.4 per cent from Philadelphia agrees with the
Philadelphia percentage in Table II, and also the 28.2 per cent
from Virginia corresponds very nearly with the parallel record
in that table which shows 27.9 per cent of the total domestic
service of Philadelphia coming from Virginia. Turning to
consider the pay of these long-service men, it is found that of
these 71 men 20 are coachmen, while 51 are "private waiters."
The following table gives their range of wages and average
wages. The general average wage will be seen to approach
close upon $9.00 a week.

TABLE XIX.

(*Domestic Service.*)

WAGES OF SEVENTY-ONE "LONG-SERVICE" MEN IN THE SEVENTH
WARD OF PHILADELPHIA.

Sub-occupation.	Range of Wages.	Average Weekly Wage.
Coachman	$8.00-$14.00 (weekly)	$10.74
Private waiter . . .	4.00- 10.00 "	8.10
	General average wage	$8.84 (weekly)

With these facts concerning service periods, nativity and wages of "long-service men," it may be interesting to compare the same facts for the men of the rank and file. With the "rank-and-file men" the service periods vary from a few days to 31 years, the average period being 4 years 6 months and some days, a considerable contrast with the 11 years and 5 months of the long-service men.

In the following table the nativity of the long-service men and that of the rank-and-file men are brought together:

TABLE XX.

(*Domestic Service.*)

NATIVITY OF "RANK-AND-FILE MEN" COMPARED WITH NATIVITY OF "LONG-SERVICE MEN" IN THE SEVENTH WARD.

Birthplace.	Per Cent of Rank-and-File Men.	Per Cent of Long-service Men.
Philadelphia	13.8 } 19.7	8.5 } 18.4
Pennsylvania	5.9	9.9
District of Columbia . .	7.2	9.9
Maryland	15.1	21.1
Virginia	34.2	28.2
Delaware	6.6	7.0
New Jersey	2.6	4.2
North and South Carolina . .	5.3	5.6

In this table as in previous ones, Maryland and Virginia are seen to be far in the lead in the matter of furnishing the domestic service of the Seventh Ward of Philadelphia. Here indeed, the Virginia record rises to a number almost twice as great as that furnished by both Philadelphia and Pennsylvania taken together; although the percentage from the State here practically agrees with that of the long-service men. The facts in regard to range of wages and average wages of coachmen and private waiters in the "rank and file" of service in the Seventh Ward are given in Table XXI, which follows:

TABLE XXI.

(*Domestic Service.*)

WAGES OF "RANK-AND-FILE MEN" IN THE SEVENTH WARD OF
PHILADELPHIA.

Sub-occupation.	Range of Wages.	Average.
Coachman	$5.00 to $14.00	$8.58
Private waiter . . .	2.00 to 8.00	6.14
	General average	$6.55 (weekly)

A comparison of this with the average pay of the "long-service men" (whose average coachman's wage is $10.74, while their average waiter's wage is $8.10 and their general average wage is $8.84, nearly $9.00), would seem to point to the possibility that length of service may have some occult connection with length of pocketbook, and that the "giving satisfaction" may not be all on one side of the line in the domestic service question. Of course it is true that a bad servant can not command high wages, also it is impossible to transform a poor servant into a good one by paying him high wages; but, on the other hand, it is true that good service can not be obtained without paying good wages for it.

Schedules giving service periods of colored *women* employed in the Seventh Ward show 591 records, only six of which were volunteered as unusual, as in the case of the long-service men given above; in view of the smallness of this number these six schedules have not been dealt with separately; but the women who have served five years and over have been isolated, irrespective of the manner in which the information was obtained, and their statements separately treated as in the case of the long-service men.

These "long-service women" who have served five years and more show 178 records; the range of service periods is from five to thirty-five years, the average being six years and eight months.

The range of service periods of "rank-and-file women" varies from one day to five years, while their average service period is found to be three years and six months, only about one-half the service period of the long-service women.

Their nativity and that of the "rank-and-file women" are given together for purposes of contrast and show the following facts:

TABLE XXII.

(Domestic Service.)

NATIVITY OF "LONG-SERVICE WOMEN" COMPARED WITH NATIVITY OF "RANK-AND-FILE WOMEN" IN SEVENTH WARD.

Birthplace.	Per Cent of Long-service Women.	Per Cent of Rank-and-File Women.
Philadelphia	12.0 } 20.3	12.8 } 18.8
Pennsylvania . .	8.3	6.0
District of Columbia	3.0	4.6
Maryland	20.3	20.5
Virginia	27.1	34.8
Delaware	14.3	6.5
New Jersey	6.8	4.1
N. and S. Carolina .	3.0	4.3
South	3.7	4.2
Scattering	1.5	2.2
	100.	100.

According to this record a greater proportion of "long-service women" come from Philadelphia and Pennsylvania, which is not the case in Table XX, contrasting nativity of the men.

The following tables show the range of wages and average wage for each of the classes of women servants here considered:

TABLE XXIII.

(Domestic Service.)

WAGES OF "LONG-SERVICE WOMEN" IN THE SEVENTH WARD OF PHILADELPHIA.

Sub-occupation.	Range of Wages.	Average Wage.	
		Weekly.	Monthly.
Cook (or laundress)	$3.00– $7.00	$4.21	$18.22
Chambermaid (or waitress) . . .	3.00– 4.00	3.50	15.17
General housework	1.50– 10.00	3.50	15.17
	Gen'l average wage	3.67	15.90

(In this table and the one following 4⅓ weeks have been reckoned to a month.)

TABLE XXIV.

(*Domestic Service.*)

WAGES OF "RANK-AND-FILE WOMEN" IN THE SEVENTH WARD OF PHILADELPHIA.

Sub-occupation.	Range of Wages.	Average Wage.	
		Weekly.	Monthly.
Cook	$2.50–$10.00	$3.99	$17.29
Chambermaid	1.50– 4.00	3.21	13.91
General	1.00– 4.00	2.99	12.96
	Gen'l average wage	3.26	14.12

By comparing the last two tables it will be seen that the wage varies less between long-service and ordinary-service women than in the case of the men. The ordinary cook's wage, $3.99, compares more favorably with $4.21, the long-service cook's wage, than does $8.58, the ordinary coachman's wage, with $10.74, the wage of the long-service coachman, and the contrasts throughout will be seen to be less pronounced in the women's than in the men's wages.

But if the wage of ordinary service and long service varies less among the women than among the men, it must be remembered that the length of service varies less among the women than among the men. The average service periods of two classes of men servants are four years six months, and eleven years five months, the one being two and one-half times as great as the other; while the average service periods of the two classes of women are three years six months, and six years eight months, the one being not quite twice the other; hence, the narrower variations in wages of women as compared with those of men would corroborate the theory of the close connection of quality of service and consequent length of service with high wages, rather than weaken that theory. Also it is true that in spite of the occasionally greater range in the wages paid to the "rank and file," the average wages of the long-service domestics, both men and women, are uniformly greater than the average wages paid to the " rank and file." Combining the average service periods of the long-service domestics with those of the " rank and file " gives us a combined average of six years and one month as the average service period of colored men servants, and four years and five months as the average service period of colored women servants in Philadelphia. Again, uniting these averages of servants of both sexes in Philadelphia, gives the *combined average service period for all colored domestics* in the Seventh Ward of Philadelphia. This combined average service period is 4.96 years, that is to say, five years lacking less than one month. It is based on 875 records:[17]

This offers a decided contrast with the average length of service of domestics the country over, which average service period, Miss Salmon states, " is found to be less than one year and a half." [18]

This contrast in service periods may be made clearer by the following graphic representation, showing length of service period of Negroes and of general domestic service in the United States, given in terms of a common unit of length.

LENGTH OF SERVICE.

GEN'L SERVICE
(ALL DOMESTICS IN U.S.)
COLORED DOMESTIC SERVICE
(IN PHILADELPHIA)

These service periods will be seen to stand to each other in the ratio of about 3 to 10, and may have some connection with the relative numbers of white and Negro domestics. It may be that the Negro service period is three times as long as the average service period, because there are three times as

---

[17] Some time after the beginning of the investigation it was found to be practicable to get two records of length of service from each individual interviewed by adding the question, " How long were you in your last place ?" This question was then uniformly asked, which accounts for 875 records of length of service from only 616 people personally interviewed. It must also be noted that the average is high, partly because the number of cases is small and includes a few cases of exceptionally long-service periods.

[18] L. M. Salmon, " Domestic Service," p. 109.

many Negro servants proportionately, and therefore three times as many chances for capable servants to be found among them. Another possible explanation of the longer period of colored domestics may be their greater docility as servants. As one employer whose name is well known in Philadelphia circles has said of colored domestics: "If you get a good class of colored people they are the most faithful, honest and biddable servants in the world." This docility which is a recognized trait of the Negro character has doubtless been developed by slavery, and it is not unlikely that it has been still further cultivated in these later days by their knowledge that losing their places in service may mean inability to get work of any kind for an indefinite period. However, if we may judge from the remarks of a certain colored waitress upon length of service, the Negroes feel that there is a point beyond which docility and a respectful bearing cease to be virtues. As she had held her own situation for twenty-two years, her remark may fairly be taken as unaffected by personal considerations. She said: "Yes, they say long service is good service, but sometimes you can't *stay* at places ; some of the ladies an' gentlemen's not very *pleasant*." An employer, on the same point, says: "It isn't the servants any more than it is the mistresses who are responsible for the frequent changes of place." She thinks that "it varies with the individual, not with the race." Many of the employers who discussed the subject with the investigator said that their experience was that colored servants were "more respectful" (six said this), "less impertinent" (2), "very anxious to please" (2), "more agreeable and obliging and have nicer manners" (4).

A third possible explanation of the longer period of service among colored domestics may be found in the fact frequently adduced by their employers, that they "are much more likely than white girls to become attached to the family"—so they naturally stay longer in one place than others do. Another employer says: "When they become fond of you they are very staunch friends," and yet another, says of them : "They are *much* more loyal and infinitely more affectionate than white servants. They have shown me absolute loyalty in service." This is significant as being the testimony of a Northern woman who had "never seen a colored servant" before she was married and who employed them for the first time on coming to Philadelphia and now, after sixteen years, "would never have any one else."

The question whether one State or one section furnishes better domestics than another State or section is interesting, and has its bearing on the point under discussion. It is possible that the Philadelphia colored people represent a higher grade socially and intellectually, than the Negroes of the South—and so, in searching for an explanation of the connection between length of service and quality of service it may be suggestive and valuable here to compare the facts already tabulated in regard to nativity with the facts in regard to ordinary and extraordinary service, to see if any indication may be forthcoming as to the locality which furnishes the best quality of colored domestic service, whether Philadelphia and Pennsylvania or the South. Such a comparison may cast light on the moot question whether Philadelphians are more likely to be well served by Philadelphia colored people or by Southerners. In the table given below, therefore, the per cent of Philadelphia colored people among long-service and ordinary domestics is compared with the corresponding per cent of Virginia-born colored domestics. Virginia has been chosen to represent the South because it is the Southern State furnishing the greatest number of domestic servants in the Seventh Ward and is perhaps the State coming most sharply into competition with the native colored domestics.

TABLE XXV.

COMPARING QUALITY OF SERVICE (AS IMPLIED IN LENGTH OF SERVICE PERIOD) OF COLORED DOMESTIC SERVANTS OF VIRGINIA AND PENNSYLVANIA.

Birthplace.	RANK-AND-FILE DOMESTICS.		LONG-SERVICE DOMESTICS.	
	Av. Service Period, 3 yrs. 6 mos. (Women.)	Av. Service Period, 4 yrs. 6 mos. (Men.)	Av. Service Period, 6 yrs. 8 mos. (Women.)	Av. Service Period, 11 yrs. 5 mos. (Men.)
Philadelphia . . .	12.8 } 18.8	13.8 } 19.7	12.0 } 20.3	8.5 } 18.4
Pennsylvania . . .	6.0	5.9	8.3	9.9
Virginia	34.8	34.2	27.1	28.2
Proportion between Pennsylvania and Virginia . . . . (Approximately.)	$\frac{19}{35}$	$\frac{20}{34}$	$\frac{20}{27}$	$\frac{18}{28}$

The proportions of Pennsylvania and of Virginia service here shown, are approximately represented by the fractions $\frac{19}{35}$, $\frac{20}{34}$, $\frac{20}{27}$ and $\frac{18}{28}$, where the numerator in each case stands for Philadelphia servants employed in the Seventh Ward, and the denominator stands for Virginia servants there employed. When these fractions are reduced to the same scale they become $\frac{34884}{64260}$, $\frac{37800}{64260}$, $\frac{47600}{64260}$ and $\frac{41310}{64260}$. Here, as will be seen, the first and *smallest* fraction stands for the *shortest service period* (three years and six months); the second fraction for the next longer service period, and so on. The values of these fractions will be seen to increase progressively, excepting the last, so that the greater values correspond with the longer service periods. The values of these fractions then, when taken in connection with the increasing service periods, would seem to indicate that the greater the proportion of Philadelphia domestics as compared with the proportion of Virginia domestics, the more valuable is the service ; that is to say that Philadelphia-born colored people appear to render the more efficient service. It should be said that the fourth fraction in the above comparison, to be consistent with the theory offered, should be larger than the third, but it must be remembered that the fourth fraction is based upon only seventy-one records and is therefore less likely to represent the facts accurately than the others which are based on a much greater number of records.

Such indications as the above approach nearer to accurate treatment of the question of quality of service rendered than it is possible to get through quoting opinions of employers. The subject is hard to treat at all adequately for the reason that all statements of degrees of excellence or of incompetency must be based on the shifting sands of opinion and upon the opinions of many different people, having different traditions, different education and home influences, different degrees of insight and different standards of excellence. Statements so conditioned must necessarily be relative and impossible to reckon up and number with any semblance of statistical precision. Still the opinions of the employers of colored domestics in the Seventh Ward of Philadelphia, a large proportion of whom have employed both white and colored help, should have a certain interest and value, even though they are not reducible to figures.

Fifty-five employers [19] in the Seventh Ward stated their views in regard to the qualities of Negro domestics and many varying opinions, both favorable and unfavorable, were expressed. The balance of testimony from these fifty-five employers, how-ever, seems to be largely in favor of the colored people rather than whites, both in regard to the service offered and in the attitude of the employe toward the employer. Only one employer stated that she preferred white to colored; she was employing colored help at that time only because she had not been able to secure satisfactory white girls. Twenty employers say that they find colored domestics quite as neat as whites, while two find them not as neat and five find them more so; "much cleaner than the Irish both in their work and in their persons;""they keep their kitchen and their own room cleaner." Ten employers think they stay for as long or longer a service period, while seven think they do not stay as long as the whites. Fourteen employers think they render as good service as whites, and eleven think their service better, or "a great deal better;" while one—although employing three col-ored servants—thinks the whites do better work and says she has colored servants "because they look more like servants." She also thinks they drink more than the whites, an opinion which, so far as the present investigator can learn, she is unique in holding, since all the other employers who discussed the point held the opposite view.

One gentleman, the business manager of one of the large first-class apartment hotels which employs thirty dining-room men, names their freedom from intemperance as one of the chief reasons why he "decidedly prefers colored help." "They give more attention to their work," he says, "are better waiters and they drink less. They can be counted upon on pay day the same as any other day, while white serving men are likely to go and drink up their pay and be useless for the rest of the day." The business manager of the Continental says the same thing, as do also all the hotels which employ colored service.

A very few employers think colored domestics "are lazy and neglect their work," while more than four times as many say

---

[19] Most of whom have employed both white and Negro domestics.

that they are "industrious" and "good workers," "splendid workers," "a great deal better workers and decidedly better cooks than the whites." One employer says on this point: "No, I have not found them lazy, at least no more so than others; there are good ones and bad ones among both white and colored." Skill in cooking was mentioned by only six employers, all of whom think colored cooks superior to other servants in this respect.

Further judgments are: "They are excellent servants and have an intuitive knowledge of what you want;" "they *do* all the things white servants wait to be told to do." Several employers agree on these points, but one says: "They have to be told to do everything, but if you keep after them, you can get the things done." The testimonial of one cook upon the virtues of "her madam" will show this matter from the domestic point of view. This cook says, "My madam gives me the key, and she never comes down to see if I'm here in the morning; she knows I'll be here; and she never comes into the kitchen to see if meals are getting along, because she knows when half-past six o'clock comes she can trust her girls to have it ready right then." One mistress said: "Trust them, and I have found they *always* prove themselves worthy of trust." Eighteen employers concur in the view that they are trustworthy and do not disappoint confidence; while three think them unreliable and untrustworthy, as compared with white servants. On this subject one employer on Spruce street said: "I think the colored people are much maligned in regard to honesty, cleanliness and trustworthiness; my experience of them is that they are immaculate in every way, and they are perfectly honest; indeed, I can't say enough that is good about them." These sentiments were held by several other employers, one on Broad street using almost the same words: "I think the colored people are very much maligned in this matter of honesty and trustworthiness; I have two colored men now who are as honest as the sun, and my cook, who also does all the marketing, is very industrious and careful —painstaking. She is a good, faithful creature, and very grateful."

In regard to the question of the pilfering of food left from the table, the concensus of opinion is heavily against the colored people. There are only three employers who have anything to say in defence of them in this particular, and six against. Their defenders say: "After ten years of experience with the colored people, I have never had a colored servant take anything, even food;" the next: "We lost more food, etc., from the treating in the kitchen, which the Irish indulge in, than we have ever missed from pilfering of colored servants," and a third, who employs both white and colored servants, says: "I know it is frequently said that the colored people take food home from the kitchen, but I have not found it so." On the other hand it is said: "They are good servants, but they *will* carry things off;" while another says that they "take food; they don't mean to be dishonest, but they don't consider that stealing, and are perfectly honest about money." Another employer says: "Unquestionably they are light-fingered about food and sweetmeats; slavery has always clothed and fed them and taught them to help themselves; we think slavery is responsible for it." Another thinks "they are like children in temptation; they can't resist sweetmeats, but never take things of value." The other two employers who spoke on this point say practically the same thing: "They are honest; they take things to eat home, but they don't count that; we never lose anything valuable." The other calls them "thieves," but evidently means pilferers of food.

In regard to their honesty, the balance is as strongly with them as, in this question of purloining food, it is against them. Eighteen employers say they are honest, and not one states the opposite. Two of these find them "more honest than white servants," and two others, already quoted, say they are "perfectly honest," "as honest as the sun." Many remarks made by domestics themselves, in the course of conversation, might be quoted as casting light on the subject, but only two will be given here. One elderly colored man, who had been a school janitor in the west end of the ward for two years, and was nearly nine years in his former place, said: "Some people say if you put your hand in a man's pocket, you're stealing; they think that's the only way; but if you loaf two or three hours every day when your boss is paying you for working, I say you're stealing just the same—stealing his time; I say we only live one day at a time, and that one day we've got to do the same as if we'd just come to that place. In summer places I've seen them so triflin'—fooling away their time, and merely because the proprietor don't see them." The same spirit was shown by a woman cook on Broad street, who took pleasure in doing good work always for " her lady," whose kindness she enlarged upon with a warmth that showed a strong affection. This woman said: " When my time comes to go home from here, it will be a pleasant thought that I have done all I can to help my kind employer." These two cases imply not only honesty in the overt act, but an entire honesty of purpose. Many similar cases might be cited.

The question of the general bearing and manners of colored domestics was discussed by many of their employers. The general opinion of the employers is that they are "more willing and obliging" than white servants. As one employer says: "The Germans drink and the Irish order you out of the house, but the colored people are more respectful and anxious to please." "They are more agreeable and obliging and have nicer manners," says another employer, and adds: "When my sister was ill, the Irish maid I had at the time refused to carry up the breakfast tray, 'because,' she said, 'it was not her business to do nursing,' and she 'wouldn't do it for ten dollars.'" So the employer herself prepared and carried up the trays until the colored girl, who came soon after, volunteered her services with: "Let *me* take up the breakfast tray, Mrs. W——. You look ready to drop," and since she came, Mrs. W—— has never had a white girl in the house. That the colored people are more willing and obliging in manner is attested by twenty employers and denied by no one, while one employer, who is connected with the University, and has had years of experience, both with white and colored servants, says of the colored people: "Whether they are better or worse than the whites may depend upon what whites you have. We had white servants for seven winters, and always employed the best Irish servants we could get; but they were so unsatisfactory that we gave them up and tried colored servants. Our experience of them is that they are infinitely cleaner than the white Irish, both in their work and personally; they are more self-respecting and better mannered—more agreeable in manners; indeed, I have found them capable of the very highest cultivation of manner. One of our men has the education of a gentleman and is improving himself constantly; the other is ignorant, but is exceedingly refined and modest in manner. Of course they have faults; they are fickle, changing from place to place, even when they are fond of their employers, and they have quick tempers, but they are truthful and honest; we have never lost a thing by them. We keep them by preference, and shall continue to do so."

Several employers agree in regard to this instinct of the colored people for good manners. One who constantly employs nine servants, and in the last twenty-five or thirty years has had only one set of white servants says: "There is much more to them than people think; our first man servant has as many of the instincts of a gentleman as anyone I ever saw." This is high praise. "They have a native, deep-seated refinement and very lovely manners," says another who has employed them for fifteen years.

A judgment which was frequently encountered and always among those employers who had had experience of both white and colored servants was that colored servants are "just like other people of their own class." One employer says on this point: "I don't find a bit of difference; some are very neat and some are very untidy; it depends *entirely* on the girl." Another says: "There are good ones and poor ones among both; it varies with the individual, not with the race." Another, in charge of a large institution, employing many servants of whom half are white and half colored, says: "My experience has been very satisfactory with the colored; they are less impertinent, but in most respects are much like white people of their own class. One is about as faithful as the other, and in the matter of neatness they are just like other people; it is six of one and half a dozen of the other. As to trustworthiness I have found certain ones are perfectly reliable— just as with other human beings." Those who are interested in this subject will doubtless see that, although these opinions of employers have no statistical value, they will have a *practical* value for many readers, and especially if they open the eyes of the Philadelphia public, or even a small part of it, to the hitherto apparently unsuspected fact that there are grades among colored people, just as there are among white people;

TABLE XXVII.

(Giving Number and Per Cent.)

CONJUGAL CONDITION OF COLORED DOMESTIC SERVANTS IN PHILADELPHIA, BY SEX AND AGE PERIODS.

Conjugal Condition.	MALE.					FEMALE.				
	Single.	Married.	Widowed.	Divorced or Separated.	Total.	Single.	Married.	Widowed.	Divorced or Separated.	Total.
15 to 20 years	46 95.8%	2 4.2%	0 0	0 0	48 100%	246 89.8%	28 10.2%	0 0	0 0	274 100%
21 to 30 years	172 56.4%	129 42.3%	1 0.3%	3 1.0%	305 100%	369 52.9%	271 38.8%	45 6.5%	13 1.8%	698 100%
31 to 40 years	60 36.4%	99 60.0%	6 3.6%	0 0	165 100%	104 28.5%	162 44.5%	88 24.2%	10 2.8%	364 100%
41 and over	22 14.7%	114 76.0%	12 8.0%	2 1.3%	150 100%	45 17.2%	67 25.5%	142 54.2%	8 3.1%	262 100%
Age unknown	2	1	0	Unknown Conj. Cond. 6	9	2	5	5	Unknown Conj. Cond. 2	14
Totals.	302	345	19	11	677	766	533	280	33	1612

This comparison of the conjugal condition of white and of colored domestics may advantageously be reduced to graphic form for clearness. The first of these diagrams presents the facts of conjugal condition among American domestics servants of all nationalities, as recorded in the eleventh census, while the second presents the same facts relating to colored domestic servants in Philadelphia.

CONJUGAL CONDITION IN ALL AMERICAN DOMESTIC SERVICE.
(*Figures of Eleventh Census.*)

CONJUGAL CONDITION IN COLORED DOMESTIC SERVICE IN PHILADELPHIA.

A study of census statistics in connection with the results of this investigation seems to show a remarkably close parallel between the conjugal statistics of men servants, white and colored. The disproportionate number of single white women is accounted for by the great number of unmarried foreign-born white women in American domestic service. This study of the conjugal condition of domestic servants seems to corroborate the opinion of those employers who found colored people "very much like other human beings."

Illiteracy.—The following table of illiteracy is based upon 576 reports:

TABLE XXVIII.

ILLITERACY AMONG DOMESTIC SERVANTS, NEGROES, OF THE SEVENTH
WARD, PHILADELPHIA.

	Male.	Female.	TOTAL.	
			No.	Per Cent.
Illiterate.				
Cannot read or write	10	60	70 ⎫	20.7
Cannot write	5	44	49 ⎭	
Literate				
Able to read and write	109	267	376	65.3
Having a trade	7	11	18	3.1
Having a trade and some higher school training	3	7	10	1.7
Having higher school training	22	31	53	9.2
Total	156	420	576	100.0

This table shows 9.6 per cent of the men and 24.8 per cent
of the women in domestic service to be illiterate in some degree,
with a total percentage of 20.7 illiterate, either wholly or in
part, while 80 per cent of the colored men and women in domestic
service have at least a common school education. Fourteen
per cent of the total count will be seen to have had some training above that of the common schools, or to have attended an
industrial school.

The illiteracy of Negro servants is about 2 per cent greater
than that of the total Negro population of the Seventh Ward.
This is doubtless to be accounted for by the fact that 70 per cent
of colored domestic servants are women, and the illiteracy of colored women is uniformly greater than that of colored men.
This will be seen by glancing at the per cents of illiteracy for
colored men and women servants, 9.6 per cent as opposed to
24.8 per cent, and in the total population 14.2 per cent as opposed
to 24.1 per cent. In the whole population the sexes are about
evenly balanced in numbers; hence, in the general average for
the illiteracy of the whole population, the rates for each sex
would bear an equal part in the general result. A comparison
of these averages shows that the men in domestic service are
somewhat less illiterate than the men in the whole population, while the women in domestic service appear to be slightly
behind the women of the whole population.

The question will arise as to the relative illiteracy of Negro domestics and of other domestics the country over. It is interesting to make the comparison. The census of 1890 gives the percentage of male illiterates in domestic and personal service as 18.9. This is the rate for all men servants in America, ten years old and over and includes all nationalties, the native whites, foreign-born whites and colored. It is less creditable than the record of the Philadelphia colored population by nearly five points, the record for Philadelphia's male Negroes ten years old and over being but 14.2 per cent. And it is only about half as creditable as the record of colored domestic men servants, their per cent of illiteracy amounting to only 9.6. (The margin of error in the last is probably large, however, since it is computed upon but 156 cases.) The census shows for female domestic service the country over, including both native and foreign white, and colored women over ten years of age, a per cent of illiteracy amounting to 24.75. Among colored women servants in Philadelphia 24.80 are found to be illiterate. The whole colored population of Philadelphia improves slightly upon this, showing for its women and girls 24.1 per cent of illiteracy.

ILLITERACY OF COLORED DOMESTICS (PHILADELPHIA) AND OF ALL AMERICAN DOMESTICS, COMPARED BY SEX.

This comparison seems to indicate that the grade of intelligence of women servants, white and colored, is practically the same, while the colored men servants are of a higher grade of intelligence than are white men servants. The investigator is inclined to think that the average of illiteracy for colored men servants, though computed on so few records, fairly represents the real conditions. It is not difficult to account for the great difference in records of colored and of white men servants when one remembers the fact so often referred to, of the crowding out of competent and educated colored men, who have been clerks, teachers and skilled workmen, and who at one time or another have found themselves in a position where they were obliged to take domestic service or nothing. Large numbers of such men in the ranks of domestic service would bring down the percentage of illiteracy very decidedly. That it should reach the point of 9.6 per cent is very creditable to the colored men servants if the figures are correct, since the per cent of illiteracy for native white males is not quite four points ahead of it, being given by the census as 5.83 per cent.

Health Statistics for Domestic Servants.—The questions "Number of days sick in last twelve months?" "Nature of illness?" were answered by 547 domestic servants. The tabulation of their reports follows:

TABLE XXIX.

(Domestic Service.)

SICKNESS AND HEALTH DURING LAST TWELVE MONTHS, BY SEX.

Health Record.	MALE.		FEMALE.		TOTAL.	
	No.	Per Cent.	No.	Per Cent.	No.	Per Cent.
Not sick at all during last twelve months .	121	79.6	293	74.2	414	75.7
Ill one week or less . .	7	4.6	33	8.4	40	7.3
Ill more than one week	24	15.8	69	17.4	93	17.0
Total . .	152	100.	395	100.	547	100.

From this table it is seen that 80 per cent of the men have not been ill at all during the year; while among the women 74 per cent have been exempt from illness. It is noteworthy that the slightest illness appears to have been conscientiously reported upon, since very nearly one-third of the men reporting illness were cases of colds or other such slight troubles as kept them ill only a day or two; while rather more than one-third of the women also scrupulously reported such insignificant illnesses. In this paper, however, the example of the Commissioner of Labor has been followed and "colds" have not been counted at all. Wherever, therefore, an illness of one or two days is reported, it is of more serious nature than a mere cold.

Of the 547 persons reporting, 3.1 per cent report serious illness, of which 2.6 per cent belongs to the women and the remaining .5 per cent to the men.

The most prevalent troubles are consumption, la grippe, quinsy, sore throat, rheumatism, neuralgia, chills and fever, or dyspepsia and "inflammation," which latter term appears to be a general name for all discomforts of the inner domestic from indigestion to peritonitis and sudden death.

Of those reporting illness seven of the thirty-one men will be seen to have been ill one week or less ; while thirty-three of the 102 women were ill one week or less. One maid reports a severe attack of la grippe but she " worked all the same," losing not one day of work in the year. And Table VII will show that this is no uncommon fact but that several of those reporting illness lose no time from work. While the women's sick list shows thirty-three ill one week or less, it shows sixty-nine who have had longer periods of illness. Among the longest periods reported are the following : "Out of work for three months on account of trouble with the eyes, an operation for cataract ;" another, out three or four months on account of weak lungs, says : " I never can work more than a few weeks to a time;" another, laid up three months with a sprained ankle ; another, "sick from March to Christmas with rheumatism ;" another, "four months sick with rheumatism, but worked ;" another, five months sick with nervous shock caused by sudden death of her husband in an accident ; one man has chills and fever from time to time all the year round ; another, "had rheumatism all winter but lost no working time." A comparison of the length of illness tabulated below will show that the records just quoted are unusual. Table XXIX gives the complete record of those who report illness within the past twelve months.

TABLE XXX.

(*Domestic Service.*)

PERSONS SICK OR INJURED, BY SEX, BY KIND OF AILMENT OR INJURY AND BY LENGTH OF ILLNESS.

Kind of Ailment, etc.	MALE.				FEMALE.			
	No.	Period of Illness.			No.	Period of Illness.		
		Days.	Weeks.	Mos.		Days.	Weeks.	Mos.
Abscess	1	.	8	.	1	1	.	.
"	.	.	.	.	1	.	2	.
Accident (to hand) .	1	.	2	.	1	2	.	.
"	1	.	.	1	1*	.	.	3
Asthma	.	.	.	.	1	.	3	.
Biliousness . . .	1	3 or 4	.	.	1	3	.	.
Chills and fever . .	1	†	.	.	1	.	2	.
Consumption . . .	.	.	.	.	1	.	.	3½
"	.	.	.	.	1	.	.	3
"	.	.	.	.	1	.	.	3
Cramps	.	.	.	.	1	1	.	.
Dyspepsia	.	.	.	.	1	‡	.	.
"	.	.	.	.	1	§	.	.
" and kidney trouble .	.	.	.	.	1	10	.	.
Erysipelas	1	‖	.	.	.	.	.	.
Eyes, inflammation	.	.	.	.	1	.	2	.
" operation for cataract . .	.	.	.	.	1	.	.	3
Felon	.	.	.	.	1	.	6	.
Headache	1	2	.	.	1	4	.	.
Injury to back . . .	.	.	.	.	1	.	6	.
Internal ailment . .	.	.	.	.	¶1	6	.	.
" "	.	.	.	.	1	.	3	.
" "	.	.	.	.	1	.	1	.
" "	.	.	.	.	**1	.	.	2
La grippe	1	5	.	.	1	1	.	.
"	4	.	2	.	1	2	.	.
"	.	.	.	.	1	.	3	.
"	.	.	.	.	1	.	4	.
"	.	.	.	.	1	.	5	.
"	.	.	.	.	2	.	8	.
"	.	.	.	.	1	††	.	.
Malarial fever . . .	1	.	3	.	.	.	.	.
Neuralgia	.	.	.	.	1	.	2	.

* Broken leg.
† Intermittent (" loses no time").
‡ " Few days."
§ Unknown (" worked all time").
‖ Unknown.
¶ Result of heavy lifting.
** Hemorrhage.
†† Unknown (" worked all time.")

TABLE XXX.—*Continued.*

Kind of Ailment, etc.	MALE				FEMALE			
	No.	Period of Illness			No.	Period of Illness		
		Days.	Weeks.	Mos.		Days.	Weeks.	Mos.
Neuralgia					1			2
"					1			3
"					1			4
Neuritis					1			2
Operation (surgical),					1			1
Pleurisy					1			2
Quinsy					1	10		
"					1	*		
"					2	2		
"					1	3		
"					1		2	
Rheumatism	1		2					
"	1	†			1	‡		
"					1			2
"					1		6	
"					1			4
"					1			3 to 9
Shock (nervous)					1			5
Sprained ankle					1			3
Stomach,"inflammation" of					1		1	
"　　"　　"					1		2	
"　　"　　"					1		3	
"　　"　　"					1			1
"　　"　　"					1		7	
"　　"　　"					1			2
Tape-worm removed					3	2		
Typhoid fever					1		2	
"　　"					1			2
Unknown	1	1			4	3		
"	1	2			1	4		
"	1	5			2	5		
"	1		1		1	10		
"	3		2		1	16		
"	2		2 or 3		5		1	
"	1	10			9		2	
"	1	15			6		3	
"	1	19			1		4	
"	1		3		3		6	
"	2			2	3			1
"	1			3	3			2
"					1			3
Total	31				102			

* Week ("worked all time").
† "All winter but worked all time."
‡ Few days.

This table is found to aggregate 415 weeks of illness during the year, to be distributed among 547 persons, giving an average loss of work time for illness of about four-fifths of a week per individual during the year.[20]

Health of colored domestic servants in the Seventh Ward during the last twelve months is shown in the diagram which follows:

HEALTH STATISTICS, FOR LAST TWELVE MONTHS, OF COLORED DOMESTICS OF PHILADELPHIA.

	0	10	20	30	40	50	60	70	80	90	100		
MALE												WELL ILL1WK. ILL	79.8 4.6 15.8
FEMALE												WELL ILL1WK. ILL	74.2 8.4 17.4
TOTAL												WELL ILL1WK. ILL	75.7 7.3 17.0

☐ NOT SICK AT ALL DURING LAST 12 MONTHS

▨ ILL ONE WEEK OR LESS " " " "

■ ILL MORE THAN 1 WEEK " " " "

---

[20] It may be of interest to compare this result with the following table taken from Professor Mayo Smith's " Statistics and Sociology," which table, the author says, is " based upon the experience of the largest and most important Friendly Society in England, which gives aid to members when they are ill, the Manchester Unity of Odd Fellows, comprising 400,000 members." The table is as follows :

Age.	Average Sickness per Individual Per Annum (in Weeks).	
	Male.	Female.
15–20 years	.666	.666
20–25 "	.737	.737
25–45 "	.995	.995
45–65 "	2.736	2.751
15–65 "	1.314	1.334

Omitting the 45-65 period, which is not fairly comparable with the ages of colored domestic servants (their average age being 30.3), it will be seen that the average illness among the English working people is nearly the same as that among colored domestics of the same age. The English Sick Benefit Society showing an average of .799 as compared with .759 for colored servants, the slight difference being to the advantage of the colored servants.

IX.

In view of the general purpose of this investigation, it is proper to discuss in conclusion the question of the improvement of Philadelphia Negro domestic service. In the first place, what remedies or improvements in domestic service have already been tried with any measure of success? The answer to this question should indicate the lines along which progress may be expected.

The only two scientific studies of the subject up to the present time, are those of Mr. Charles Booth and of Miss Salmon, who in 1897 published her 300-page book entitled "Domestic Service." Mr. Booth's treatment of the subject is purely statistical, simply stating and grouping facts; it has no theory of betterment to offer. But Miss Salmon, besides giving statistics of American domestic service, also treats the question in its historical aspects and considers it philosophically and practically, with an eye to its probable future development and to possible remedies for present difficulties.

Hence the best, perhaps the only answer, to the above question now to be found in print is that given by Miss Salmon in the closing chapters of her book; and a brief abstract of those chapters is therefore given here, with her permission.

Before suggesting any plan of betterment, Miss Salmon enumerates and discards various "doubtful remedies," such as the removal of all difficulties by the application of the golden rule, employing the system of service books in vogue in Germany, introducing domestic training in the public schools, and other methods. All these plans fail, says the author, because they assume that the adjustment to be made is a purely personal one, whereas larger relations—political, economic, industrial and social—are, in point of fact involved; and she believes that reform in domestic service, if it is to succeed, "must be accomplished along the same general economic lines as are reforms in other great departments of labor." She shows that domestic service, though apparently isolated from other departments of the world's work, has been powerfully affected by inventions, by political revolutions and social changes, by the commercial development of the country and the introduction of the factory system, which took out of the household once and for all the making of men's garments, many kinds of woolen wear, boots and shoes, hats, gloves, etc., together with the preparation of many kinds of food now made chiefly in factories —cheese, canned vegetables, ice cream, etc.

Having shown that domestic labor is not isolated but forms an integral and closely interwoven part of the social fabric, the author turns to consider possible remedies which can succeed only as they harmonize with the all-pervasive economic tendencies of modern times. Miss Salmon first enumerates these tendencies and declares them to be:

" 1. The tendency toward concentration of capital and labor in industry, shown in pools, trusts, department stores, etc.

" 2. The tendency toward specialization in every department of labor.

" 3. The tendency toward collective action growing from (1) and (2).

" 4. The tendency toward profit-sharing and similar methods constantly becoming more far-reaching.

" 5. The tendency toward greater industrial independence of women."

The first of the remedies suggested by Miss Salmon as running in harmony with these tendencies is specialization of household employments. This is an important point deserving of most careful consideration. It is true that all advancement yet made in household employments has involved division of labor and unconscious co-operation; as, for instance, when spinning and weaving, once done by the women at home, was removed to the factory ; next, when the sewing machine took the making of underclothing largely out of the home and made of it the "white goods" industry. Cheese, a home product till 1860, is now wholly factory made.

It is important to notice that all these articles, both of food and clothing, though at first more expensive when factory made, are now both better and more cheaply made outside the household. The presumption is that other articles now in a 'ransition state (such, for example, as glass-canned fruits and preserves, jellies, pickles, bread, cake, pastry, pressed meats, condensed milk, butter, etc.) would soon be among those things made both *better and more cheaply* out of the house than within, were the demand for them sufficient. These things, if purchased through women's exchanges, are more expensive only because the "demand for them has thus far been limited." The author believes that their cheapening would follow upon their greater demand, together with improved quality, as has been the case with clothing, etc. She shows further that the delivery of practically all articles of food ready for the final application of heat is possible through business enterprise and scientific experiment, and believes that this would go a long way toward solving the "servant question" by taking most of the domestics out of the house and thus lessening the strain of personal relations of employer and employe. Employers would welcome such a change. The situation would be improved for the employes also, since many women could retain their homelife and at the same time earn money and support their families. [21] This change, it is pointed out, "is in direct line with the tendency toward specialization everywhere else found, in that it enables each person to do exclusively that thing which she can do best; it allows the concentration of labor and capital and thus economizes and secures the largest results; it retains the woman's homelife without sacrificing her bread-winning opportunities; it improves the quality of products, thus made under the most favorable conditions; it brings the work of every cook into competition with the work of every other cook and thus incites improvement; it applies the principle of unconscious co-operation and thus harmonizes with other business activities."

That the laundry department also could thus be taken outside the household will not be questioned, since Troy laundries already do many articles better and more cheaply than can be

---

[21] A long list of bread-winners among women is given ("Domestic Service," page 219 *et seq.*) showing how women are wholly or partly supporting their families by preparing in their homes articles of food for sale in neighboring large cities, each woman usually making large quantities of only one or two articles, e. g., Saratoga potatoes, sold in large quantities to grocers, jams and pickles, chicken salad, cake, etc.

done at home. Troy prices would lessen with increased demand and competition among laundries.

The care of lawns, gardens and orchards in summer, and of furnaces in winter, also tends to become a business in itself; and many cases are recorded of men who care for eight or ten different furnaces, or who have charge of from ten to fifteen lawns or gardens, and of women who wash windows once a week for a large number of families.

There are many reasons why this tendency should develop. It has much in its favor, while the only objection to it—that the cost of living would be increased—is not valid, since it is certain that the added expense would only be temporary, as in the case of factory-made garments, and would finally operate decidedly to cheapen living expenses.

The second possible remedy suggested is profit-sharing, and its application to housework is interesting. "It is possible," says Miss Salmon, "to fix a sum, as $50 or $100 for monthly expenses, including food, fuel, lights, a *pro-rata* for guests, etc. If by care in the use of materials the expenses amount to but $45 or $90 monthly, the $5 or $10 saved can be divided according to a proportion previously agreed upon, between the employer and the employees; the cook, who is in a position to save most, receiving the greatest percentage of the bonus."

Domestics thus become interested partners in the concern and with most satisfactory results. Miss Salmon states that this is not untested theory but has been successfully practiced and actually does place the household on a business basis.

A third possible remedy proposed is thorough education in household science. It is maintained that the organization of a great professional school fully equipped for the study of domestic science and open only to graduates of the leading colleges and universities would start household science in the right direction —that in which advancement in all other occupations has been made —and thus make possible true progress and further harmonious development in this "belated industry." [22]

The result, should these remedies be applied on a large scale, Miss Salmon believes would be far-reaching and of inestimable value. She says: "This readjustment of work and the

---

[22] So called by Miss Addams in a recent address.

willingness of large numbers of women to work for remuneration would be as productive of improvement in all household affairs as division of labor has been elsewhere. A far-reaching benefit is suggested by Maria Mitchell when she says:—'the dressmaker should no more be a universal character than the carpenter. Suppose every man should feel it his duty to do his own mechanical work of all kinds—would society be benefited?—would the work be well done? Yet a woman is expected to know how to do all kinds of sewing, all kinds of cooking, all kinds of any "woman's work," and the consequence is that life is passed in learning these only, while the universe of truth beyond remains unentered.' It must be said in conclusion," the author continues, "that little can be accomplished in domestic reform except through the use of means which already exist, developing these along lines marked out by industrial progress in other fields."

This brief extract gives the gist of the best thought thus far devoted to the subject. Now, we must ask ourselves, how can all this be applied to Negro domestic service in Philadelphia? What facts now existing in service there can be laid hold of and developed along these lines of progress observed in other fields of industry?

Most of the facts of Negro domestic service which are amenable to such adaptation and development are to be found under the head of specialization of employments. Considerable outside service is already being done by colored people in Philadelphia. The degree to which laundry work, for example, has been removed from the household may be seen by the fact that there are but thirty-one private laundresses in the ward, while 1097 colored women in the ward support their families by taking in washing or doing "day's work," as they call washing by the day at the employer's house. There is every evidence that sending out the washing instead of keeping a laundress as one of the regular domestics is more satisfactory both to employer and employee; for the laundress would rather do the work at home, and often must do it there or not at all when there are young children in her family, while the employer gains a peaceful Monday and Tuesday by having the work done out, besides saving the slight but constant expense of coal and washing supplies. Aside from these 1097 individual laundresses in the ward, there are also two regular laundries managed by Negro families, where all the working members of the family are busily employed for six days in the week with the work of a large number of families. Such colored people as these are justly jealous of the work given to Chinamen, while many native Negroes cannot get work to do. There is no doubt that successful and excellent laundries would grow up under the management of Philadelphia colored men and women if employers could be satisfied to "put the washing out" and to admit the possibility of having clothing laundered on some other week day than that which was usual in the Plymouth colony. The domestic economy of America to-day is more complex than was that of the Plymouth colony, and we can very easily make due allowance for the fact by letting our laundresses choose their own "Monday."

Another branch of domestic work showing the specializing tendency is that known as "general work," which with men servants usually denotes care of furnaces, cleaning the front of the house, etc. Nearly all of these men do such work for a considerable number of families and devote their entire time to it. One man was encountered who was in charge of the furnaces and "outside work" of not less than eight different establishments. In this direction employers could easily co-operate to effect further specialization, as only a little over two per cent of Negro male wage-earners are at present general workers. It was observed that such men were found almost exclusively in the more fashionable and wealthy quarter, while elsewhere the waiter manservant undertook the outside work as part of his duty. The specializing tendency in this department of Negro service is much less marked than in the laundry work. Still progress in the right direction is practicable, since the tendency, though not greatly developed, still exists.

A much more significant fact in the matter of specialization of work is the presence in the Seventh Ward alone, of eighty-three colored caterers and cateresses, whose employment by families who entertain to any extent surely diminishes the need in those families for the services of such large numbers of domestics as would otherwise be employed by them. The use of such outside professional help is clearly a development in the right direction and the service thus secured is manifestly

better, because skilled. It is equally evident that it is cheaper
to employ a caterer periodically than to keep an extra number
of trained domestics permanently employed in the household
for such occasions. Here again, then, specialization is found
actually at work among the colored people of Philadelphia.

A fourth instance of it which is found in the city is worth
citing. This is a Woman's Exchange. The preparation of
foods, such as fruit in glass jars, preserves, jellies, pickles,
etc., and the making of simple garments, underwear, aprons,
shirt waists, baby's caps, etc., are the kinds of work specialized upon by the "Exchange for Women's Work," located at 756 South Twelfth street, in connection with the
parsonage of Bethel Church. This Exchange is outside the
Seventh Ward, but is so notable a case of the tendency here
discussed that it seems well to mention it. The articles offered
for sale are of excellent quality and are sold at moderate
prices. The investigator has noticed, in a high grade provision store on Chestnut street, not far from Rittenhouse
Square, that jellies, jams and fruits are offered for sale bearing
conspicuous sale cards marked, "Miss ———'s Pickled
Peaches," "Miss ———'s Currant Jelly," etc. This suggests
that there might be an exchange for *colored* women's work at
such provision stores and high grade groceries if the proprietors
could be induced to co-operate, as many of them doubtless
could be by judicious and business-like suggestions from their
leading customers or from some well-known and influential
organization of women. Colored women who have unusual
skill in the preparation of any kind of foods might in this way
be able to place their goods advantageously, greatly to their
own benefit and also to that of the community of which they
form often an unemployed part.

To sum up : the facts of colored domestic service which can
be laid hold of and developed along the lines of specialization
of household work then, are these facts connected with
"Extra Service" : (1) Laundry work can be done more conveniently and as cheaply or more cheaply outside of the house
than within it, and many excellent laundresses among the
married colored women are anxious to get such work to do.
(2) "Outside work," furnace work, etc., can similarly be done
by men making it their business, and a man servant thus be

left free for other duties or dispensed with altogether. (3) Patronage of caterers rather than the employment of supernumerary domestics is a step tending to simplify household work in large establishmencs and the employment of competent *colored* caterers a step tending to simplify the problem of unemployed colored men in Philadelphia. (4) Anything tending to extend the patronage of exchanges for women's work, and, by inducing competition in such work, to cheapen articles so offered for sale is a step in the direction of taking food preparation outside the household, and anything tending to secure a steady sale for the work of skilled *colored* cooks in such exchanges is a step in the direction of solving the "colored unemployed" problem of Philadelphia with all the degradation and suffering implied in that problem.

In regard to the second possible remedy proposed by Miss Salmon, it can only be said that the method of profit-sharing is as practicable with colored as with white or foreign employes —perhaps more so since colored domestics are proverbially "anxious to please."

The third possible remedy suggested—thorough education in household affairs—aims to remove the odium now attaching to domestic service and to attract competent people to the employment by raising it to the rank of a profession. The Philadelphia colored people have already thought this subject through for themselves. A woman physician who is well known in Philadelphia, one of the most intelligent and interesting women of either race, said to the present investigator: "If domestic service were made more honorable, more tolerable, more human, it would not be so unpopular. If we had good training schools for service it would become an honorable branch of business. Mr. Booker Washington believes in ' putting brains into common work,' and that is just what I say about domestic labor. If a girl is taught to cook skillfully and to buy economically she becomes a dignified laborer. A trained worker is always honorable and dignified. I have often said there should be a school to train domestics. Many girls want to work who can't get the opportunity. If you ask them ' What do you understand doing ?—What do you represent?' they say, ' I don't know how to do anything well;' it is a most lamentable answer and a most common one. But they *want* to learn; if you ask, 'Would you go and work for fifty cents a week and be trained?' they will say: 'yes, willingly.' And I believe that we should have a school of instruction with a regular course, where graduates who reach a certain degree of excellence get a certificate of efficiency. Let this school be an employment bureau also. Such an arrangement would be a help both ways, to the employes and to the competent among the employed."

That this idea of Dr. ——'s could be made workable seems unquestionable when we study the situation in London as shown by Mr. Booth. There the girls from the workhouse schools, who have only the merest rudiments of training in household affairs, are nevertheless in such demand in London service that, as Mr. Booth says:[23] "There is no difficulty in finding places for the girls from the workhouse schools as the demand far exceeds the supply." The M. A. B. Y. S. (Metropolitan Association for Befriending Young Servants) has organized an employment bureau where these young servant girls may be engaged, and at this office the protection of the girl is insured by obliging the mistress to sign a form of agreement stating the number in her family, work required, wages paid, privileges granted, etc. The detailed workings of this bureau and its friendly connection with the girls after their places are secured are set forth fully in Mr. Booth's book. The chief thing to be noted here is the remarkable demand which actually exists for girls having any training at all, which fact leaves little doubt that the training does distinctly add to the value of the servant. A training school for domestic training could easily be established in Philadelphia in connection with institutions already organized. The best known colored institute in the city of Philadelphia is already doing admirable work in manual training and the teaching of trades from the building trades to millinery and dressmaking. Would it not be practicable to add courses in domestic science and economy, chemistry and sanitation, etc., *to which only graduates of the institute should be admitted* and where certificates should be granted only to graduates attaining a certain rank in their work, both theoretical and practical? An employment bureau in connection

---

[23] "Life and Labour of the People," Charles Booth, Vol. 8, p. 215 and following.

with such a training school could be undertaken on a fair business basis by some philanthropic or civic association, to insure fair treatment, as is done by the M. A. B. Y. S. in London. Such a plan would undoubtedly be facilitated by the presence at the head of this particular institution at the present time of one of the most gifted and progressive women in Philadelphia, whose views on domestic service are the leading ones in modern domestic reform.

In closing this paper it may be well to point out that these suggestions, all of which are in line with the views of the best thinkers upon the subject of reform in the administration of household matters, would obviate in large measure the greatest difficulties in the domestic service of to-day. What are these difficulties? In England the two greatest, in the opinion of Mr. Booth, are the dullness of the domestic servants' life and the difficulty of the personal relations between employer and employed. The same is true of American domestic service, with the added drawback of loss of social standing, which in this country is the greatest objection of all, though hardly consciously felt in England. When the domestic becomes a "trained worker, honorable and dignified," this great objection will be removed, and it is clear that minimizing the number of domestics employed within the household would do away in large measure with the difficulty of the personal relations between mistress and maid, while the domestics thus set free to perform their special work according to their own methods, and in their own homes, would have no more reason to complain of the dullness of such life than a dressmaker or milliner would have. With the removal of these obstacles, better ability would enter domestic service, and the industry would become more honorable as well as more endurable and attractive to domestics, who we sometimes forget are also human beings, and naturally wish to live the lives of human beings.

INDEX.